Unearthing Gotham

Yale University Press • New Haven & London

Anne-Marie Cantwell and Diana diZerega Wall

UNEARTHING GOTHAM

The Archæology of New York City

Designed by Nancy Ovedovitz and set in Galliard Oldstyle type by
B. Williams & Associates. Printed in the United States of America.

Library of Congress Cataloging-in-Publication Data
Cantwell, Anne-Marie E., date.
Unearthing Gotham : the archaeology of New York City /
Anne-Marie Cantwell and Diana diZerega Wall.
p. cm.
Includes bibliographical references and index.
ISBN 0-300-08415-3
1. New York (N.Y.)—Antiquities.   2. Excavations (Archaeology)—
New York (State)—New York.   3. New York (N.Y.)—History.
4. Natural history—New York (State)—New York.   5. Indians of
North America—New York Region—Antiquities.   I. Wall, Diana
diZerega.   II. Title.
F128.39.C36 2001
974.7'101—dc21   2001000359

A catalogue record for this book is available from the British Library.

The paper in this book meets the guidelines for permanence and
durability of the Committee on Production Guidelines for Book
Longevity of the Council on Library Resources.

10 9 8 7 6 5 4 3 2 1

Unearthing Gotham: The Archaeology of New York City is the first annual Friends of Yale University Press Book. In recognition of the generous and continuing support of the members of the Publisher's Council, the Press dedicates this publication to them.

The Josef and Anni Albers Foundation

David J. Bodney

George P. Brockway

Robert L. Crowell

Joseph F. Cullman 3rd

William H. Draper III

Edward P. Evans

Deborah J. Fennebresque

Richard F. French

Jamie and Andrew Gagarin

Victor Grann

Thomas H. Guinzburg

Arthur T. Hadley II

V. W. Henningsen, Jr.

G. D. Edith Hsuing

Lawrence Hughes

Eleanor H. Jorden

James M. Kemper, Jr.

Donald S. Lamm

Louis L. Martz

Alfred L. McDougal

Ruth R. McMullin

Jim Ottoway, Jr.

Jaroslav Pelikan

Jules D. Prown

Joseph Verner Reed

Joanna and Daniel Rose

Daniel H. Rosenblatt

Arthur J. Rosenthal

Ronald G. Sampson

Jack Schulman

Anthony M. Schulte

Will Schwalbe

Gaddis Smith

Harry H. Wellington

Wilmot F. Wheeler, Jr.

Peter Workman

July 2001

Contents

ix   Acknowledgments

Part 1: Introduction

3   CHAPTER ONE
The Archæology of New York City

15   CHAPTER TWO
Digging in New York

Part 2: The Deeper Past

35   CHAPTER THREE
The Creation of the World: The Paleoindian Period,
11,000–10,000 B.P.

46   CHAPTER FOUR
Settling Down in the Archaic, 10,000–3,700 B.P.

62   CHAPTER FIVE
Funerary Pyres on Long Island: The Transitional,
3,700–2,700 B.P.

73   CHAPTER SIX
Tidewater Trade and Ritual: The Early and Middle Woodland,
2,700–1,000 B.P.

93   CHAPTER SEVEN
Tethered to the Land: The Late Woodland, 1,000–400 B.P.

Part 3: The Recent Past

119   CHAPTER EIGHT
A Tumultuous Encounter: "Some Monster of the Sea"

149   CHAPTER NINE
The Arrival of the Global Economy

167   CHAPTER TEN
Daily Life in New Amsterdam and Early New York

188   CHAPTER ELEVEN
Urban Space in the Colonial and Post-Revolutionary City

206   CHAPTER TWELVE
Daily Life in the Nineteenth-Century City

224   CHAPTER THIRTEEN
Building the City: The Waterfront

242   CHAPTER FOURTEEN
Building in the City: Early Urban Backyards

257   CHAPTER FIFTEEN
Beyond the City's Edge

277   CHAPTER SIXTEEN
"We Were Here": The African Presence in Colonial New York

Part 4: Conclusion

297   CHAPTER SEVENTEEN
Common Ground

303   Notes

331   References

355   Index

373   Illustration Credits

Acknowledgments

When we began to write this book about the archaeology of New York City, we thought it would be interesting and easy to do. But although the process turned out to be interesting, it certainly wasn't easy. First of all, we found it extremely difficult to turn this gargantuan subject into a coherent narrative. We also wanted to write a book that would appeal to both general readers and more scholarly ones. This proved to be a daunting task. Our solution was to tell the story of the city's past in a readable, nonscientific way but to include full references for those readers who wished to delve more deeply into particular issues.

We recognize that we could not have written this book without the help and support of our colleagues and friends, many of whom contributed in important ways to the study of the city's archaeology. Here, while accepting full responsibility for all errors of fact and interpretation, we acknowledge our debts to them.

We were fortunate in receiving support at various stages of the project from Peter Neill, Judy Sandman, Annette Weiner, and Sally Yerkovich. For reading and commenting on various parts of the manuscript in its early stages, we are grateful to T. O. Beidelman, R. Joseph Dent, Robert Funk, Robert Grumet, Lucianne Lavin, Arnold Pickman, Anthony Puniello, Nan Rothschild, Robert Schuyler, Janet Siskind, Ralph Solecki, Lorraine Williams, Rebecca Yamin, and Sally Yerkovich.

For discussing their own work with us or for reading and commenting on sections of the manuscript that covered their work, we thank Albert Anderson, William Askins, H. Arthur Bankoff, Leonard Bianchi, Michael Blakey, Eugene Boesch, Patricia Bridges, Elizabeth Chilton, Diane Dallal, R. Brian Ferguson, Karen Flinn, Joan Geismar, Allan Gilbert, Wendy Harris, Roselle Henn, Jean Howson, Meta Janowitz, Edward Kaeser, Herbert Kraft, John Krigbaum, Alyssa Loorya, Daniel Pagano, Edward Rutsch, Robert Schuyler, Annette Silver, Carlyle Smith, Linda Stone, Stanley Wiesniewski, and Frederick Winter. It's a pleasure to have such good and generous colleagues.

For facilitating our research, we thank the staff at the African Burial Ground's Office of Public Education and Interpretation (especially Sherrill D. Wilson and Emilyn Brown), the American Museum of Natural History (especially Belinda Kaye and Anibal Rodriguez), the City University of New York Libraries, the Nassau County Museum (especially Ron Wyatt), the Museum of the City of New York (particularly Marguerite Lavin), the National Museum of the American Indian (especially Nancy Rosoff), the New Jersey State Museum (especially Karen Flinn and Lorraine Williams), the New York City Landmarks Preservation Commission (especially Daniel Pagano), the New York City Municipal Archives (especially Kenneth Cobb), the New York Genealogical and Biographical Society, the New-York Historical Society, the New York Public Library, New York University Library, Rutgers University Libraries, and the South Street Seaport Museum (especially Diane Dallal and Paula Mayo).

We are grateful to Nikoleta Katsakiori for her help in researching chapter 10.

Special appreciation goes to the City College of the City University of New York and the Rutgers University Faculty Academic Study Program for their support. We also thank Fred Myers and the Department of Anthropology at New York University.

Many friends and colleagues were particularly helpful in providing illustrations for the book. We thank H. Arthur Bankoff, Edith Coleman, Diane Dallal, Karen Flinn, Carl Forster, Joan Geismar, Allan Gilbert, Herbert Kraft, Tamara Jubilee-Shaw, David Oestreicher, James Rementer, Nan Rothschild, Annette Silver, Ralph Solecki, and Lorraine Williams. We also thank Kervin Maule for taking new photographs for the book and Arnold Pickman for his help in making graphs.

Our association with Yale University Press has been a consistent pleasure. We are grateful to Harry Haskell, our editor, for all his efforts and for sharing our vision of the book. We appreciate the invaluable help that Jenya Weinreb provided as manuscript editor. Additional thanks go to Alexa Antanavage and Susan Smits for their help in rounding up the illustrations and permissions. We are also grateful to Nancy Ovedovitz, our designer, for making the book so attractive.

We acknowledge with great pleasure our intellectual debts to Bert Salwen and Howard D. Winters, our professors at New York University.

We also recognize our debts to our informants, the generations of people who lived in what is now called New York City. The traces of their ways of life became the archaeological record and the basis of this book.

Most of all, we thank our families and friends, without whose support we would never have finished this project. We dedicate this book to them.

PART I

Introduction

We delight in the promised
sunshine of the future.
— Cadwallader Colden

CHAPTER ONE

The Archæology of New York City

New York City is one of the most intricate products of the human imagination. Today it ranks among the modern world's greatest financial, media, and cultural capitals. It is a city everywhere renowned for its glamour and its influence. What happens in New York is immediately reported to millions of people all over the world. And yet, what few realize as they follow events in this great modern city is that New York is also the oldest major city in the United States.

Unlike the nation's other early cities or many of the well-known Old World cities that exude a cherished past, New York rarely uses its history in constructing its identity or in stimulating its economy. Perhaps because the city has always been a place where people have come to build new lives, New York and its citizens have rarely wanted to look back. Instead, the past for them often either lies in the way of progress or is enshrined in memory in some other part of the world. For that reason, many people find it hard to think of archaeology in the context of New York. Both archaeology and the past are things that happen elsewhere; the present and future are in New York. And so the very idea that we propose here, the archaeology of New York City, seems odd, in fact an oxymoron. But that oxymoron is exactly what this book is about.

However incongruous it may seem, New York has a deep past, both literally and metaphorically. The land on which the modern city is built has an eleven-thousand-year human history that is largely unknown to the millions who walk its streets every day or to the hundreds of millions who watch its news, its trends, and its stock markets. Much of that past has been recovered by generations of archaeologists working quietly but determinedly over the past century. Their work has intensified since the 1970s, when the practice of archaeology in the United States was transformed. That transformation has led to a vastly increased knowledge of the city's past, which only now lets us tell a very different New York story than the one splashed across television and movie screens.

In the pages that follow, we take the modern city of New York, all five boroughs and 325 square miles of it, and view it as one vast archaeological site to be examined in its entirety through time. We use archaeology to study many of the people who once lived or worked anywhere within the limits of what is today the modern city, from its earliest inhabitants up to twentieth-century dwellers. As archaeologists, we explore not only urban life throughout the modern city's history, but also life in the earlier, pre-urban past. This approach allows us to tell a continuing story of many of the different peoples who have lived on this same piece of land for thousands of years. It also lets us describe the distinctive ways each of these groups related to the land and how the land itself changed over the millennia.

Although for many people the story of New York begins in 1524, when Giovanni da Verrazano sailed into what is now New York Harbor, the land that he and his crew saw spread out before them had been occupied since the end of the Ice Ages, when the first pioneering Indians arrived around eleven thousand years ago. Starting with that beginning, we follow the changing landscape and the many human groups who lived in what would become New York.

We look at New York the way archaeologists look at any archaeological site. That is, we regard as important each small site buried beneath the modern city, be it an English colonial tavern in lower Manhattan, an eight-thousand-year-old Indian settlement on Staten Island, a colonial farm in Queens, a seventeenth-century Indian community in the Bronx, nineteenth-century middle-class homes in Brooklyn, or an eighteenth-century African cemetery on Broadway. Some of the sites we discuss are located in the Wall Street area; others are in city parks, in tree-lined residential neighborhoods, or along the industrial waterfront. Each is important because it is part of the larger site that is the city itself (figs. 1.1, 1.2).

Viewing a modern city as an archaeological site and studying both its urban and its pre-urban past constitute a radically new way of looking at an American city. It is not only novel but also intimidating to consider New York today, with its millions of people carrying out their daily tasks on its surface, as a site that contains hidden beneath it the material remains of the ways of life of hundreds of generations of earlier peoples who once carried out *their* daily tasks there. And yet we firmly believe that this perspective provides a unique opportunity to contribute significantly to the ongoing creation of New York's identity and to the broader national one as well. This is because of the peculiar nature of cities and archaeology.

Archaeology provides a singular approach to the human past. Archaeologists, no matter where they work, reconstruct past environments and landscapes and study the actual objects that people made, used, and left behind. They carefully uncover broken pottery, trash pits, spear points, ornaments, food scraps, agricultural fields, privies, and

1.1. Modern-day New York City, showing the locations of some archaeological sites in the Bronx, Brooklyn, Queens, Staten Island, and upper Manhattan.

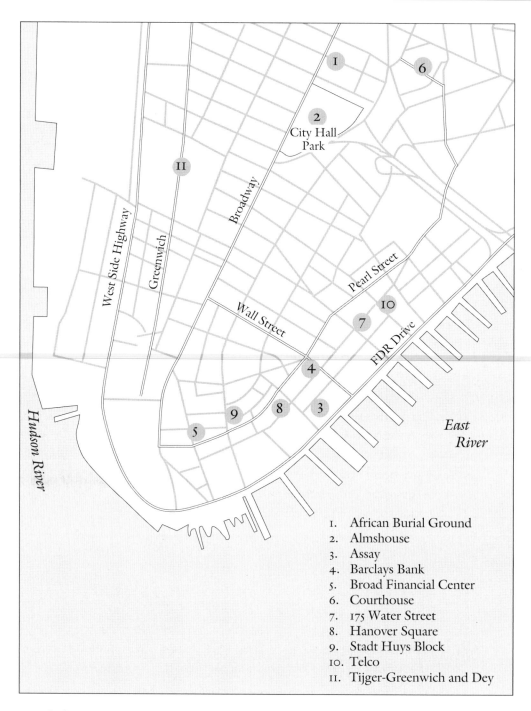

1.2. *The locations of some archaeological sites in lower Manhattan.*

1. African Burial Ground
2. Almshouse
3. Assay
4. Barclays Bank
5. Broad Financial Center
6. Courthouse
7. 175 Water Street
8. Hanover Square
9. Stadt Huys Block
10. Telco
11. Tijger-Greenwich and Dey

hearths. And they map and explore houses, temples, landfill, pyramids, and military forts. For archaeologists, all these finds, the humble and the grand, the fragmented and the whole, have meaning because their creation, use, and disposal were deeply embedded in the social, economic, and symbolic worlds of the peoples whose ways of life they are studying. And it is this deeper meaning that they wish to understand. For them (as for us) an archaeological excavation is not a treasure hunt. Rather, it is a scientific search for information that will help us re-create the lives of earlier peoples in order to reach a deeper understanding of the human predicament.[1]

Archaeologists want to *understand* the past, not only because the journey to that understanding can be an exciting intellectual challenge, but also, and more important, because they believe that the past has significance for the present. All societies live with the legacy of the past; decisions that were made and actions that were taken centuries or even millennia ago still affect lives today. And as the legacy of the American past continues to be redefined, archaeologists hope that their discipline is making a unique contribution to this ongoing process.

In many ways, modern, living cities are the perfect laboratories for archaeologists to learn about that deep legacy of the American past. Cities, after all, have played an increasingly important role in American life ever since the first European settlements. As of 1990, 75 percent of the American people could be found living in metropolitan areas.[2] In excavating in cities, archaeologists can investigate the development of urbanism in America. Yet in treating a major city as an archaeological site, they can study far more than urbanization. Modern metropolises like New York have sprawled over earlier colonial farms and villages as well as more recent suburbs; they have also spread across land that had been occupied by Native Americans for millennia. Therefore, although modern American cities may be young cities by Old World standards, as archaeological sites they are made up of the remains of thousands of years of buried human history.

As American cities like New York grew, they attracted millions of people who came to live and work in them. Multitudes more passed through them at some point in their lives. Many urban areas served in the past, as now, as points of entry for immigrants from foreign countries, places of hope for those fleeing rural poverty, places of promise for the ambitious young, ports of trade for businesses from all over the world, and cultural and administrative centers for all. But cities are also marked by slums and sweatshops. And some of the older cities were once places where the oppressed were forced to live and work in bondage. So cities have also been places of poverty, misery, disease, and dissension. By their very nature, cities like New York are cosmopolitan places, filled with competing ideas and made up of people from different backgrounds, ethnic groups, social classes, religions, and occupations. They are densely populated, with buildings, people, and public spaces cheek by jowl. The land is valuable; it is used over and over again and is frequently subdivided into smaller and smaller parcels that are used by more and more people as each group builds on the remains of the last.[3]

Because of the nature of the archaeological record, archaeologists are able to study this astonishing array of human experience in the city. They can bring forward into modern consciousness not only the daily lives and actions of those featured in published histories and other documents, but also the lives of those forgotten or ignored in the written record, including children, laborers, shopkeepers, enslaved workers, housewives, and members of minority groups. And they can re-create the complex history of the hundreds of generations of Native Americans who lived in the area long before the European colonizations began. They can thus provide a tangible past for almost everyone. In other words, we believe that an archaeological study of the city provides an unparalleled opportunity to study the American past in all its richness. In this book, we take that opportunity for New York, one of the oldest, largest, most densely populated, and most heterogeneous of American cities.

For archaeologists and non-archaeologists alike, one of the most compelling things about the archaeological record is that it is tangible. Archaeologists reclaim from the earth the material traces, the physical palpable evidence, of the past. They recover artifacts and also the remains of people themselves—human burials. Because of this, their work has a special immediacy. Human burials, especially, are so evocative that they can easily be transformed into powerful symbols for the living. As for the artifacts, many are of the humble everyday sort. Yet when they are viewed today, their very universality of function, although the objects may have changed in form or material, gives us an immediate and forceful connection with the past. In looking at these relics, imbued with the meanings of their times, we are inspired to ask the age-old questions "Who am I?" "Who is my neighbor?" "Where did we come from?" and, more important today, "Who are we as a people?"

Because of this unique ability to bring into modern memory the lives of those long forgotten or ignored, archaeology in New York and elsewhere in the United States is not simply an academic exercise. On the contrary, archaeology can help us address the important questions that have always faced New York and the rest of the United States and which are especially troubling at this point in our history as a people: Can we, a people made up of citizens from so many different cultural backgrounds, create a national identity, one with meaning for all? Can we find strength and not weakness in our diversity? Are we a people? Obviously the archaeological study of American cities like New York cannot possibly answer these questions on its own. But it can, we believe, help us document, understand, and respect a long and complex American past.

A Nation Acts to Protect Its Past

Over the centuries, many Americans have been ambivalent about the past. Certainly in the early part of the nation's history, some people emphatically did not want a past. They saw themselves as a pragmatic people who focused on the present and the future. Cadwallader Colden, mayor of New York City in the 1820s, epitomized these attitudes. In comparing the United States to Europe, he argued, "Did we live amidst ruins [and evidence of] present decay, . . . we might be as little inclined as others, to look forward. But we delight in the promised sunshine of the future, and leave to those who are conscious that they have passed their grand climacteric to console themselves with the splendors of the past."[4]

Most Americans today are less adamant in denying the past. In fact, many of them long for tradition and a sense of rootedness. In writing about these longings, historian Michael Kammen argues that they are "more likely to increase . . . in times of transition, in periods of cultural anxiety, or when a society feels a strong sense of discontinuity with its past." He goes on to contend that these periods of cultural anxiety have occurred cyclically in the United States. Some earlier crises were related to the development, in the late nineteenth century, of American archaeology and the establishment of the historic preservation movement in the United States. The era after World War II, when modern archaeology emerged, is also one that Kammen and others, including ourselves, would argue was one of national cultural anxiety, marked by "worries about security, freedom, swift social change, and a sense of radical discontinuity with the world as it had hitherto been known." In many ways, the national soul-searching over multiculturalism and the rise of "identity politics" might be seen as expressions of this cultural anxiety.[5]

It is not surprising, therefore, that the developing importance of archaeology in the United States is closely tied to this ongoing period of national questioning, this "sense of radical discontinuity." For this reason, the lineage of archaeologists working today in modern American cities is very different from that of their peers digging in the cities of the ancient worlds. Instead, it is directly related to a number of changes, culminating in the 1960s and 1970s, within the fields of social history and American archaeology, within the environmental and historic preservation movements, and within the wider society of which these are a part.

Before that period, most archaeologists working in the United States had focused their work on the histories of Native American societies during the millennia before the European invasions of the continent. They excavated sites associated with the mound-building cultures of the Midwest and Southeast, the Pueblo societies of the Southwest, and those of the earliest peoples all over the continent. But by the 1930s,

for many years, and his work at Neanderthal sites in Southwest Asia is known world-wide. Yet his long and distinguished career had actually begun in Queens in the 1930s and 1940s, when he and his friends tried to salvage sites all over the city before they were destroyed by developers' bulldozers. Throughout his career, he has continued to write about the archaeological discoveries that he made as a teenager in the New York area.

Salwen, a professor at New York University, was the group's crusader. Originally trained as an engineer, he had come late to archaeology. At the age of thirty-seven he enrolled as a graduate student in the anthropology department at Columbia University, where he studied with Solecki. Salwen was more than a respected and influential scholar. He also had a long history of political activism (he had been blacklisted for union organizing during his engineering days), which he brought to his new career. Arguing that archaeologists should fight to protect sites and should educate both the public and government officials about the importance of archaeology, he became a national leader in the preservation of the country's archaeological heritage. His activism and his charisma were both crucial factors not only in the success of the Stadt Huys Block project but in archaeological projects in urban areas throughout the country. He later became known as the father of urban archaeology.[7]

Rothschild and Wall had studied with Salwen at New York University and were just beginning their careers in archaeology. Rothschild had recently finished her Ph.D. dissertation and had started teaching at Hunter College in New York; Wall was still in graduate school and was about to begin her dissertation (fig. 2.1). Although they had both worked with Salwen at a number of small sites in the city, neither they nor anyone else in New York had ever attacked a site on the scale of the Stadt Huys Block.

The archaeologists agreed with the Landmarks Preservation Commission that the Stadt Huys Block was a perfect archaeological test case: not only did it have the potential for revealing remains of seventeenth-century Dutch New Amsterdam, the first European settlement in the city and one of the country's earliest, but the site would also have enormous visibility—it was located smack in the middle of the financial capital of the world. Any traces of seventeenth-century New Amsterdam that could be found among the skyscrapers of the Wall Street district would capture the imagination of even the most blasé politician and help make the case for urban archaeology not only in New York but throughout the country. This was the site worth going to bat for.

The commission proposed that if the bank would finance an archaeological project at the Stadt Huys Block, the requirements for rescinding landmark status would be satisfied. After a great deal of heated discussion, the bank finally agreed. New York City's first large-scale archaeological project got under way in 1979, with Rothschild and Wall as co-directors and Salwen as senior adviser. Although the archaeologists were elated by the success of the negotiations, they were also anxious. What if, after all their efforts, intense urban development had already destroyed the site and they found nothing of importance?

The Stadt Huys Block project began as all archaeological projects begin anywhere in the world. Well before a shovel broke ground, Rothschild and Wall had to find out as much as possible about the site. On a five-thousand-dollar budget, they had to do two things. First, they had to understand the history of that piece of land, from the arrival of the Native Americans until the moment the excavations began. They also had to identify those parts of the site where traces of the lives of earlier people were most likely to have survived intact as well as those parts where those traces had probably already been destroyed. Then, using both sets of information, they would decide whether there was likely to be anything left on the site worth excavating and, if so, where they would concentrate their digging efforts.

In July 1979 they assembled a small research team, which spread out to government agencies, libraries, archives, and historical societies all over the city. The researchers pored over local histories, old maps and atlases, early travelers' accounts, accounts of the Native Americans who were here when the Europeans arrived, census records, records of soil borings, tax records, building records, deeds, and city directories.

By the time they had finished, the archaeologists had discovered that they were dealing with a very complex site. It was made up of as many as twenty-one separate properties, each of which had its own history of land use. Over the past three and a half centuries, thousands of people had lived or worked on the site, and dozens of structures had been built there and then torn down. The geography of the site was also complex. Although the block today is inland, in the seventeenth century it was a waterfront property on the East River shore: the three blocks that now separate the site from the river are landfill installed in the intervening centuries. Long before the Europeans arrived, then, Native Americans might have used the site as a fishing station.

2.1. Nan Rothschild (right) *and Diana Wall, the co-directors of the Stadt Huys Block Project, 1979.*

In the 1620s the Dutch built their fort close by, at the tip of Manhattan Island, and the site became Dutch territory. By the 1640s their settlement had spread north along the shore to the site area, across the stream that the Dutch would first turn into a canal and that the English would later fill in to become Broad Street. In 1641 the Dutch West India Company built its tavern, the Stadt Herbergh, on the site (fig. 2.2). This building was converted into New Amsterdam's Stadt Huys, or State House, when the frontier town became a municipality in 1653, and it continued fulfilling that function after the British conquered New Amsterdam in 1664 (fig. 2.3). Even before the conquest, though, the Stadt Huys had been joined by many other buildings in the young, growing city. Later on, in 1670, the English governor Francis Lovelace built a tavern, the King's House, right next door (fig. 2.4). The King's House served as a temporary city hall be-

2.2. "The City of New Amsterdam located on the Island of Manhattan in New Netherland," showing the frontier town from the East River, ca. 1650. The large building toward the right is the Stadt Herbergh. The three matching buildings in the middle of the view are warehouses; the one on the right was owned by Augustine Heermans. The small house to the right of Heermans' warehouse was owned by Dutch colonist Cornelis van Tienhoven. The house five buildings to the left of Heermans' warehouse belonged to surgeon Hans Kierstede.

NIEUW AMSTERDAM OFTE NUE NIEUW IORX OPT TEYLANT MAN

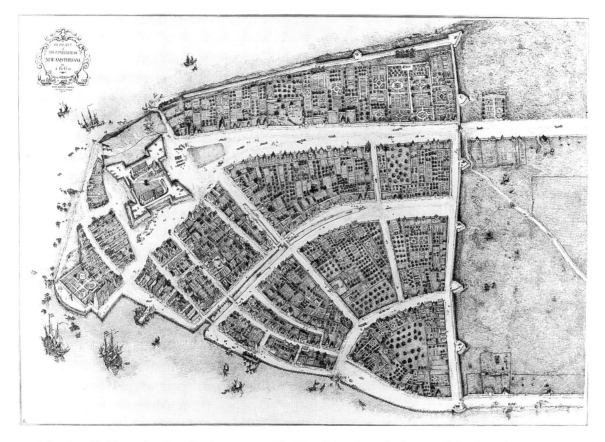

2.3. The Castello Plan, showing the city ca. 1660. The East River is at the bottom of the view; the natural shoreline has been replaced by a seawall. The Stadt Huys Block is to the right of the canal, which is today's Broad Street. The wall that forms the city's rightmost boundary is at today's Wall Street. Collection of the New-York Historical Society, negative number 57812.

tween 1697, when the dilapidated State House was declared unsafe for use, and 1703, when the new city hall at the corner of Wall and Nassau Streets was finished.

The records showed that throughout the eighteenth century, the small lots that made up the larger land parcel housed the homes and workplaces of a cross-section of early New Yorkers, including brokers and merchants, attorneys and druggists, printers and booksellers, ship masters and accountants, painters and glaziers, bootmakers, coopers, tailors, and even boardinghouse keepers. But in the first half of the nineteenth century the character of the neighborhood changed: people moved their homes away from what was becoming the city's business center, a commercial area filled with warehouses and countinghouses reflecting the city's growing importance as the new nation's premier

2.5. The Stadt Huys Block in 1979, while excavations were under way. Broad Street is to the left of the site.

rubble and slowly uncovered the basement floors of the buildings that had recently stood on the site. Then the backhoe lifted up the floors and revealed what the archaeologists fervently hoped would prove to be an archaeological site (fig. 2.5).

With their crew of fifteen, a tight budget, and a three-month time limit, the archaeologists knew they couldn't waste a minute. In this short time and within their budget, they had to accomplish two things: they had to test the site to find its rich areas, and then, assuming that such areas existed, they had to excavate them as carefully as possible. Using their background research as a guide, they divided each of the ten promising lots into two parts—those closest to the street where early buildings had once stood, and those toward the center of the block where backyards had once been.

To see if any archaeological remains were present, the crew laid out a test cut in each part of the lots and then, with trowels and shovels, excavated the test cuts as archaeologists do everywhere (fig. 2.6). They peeled back the soil, layer by layer, within each test cut. Each layer, or stratum, that they excavated represented a specific event in the past, perhaps from a householder throwing out some trash in a backyard or filling up the hole of a privy pit, or from the East River flooding its banks and leaving behind a layer of sand or silt as it receded. Following what archaeologists call the Law of Stratigraphic Association, the crew knew that when they found artifacts together within a stratum, those artifacts had been deposited in the ground at the same time and as part of the same event. These associations provided context, or provenience, for the artifacts. When the archaeologists later examined them in the laboratory, they could use all the artifacts from a single layer to make inferences about, for example, the eating habits of a particular household at a particular moment in the history of early New York.

The crew, like archaeologists everywhere, knew the central paradox of archaeology: as you excavate a site, you destroy it. Once the archaeologists leave the field, their records and the artifacts are all that are left of the excavations. They therefore spent almost as much of their time recording information about the excavations as they did

2.6. An archaeologist excavating at a New York City site, 1981.

digging, in order to document the test cut and layer of soil where every artifact was found.

As they worked, crew members "screened" or sifted the soil they had excavated through quarter-inch wire mesh and picked out all the artifacts left behind in the screen (fig. 2.7). The artifacts—including glass and ceramic sherds, pieces of brick, buttons, pins, animal bones, and even fish scales and coffee beans—were put in an artifact bag assigned to that specific soil layer. Sifting was easy when the soil was dry and sandy, for then it fell freely through the mesh, but it was much harder when the soil was damp or claylike. Then the crew had to "wet screen," using water from hoses hooked up to nearby fire hydrants to wash the soil through the mesh. The icy-cold water, though refreshing at the beginning of the excavation while the days were still warm, became brutal with the approach of winter.

When the weather got cold, the crew needed shelters to protect themselves and the site. These shelters were simple affairs, made of wooden frames covered with polyethylene sheeting, but they did keep out the wind. On the worst days, however, neither the shelters nor the crew's down jackets, thermal underwear, and heavy work boots and gloves provided enough protection from the cold. They had to use kerosene heaters, and at times the fumes inside the shelters were nauseating. On those days the crew

2.7. Archaeologists screening at a New York City site, 1991.

needed frequent breaks and would run to the heated trailer that served as the field office for hot coffee or yet another pair of socks.

The crew soon found out that excavating in the city was not as civilized as they had anticipated. Although they did not camp out in tents or use machetes to cut their way through the jungle like their colleagues working in more remote places, they had other, distinctively urban problems to contend with. One was site security. Several times, despite the presence of security guards, the crew arrived in the morning to find that vandals had looted the site during the night. These pothunters had ripped through half-excavated features like privies or wells, hunting for such artifacts as bottles to sell or add to their own private collections. Not only were the pothunters trespassing and stealing property; they were also destroying the city's heritage. From the crew's perspective, the damage was crushing. Their painstaking work to excavate that feature had been for nought, and they would never even know what they had lost.

The crew faced other kinds of problems as well. One crew member, digging near the security fence, saw a blood-filled syringe, most likely carelessly discarded by a drug user, fly over the fence and land in his excavation unit. Another day, a mugger with a snatched purse still in hand ran across the site with police in pursuit. Occasionally, male passersby, seeing what looked like a construction site and therefore part of the world of men, would slip behind the fence to urinate. Some of them were taken aback when they realized, too late, that women were working behind that fence as well.

The excavations captured the imaginations of thousands of New Yorkers, who were astonished to learn that something might lie beneath the Wall Street district. Mayor Edward I. Koch held a press conference at the site, and the archaeologists found themselves being interviewed on radio and television and in newspapers and magazines. As word of the excavation spread, office workers looked down from windows in surrounding skyscrapers and followed its progress during morning coffee breaks. Lawyers, secretaries, tourists, brokers, schoolchildren, messengers, and cab drivers all stopped to peer through holes in the plywood fence. Many asked questions, shouted out advice, or tossed out an occasional sexual taunt at the women who were digging at the site. Unfortunately, the crew could not always take the time to stop work and explain that they were not looking for gold, oil, or even Peter Stuyvesant's wooden leg, but instead they had embarked on a scientific mission to uncover the lost past.[9]

As the field season progressed, it became clear to Rothschild and Wall that their initial fears of not finding anything important at the site were groundless. In fact, the site was even richer than they had imagined in their wildest dreams. They began to worry that there wasn't enough time and money to do it justice. The crew, excavating in the old backyard areas, uncovered a slew of features—privy pits from old outhouses and cisterns for water storage—dating from the seventeenth through the nineteenth centuries. Many of these features had been filled in with refuse after having been abandoned, making each of them a treasure trove. The food scraps, broken dishes, and manufacturers' debris left behind all documented everyday life on the block at different points in its history.

The crew began to test the areas near the front of the lots, where the oldest buildings had once stood. In the spot where the Landmarks Preservation Commission had dug a decade earlier, they tested to see if the old stone foundation walls were in fact from the Dutch Stadt Huys. In all, they put in seven test cuts alongside the walls in the Stadt Huys area, in places that had not been disturbed by the earlier excavations. Although they found artifacts that might well have been made in the seventeenth century, they also found artifacts in the same soil layers that had been made at least a century later, in the late eighteenth century. The wall thus had to have been built in the late eighteenth century and was not part of the Stadt Huys at all. Somewhat daunted, the crew nevertheless continued their methodical sweep across the site in those areas close to the street. Most of all, they hoped to find old basement floors still covered with artifacts left behind by the people who had once lived or worked in the old buildings.

Archaeologists' most cherished myth about fieldwork is that the best finds always turn up at the end of the project, when time is running out. This, alas, proved true at the Stadt Huys Block. As the end of the three-month field season approached, the crew digging in one test cut near the street noticed that they were finding plenty of seventeenth-century broken clay tobacco pipes and wine-bottle fragments, and very little else. This combination of artifacts is exactly what would be expected at an early tavern site. The test cut was located on the lot that they knew had been the site of the King's House, the tavern built by Governor Francis Lovelace in 1670 (see fig. 2.4). The crew began uncovering the remains of a stone foundation wall and a wooden floor, and they realized that they were digging inside the tavern's basement. But they knew that their time was up, and that construction might soon destroy this fragile remnant of colonial life. And so, on a gloomy New Year's Eve, with most of the tavern remains still unexcavated, they left the site, as they were required to do by the agreement between the Dollar Savings Bank and the Landmarks Preservation Commission. Although they had surrendered the site, they had just begun to fight for it.

In the new year, 1980, Rothschild, Salwen, and Wall met again with the staff from the Landmarks Preservation Commission. They reported the results of the excavation and outlined their concerns about the future of the tavern. The commission's staff agreed that it was inconceivable that these, the only extensive remains from seventeenth-century New York that had ever been found, would soon be destroyed by bulldozers. After a public hearing and a series of stormy meetings with representatives from the Dollar Savings Bank and other groups involved in constructing the new building, the parties reached a compromise: the developer would be able to start work on the foundation of the new building as originally planned, but the archaeologists would get more time and money to excavate the tavern. The agreement gave Rothschild and Wall a new budget of $35,000 and access to the tavern area for twenty-five excavation days while construction went on around them. The developer also agreed to install an archaeological exhibit in the new building's plaza.[10]

The archaeologists returned to the field and worked intermittently at the tavern, coordinating their work around the weather and construction schedules. Together, the tens of thousands of artifacts found at the tavern constituted the largest collection of materials from a seventeenth-century site that had ever been excavated in New York. By the end of the spring, the archaeologists had finished their excavations and yielded the site to construction workers.

Although the archaeologists had left the field, their work was far from over; they just shifted the operation to the laboratory, which had been up and running since field-work began. The fish warehouse had been wired for electricity, but there was still no running water; the crew drew water from a nearby fire hydrant to wash the artifacts. They worked inside the old fish refrigerator, which was very well insulated. In the winter, they used electric heaters to warm the lab; when summer came, they switched to fans. For the Stadt Huys Block, as for most projects, the level of effort expended in the laboratory was about three times that spent in the field. The crew began by washing the tons of muddy artifacts that had been discovered. Then they sorted the artifacts for analysis and identified them, counted or weighed them, and recorded the dates when they were made.

At the same time, the field archaeologists began to pore over the field records to reconstruct the site's stratigraphy. Others did additional historical research to help answer new questions raised by the excavations. A computer specialist designed a program to handle the huge amounts of artifact data, and team members began entering the data for analysis. Conservators began stabilizing some of the more fragile artifacts, such as coins, seventeenth-century leather shoes, and bone combs and toothbrush handles. Artists and photographers created a pictorial record of the excavations and its finds. Other specialists studied the animal bones and seeds from the site to reconstruct the environment in early New York and the food preferences of the people who had lived there. It was only

2.8. The new building at 85 Broad Street, where the Stadt Huys once stood, in the year 2000. The small buildings in the left foreground are nineteenth-century structures.

after all these analyses had been completed that the archaeologists could begin the long and arduous task of synthesizing the results of all three lines of investigation—the field data, the artifacts, and the historical research—into their six-hundred-page scientific report interpreting the archaeology of the Stadt Huys Block.[11]

Long before the report on the excavation at the Stadt Huys Block was completed, the new office tower (now known as 85 Broad Street) was finished, and Goldman Sachs, its primary tenant, had moved in (fig. 2.8). Today this investment banking and brokerage house sits on the very spot where, three hundred years ago, revelers had gathered at the King's House next door to New York's first city hall. Yet the block sports a visible reminder of its history and of the archaeological excavations: the locations of both the Stadt Huys and the King's House are outlined in colored paving stones in the building's plaza, and parts of the tavern's foundation wall have been reconstructed underground, where they can be seen through windows set flush into the plaza's pavement.

Digging in New York Today

Fortunately for archaeology in New York, the excavations at the Stadt Huys Block were a great success. The archaeologists found more than two tons of artifacts documenting the block's history from earliest Dutch colonial times through the nineteenth century. Their most spectacular finds were the thousands of seventeenth-century artifacts from the King's House Tavern—rare tangible testaments to a way of life in early New York that many feared had been lost forever (fig. 2.9). Because of the project's success, no one could now claim that it would be a waste of time and money to require archaeological excavations in heavily urbanized New York. As a result, archaeology has gone on to become a permanent part of the city's landscape.

Today archaeological projects in New York are mandated not only by the National Historic Preservation Act but also by the City Environmental Quality Review (CEQR) process. This process comes into play whenever a developer—either private or public—applies for a zoning variance from the city. Private development projects are overseen by the Landmarks Preservation Commission, and city projects are overseen by the city agency undertaking the development.

Because most development in the city is in private hands and the federal legislation does not apply, CEQR has sometimes been an archaeological bonanza. It was especially effective during the bull-market years of the 1980s, when there was a construction boom in the old part of the city. Many developers applied for zoning variances and consequently had to have their projects reviewed. A few had to grit their teeth and pay for excavations in order to get the permits they needed from the city. The scale of these archaeological projects matched the scale of construction during those prosperous years, when developers were building enormous office towers covering entire city blocks. Millions of dollars were spent on these archaeological projects, and millions of artifacts were recovered.

But those were the boom years. Since the 1980s developers have been cutting back the scale of their projects in the old part of the city. Often their plans call for more modest, "as-of-right" buildings that are usually not reviewed for their impact on the environment. These projects thus can destroy archaeological sites with impunity.

Yet CEQR can apply to smaller projects as well. In the late 1980s, for example, a developer wanted to build a row of single-family houses in Greenwich Village. Although the houses were small in scale and well within the zoning regulations for the neighborhood, the developer also planned to build an underground garage. For that he needed a special permit, and his entire project therefore fell under the city's environmental review. After reviewing his plans, the Landmarks Preservation Commission required an archaeological study, and a small-scale archaeological excavation was soon recovering glimpses of middle-class family life in the nineteenth century.[12]

The CEQR process does not always work smoothly, however. One site, at 17 State Street, became a cause célèbre for preservationists, archaeologists, and developers alike. This story began simply enough in 1985, when the William Kaufman Organization

2.9. A few of the artifacts, dating from ca. 1700, from the King's House Tavern at the Stadt Huys Block: bottles, tobacco pipes, and marbles. The bottles in the back row are made of red earthenware; those in front of them are made of glass.

started preparations for building a forty-two-story office tower with spectacular views of New York Harbor. It applied to the Department of City Planning for a zoning variance, and the project began to be reviewed under CEQR. The Landmarks Preservation Commission's archaeologist flagged the project for a background study because it was slated for a block in the heart of Dutch New Amsterdam. In early 1986 the developer hired an archaeologist to begin the study, but before it was even started, and for reasons that are still disputed today, the developer obtained a permit to excavate for the foundation of an "as-of-right" building, which required no environmental review. Bulldozers began digging for the building's foundation, destroying any archaeological site that might have been there. Archaeologists and preservationists were alarmed not only because a particular potential archaeological site had been destroyed, but also because the CEQR process itself was threatened. If one developer could violate the environmental review procedure and get away with it, why would any developer ever comply with CEQR?[13]

The case went to the city's Board of Standards and Appeals, which at that time mediated between developers and the Department of City Planning. The board held a public hearing at which the Landmarks Preservation Commission testified on the importance of CEQR in protecting the city's archaeological heritage. The commission proposed that the developer receive its zoning variance only if it agreed to create and maintain a small museum on New York City archaeology at the site. The developer agreed. In discussing the affair later, the developer, Melvyn Kaufman, said, "We were punished, so to speak. . . . The city made all kinds of terrible threats. I said: 'What do you want us to do? I can't put it back. You want to shoot me? Shoot me.'"[14] In 1990 Kaufman established *New York Unearthed: City Archaeology,* a public exhibit that opened in a small building in the plaza at 17 State Street and which is now administered by the South Street Seaport Museum.

On the whole, CEQR has been quite successful. In the years since the Stadt Huys Block project, scores of archaeological projects have been undertaken in New York. Today's projects are organized and run in much the same way as the Stadt Huys Block project. Although a few avocational archaeologists, university field-school students, and volunteers are still digging in backyards and parks and other less developed parts of the city, archaeology in New York today is largely contract archaeology. As such, it is required by governmental regulation to be done by archaeologists who are "professionals," who have advanced degrees in their specialty, and who make their livings from it. Not only has there been a quantum leap in the number of professional archaeologists working in the city—there are now almost a hundred of them—there has also been a quantum leap in the number of sites being excavated.

In spite of all the regulations, however, the city's archaeological sites still have relatively little protection. Any kind of ground disturbance—planting a garden in a park, putting a swimming pool in a backyard, building a road, laying a sewer line, or constructing a skyscraper—can destroy an archaeological site. Unfortunately, most new construction done in the city is not covered by any of the environmental protection laws. Most construction projects are not federally funded and do not require a federal permit or a city zoning variance. In 1991, for example, a surprisingly small number—fewer than 3 percent—of new building projects in the city underwent CEQR. Wittingly or not, then, construction in the city today often legally destroys important archaeological sites, as it has always done throughout the city's history.[15]

Over the past century—both before and after the environmental regulations—professional and avocational archaeologists have uncovered surprising evidence of New York's long-buried and neglected past. We begin its story with the oldest site, Port Mobil, on Staten Island's industrial waterfront.

PART **2**

The Deeper Past

CHAPTER THREE

The Creation of the World: The Paleoindian Period, 11,000–10,000 B.P.

In 1679 Jaspar Danckaerts and Peter Sluyter sailed from Amsterdam for the English colonies, hoping to find a place in America where their small religious community could practice its faith in freedom. They were Labadists, fiercely dedicated to the gospels, simple living, and the sharing of worldly goods. When their ship, *The Charles,* sailed into the Narrows, the frontier city at the head of the harbor was in the hands of the British. This European outpost, now called New York, had grown rapidly from its modest beginnings, more than fifty years earlier, as the Dutch colony of New Amsterdam (see fig. 2.4).

Yet along with the newcomers living in the area were those for whom the new port city was not part of a New World. For them it was part of a world that, though currently in turmoil, had long been theirs. These were the Munsees, a branch of the Lenape (or Delaware, as they are sometimes also known). The raw colonial city that some called New York was an intrusion into their ancestral territory, Lenapehoking. In a few more decades, most of the Munsees would have begun their long westward journeys in search of a new homeland. With the city's expansion over the next few centuries, they and the hundreds of generations of Native Americans who had been there before would be largely forgotten by the New Yorkers who replaced them.

At the time that the two Labadists arrived in New York, some Munsees were still in the city. Among them was Tantaque, an eighty-year-old man originally from Long Island. He was a well-known figure in early New York, for he was a generous man and, in his younger days, had often given fish to starving Europeans. On October 16, 1679, Tantaque came to Manhattan from New Jersey, where he had been staying with relatives, to pay a visit to Danckaerts and Sluyter. He was a frequent visitor at the house where they were staying, not far from the King's House on Pearl Street.

3.1. A petroglyph of a tortoise discovered in the New York Botanical Garden in the Bronx. The petroglyph's age is unknown.

Danckaerts' journal details the extraordinary encounter that took place that October day between the two followers of the French mystic Jean de Labadie and the aged Lenape. They asked Tantaque, "Where did your father come from . . . and your grand-father and great grand-father, and so on to the first of the race?" Tantaque replied by telling them the story of the creation of the world. According to Danckaerts, he

took a piece of coal out of the fire where he sat, and began to write upon the floor. He first drew a circle, a little oval, to which he made four paws or feet, a head and a tail. "This," said he, "is a tortoise, lying in the water around it," and he moved his hand round the figure, continuing, "this was or is all water, and so at first was the world, or the earth, when the tortoise gradually raised its round back up high, and the water ran off of it, and thus the earth became dry." He then took a little straw and placed it on end in the middle of the figure, and proceeded, "the earth was now dry, and there grew a tree in the middle of the earth, and the root of this tree sent forth a sprout beside it and there grew upon it a man, who was the first male. This man was then alone, and would have remained alone; but the tree bent over until its top touched the earth, and there shot therein another root, from which came forth another sprout, and there grew upon it the woman, and from these two are all men produced" [fig. 3.1].[1]

For archaeologists working today, more than three hundred years after Tantaque and the Labadists sat in that house in lower Manhattan and discussed the nature of the universe, the story of the land and its first inhabitants is a very different one. It is based not on oral tradition but on the combined efforts of many scientists, including geologists, paleobotanists, and paleontologists as well as archaeologists. For them, the land on which modern New York sits and the harbor it faces appeared not from the back of a rising tortoise, but from a different, though equally dramatic, event: the northward retreat of the vast ice sheets that had covered the area during the Wisconsin, the last of the great North American Ice Ages. With that retreat, the land that was to become the site of one of the largest cities in the world was ready for its first human inhabitants.

The First Inhabitants

Twenty-one thousand years ago, during the height of the Wisconsin, the New York area was uninhabitable. Tons of glacial ice covered the entire Northeast. In some areas the ice was more than nine thousand feet thick. The southernmost fronts of the vast glacier reached down to what today are Long Island and Staten Island. South of that was tundra. In those days, the locale was unrecognizable in other ways. It was an inland area, 120 miles from the shores of the Atlantic Ocean. Because sea levels at that time were at least three hundred feet lower than they are today, vast areas of the continental shelf were exposed to the south and east of what is now New York Harbor (fig. 3.2). The Hudson River cut deeply through the open land on the continental shelf on its way to meet the distant ocean.

3.2. The modern shoreline and the relative positions of the 20 m, 40 m, and 80 m isobaths, which represent the approximate locations of the ancient shorelines 6,000, 8,000, and 11,000 years ago, respectively.

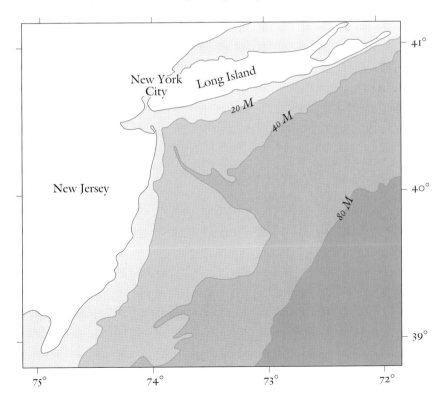

Then, as part of a worldwide warming trend, the ice sheets began receding north-ward, leaving behind huge glacial lakes of meltwater. The sea levels began their slow rise, and the continental shelf was gradually drowned by the advancing Atlantic Ocean. New York remained inland, however, and would stay so for many more thousands of years.

As the land became more hospitable, the first humans to set foot in what is now New York City arrived, around eleven thousand years ago. Their name for themselves has long been lost, but archaeologists call them Paleoindians. They entered a truly new world, one made up of lakes, marshes, and forests dominated by spruce, fir, pine, birch, alder, and some oak. These were not closed forests; they were parklands with open areas of tundra vegetation. Herds of moose, elk, mammoth, mastodon, and cari-bou roamed freely. This landscape has no modern analogue on the planet today. Many of the animals the early pioneers encountered have long been extinct, and the kind of forest they entered is no longer found at such southerly latitudes. That early New York would have been just as unrecognizable to Danckaerts and Tantaque as it would be to us.[2]

There are no clear signs telling archaeologists exactly when the Paleoindians arrived or what route they took to get there. These pioneers probably made their way up from the south or across from points west. Some traces of their passage may well lie some-where out on the immense reaches of the continental shelf that is now submerged be-neath the Atlantic Ocean.

Even more questions remain unanswered about the arrivals of the first Paleoindians, or their predecessors, in the Americas. The story begins sometime during the Pleis-tocene, the time of the Ice Ages, when small family groups of migrating peoples, per-haps arriving in several waves, colonized the Americas. Many archaeologists believe that these first Americans entered the Western Hemisphere by crossing the Bering Land Bridge, an immense tract of land that at that time connected Siberia with Alaska. The rising sea levels at the end of the Pleistocene have long since covered that point of en-try, and the land bridge itself now lies beneath the waters of the Bering Strait. Because of recent discoveries in South America as well as in North America, the problems of dating these early arrivals, determining the number of migrations, or even plotting the routes into the Americas have become some of the most hotly contested and keenly followed issues in archaeology today, with no clear consensus on any one of them.[3]

The Paleoindian period provides the strongest evidence that archaeologists have for understanding the lives of early Americans in the continental United States. Sites for the earliest Paleoindians, a people archaeologists call Clovis (after the site in New Mexico where they were first recognized), have been discovered in the Plains and the Southwest with radiocarbon dates clustering between 11,200 and 10,900 B.P. and in the

Northeast with radiocarbon dates ranging between 10,700 and 10,200 B.P. Whether these Paleoindians, or their ancestors, were the first people to arrive in the continental United States is not yet known. The search for the first Americans is far from over. Some archaeologists believe that a few sites may date to a somewhat earlier period. The data are controversial, and the jury is still out on them.[4]

The debates on these issues will probably rage for decades to come, but the one point on which most archaeologists agree is that in Clovis times there was, in archaeologist Brian Fagan's words, "a veritable explosion in the number of archaeological sites throughout North America." Paleoindians are the earliest people to have left undisputed "archaeological footprints" across the country. These footprints are the best guide that archaeologists have in trying to re-create the human experience at the time that North America was being explored and settled.[5]

What we currently know about Paleoindians suggests that they spread rapidly throughout the continent in the final centuries of the Ice Ages. These pioneering American families would have had to surmount formidable geographical obstacles, adapt to a variety of environments, and maintain their group size as they settled into this scarcely inhabited and unfamiliar continent. They did this without guns, wagons, horses, steel axes, guides, or any of the other paraphernalia of more recent pioneers. Their experiences are so foreign to those of the modern world that it is sometimes difficult for us to appreciate the enormity of the challenges they faced or the scope of their achievements.[6]

Although Clovis sites have been found throughout the country, they are few in number, because not many places have survived the natural and human disturbances to the landscape over the past eleven thousand years. This makes it all the more astonishing that one of the few sites that can testify to that great human undertaking, the exploration and settlement of North America during the period when the glaciers were finally retreating, was found in the modern urban sprawl that is New York City.

A Discovery on the Waterfront

The story of Paleoindians in what is now New York City is a fragmentary one, based on some broken stone tools that these early Americans left behind at a campsite almost eleven thousand years ago. At the same time it is also the story of some modern New Yorkers who, against all odds, found those long-abandoned tools along New York's industrial waterfront on Staten Island. The credit for this major discovery belongs to a small group of avocational archaeologists who had spent years documenting their city's ancient past during a period when no professional archaeologists were interested.

By the 1950s, traces of the Paleoindian presence were increasingly turning up in the East, and sites were being discovered in the Hudson and Delaware River Valleys. But

Port Mobil annually or if they stayed in the area only that one time. In addition, we do not know what animals the Paleoindians killed and butchered because no food remains were recovered from the site.

Although it is tempting to picture these Paleoindian hunters, armed only with their spears, stalking a mastodon across land that is now in the shadow of the World Trade Center, it is unlikely that such a dramatic encounter ever took place. In fact, the relationship between these now-extinct megafauna and early peoples is an enigmatic one. Certainly, mastodon remains are fairly common in the East. In New York City they have been found in peat deposits in the Harlem River and upper Manhattan. But no mastodons have ever been found in association with any Paleoindian artifacts. There is no evidence that Paleoindians anywhere in the East depended on these massive animals for food or focused their lives around hunting them. Although mastodons may have been hunted or scavenged, they probably played a minor role, at best, in the Paleoindian larder. They may have played a more prominent role in Paleoindian mythology, or the Paleoindians and these great beasts simply may have ignored each other.[14]

Most archaeologists argue these early peoples more likely hunted smaller, more readily available game (such as caribou, fox, marten, or hare), using the meat for food and the hides for clothing. Although Paleoindians are sometimes referred to simply as hunters, there was much more to their diet than meat. Evidence from nearby Pennsylvania shows that the Paleoindians there ate fish as well as a variety of plant foods, including hawthorn plums, ground cherries, grapes, and seeds. Such foods were probably also gathered, stored, and eaten by the Port Mobil peoples at some point in their seasonal rounds.[15]

Port Mobil itself was more than just a hunting station. The items found there included not just weapons, but also scrapers for working on wood and animal skins, knives used for a variety of tasks, and drills and gravers for working on bone or antler. This wide range of tool types suggests that small groups of men, women, and children may have come to the area, stayed for a while, and worked at a number of different activities before moving on. The women may have used the scrapers to prepare the hides brought in from the successful hunt. They could then start the long and arduous process of transforming the hides into the boots and clothes that every family member needed for survival, or into the equally essential bedding and tent covers.

In trying to reconstruct the ways of life of past societies, archaeologists frequently turn to studies of modern groups for useful analogies. In this case, we have used analogies from modern hunting-and-gathering groups to interpret these stone tools in terms of the Paleoindian economy and division of labor. Modern analogues lead us to assume that hunting, heavy butchering, and some toolmaking were part of the working world of men, while food preparation, child care, the manufacture and care of clothing, other

3.4. A drawing of a reconstructed Paleoindian settlement at the Adkins site in Maine. The pioneering Paleoindian families who stayed at Port Mobil may have lived in similar homes.

kinds of toolmaking, and the gathering of plant foods were part of the working world of women. Ritual and healing activities, as well as education of the young, could be part of either world. It is likely, however, that these divisions were far from rigid—flexibility for group members in the face of changing circumstances, as well as individual abilities and preferences, surely figured into the equation—and that cooperation among all members of the group was an integral part of these societies.[16]

Although the imperishable stone tools are the only surviving remains of the encampments at Port Mobil, the lives of these people contained much more. They had not only the vegetable foods that were part of their diet, their shelters (fig. 3.4), the drying racks where meat and fish were smoked or clothing aired, and their warm clothing, but also the traditions they passed on from generation to generation, the strong emotional ties that bound families together, the rituals that eased the uncertainties of life and death, and even the names they gave to the features of the landscape. These aspects of their lives, for now at least, are hidden from us, but we know they were there.[17]

Settling Down in the Archaic,

10,000–3,700 B.P.

In the New York City area, as elsewhere in the Northeast, sweeping environmental changes marked the millennia that followed the end of the Ice Ages. These were also times of great cultural innovation, as people adjusted to this changing world. During this period, which archaeologists call the Archaic, Native Americans acquired new tools, adapted to newly available plant and animal foods, practiced new rituals, and began to see their relationships to the land and their neighbors in new ways. Based on what we know of these cultural achievements and environmental changes, we have subdivided this long Archaic period into three cultural periods: Early Archaic (10,000–8,000 B.P.), Middle Archaic (8,000–6,000 B.P.), and Late Archaic (6,000–3,700 B.P.).[1]

The Empty Quarter? The Early Archaic

The seas were still rising ten thousand years ago, still in the process of drowning the flat continental shelf where Paleoindians had probably once set up their camps. New York City was still inland then, with sea levels at least 150 feet below their present stand. It would be another six thousand years before the rising seas finally reached near-modern levels. The Hudson River, so casually crossed today by bridge or tunnel, was a dramatic fjord then, the world's most southerly, still cutting its way through the exposed continental shelf to the distant seas. And the city's great harbor, through which countless ships would later bring millions of immigrants, had yet to be formed.

The landscape was markedly different in other ways, too. Glacial lakes were becoming marshes and swamps, and offshore islands and estuaries were common features of the landscape. Many of the large animals that had so dominated the land in Paleoindian times were gone. Mammoth and mastodon were now extinct, while others, like moose and caribou, had migrated north, following the glaciers.[2]

For many archaeologists working in the Northeast in the 1950s and 1960s, one of the most significant aspects of these early post-glacial times was that human populations seemed to have simply disappeared. No archaeological sites from this period had been found anywhere in the region. And so this area, today one of the most densely populated in the world, was envisioned as an almost "empty quarter" during those post-glacial centuries. The best explanation for this phenomenon seemed to be an environmental one. Archaeologists argued that the landscape may have been a nearly silent, closed pine forest, offering limited numbers of seeds, nuts, or tubers not only for humans but also for the game animals on which they depended, like white-tailed deer and turkey. For these reasons, the argument continued, the Northeast was abandoned, albeit temporarily, after Paleoindian times. One geologist even suggested that the swarms of insects associated with pine forests might have made the area too miserable for human habitation.[3]

This apparent desertion of the area raised a number of questions about the whereabouts of the descendants of the Paleoindians. Had they moved on to other parts of the continent, which offered better opportunities for their hunting-and-gathering way of life? Had they migrated north, following the paths of the retreating glaciers, to hunt the animals of the taiga and tundra, such as moose and caribou? Or had a disaster in those distant times dramatically reduced their population?

Whatever the reasons, it appeared to many archaeologists that New York and most of the Northeast had become an empty quarter for an enormous stretch of time, lasting anywhere between two thousand and four thousand years. And then, six or eight thousand years ago, the archaeologists believed, the environment began to change, producing a landscape dominated first by oak-hemlock forests and then by oak-hickory ones. These forests, unlike the earlier pine-dominated ones, would have attracted significant populations of white-tailed deer, turkey, and other game that eat mast, the nuts found on the forest floor. The continued presence of these mast-eaters, along with the highly nutritious nuts themselves, presumably transformed the region into an attractive place for later Archaic peoples, who migrated there from other parts of the continent and resettled the area.[4]

While the professional archaeologists in the Northeast were busy reconstructing post-glacial environments in an attempt to explain the apparent absence of Early Archaic sites in the region, their colleagues in the Southeast were finding a number of extraordinary stratified sites, in the North Carolina Piedmont and in Tennessee. Not only were those archaeologists able to demonstrate that those regions were occupied in the Early Archaic and subsequent Middle Archaic times, they were also able to track changes in spear-point styles over long periods of time. They could use this sequence of point types to date sites that couldn't be dated by other means (fig. 4.1). So, for the Southeast, there was a continuity of Native American life from Paleoindian times on, a continuity in sharp contrast to the seemingly abandoned Northeast.[5]

Albert and Robert Anderson, Joseph Bodnar, Donald Sainz (all of whom were involved in the Port Mobil finds), and their friend Donald Hollowell were following the accounts of these discoveries in the South with great interest. They knew that distinctive spear points, commonly called bifurcates because their bases are divided in two, were turning up at some of these Early Archaic sites in the South (see fig. 4.1). In fact, these points seemed to be almost a signature for that period.

These Staten Islanders had been exploring along the western shores of the island. In the 1960s the area where they were digging was still so undeveloped that Albert Anderson recalled feeling that he was lost in an earlier time as he trapped woodchucks, harvested oysters, and gathered wild greens for salad. And it was there that Anderson and his friends began finding a number of sites with spear points, bifurcates and others, that in the Southeast were the hallmarks of the Early Archaic (fig. 4.2).[6]

Although the Staten Island group's Port Mobil finds had been exciting because they were the oldest ones in the city, their Early Archaic finds proved to be far more important. Because of them, the prevailing view of the Northeast as an empty quarter began to crumble. The four Early Archaic sites the avocational archaeologists found—Ward's Point (see fig. 1.1), Richmond Hill, H. F. Hollowell, and Old Place—forced many professional archaeologists to rethink their views of post-glacial life in the Northeast. These sites were striking in other ways, too. Unlike Port Mobil, where the artifacts recovered were surface finds, these Early Archaic discoveries were made in situ, in deeply buried stratified sites. The artifacts' relationships to each other could thus be examined, and any charcoal associated with them could be dated.[7]

The Staten Islanders were thrilled by their discoveries. One of them, Donald Hollowell, even pawned his guitar to raise the money for radiocarbon dating to prove the sites' antiquity. Recognizing how important these sites were, they contacted William A. Ritchie, the state archaeologist at the New York State Museum and Science Bureau, and went to Albany to show him what they had found. At that time, Ritchie was the senior figure in professional archaeology in New York State. He had spent years excavating and analyzing sites and had published dozens of works on New York's past. He was also an expert on the Archaic and, at the time of the Staten Island finds, was one of the leading proponents of the cultural hiatus theory. He was convinced that the area had been largely abandoned for more than four thousand years.[8]

Ritchie's interest was piqued by the discoveries, and he came to Staten Island along with Robert Funk, another expert on the Archaic, who later succeeded him as state

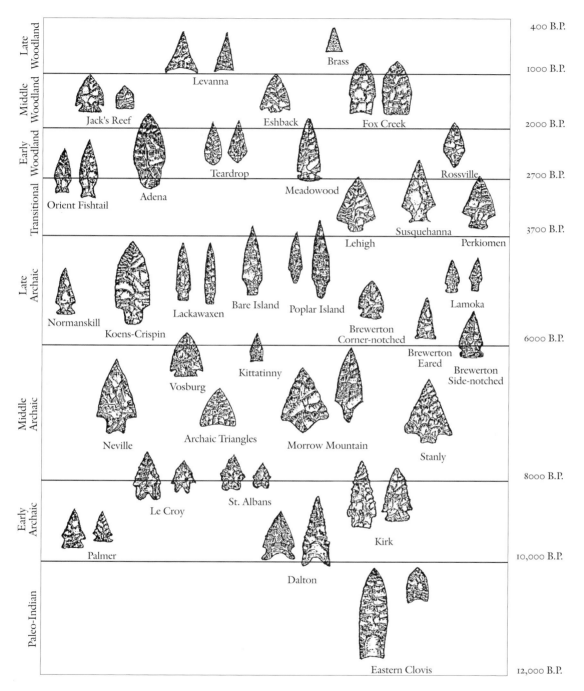

4.1. *The chronological sequence of some of the styles of projectile points for spears and arrows favored by hunters in the Northeast.*

1   2   3   4   5   6

7   8   9   10

11   12   13   14   15

16   17   18   19   20   21

22   23   24   25

26   27   28   29

30   31   32   33

archaeologist. As Anderson remembered it, they all sat down at his kitchen table, looked at all the records, drawings, and artifacts, and then went out to inspect the sites. After examining all the evidence, Ritchie and Funk were convinced that these discoveries were so important that the entire concept of an empty Northeast during the Early Archaic had to be reevaluated. With the cooperation of the Staten Islanders, Ritchie and Funk analyzed the four sites and wrote their landmark paper on the Early Archaic, in which they described these "many novel and significant data."[9] The empty quarter was empty no longer. The descendants of the Paleoindians had by no means abandoned the area. They were still there, adapting their lives to the continuing and dramatic changes in their world.

Ward's Point

Of the four sites found, Ward's Point offers the clearest view of life in those distant times. The site is located at the southwestern corner of the city, opposite the place where New Jersey's Raritan River meets the Arthur Kill and together they enter New York Harbor. Today, standing near the site on a clear summer's day and looking west, you can see sailboats racing along the kill and, off to the south, the cruise ships, cargo containers, oil tankers, and all the other traffic of the busy harbor. But the world was vastly different during the Early Archaic. The Arthur Kill was a smaller stream then, and parts of today's great harbor were still exposed land masses, crossed by creeks, bisected by the Hudson, and marked by lagoons and forested areas.

The Early Archaic occupation at Ward's Point was deeply buried beneath layers of deposit left behind by more recent groups of Indian peoples who had lived and worked in the area. In the lowest level of the site, Zone 5, the Andersons and Hollowell uncovered a surprisingly intimate view of domestic life eight thousand years ago.

The archaeologists discovered several hearths at the site. These fires not only gave warmth, light, and protection from marauding animals; they were also the focus for a number of daily tasks that took place around them. Cooking was evidently one

4.2. Typical tools used by men and women staying at Ward's Point during the Early Archaic: (1–2) Kirk Stemmed points; (3) broad-stemmed point; (4, 6, 10–11, 13–15) Kanawha Stemmed points (bifurcates); (7–9) LeCroy Bifurcated-Base points; (5) damaged bifurcated-base point; (12) small-stemmed point or drill; (16–18) end scrapers; (19, 26) ovate knives; (20, 24) flake knives; (21, 25) side scrapers; (22) small stone tool of unknown function; (23) small spokeshave scraper; (27–28, 30–31) chopping tools of various sizes and shapes that were most likely used as heavy hide scrapers; (29) possible bannerstone fragment; (32–33) bifacially flaked and partially ground celts.

of them, because the team found large amounts of fire-cracked rock scattered close to the hearths. Reddened and broken stones such as these are evidence for stone boiling, one of the oldest cooking techniques in the Americas. This cumbersome method involves gathering stones, each roughly the size of a plum, and then heating them in a hearth. When the stones are red-hot, the cook pulls them out of the fire with sticks and then drops them into a skin or bark container filled with water and whatever else is being cooked that day, such as meat, seeds, nuts, fish, or greens. The hot stones bring the liquid to a simmer, and then, as they begin to cool in the pot, they are scooped out and replaced by a fresh batch of hot ones until the meal is ready.

Although we know that someone at Ward's Point was using this method to cook meals, we do not know what the people were eating. No remains of plants or animals were found at the site. It may well have been a meat stew that the cook set to simmer by the fires, because there were broken spear points nearby as well as some knives that could have been used to butcher the kill (the artifacts mentioned in the following paragraphs are pictured in fig. 4.2).

The women at Ward's Point were doing more than boiling their families' meals. They were also transforming the hides acquired from the men's successful hunts into the clothing, boots, bedding, and tent covers that were essential for their families' survival. Hide preparation is a long and arduous task, and a number of tools associated with it were left behind at Ward's Point. There were heavy scraping tools for the initial "defleshing" of the skin and smaller scraping tools for the later, more delicate, stages of hide working.

Certainly, some members of the group were hunting in the vicinity of Ward's Point, for the Staten Island team found a number of spear points, thirty-six in all, including the bifurcates that had first generated their excitement. But these Early Archaic hunters were also working on their equipment at the site. In fact, the areas surrounding the hearths appear to have been workshops. Scattered around the hearths were a number of tools of the sort used to make other tools—hammerstones to rough out the shape of a stone tool before the more careful flaking was done with bone or antler to turn it into a spear point, chert cores ready to be shaped into tools, and a spokeshave to straighten the wood for a spear shaft.[10]

Someone at Ward's Point sat near the hearth laboriously grinding stones to make celts, tools that would later be used in woodworking.[11] He may have planned to make a canoe that would carry the group and their gear on to their next encampment. But for some reason he never finished the job; four half-done celts were left behind in the workshop area. We don't know how long these Early Archaic peoples stayed at Ward's Point. Nor do we know if this site was part of their territory to which they returned on a seasonal basis or if they were just passing through.

The Early Archaic occupation at Ward's Point is only a small part of this large and magnificent site, which is now a National Historic Landmark. For thousands of years after these Early Archaic peoples put out their fires and moved on, other Indian peoples continued to come to Ward's Point to live and to bury their dead. Native Americans were still living there in the eighteenth century, when European colonists were farming nearby. Because of Ward's Point's long and important history, we take up its story again in later chapters.

The discovery of the Early Archaic sites in Staten Island did more than add a small chapter to the eleven-thousand-year history of New York City. It helped archaeologists rethink the history of the entire region and the ways in which past human societies responded to the post-glacial world. In the decades since the Andersons, Bodnar, Hollowell, and Sainz made their discoveries, other Early Archaic sites have been found throughout the Northeast. Many of these more recent finds were made by professional crews using modern technologies, and their results have led to an understanding of what the environment was like in those years.

These more recent environmental reconstructions done by archaeologists and palynologists suggest a less bleak and more complex picture in New York and elsewhere in the Northeast. The pine-oak forests were probably much more limited geographically than had been previously thought, and the rest of the landscape was likely marked by considerable environmental diversity, with a mosaic of wetlands, oak stands, and a variety of other plant resources. This environmental diversity, some archaeologists now think, may have made this area an attractive and hospitable quarter for both human and animal populations.[12]

The debates about Early Archaic peoples have now shifted from environmental explanations for their disappearance to estimates of their population size and questions about their adaptations to this post-glacial landscape. Part of our difficulty in trying to reconstruct the lives of these people is that their environment, like that of the earlier Paleoindian peoples, has no modern analogues. It is completely beyond modern experience and is, in that sense, a true terra incognita for scientific exploration.

Exploring this unknown terrain can be as treacherous as it is exciting. Because we have so little data—just a few stone tools, hearths, and patchy environmental reconstructions—it can be tempting to fall into the trap of environmental determinism. That would be a mistake. These ancient societies were not controlled by their environment, nor were people's lives determined by it. They, like any group of people, ancient or modern, were powerful actors in their relationship with their environment. As historian William Cronon put it, the "environment may initially shape the range of choices available to a people at a given moment, but then culture reshapes environment in responding to those choices. The reshaped environment presents a new set of choices for cultural reproduction, thus setting up a new cycle of mutual determination."[13] It is this cycle of mutual determination that archaeologists are now working to understand.

Oystering along the Hudson: The Middle Archaic

Of all the traces left by the aborigines along the New York seacoast,

the most abundant and familiar are the shell heaps—the beds of refuse

marking the the sites of ancient villages, camps and isolated wigwams.

—M. R. Harrington, 1909

By the beginning of the Middle Archaic, eight thousand years ago, the forests were filled with oak, chestnut, and hemlock trees. The seas were still rising, although not as rapidly as before, and the coast was still distant on the horizon. There are large gaps in what we know about life in the New York City area during this long period. For the first time, however, we see signs of the close relationship between the human populations and the seas and estuaries that would soon become prominent features of their world—a relationship that would continue for the next eight thousand years.[14]

Our most visible clues to this long-term connection with the coastal waters are the shell middens that until recently had been a conspicuous part of New York City's landscape. These shell heaps are complex affairs and may be more than just refuse left over from a meal of shellfish. They could be refuse from fish bait or shell bead making, places for human burials, or simply piles of shell put in place to stabilize the terrain.[15]

These ancient shell heaps have captured the imaginations of the city's residents throughout New York's history. Dutch colonists were intrigued by a large shell heap near the Fresh Water Pond, or Collect, in lower Manhattan. Among the later citizens captivated by these middens was Daniel Tredwell. When he died at the age of ninety-five in 1921, his obituary in *The New York Times* described him as Brooklyn's oldest businessman. Like many prominent men of his day, Tredwell was a polymath. At various times in his life he was a reporter for Walt Whitman's newspaper, *The Brooklyn Daily Freeman,* a chief clerk of the Supreme Court of Brooklyn, and an author of a number of books, including *A Plea For Bibliomania, A Sketch of the Life of Apollonius of Tyana,* and especially *Personal Reminiscences of Men and Things on Long Island*. In that volume, he includes entries from a diary that he kept before the Civil War, when as a boy he would go with his family to explore the shell heaps. One excerpt, in particular, shows how these middens could seize the imagination. The entry for Friday, September 20th, 1839, reads in part:

> Went out to the bay yesterday with my father. This is a favorite recreation of his. . . . On the way out we pass many Indian shell heaps bleached as white as snow, which they much resemble at a distance. Some of them on the banks of the creek extend from fifteen to thirty feet upon the bank and under the water, in many instances entirely across the creek. These shell heaps, long ere this, had excited our curiosity and we had proposed all manner of questions concerning their authors. These questions my father did not and could not satisfactorily answer, and we were consequently unsatisfied, and hence there was a constantly recurring inquiry. My father is greatly interested in these shell heaps, their contents and their authors . . . and he was pleased to observe the interest manifested by us.[16]

Today, more than 150 years later, archaeologists still have "all manner of questions concerning their authors." One of them involves timing. When did the peoples who lived in this area first start harvesting oysters and other shellfish from the surrounding waters? So far, the oldest clues we have come from a nearly seven-thousand-year-old Middle Archaic shell midden site. Although earlier societies may have gathered these mollusks, no evidence exists to show that they did. Any ancient coastal middens they may have left behind would have long since been buried by the rising waters of the Atlantic.[17]

The evidence we do have comes from Dogan Point, a Middle Archaic midden on the banks of the Hudson River about thirty miles north of the modern city's limits. Then, as now, the Hudson was an estuary as far north as Troy, New York. During the Middle Archaic, the saline levels in the Hudson were such that the lower reaches of the river could support abundant oyster beds. At Dogan Point, on the bluff and just below it, archaeologists discovered large shell middens, in this case made up of oystering debris left behind by Middle Archaic and Late Archaic peoples. Although shell middens still exist all along the Atlantic Coast as far south as Florida, Dogan Point is especially significant: its radiocarbon dates, ranging from 6,900 to 4,400 B.P., make it the oldest shell midden found on the Atlantic Coast.[18]

Even though we know that people were harvesting oysters back then, the significance of oysters in their diets remains uncertain. Some archaeologists argue that because oysters have so little caloric value, it is unlikely that they were ever a major part of the diet of these ancient societies. Some modern studies estimate that a pound of shelled oyster meat adds up to only 475 calories. If that is the case, and if oysters did play a major role in the Archaic diet, then an average adult would have had to eat a staggering number of oysters, about 250 a day, to maintain daily caloric requirements.

For any population, even a small one, that was dependent on oysters, the numbers that would have to be gathered and shucked would be considerable.[19]

Nonetheless, oysters may have been important as a source of protein, with other foods meeting caloric requirements. Oysters may have been more important at those times of the year when other foodstuffs were not readily available. Some archaeologists have even suggested that they were starvation food, especially important in late winter or early spring, when richer game and nuts were unavailable. Oysters could also have been smoked or dried at the shellfish-gathering stations, to be taken away and eaten another day or traded with inland groups for desirable commodities. Alternatively, they may have been delicacies eaten, fresh or smoked, for the sheer pleasure of their taste.[20]

Long after the Middle Archaic peoples had moved on, other peoples continued to come to the area to harvest oysters and other shellfish, leaving behind shell middens throughout the region. In fact, they were still doing this as recently as the nineteenth century. We shall return to such middens in subsequent chapters, as we try to understand life in an area whose landscape was gradually yet inexorably being transformed from an inland territory into a coastal one.

There is little evidence of Middle Archaic life in the city proper. Spear points dating to this time period were discovered in a few sites on Staten Island (see fig. 4.1), but these artifacts were not found in any clear archaeological context. Without such context, it is difficult to use these artifacts to reconstruct the lives of the people who made and used them. These Middle Archaic peoples may have spent comparatively little time inland, which is what the land that makes up New York City was at that time. They may have chosen to spend much of their time on the continental shelf, where all traces of their presence would have long since been drowned by the rising seas.[21]

To the limited and generalizing eye of the modern observer, the way of life during this long period—almost ten times as long as the United States has been a nation—appears to be an unchanging one made up of hunting, fishing, and gathering of plants and shellfish. Every now and then this pattern is altered slightly as archaeologists recognize the appearance of a new style of spear point, a new type of tool, new raw materials suggesting new trade routes, or an increase in shellfish eating. But the people living over the course of those many centuries may have seen many changes—not only in their economic lives, but in their social and ritual ones as well—that have either left no traces or whose traces we have yet to find.

From other sites in the Northeast and Middle Atlantic we have a general impression of people settling down and of populations increasing in size. But this is only an impression. We have no knowledge of their seasonal rounds, their social or ceremonial lives, their contacts with neighboring peoples on the now-drowned coast or further inland, or of their relationships to the land. Much of the evidence that might have documented this two-thousand-year period was destroyed in the past two hundred years of urbanization.

A Familiar Landscape: The Late Archaic

By the time the Late Archaic began, six thousand years ago, sea levels were about sixty feet below their present level. The area must have been an attractive place for the people living there, for the surrounding forests were rich deciduous ones, with large stands of oak and chestnut. Deer, bear, raccoon, and turkey were common, along with flocks of migrating birds, and the rivers and the approaching coastal waters offered many and varied fish and mollusks.

Traces of these Late Archaic peoples remain all over the city. The population seems to have been much greater, not only there but throughout the whole Northeast, than in earlier times. Perversely, although we have abundant artifacts from this period, we seem to have few clues to Late Archaic Indian life.[22]

A few shreds of evidence for the Late Archaic come from two sites in Manhattan that were excavated at the beginning of the twentieth century.[23] Both sites are on the northern part of the island along the shores of the Hudson River. These must have been particularly agreeable spots, because Native Americans continued to live there generation after generation, even after the Late Archaic. Artifacts representing thousands of years of the city's Indian heritage have been discovered at both sites. Indeed, Native peoples were still living at one of the sites when the Dutch were building their colony at the southern tip of the island. Even today, the breathtaking views of the Hudson from these sites attract modern New Yorkers, despite all the flotsam and jetsam that now burden the river.

The more southerly site, Tubby Hook (see fig. 1.1), is a shell midden located alongside the old Hudson River Railroad tracks, near the foot of what is now a busy commercial street in Washington Heights. The site is at the base of what was once a rocky ravine close to the river. These days, some of New York City's homeless population have set up their own encampments nearby. Inwood (see fig. 1.1), the other site, is in a city park at the northern tip of the island. In addition to a midden, there are rock shelters nearby where Late Archaic and other peoples stayed briefly and where modern people still seek shelter.

Shellfish were part of the Late Archaic economy at both sites. Although the importance of shellfish is unclear, the middens themselves may have contributed to the sites' prolonged appeal. Middens can create and maintain what archaeologists call a "disturbed environment," one that provides a fertile ground for the colonization of an area by such plants as marsh elder, goosefoot, or sunflower, which produce edible seeds in the fall. The presence of these nutritious wild plant foods would have added to the attractions of these sites, making them especially desirable places to return to in the fall. Because many archaeologists think that the gathering of shellfish and plants was part of the working world of women and children, these sites may reflect their contributions to the family economy.[24]

Scattered among the oyster shells at both sites were artifacts, including Late Archaic spear points and knives, that reflect the contributions that the men of the group were making during the same period. Stone axe heads are also common finds at sites throughout the city, highlighting the growing importance of woodworking tasks in making canoes to travel on the Hudson and other waterways, building fish weirs in the local waters, or constructing more substantial homes (fig. 4.3; see also fig. 4.1).

Also turning up at sites throughout the city is another Late Archaic artifact, commonly called a bannerstone (fig. 4.4). For many years archaeologists all over the country were curious about the purpose of these beautifully polished stone artifacts, some grooved, others wing-shaped with a hole drilled through the middle for the insertion of a wooden shaft. Among them was Alanson Skinner, who was one of the first professional archaeologists to work in the city and who, with Amos Oneroad, dug at both Tubby Hook and Inwood (fig. 4.5). Skinner recognized the bannerstones' antiquity, puzzled over their function, and finally concluded that there "seem to be neither records nor plausible theories as to their use." Because of their drilled holes, some early archaeologists speculated that these mysterious artifacts had once been mounted on wooden shafts and served as the Native American equivalent of a royal mace or standard. Others wondered if they were early musical wind instruments, and one early archaeologist even started to write a musical composition for them. But further archaeological work over the years produced a more prosaic explanation. Bannerstones have since been found in situ at Late Archaic sites along with the remains of other components of spearthrowers, weapons that are sometimes known as atlatls. The bannerstones, then, were neither ceremonial flags nor stone flutes but instead were carefully crafted weights designed to fit on the wooden shafts of the spearthrowers. A spearthrower so weighted would be a very forceful propel-

4.3. Stone axes discovered in upper Manhattan at the beginning of the twentieth century. These tools could have been used for making dugout canoes, shelters, or fishing weirs, or for other woodworking tasks.

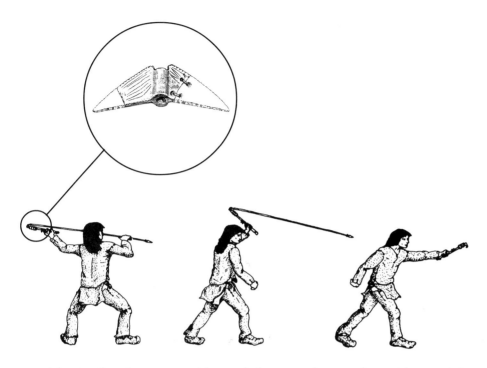

4.4. A hunter throwing a spear with an atlatl, or spearthrower, along with an artist's reconstruction of a broken bannerstone, or atlatl weight, found on the banks of the Harlem River in upper Manhattan during the early twentieth century.

ling device, with a strong whiplike effect. Modern experiments suggest that banner-stones may also have served as "silencers," diluting the sound waves of the propelled spear. By Late Archaic times, these powerful weapons had become a common part of the arsenal of local hunters.[25]

There are not enough sites in the city to decipher the annual economic cycle of the Late Archaic peoples who lived and worked there. Based on discoveries made in neighboring regions, we doubt that they were always on the move. At this time, populations throughout the Northeast were settling down within territories that were becoming more and more clearly defined, and this was probably the case in coastal New York as well. We can speculate that the Late Archaic peoples had a warm-weather main base camp or village, from which they went to spring and fall fishing stations and to places for gathering wild plants. The fall may have been a particularly important time for gathering nuts and seeds to tide them over during the leaner months ahead. They probably also went to local shellfishing stations in the summer and at emergency times during the year. In the winter, they may have spent time at sheltered hunting settlements in the interior. In addition, they probably also visited neighboring groups of kin or allies to exchange goods and to maintain social and political relationships. Presumably, they also held a number of ceremonies during the year that were important for their physical and spiritual well-being. Unfortunately, no evidence for that important aspect of their lives has been recovered at the handful of Late Archaic sites found in the city. As for the names they gave themselves and their territory, or the styles of their houses, clothes, ornaments, or hair, we must rely largely on our imaginations (fig. 4.6).[26]

We do have some hints of the wider social world of these Late Archaic peoples. These come from the spear points and knives abandoned during that period. Although many of these tools were made from such local stones as quartz, many others were made from argillite, a stone most easily found in the interior, in the central Delaware River Valley. We don't know whether the finished tools or only the raw materials came from there. Other raw materials and tools, foods, ideas, and even marriage partners probably also moved easily along these routes to the west and up the equally navigable routes to the north.[27]

4.5. Alanson Skinner (left) *with Amos Oneroad, a member of the Menominee tribe, in 1922. Together they dug at the Tubby Hook and Inwood sites, and at the Throgs Neck and Clasons Point sites in the Bronx, while working for the newly formed Museum of the American Indian, now the National Museum of the American Indian, Smithsonian Institution.*

Throughout eastern North America, the Late Archaic period seems to be, on the one hand, a time of increasing social interaction among various groups marked by exchanges of ideas, tools, and raw materials, and, on the other hand, a time of increasing regionalism and settling down. It was also a time of elaborate burial ceremonies. But it is not until the following period, the Transitional, that we have any evidence of ritual life in what is now New York.[28]

In looking at the archaeological record, we begin to see a dramatic difference in the lives of the people whose history we have been following and an equally dramatic change in their landscape. By the end of the Late Archaic, thirty-seven hundred years ago, the rising sea levels were close to their present position. The land that would make up the modern city was no longer inland; it was now on the coast. In fact, the shape of the coastline and the enormous harbor so familiar to the Late Archaic peoples moving about the area were essentially the same landscape that Giovanni da Verrazano and his crew saw when they sailed into New York Harbor in 1524. Beginning with the Transitional period, that coast and harbor would play increasingly important roles in the lives of the peoples who lived around them.[29]

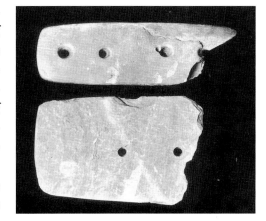

4.6. Two stone gorgets found at the beginning of the twentieth century in upper Manhattan. These ornaments were strung on a thong and worn around the neck.

Funerary Pyres on Long Island:
The Transitional, 3,700–2,700 B.P.

Until now this book has, by default, focused on the more mundane aspects of the lives of the Native Americans who once lived and worked in what is now New York City: their arrival, their diet and technology, and the changes in the land around them. All these things, ordinary though they may be, are of great importance in trying to re-create the lives of these early peoples. But we long to know more about other, extraordinary matters: the social and ritual bonds that united these people and gave their lives meaning.

We frequently feel frustrated by our failures to find the evidence for these more elusive parts of the human past. In a world that is becoming increasingly homogenized on a global scale, it seems especially important to record, understand, and appreciate ways of dealing with the human condition that are beyond modern experience and otherwise beyond recall. Unfortunately, the significance of this part of the past is matched only by the difficulty in finding it. In New York, the earliest evidence of this sort comes from a period known as the Transitional and a culture known as Orient. Because of a series of spectacular discoveries made right before World War II, we can begin to reconstruct some of the complex funerary rituals and ideas of a collective guardianship of the land that the Orient peoples held some three thousand years ago.[1]

There were a few hints of this Orient culture back at the beginning of the twentieth century. But to most archaeologists at that time, Orient seemed to be one of the more prosaic parts of the area's past. The first glimpses of this culture were hardly promising. Its defining characteristic was a distinctive style of artifact, one we now call "Orient fishtail," which had been turning up all over New York City and the surrounding coastal areas. Many of these fishtails were spear points, although some had been transformed into knives, drills, and other hafted tools. These tools, extremely graceful to the modern eye, were long, slender, and waisted, ending in a flaring "tail," usually chipped out of local white quartz or quartzite (fig. 5.1; see also fig. 4.1). But many of these fishtails were random surface finds with no clear context. Archaeologists knew that at some point unknown peoples had used these graceful tools in the city, often for hunting, but no one knew when these people had lived or anything else about them.[2]

Almost the only other thing known about the people who had made these points was that they lived before clay pottery became common; the fishtails had been found associated with fragments from stone cooking pots (fig. 5.2). These heavy, sturdy "kettles" were carved out of a soft stone, commonly known as soapstone or steatite, that came from quarries in Pennsylvania, Connecticut, and Rhode Island. The pots usually had lugs for handles and occasionally had incised decorations along their rims. We now know that both the fishtails and the stone pots were popular in the Transitional period, right before pottery making became widespread in the following Woodland period.

Steatite bowls are the signs of a new way of cooking, one that was far more efficient than the cumbersome stone-boiling techniques used earlier. Steatite pots, which retain heat efficiently, could be put directly on a fire. Because these pots were heavy, some weighing well over twenty pounds, their use might also mean that the Orient peoples were settling down in one place for longer periods of time than their predecessors.[3]

Alanson Skinner had found many examples of these fishtails and pots, both when he was a boy digging in his native Staten Island and later, in 1918, when he was excavating the Throgs Neck site in the Bronx for the newly formed Museum of the American Indian. While digging a seventeenth-century Native American village at Throgs Neck (see fig. 1.1), he found artifacts, including Orient points, in trash pits dating to a much earlier time. He was unimpressed by these points, however, and dismissed their makers as a "poor people, these old pit-diggers . . . in the light of their successors."[4]

As it turned out, "these old pit-diggers" were vastly underrated by Skinner and all those who had been more taken with the tools and pottery found in the villages of more recent Indian peoples. But to be fair to these early archaeologists, if all they had were

5.1. These distinctive white quartz Orient fishtails from the Jamesport site are typical tools used by peoples in the greater New York metropolitan area during the Transitional. Although they were most commonly used as spear points, some were transformed into knives, scrapers, or drills.

5.2. This steatite pot, now restored, was found in Greene County, New York. Fragments of similar stone pots have been found in New York City.

broken quartz points and fragments of stone pots, then it is no wonder they considered the Orient culture a bit plain compared to the more elaborate later cultures. Yet as the study of the Orient makes clear, it is a mistake to judge the richness and sophistication of a culture by the complexity of its technology alone.

The problem for Skinner and other early archaeologists was that no signs of Orient ceremonial life had yet been found. Years later, in the 1930s, a group of avocational archaeologists found the missing evidence. Outside the city, they discovered an extraordinary series of hilltop cemeteries where Orient peoples buried some of their dead. In reconstructing the rituals that once took place on those hilltops, we can catch glimpses of the complex system of beliefs that so profoundly marked the lives of these ancient peoples.

"These Remarkable Structures"

To see the evidence of early ceremonial life in the general metropolitan area, we have to head past the modern cemeteries that make up so much of the city's eastern boroughs of Queens and Brooklyn, past La Guardia and Kennedy airports, and follow the path taken by many affluent modern New Yorkers as they flee summer in the city. There, near some of today's fashionable resorts on the eastern end of Long Island, the clues to Orient rituals were found.

The first reports of these sites were sketchy. Four cemeteries, each on a hilltop overlooking the water, had been discovered: Orient I, Orient II, Jamesport, and Sugar Loaf Hill (fig. 5.3). According to the first accounts, these sites contained great mortuary pits, cremations, heaps of red ocher, and large numbers of grave offerings, including fishtail points and steatite pots. These remarkable discoveries were the culmination of years of work done mostly by Roy Latham, Nathaniel Booth, and Charles Goddard, avocational archaeologists who had worked in that area for years.[5]

Latham, a farmer all his life, was especially fervent about archaeology and about many other things—in his eighty-eighth year alone, he collected and mounted more than six thousand moths. He and his cohort had been working for decades in the region, always checking plowed fields for "relics" and then digging in areas that looked promising. And their efforts paid off. They discovered the first evidence of the great burial ceremonies held by the Orient peoples, who had been so summarily dismissed at the beginning of the century. Booth wrote, with some understatement, of the group's elation at their discoveries: "Great interest was manifested in the work by those who participated in their exploration."[6]

Although earlier Archaic burials, including cremations, had been found in other parts of the Northeast, nothing so early or so complex as these hilltop Orient cemeter-

5.3. View from the summit of the Sugar Loaf Hill site looking southwest. Sugar Loaf Hill, like the other Orient mortuary sites, was on high ground, with both views of the water and visibility from the water.

ies had ever been found in coastal New York. By any standards, these were spectacular finds. But it is not easy to decipher the records of the avocational archaeologists, and for that reason much of Orient may always elude us.[7]

Early on in their explorations, the avocationals began corresponding with William A. Ritchie. He analyzed a few of their finds for them and became increasingly intrigued by their reports of elaborate burials on high hills in eastern Long Island. Unfortunately, because of the ways they had dug and recorded these sites, it was hard for Ritchie to interpret their accounts. Later, in the 1950s, Ritchie began his own fieldwork in the area under the aegis of the New York State Museum and Science Service Bureau in an attempt to understand what he called "this intricate and intriguing subject." He hoped to find another hilltop cemetery and excavate it using professional techniques. He also wanted to go back to the original sites to see if the avocational archaeologists had missed any intact areas that he could excavate.[8]

While looking for these cemeteries, Ritchie and his team found several small Orient habitation sites, some of which included small burial plots. The Stony Brook site contained an infant's grave, and the Cutchogue site had what may have been a small family burial plot. But these were modest living sites, not the dramatic hilltop cemeteries with great mortuary pits that he had hoped to find. He and his crew trenched more than a dozen promising hills in the region, to no avail. To this day, no other extraordinary hilltop cemeteries have been found. The four that Latham and his group dug may be the only ones that were ever built.

Ritchie did have some luck at the Jamesport and Sugar Loaf Hill sites. He found and excavated some areas that the avocationals had missed (figs. 5.4 and 5.5; Ritchie labeled them "unmolested features"). Combining his new information with the avocationals' reports, Ritchie went on to reconstruct some of the ceremonial life of this ancient society. Much of what we know about Orient today, we know from Ritchie's own fieldwork and his painstaking analysis of the earlier finds.[9]

The funeral rites practiced by the Orient people were extremely complex. They dug several different kinds of graves into the hilltops. Some were individual graves about six feet in diameter and three to eight feet in depth. Others were large communal mortuary pits, averaging twenty by thirty feet in area and five to eight feet in depth. Burials in both individual and communal graves apparently took several forms.[10]

No complete skeletons were found at any of the cemeteries. The reason for this, Ritchie maintained, is that the highly acidic soils at these sites claimed such fragile organic materials as unburned human bone. When he was excavating at Sugar Loaf Hill, Ritchie discovered an undisturbed corner of the great mortuary pit. In it, he found a

5.4. Features excavated by William A. Ritchie at the Jamesport site.

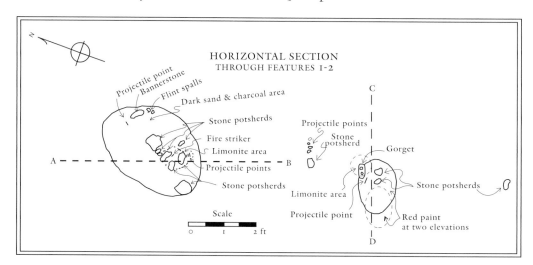

5.5. Feature 1 at the Jamesport site. The arrow points to a group of projectile points discovered in situ. Fragments of broken, or "killed," steatite pots are in the center of the picture. The outline of the original pit can be seen on the left. The dark soil above the broken line on the wall of the trench shows where the original excavators had dug. The lighter soil below is undisturbed.

smaller pit, six by four and a half feet in size, with a cache of artifacts carefully placed at each end. Although he found no human remains in the middle of this pit, he surmised that a burial had originally been placed between these two caches and that the bones had been "completely dissolved within the strongly acid medium (pH 5.5, as measured . . . with the Hellige Truog soil reaction test method), during the approximately 3,000 years of its interment."[11]

Cremated bone could, however, survive those intervening millennia even in such acidic soil. Although the avocationals had reported finding cremated human remains at the sites, it is not clear how much was actually recovered or where in the grave pits the remains were found. At one point, the Long Island group had shown fragments of burned bone to Ritchie, who confirmed that some of it was human. But Ritchie's analysis revealed that the Orient burial practices were far more complex than anyone had imagined. He discovered that not all of the fragments of burned human bone that Latham showed him were the remains of cremations in the flesh. Some were from the burning of old and dry human bones. It appears, then, that there were both in-flesh burials and two kinds of cremation burials. To make things even more confusing, reports indicate that there may also have been a "bone burial" consisting of the bundled bones from which the flesh had already decomposed. With the scanty information available, we have no idea how many people were once buried in these sacred places, how many were given simple burials and how many were cremated, or what their ages and sexes were.[12]

The accounts of the avocationals' work suggested that a number of features were discovered in these cemeteries, including masses (up to several bushels) of red ocher (a pigment made from iron oxide), "hearths," and piles of broken steatite pots. Each of these features was apparently associated with at least one cache or group of burial offerings. It may be that each cache of grave goods was left as an offering for a specific individual, but there is not enough information to say even that with any degree of certainty. Ritchie, understandably somewhat testy, outlines why he had so many problems interpreting the Orient culture: "Many of our problems would surely be less acute if the excavation methods employed by the finders of these cemeteries had been more adequate, and if offers of professional assistance had been accepted. The work was done by digging a series of deep shafts into the productive areas and enlarging them at the bottom until nothing more could be found, the holes being completely filled in at the close of each day's work. It was thus impossible to observe most of the details which could have led to a true comprehension of these remarkable structures."[13] Difficulties notwithstanding, these cemeteries are truly "remarkable structures," and they provide the only real clues to understanding just how noteworthy the Orient culture was.

"A Pervading Aura of High Religious Drama"

When archaeologists look at burials, they are looking at only a small portion of a funerary rite. Much of the ceremony, let alone the grief of the mourners, will leave no material record. In addition, the funeral itself is only part of the larger and more complex events that follow the death of a community member. But even with these limitations, the analysis of burials is still one of the best windows we have for understanding the rituals of the ancient world. For the Orient culture, that window is small indeed. Nonetheless, we can make some reasonable assumptions about what happened in those "remarkable structures" three thousand years ago. What we have to work with are the reported fireplaces, steatite pots, caches of grave offerings, red ocher, and the hilltop cemeteries themselves.

Ritchie argued that the fireplaces at the sites were not hearths at all but simply piles of ash and charcoal along with pieces of burned deer and bird bone. Occasionally, they also included fragments of burned human bone. He found no evidence that fires had ever actually burned in any of the mortuary pits; no scorched or reddened earth was reported from any of the pit floors. It looks as though the funerary fires were lit outside the pits, presumably somewhere on the hilltops. When these fires finally burned out, the ash deposits were carefully collected and brought into the great mortuary pits, where they were ritually scattered over the remains of the honored dead and their grave offerings.[14]

Stone pots were common offerings to the dead at these cemeteries. But curiously, the pots had all been "killed"—either broken into pieces or marred by a hole punched out of the bottom—before they were placed in the mortuary pits (see fig. 5.5). Archaeologists suggest that objects are sometimes ceremonially broken and then placed in graves in order to release the spirit of the artifact, prevent its improper use, or claim it for the dead. The smaller stone bowls were frequently placed upright in masses of powdered red ocher along with other grave goods. The larger pots were frequently shattered, with their sherds scattered throughout the mortuary pit among the individual graves.[15] It looks, then, as though some of these pots were placed there as offerings for specific individuals while others were left as collective offerings for the group as a whole. But whether large or small, the pots, which ranged from less than a pound to well over twenty-four pounds, all showed signs of use—they were covered with soot on the outside and encrusted with grease on the inside. They were probably not carved as special grave furniture but had already been used in the world of the living before they were broken and placed in the world of the dead.

Both the stone pots and the "fireplaces" were often associated with at least one cache of burial offerings. Although there was some variation from cache to cache, each one usually included a cosmetic kit made up of paint stones, that is, pieces of hematite or graphite (or both) that were used as pigments, and paint cups to work them. Many of these paint stones showed signs of rubbing, indicating that the Orient peoples had decorated their faces, bodies, or clothing in these red and silver-gray colors. Some pieces of jewelry—stone or shell pendants and other ornaments—were also occasionally found with the burials. Although we have no idea how the Orient peoples dressed or looked, these cosmetics and jewelry suggest that their appearances mattered to them in their lifetimes and perhaps in their afterworld as well.

In addition to a cosmetic kit, most caches also included a fire-making kit (iron pyrites with quartz strikers), a woodworking kit with adzes and celts, a hunting kit made up of spear points and knives (most of which were Orient fishtails), and steatite pot fragments.[16] Although we can't be sure, it is tempting to think that the mourners placed these objects, as well as the burnt offerings from the funerary fires, for the dead to use in a world not too dissimilar to the present one. After all, the offerings were the kinds of things used for everyday activities.

We are not sure what the bushel loads of powdered red ocher may have signified. Red ocher has been a common burial offering for thousands of years, not only in North America but throughout the world, and there has been a great deal of speculation about its symbolic meaning. Some archaeologists suggest that the pigment is associated with shamanic ritual practices common to many small-scale hunting-and-gathering societies. Others note that in more recent times in the Northeast, many Indian peoples associated the color red with blood, fire, and the emotional qualities of life and that the color may have had a similar symbolic meaning in earlier times. Still others point out that the iron salts in ocher have healing and antiseptic properties, which may have been significant in the past. Although it is tempting to suggest that these qualities of life—well-being, renewal, and animation—explain the presence of these masses of red ocher in the graves, we do not know for sure.[17]

One of the curious things about these hilltop cemeteries is how isolated they seem to have been from the everyday world of the Orient people. Ritchie and others have found sites where Orient peoples once lived and worked (some of which had their own small family burial plots), but they are miles away from these cemeteries. Perhaps the hilltop cemeteries were reserved for the honored dead, who may have represented only a small percentage of a much larger and dispersed population. We have no way of knowing the precise relationship between the hilltop cemeteries and coeval Orient peoples, including those whose broken and abandoned tools Skinner and others have found in New York City. But the religious core behind the ceremonies held in these sacred precincts would surely have been familiar and important to the members of the smaller local groups that together made up the Orient culture.[18]

In considering the available, albeit meager, evidence, it seems that these hilltops, each commanding views of the water and figuring prominently in the landscape, may have been sacred precincts for a scattered Orient population. It was to these hills that the mourners brought their dead, and it was there that they held elaborate funerary rites before final interments were made. We don't know if the Orient peoples walked to these hills, carrying their dead with them, or whether they came by boat. Certainly, all four cemeteries were easily accessible by water, and the large number of woodworking tools found at Orient sites throughout the greater area, including New York City, indicates that they had the technology to build wooden water craft.

The hilltops may have been chosen for certain attributes—high ground, proximity to the water, views of the water, or visibility from the water—that were important to the Orient peoples and were incorporated into the rituals that took place there (see fig. 5.3). The very construction of the great mortuary pits, each aligned on an east-west axis, would have involved an organized effort by members of a lineage or a larger community: the pits were dug by hand, without metal tools.

Much of the available evidence for interpreting these funerary practices is far from conclusive, and many questions remain. Was only a small percentage of the total Orient population in coastal New York given this special treatment? If so, why were those particular individuals so elected? Were there large mass funerary rites, with mourners from a wide region bringing their recently dead as well as their long-dead to these hills for elaborate ceremonies, followed by final interment and the closing of the great pits?

If so, where were the long-dead kept until they were brought to their final resting places? Alternatively, did mourners come to the cemeteries shortly after each death and conduct a separate ceremony for each individual? Were the great mortuary pits originally charnel houses, roofed in some fashion to protect the dead already there and then reopened for burial ceremonies each time a member of the community died? Surely there must have been closing ceremonies when the pits were filled in, for scattered throughout the fill in all the pits were additional pieces of ritually broken steatite pots. Who broke them? Were they from the final ceremonial feasts? And what prompted the closing of these great pits? Presumably, a spiritual leader, shaman, or family head must have conducted these ceremonies. What powers and other authority did that person have?[19]

Ritchie felt that these cemeteries had "a pervading aura of high religious drama, in marked contrast to the impression of prosaic everyday life conveyed . . . in the settlement sites of the same people." He also felt that there was much "lost symbolism, some of it of more universal nature, in which high places, the east, the sun, fire and red ocher figure as elements of a vigorous religious movement, apparently focused upon the perpetuation of life after death, and the care and welfare of the deceased."[20] That may well be, but funerals are also about the living and their relationships with the supernatural as well as with each other. Although we can detect little about their relationships with the supernatural, other than the fact that the hills seem to be sacred spaces, we can consider what powerful statements about their own society the Orient peoples were making as they stood among their funerary pyres.

A Different Sense of Place

Archaeologists have long noted that by the end of the Archaic, many societies, not only in the Northeast but throughout eastern North America (the region east of the Mississippi River), had begun building elaborate formal cemeteries as distinct either from isolated graves scattered across a landscape or from individual graves randomly placed within a settlement. Some archaeologists working in other parts of the country have speculated that the appearance of such cemeteries, this "collective representation of the dead," coincides with profound social changes, including the emergence of concepts of hereditary control over vital natural resources by particular families or lineages living in certain territories. They suggest that these lineages might symbolize their territorial ownership or control of these resources by placing the remains of their ancestors in prominent burial grounds. These noticeable cemeteries and the accompanying ceremonies in honor of dead group members would clearly show their hereditary rights to the land. Another archaeologist, analyzing burials in a different part of the world, has made

technological innovations never occur in isolation; they reverberate throughout the entire social system. For archaeologists, pottery may mark the beginning of the Woodland period, but for the peoples in the Northeast the adoption of pottery may have led to changes in the division of labor, shifts in trade routes away from steatite quarries, changes in child care, improved overall family nutrition, and population increases. It may also have been part of the increasing trend toward a more sedentary way of life that began in the last stages of the Archaic. This trend in turn led to territorialism and a focus on local food resources, on the one hand, and, on the other hand, the formation of alliances with adjacent peoples for needed raw materials, foodstuffs, or other goods. This more settled lifestyle would also mean easier and more comfortable lives for the elderly, the infirm, and the very young.

The advent of pottery, that major technological breakthrough, is not the only story of the Woodland peoples, but it is a significant one. And so, before discussing the distinctive social and natural landscapes of the Woodland peoples, we start with this container revolution and its implications.

Archaeologists are not sure whether pottery developed in the Northeast in situ or spread there from the Southeast and Great Lakes cultures.[3] Once pottery first appeared, it quickly replaced the older steatite vessels used by the Orient peoples, and with good reason. Clay, the raw material needed to make these new pots, was much easier to obtain than steatite, which required trading partners or trips to distant quarries. Although these new clay pots were more fragile than their steatite predecessors, they were also lighter, less bulky, and easier to make.

The earliest Woodland potters usually began by mixing clay with crushed-rock temper to strengthen their pots. The clay was rolled into strips, which were then coiled to shape the vessel—usually a pot about a foot high with a pointed base that could be propped up in warm coals or buried in the ground near the fire (fig. 6.1). The coils were smoothed over, and some of the pots were "paddled" into shape with wooden paddles. The earliest pots, which could hold about a gallon, were plain. But later potters impressed designs into the still-wet clay with netting or with sticks or paddles wrapped with cord, or else they stamped and incised designs into the clay. The pots were probably first air-dried then fired, mouth down, over hot coals in an open pit, and finally slowly cooled so that they would not crack.

Woodland potters, like potters everywhere, were artisans experimenting with the shapes and decorations of their vessels and sometimes copying those of their neighbors. Because the different kinds of designs and shapes would go in and out of fashion over time, archaeologists can plot these changes and go on to develop regional chronologies that can then be used to date sites and study regional influences.

We can do this in coastal New York because of the work of Carlyle Shreeve Smith,

6.1. Drawings of an Early Woodland pot (left) *and a more elaborately decorated Middle Woodland pot* (right) *used by Woodland peoples in the Northeast. Sherds from broken and discarded pots similar to these have been found in the New York City metropolitan area.*

one of the few professional archaeologists working in the city in the mid-twentieth century. Smith developed a regional chronology based on pottery, which, although modified over the years, is still useful half a century later. He created order out of the chaos of local archaeology in the years immediately preceding World War II, when scientific dating techniques had not yet been developed.

Working with incomplete field notes from the turn of the twentieth century, old museum collections, and materials from sites that he and his friends had dug in their youth, Smith accomplished the monumental task of organizing the twenty-three centuries of the Woodland period into a coherent chronological framework, which we follow here. He used the direct historic approach—beginning with the known and then working backward in time—an approach sometimes called "upstreaming." Beginning with the most recent sites, those with evidence of European contact, Smith carefully worked backward until he reached and identified the earliest pottery-using peoples, who lived at a time known today as the Early Woodland.[4]

The Early Woodland (2,700–2,000 B.P.)

Trying to understand Early Woodland life in coastal New York is like trying to solve a jigsaw puzzle with most of the pieces missing. We know that these early pottery-making peoples were living there because sherds from their pottery have turned up at various shell middens scattered along the coast. The only site that gives us any hints at all about life during those seven hundred years is the North Beach site (see fig. 1.1), located where La Guardia airport is today. But even this, our best evidence, is sketchy —all we have are a few artifacts hastily rescued from a refuse pit in the 1930s, just before the grading operations for the new airport destroyed the site. A variety of discarded and broken tools were salvaged at that time: pottery sherds, hunting equipment, woodworking and hide-working tools, paint stones, bone awls that could be used in basket making or for punching holes in hides to make clothing, and a few bone needles. The diversity of these tool types and their everyday functions suggest that North Beach may have been a base camp for a small family group.[5]

Beyond this meager evidence—a few artifacts from North Beach and several other sites—we know frustratingly little about the Early Woodland peoples. We have no clues to help us understand the economic, social, or religious life of the many generations who lived in coastal New York during those centuries. But we do know something about life along the coast during the Middle Woodland period, which began two thousand years ago.

The Middle Woodland (2,000–1,000 B.P.)

Compared with earlier eras, we have far more sites documenting Middle Woodland life along the coast. Although evidence from these sites indicates considerable changes from Archaic and Transitional times, it also shows a life that is in many ways oddly at variance with contemporary societies in other parts of eastern North America. In fact, the coastal area sometimes seems like an outlier, a province both physically and culturally isolated from the great river valleys of the interior, where culturally complex societies, collectively known as Hopewell, were developing. These mound-building cultures, especially the one known as Ohio Hopewell, had complex mortuary systems for their elites that included elaborate burial mounds filled with ornate offerings and symbols of high status made by highly skilled artists and artisans. Many of these offerings —the sculptures, pottery, ornaments, and other artifacts—are of such high quality by modern standards that they are displayed in major museums and included in art history books. These societies differed from one another but were connected by vast trading networks that crossed much of the continent—networks along which rituals, ideas, raw materials, and trade goods all flowed. Some of these Middle Woodland peoples living in the interior had added small-scale gardening to their local economies and were growing tobacco and squashes as well as domesticated varieties of native seed plants like sunflower, marsh elder, goosefoot, and knotweed.[6]

Yet little of this "cultural florescence" appears to have developed in the New York coastal area or, for that matter, in much of the Northeast. Evidence from sites in tide-water New York suggests that the Middle Woodland peoples there lived in small-scale, largely egalitarian communities, supported by a hunting, fishing, and gathering econ-omy, with a comparatively modest funerary style and material culture. Some archaeolo-gists and other observers, attracted by the aesthetic quality of some of the Hopewell objects or by the very idea of social complexity, have dismissed the coastal area and much of the Northeast in Woodland times as dreary and uninteresting, or, as archae-ologist Dena Dincauze has complained, as "a marginal, culturally retarded outlier of the eastern United States."[7]

Nevertheless, as we try to interpret the evidence from these Middle Woodland sites discovered in the city, it becomes apparent that during those years there was a thriving adaptation to a rich coastal environment. Although the Middle Woodland peoples may have lived in small-scale societies without symbols of high status and other aesthetically pleasing objects, they were by no means living in social isolation. They had contacts with neighboring groups and possessed objects that, though perhaps plain compared with some of those produced by Ohio Hopewell and other Midwestern peoples, were valuable to them. More significantly, these people were far from oblivious to some of the ideas and rituals spreading throughout the rest of eastern North America. The ar-chaeological evidence clearly shows that they embraced some (though not all) of these new rituals.

This is what makes the Middle Woodland in New York so intriguing. The coastal peoples were not huddled in an isolated backwater at the edge of the continent. On the contrary, they were aware of events in the more sophisticated cultures in the interior, a region less than a month's journey away by canoe and portage. Nonetheless, they pur-sued a markedly different cultural trajectory than their contemporaries did. In trying to understand why this is so, it becomes clear that the study of Middle Woodland life along the coast, this "marginal, culturally retarded outlier," is by no means merely a parochial matter. It leads to fundamental issues concerning the inevitability or even desirability of "progress," the idea of marginality itself, and the significance and appre-ciation of societies that may be small in scale but which turn out to be surprisingly intricate.[8]

Tidewater Trade and Ritual

In the 1950s and 1960s, several avocational archaeologists began making a number of finds at Middle Woodland sites in the Bronx and in Queens that hinted at contacts with regions beyond tidewater New York. Many of these discoveries were made by Edward Kaeser, a Bronx native and self-trained archaeologist whose publications remain benchmarks for professional archaeologists working in Woodland studies in the Northeast.

Kaeser made one of the most curious of these Middle Woodland finds in the Bronx at Morris-Schurz (see fig. 1.1), one of a number of sites along the shores of Throgs Neck, a peninsula jutting out into the East River and Long Island Sound. The area today is a quiet pocket of land, marked by houses, schools, and beach clubs and bounded on three sides by a heavily traveled expressway and the approaches to two major bridges. The fourth side, and the one closest to the site, faces the East River and its busy coastal traffic—not only barges and ships but also the countless pleasure boats that always seem to be circling the city. Fifteen hundred years before Kaeser's excavations, Middle Woodland peoples had stayed there for a while. When they moved on, they left behind traces of their own voyages and enterprises, including Kaeser's curious find.[9]

Because much of the site was on the property of a private beach club, Kaeser had been digging only on those rainy and off-season weekend days when the beach was deserted. As the work progressed, back in 1958, he was finding a variety of everyday Middle Woodland tools and pottery. But then he discovered something that wasn't typical at all—an eight-foot circle almost completely outlined by waterworn cobbles. Kaeser speculated that he had unearthed the foundation of a dwelling of some sort and that the gap in the stone circle marked the entranceway. As he continued digging in the refuse that filled the enclosure, he found something even more singular—a stack of more than 150 plates of sheet mica.[10]

This cache is highly unusual. Sheet mica is not native to the region, and although archaeologists have discovered small quantities of it at other Middle Woodland sites in New York, no other cache, of this or any other size, has ever been found. The mica plates at Morris-Schurz had to have been brought from some distant place and left there, by accident or design, never to be seen again until Kaeser found them well over a thousand years later.

Although this cache was the most unusual find, Kaeser also found other "exotics" along this stretch of coast. These were ordinary objects, such as stone spear points, knives, and fragments of pottery storage and cooking vessels, that had been made in unusual ways (fig. 6.2). There were, for instance, large lanceolate and stemmed spear points and knives, a type that archaeologists today call Fox Creek (see figs. 4.1 and 6.2). These are typical for the time and region, but some of them were made from a distinctive reddish-purple argillite that isn't native to the area. And among the usual everyday Middle Woodland pottery sherds at the site were some with unusually elaborate designs: the bodies of the pots were marked off into zones, which were then filled in with various geometric designs. More mica, reddish-purple argillite Fox Creek spear points and knives, and zoned pottery sherds were also recovered by other avocational archaeologists, who were digging in an adjacent boatyard and beach area that was about to be bulldozed for new housing and at a number of other Middle Woodland sites throughout the city.[11]

In the years since these discoveries were made, other archaeologists have searched for the sources of these exotic goods. One of them, Annette Silver, identified the reddish-purple argillite as a Delaware River Valley Mesozoic stone from a source not far from the modern city of Trenton, New Jersey. The unusual zone-decorated pottery designs resemble, and may have been inspired by, those used on some of the pottery found at the large Abbott Farm site (figs. 6.3 and 6.4; see also fig. 6.2). That site is on the Delaware River just outside Trenton, not far from the argillite source. Quantities of mica were also found at Abbott Farm, and both that mica and the coastal New York mica have been traced to a source in southeastern Pennsylvania, some fifty or sixty miles away from Trenton.[12]

These exotic goods help us trace the larger world of which these coastal peoples

6.2. "Exotic" artifacts found at the Morris-Schurz site in the Bronx. Top left and bottom, *Abbott-like decorated sherds;* top right, *a Fox Creek reddish-purple argillite point.*

were once a part. Although these valuables reveal a relationship with peoples in the Delaware Valley, the actual nature of that relationship is not clear. They could have belonged to one large dispersed kinship group, been friendly allies, or merely known of each other through intermediaries. There may have been social or religious occasions when they gathered, feasted, and then traded or exchanged gifts that included such important goods as mica plates and argillite points.[13]

It is sometimes difficult for us today, enmeshed as we are in modern systems of values and prestige, to project ourselves back in time and try to understand the very different value systems of people who lived in the distant past. And these particular objects —reddish-purple argillite, pieces of mica, and pottery sherds with zoned designs—are so foreign to modern concepts of what constitutes value, wealth, or even beauty, that they could easily be dismissed. But that would be a mistake; these ordinary-looking objects are a guide to understanding some of the values and belief systems that prevailed in coastal New York nearly two thousand years ago.

The distinctive reddish-purple argillite points may have been "sumptuary implements," or everyday tools transformed into valuable objects by virtue of having being made from exotic or symbolically rich material.[14] Successful hunters or fishermen may have used them as badges of their accomplishments or as signs of group membership. Their distinctive color may well have given them value or added to their symbolic worth. But whatever their specific role may have been, they were clearly valuable possessions.

The ornately designed Abbott-style pottery has a spotty distribution, not only in coastal New York but in the general Middle Atlantic region as well, and never comes close in numbers to those of the plainer, more everyday pots. One archaeologist, Michael Stewart, has speculated that these vessels may have been used at large seasonal ceremonies and that their elaborate designs may have "provided a symbolic message to the gathered groups . . . to express solidarity among coastal Algonquian peoples."[15] The pots may also have been used for other kinds of special meals or during important rituals, or may have been made and used only by certain families who had the right to employ these designs.

6.3. An Abbott Zoned vessel with incised decorations found at the Abbott Farm site, near Trenton, New Jersey.

The 150 sheets of mica abandoned on that house floor are a different matter altogether. Mica is rare in coastal New York, and although it may have arrived along the same routes that brought the pottery designs and the argillite, it originally came from a more distant source. Large quantities of mica plates, numbering in the hundreds and resembling the Morris-Schurz cache, have been discovered in Hopewell burial mounds in the Midwest. Some archaeologists, using practices of more modern Indian peoples as analogies, have argued that mica plates such as these were ritual paraphernalia, used as mirrors for shamanic healing and divination in funerary and other rituals during Middle Woodland times. Although we may never know the specific purpose of the unclaimed cache that Kaeser found along the East River, it seems likely that it was brought there to be used by spiritual leaders. The presence of that mica, as well as the other mica plates found in the city, suggests that these coastal peoples may have shared ceremonies and religious and philosophical views of the world with their contemporaries throughout eastern North America.[16]

6.4. A drawing of a vessel with distinctive incised curvilinear designs. This pot, which may have been used on ceremonial occasions, was found, along with sherds from similar pots, in the Bronx. Reprinted from Julius Lopez, "Curvilinear Design Elements in the New York Coastal Area," Bulletin of the Archaeological Society of Connecticut, no. 28 (February 1958), courtesy of the Archaeological Society of Connecticut.

Other important rituals were also entering coastal New York at that time. Kaeser found a small fragment of a stone smoking pipe at Morris-Schurz, and two or three additional pipe fragments were found at other sites in the city. The practice of smoking itself probably spread to the coast from the interior, where archaeologists have discovered pipes used as early as Late Archaic times. The presence of these pipes, however, does not mean that the coastal peoples were growing, importing, or even smoking native tobacco, *Nicotina rustica*. Although native tobacco, which is stronger than the kinds common today, was grown and smoked in the interior by this time, so were a variety of other plants, including hemp, sumac, and fleabane flowers. These plants and the act of smoking itself were part of a widespread pipe ritualism, which even today, well over a millennium later, is still an important part of many Native American ceremonies. Traditionally, smoking can sometimes be a prayer or gift to the spirits, inviting them to attend or witness an important ceremony. These fragments of broken pipes suggest the importance of these smoking rituals, which once linked the coastal peoples with the spirit world.[17]

Other important rituals taking place in the interior were not adopted in the New York area. When many people, including archaeologists, think of Hopewellian societies, they tend to focus on elaborate funerary ceremonies, groups of burial mounds

of the deer, for implements, and pieces of turtle shell for ornaments. Last, but not least, he had a paint receptacle made from the lower jaw of a [lynx], which contained red paint that might be used when he appeared before the braves on the shores of the other land.

What a scene that must have been when that little wanderer was placed beneath the ground that he had trod for so short a time! We can imagine the heartaches and the lamentations that accompanied the unfettered soul as it journeyed upward on the wings of the morning.[20]

Certainly, some of Pepper's phrases seem loaded with racial and gender stereotypes that are offensive to the modern ear. But although some of his interpretations now seem fanciful and sentimental, many of them still stand.

Today, a century after his discoveries, we know much more about that burial that took place at Ward's Point well over a thousand years ago. In the 1990s, physical anthropologist Patricia Bridges reexamined the child's bones using the newly developed techniques of paleopathology. Her study showed that the outer bones of the cranial vault, and the margins of the eye orbits, were thinned, exposing the underlying porous bone. From these characteristic "pinprick" lesions she could diagnose that the child had a mild but clear case of porotic hyperostosis and cribra orbitalia. Although these conditions are often symptomatic of iron-deficiency anemia, that seems unlikely in tidewater New York, with its great resources of iron-rich marine foods. A more likely explanation is that the child suffered from an infectious disease or a parasitic infection that came from drinking contaminated water or eating raw fish. Whatever the sickness, it was a mild one, and Bridges estimated that the child died at the age of six from other unknown causes. The child's youth makes it impossible to verify Pepper's assumption that it was a boy.[21]

The sheer number of offerings found in the child's grave is extraordinary for this area. Other Middle Woodland burials in the city, even those of children, rarely have any grave furniture at all. Many of these objects are the kinds of things that are almost never found at sites along the coast. Their exoticism suggests that they were valuable to the mourners who placed them in the grave.[22]

As Pepper suggested, many of the child's ornaments reveal links with distant peoples or places. The necklace wound around the child's neck was made up of hundreds of shell beads, mainly *Olivella* species. These are native to the warm coastal waters from Florida up through Virginia, and they are the only such southern marine shell beads ever found at a Woodland site in tidewater New York. Although we are not sure what the copper ornament that Pepper found on the child's face was—it had long since disintegrated and all that remained were the telltale greenish stains—we know that the ornament must have been imported. Copper itself is not native to coastal New York, and copper artifacts are extremely rare along the coast.[23]

The smoking pipe that had been placed on the child's head is also exotic (fig. 6.5). Although fragments of several other pipes have been found within New York City limits, this steatite platform pipe, unlike them, resembles the Hopewell pipes of the Midwest. We simply do not know whether this particular piece came to Ward's Point by barter from the midcontinent, as Pepper suggested, or by other means. Similar Hopewell pipes are frequently found in burial mounds, and some archaeologists suggest that they may have been part of the funerary ceremonies. This pipe, as well as the chunk of mica that had been placed under the child's jaw, may have been part of ceremonies held for the child before the grave was finally closed.[24]

These particular grave goods—the beads, the copper ornament, the mica, and the pipe—were only a small part of the valuables buried with this six-year-old. Also marking this grave as extraordinary were all the other gifts, some utilitarian like the weapons and tools (although many were made from exotic stones), others apparently ritual like the quartz crystal and the red paint in the lynx's jaw. Presumably perishable offerings were also placed in the grave.

The burial of this child remains puzzling today, more than a century after its discovery. Who was this child who was buried so differently from everyone else? Who were the mourners who placed all this wealth in the grave? How and why did these particular valuables reach the coast?

Unfortunately, there are no ready answers, only conjectures leading to more questions. Because of the unique nature of the burial, some archaeologists have speculated that this six-year-old was foreign, the child either of a family of recent migrants or of visitors from the interior who had come to the coast looking for trading partners or allies. In either case, the parents could have been people of means who followed their own native burial customs. But the parents or other mourners could also have been local people who had somehow acquired these valuable objects and then buried them with the child. We have no real clues as to their identity. Nor do we know why all this wealth was placed in the child's grave, thus removing it from the world of the living. Certainly, Pepper could be right in suggesting that these objects were left for the child to use in the

6.5. This pipe was among the exotic offerings placed in the grave of the child buried at Ward's Point. Some archaeologists speculate that such pipes may have been used during funeral rites.

afterworld, but they could also have been left as declarations of respect for the parents, testaments of grief, or symbols of the family's or the child's prestige. The possibilities are endless, and it may be that the many questions about this unique burial will be answered only if we find more sites from this critical time period.[25]

Even if we never learn the end of this particular story, this child's grave—by virtue of its being filled with so many valuable, unique, and foreign offerings—underscores by comparison what some archaeologists see as the drab, unspectacular, and utilitarian aspects of the Middle Woodland in coastal New York. And despite their uniqueness in New York, the offerings buried with the child are quite different from those found with elaborate burials at sites on the other side of the Appalachians or even in western New York. At those burials, there are clear markers of social difference, and some individuals, presumably elites with social and political importance, are buried with grave goods so elaborate that they would make the artifacts here seem pedestrian. But there are no such status markers at sites along the coast. On the contrary, the impression is of a society whose essence is largely egalitarian.[26]

It is apparent that the peoples living along the coast were pursuing a very different cultural pathway than many of their contemporaries in the interior were. Although we don't have anywhere near the amount of evidence needed to explain the factors that led to their distinctive Middle Woodland lifestyle, we think that part of the answer lies in the rich estuarine environment in which the Middle Woodland peoples lived. For if their material world was plain and their social world modest, their natural world was exuberant. And that natural bounty, we suspect, may have been a critical factor for them as they developed their successful and prosperous, albeit "unspectacular," adaptation to tidewater New York.

The Land and Sea Around Them

New York's shoreline is enormous; almost six hundred miles of it outline most of the boundaries of the modern city. Today it is largely made up of decaying urban waterfronts, city parks, abandoned piers and warehouses, commercial and industrial areas, luxury housing, airports, public beaches, marinas, and the many expressways that ring the city. Over the past few centuries, the coastal waters themselves have been polluted with tons of sewage and industrial waste. Ongoing attempts to clean the harbor have turned up vast quantities of every imaginable kind of refuse, including a dead giraffe, a grand piano, and human bodies, mixed in among the tons of debris.[27]

It is hard today to imagine that these densely urban and polluted shores of coastal New York and southern New England were once part of an incredibly rich ecosystem. In fact, throughout the millennia, beginning with the end of the Archaic, the shoreline, harbor, and adjacent habitats were major factors in the economy of the many peoples who lived there. What we see throughout the entire Woodland period is a highly successful adaptation to this rich coastal environment.

For these Woodland peoples, the environment in which they lived, worked, and conducted their rituals was an important part of their lives. Although it may have imposed limitations, it also offered opportunities, some of which they took, and the cultural choices they made, in turn, affected the world around them. In trying to reconstruct this lost world, we rely on the work of archaeologists, paleobotanists, biologists, and ecologists who have studied both ancient and modern ecosystems, and on the writings of some of the earliest European colonists in the area.[28]

The success of much of the Woodland way of life is directly related to the reduction in the rise of sea levels that began around four thousand years ago, near the end of the Late Archaic, and the accompanying stabilization of the estuarine environments. This slowing down of the rising seas set in motion a chain of events culminating in the development of mudflats and salt marshes along the coast and at the mouths of rivers. These saltwater marshes, and the fresh- and brackish-water marshlands in adjacent areas, had an enormous impact on the economic and social lives of the Woodland peoples. Some archaeologists, such as Lucianne Lavin, have argued that the development of the marshlands that stretch across the coasts of New York and southern New England ultimately made this "one of the most productive landforms in the world, rivaling intensive agricultural lands in food productivity."[29]

Shellfish—oysters, hard- and soft-shell clams, scallops, mussels, whelk—and crustaceans like lobsters and crabs were there in abundance. The statistics on oysters alone are staggering. The area that includes New York Harbor and parts of the lower Hudson estuary had 350 square miles of oyster beds. Some biologists have argued that these beds alone once produced more than half the world's supply of oysters.[30]

But shellfish were the least of this coast's wealth. The area near today's Statue of Liberty was once a playground for seals, and whales and porpoises swam nearby. Vast annual runs of anadromous fish—inland-spawning saltwater fish, such as sturgeon, shad, striped bass, alewife, and other herrings—started arriving every April. Sturgeon are substantial fish, capable of weighing as much as five or six hundred pounds each (although many are smaller, averaging several hundred pounds). As for striped bass, they range from ten to fifty pounds each, and even today there may be as many as 17 million of them in the Hudson River alone—more than double the city's human population.[31]

Anadromous fish were an especially important food in a number of ways. Not only were they found in vast numbers, but their large fat reserves made them extremely nutritious. And because their movements were predictable, Woodland peoples could schedule their seasonal rounds accordingly. The fish were so plentiful during their runs that large groups of people could gather together to fish and process the catch (fig. 6.6). There were also eels, flounder, sheepshead, blackfish, bluefish, and a long litany more.[32]

The numbers of birds in the area, even today, are astounding. The New York coast is on the great Atlantic flyway at a point where flocks from the North Atlantic coast meet with those from the Canadian and Michigan prairies. These millions of migrating ducks, geese, and other shore birds, attracted by the teeming marsh life, stop over in New York in the spring and fall on their great north-south passages.[33]

Other birds are around throughout the year, feeding in the ponds and grasses and adjoining woodlands. Early Dutch settlers, who saw part of this coastal ecosystem before its metamorphosis, were amazed that these birds "fill also the woods so that men can scarcely go through them for the whistling, the noise and the chattery. Whoever is not lazy can catch them with little difficulty." There are accounts of turkeys weighing more than forty pounds apiece. And rivaling every species in abundance was the now-extinct passenger pigeon (fig. 6.7).[34]

The marshlands, and the adjacent forested upland regions, were home to white-tail deer and bear, many smaller mammals, and such reptiles as turtles. The forests themselves were filled with oak, chestnut, hickory, butternut, and walnut trees, all of which bore nuts that could be stored for the winter ahead. And a profusion of other plants grew in both the open and forested areas. There were hackberries, sugar maples, sassafras, red mulberries, persimmons, crab apples, cherries, elderberries, blackberries, strawberries, and wild grapes. And then there were pokeweeds, knotweeds, fiddle-head ferns, Jerusalem artichokes, milkweed and cattail shoots, black plums, currants, wild leeks, and rose hips, among many more.[35]

Many of these plants have medicinal properties, and healers may have brewed them into teas or made them into poultices to ease pain or cure all sorts of ailments. Healing practices of more recent Indian peoples in the area suggest, for example, that elderberry tea may have been used to cure an infant's colic, that the sap from black walnut trees may have been rubbed over inflamed areas to reduce swelling, and that strawberries may have been crushed and then rubbed on the face to improve a troubled complexion.[36]

6.6. These grooved stone plummets or net sinkers, discovered in upper Manhattan, were commonly used in fishing. The many plummets found at sites throughout the city attest to the importance of fishing in Native American economies.

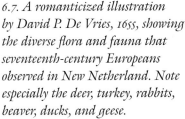

6.7. A romanticized illustration by David P. De Vries, 1655, showing the diverse flora and fauna that seventeenth-century Europeans observed in New Netherland. Note especially the deer, turkey, rabbits, beaver, ducks, and geese.

Regional plants were also important sources of raw materials for more recent Indian peoples, and many of them were probably also used by earlier peoples. Trees would have provided lumber for canoes and house frames and sheets of bark for house coverings. Hemp and milkweed, as well as strips of cedar and hickory bark, could be transformed into twine and rope. Women and old men may have spun hemp into threads, which they then wove into fishing seines and nets to catch the vast spring runs of fish entering the area. Women may have woven milkweed, nettle, or cattail into mats to line the floors and walls of their houses or into fabrics for their clothing, and they may have fashioned hemp and grape vines into baskets and bags for storing all sorts of goods (fig. 6.8). Mothers may have used clean sphagnum moss to "diaper" their babies. And artisans may have used local plants, such as goldenrod and grape, to produce vibrant dyes to decorate their house mats, baskets, bags, and clothing.[37]

When this vast array of plant foods is added to the fish, fowl, and mammals found along the coast, the potential amount of available provender for human populations is astounding. Overall, coastal New York is distinguished by its great diversity of species, the large populations within those species, and a great diversity of available habitats. The mosaic of habitats within walking distance for the Woodland peoples—the coasts, marshes, mudflats, sheltered estuaries, meadows, forests, uplands—each with its own abundance, would have been an important factor in Middle Woodland subsistence strategies. Small wonder that a Dutch colonist rhapsodized, "I admit that I am incompetent to describe the beauties, the grand and sublime works, wherewith God has diversified this land."[38]

6.8. Three plants commonly used by Native Americans in the seventeenth and early eighteenth centuries for making various textiles, including cordage, nets, household mats, baskets, bags, and clothing.

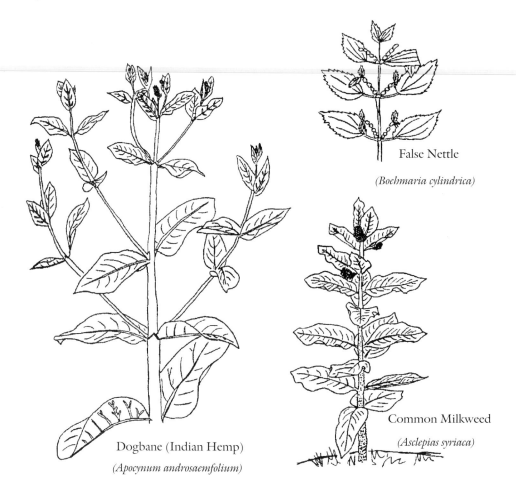

False Nettle

(Boehmaria cylindrica)

Common Milkweed

(Asclepias syriaca)

Dogbane (Indian Hemp)

(Apocynum androsaemfolium)

Although we have no hard evidence from archaeological sites for this environmental reconstruction, all the information we do have indicates that coastal New York was an extremely attractive place for Woodland peoples to live. But we emphasize that reconstructions such as this are by their very nature idealized and do not represent the environment as it actually was at any given point in time. Ecosystems are never stable. During the span of the Woodland, certain periods were drier or colder, warmer or moister. These shifts would have affected the abundance of individual species at any given time, and the Woodland peoples would have had to adapt to those shifts. There were certainly lean times for them as well as bountiful ones. We have no way to document the impact that the Middle Woodland peoples had on the local environment. But it is important to remember that they did have an impact, one that may or may not always have been benign.[39]

Unfortunately, the information that would tell us what specific subsistence choices the Woodland peoples made from this abundance is just not available. We haven't enough evidence to reconstruct their annual economic cycle, although it seems likely that this rich environment would permit an increasingly sedentary way of life for them, one within recognized territorial boundaries where they could hunt, fish, gather shellfish, collect wild plants, and enjoy life. In times of peak abundance, family groups may have joined with other families to take advantage of the great fish runs, bird migrations, and other resources. They may have feasted, exchanged gifts, performed rituals, settled feuds, and renewed alliances on those occasions. They may have moved to sheltered deer-hunting settlements for the winter months. At other times, smaller family or task groups may have gone off from the main settlement to short-term work camps.[40]

Many of the Middle Woodland sites in the city are at the mouths of estuaries, streams, bays, and coves, the very areas where the peoples living in them could take full advantage of the rich mosaic of habitats and of the many water routes that interlace the region. But they may have chosen to live in these spots for other, noneconomic reasons. Modern New Yorkers are impressed by the extraordinary views of land and sea that many of these sites offer. Aesthetic and spiritual considerations may also have influenced Woodland peoples as they built their settlements along the coast more than a thousand years ago.[41]

All this natural bounty does not mean that the Middle Woodland peoples were living in an Eden-like environment or in an egalitarian paradise. The usual human ills would have been no more strangers to them then than they are to any other people. And there were certainly differences based on birth, age, sex, personality, and ability. But overall, what we see in coastal New York are small-scale societies with a relatively prosperous hunting, fishing, and gathering economy. Apparently, they had no need for elite individuals to organize their forces of production and distribution. They may have had a simple lifestyle and a modest material culture compared to many of their contemporaries in the interior, but they nonetheless lived very well, with their own systems of value and an important ritual life that they shared with much of eastern North America. More important, they lived largely free from group conflict and the demands of social complexity.

Although they probably knew something about the more elaborate lifestyle that marked the Hopewellian societies in the interior, they apparently felt no pressure to follow suit. They lived the way they did not because they didn't know what was good for them but because cultural and environmental factors, as Dena Dincauze pointed out, "made social complexity unattractive, unnecessary, or maladaptive" to them. In trying to understand tidewater New York in Middle Woodland times, it is important, as Dincauze warned in another context, to keep in mind that "Euro-American values of dominance, competition, size, and wealth [can] blind us in important ways to the achievements of people who do not, or did not, share those values. . . . [The] interesting matters are what people did and how they did it, not whether they failed to do something bigger, fancier, or more expensive."[42]

Certainly, for the Middle Woodland, one of the most "interesting matters" is the cultural trajectory that these coastal peoples pursued in the first millennium A.D. It may be that as they settled down at these sites that line the modern city's bays and estuaries, they were also laying down the roots of that social order that the Europeans encountered much later, in the seventeenth century. At that time, one colonist observed of his Indian neighbors, with some curiosity, that "there is little authority known among them . . . they live almost all equally free." Another noted, "It is not with them as it is here in Holland, where the greatest, noblest, and richest live more luxuriously than a . . . common man." In fact, they were known to be "extraordinarily charitable one to another, one having nothing to spare, but [they] freely impart it to [their] friends. . . . they share one to another, leaving themselves commonly the least share."[43]

CHAPTER SEVEN

Tethered to the Land: The Late Woodland, 1,000–400 B.P.

The Late Woodland, which began a thousand years ago, is the last great era when Native American peoples dominated the region. A number of changes were taking place in their lives during those years—some modest, others revolutionary. For archaeologists studying these six centuries, it is not at all clear how uniform an impact these changes had on the various groups living in the area. Much of that uncertainty revolves around the nature of the landscape at that time and the relationship of the local people to it. These questions take on added importance because, by archaeological convention, the Late Woodland ends with the establishment of the first European settlements in the region. Thus the people who watched the first European ships sail into New York Harbor were Late Woodland people. Their descendants are known today as the Munsee, a branch of the Lenape or Delaware.[1]

A study of the Late Woodland inevitably leads us to revisit one of the most alluring of all American origin myths. In this stirring tale, the Europeans discovered a New World and built cities and farms in its wilderness. They brought civilization to "this forested glory of primitive America," a wilderness that until then had been inhabited by a few "savages," who were also "wild" and part of this primeval world. This vision of a nearly vacant, pristine land, "needing only an axe to make it habitable," became part of the national heritage. But this myth, with its roots in prejudice and politics, is under fire these days. For obscured beneath its poetic and patriotic appeal, as many scholars are now pointing out (and as Native Americans have long done), is the hard fact that the land already was, and for millennia had been, occupied by a number of Native American groups, each with its own long and complex history and each having left its imprint on the land. The archaeology of Late Woodland New York, then, leads us to challenge the mythical vision of the past at the same time that it leads us to understand and appreciate the Indian past for its own sake. In so doing, it helps us to envision the distinctive landscape that the Late Woodland peoples created in coastal New York during those centuries.[2]

One of the important technological changes during this period was in weaponry. By now, hunters in the Northeast were increasingly relying on the bows and arrows in their arsenals. These were far more formidable weapons than the spears of earlier times. Arrows, fitted with triangular stone arrowheads (see fig. 4.1), have a longer range and are more accurate; hunters could now shoot game (or enemies, for that matter) from distances of up to thirty or forty yards. In addition, arrows could be shot with a rapid-fire technique: a number of them could be carried in a quiver and the bow quickly reloaded as needed.[3]

There were also changes in everyday cooking and storage equipment. Potters throughout the region were now decorating their pots with new and more elaborate designs, and the pots themselves were bigger, rounder, and more thinly walled than their Middle Woodland predecessors (fig. 7.1). These new pots would have been ideal for simmering soups, gruels, or stews and for storing all sorts of foods, including those based on a triad of new foods that were now part of the diets of some Late Woodland peoples. These new foods—maize, beans, and squash—were the product of one of the most far-reaching (and, for archaeologists, controversial) of all Late Woodland innovations, the adoption of swidden, or slash-and-burn, agriculture.[4]

The introduction of full-scale farming in Northeastern economies had consequences that reverberated throughout the lives of those who adopted it. One of the most profound, and the one that most concerns us here, was the way many farming people arranged themselves across the landscape. Although residential flexibility can be an important factor for many hunting-and-gathering societies—people need to be in the right place at the right time to exploit critical food resources—this is not the case for full-scale farming communities. With a *major* commitment to agriculture, people become much more tethered to the land. Fields have to be cleared, prepared, and planted at the right time, and then they have to be weeded and protected from marauding deer, raccoons, and other raiders. The crops have to be harvested at the right time and then dried and stored to provide food for the lean winter months. Archaeologists working in some of the inland riverine areas of the Northeast see clear evidence of this tethering to the land in the establishment of large year-round, agriculturally based Late Woodland village sites, each made up of a number of large multi-family houses.[5]

7.1. A Late Woodland pot found in upper Manhattan by Reginald P. Bolton and William L. Calver at the beginning of the twentieth century.

Yet archaeologists are divided about whether these two major innovations so often causally (and often casually) linked together—farming and village life—ever reached coastal New York and southern New England. In contrast to some of the more inland areas of the Northeast, relatively little maize has been recovered from sites along the coast, and there is no clear evidence for large Late Woodland villages on the scale of many of those inland. Nevertheless, a number of seventeenth-century European accounts describe Indian farming villages in coastal areas. These accounts, as well as discoveries made inland, have led some archaeologists to argue that agriculturally based villages had existed along the coast over a long period, dating back well into Late Woodland times.

Other archaeologists maintain that these major changes—the shift to agriculture and the concomitant shift to settled village life—simply didn't take place along the coast in Late Woodland times. Instead, village life developed only later, as a response to the European arrivals. After all, they claim, contact between indigenous populations and Europeans frequently stimulated dramatic changes in local economies and cultures all over the world. In this case, their argument continues, Munsee populations moved into coastal areas from more inland ones to take advantage of the new trading opportunities opened up by the European presence. During the Late Woodland, the coastal area was hardly occupied at all. Neighboring groups visited it only sporadically for brief seasonal shellfishing or other food-gathering forays.[6]

This controversy goes well beyond scientific interest in archaeological questions—the necessary relationships between village life and agriculture and the variability of local economies within ecologically complex regions. It also goes beyond the millennia-long narrative of the people who once lived on the piece of land whose history we have been tracing. Because the final years of the Late Woodland constitute the period right before the Europeans arrived and started building New Amsterdam, questions about the economy and village life inevitably become entangled with the enduring images of a primeval landscape. As a result, a number of scientific questions arise: Was New York largely vacant during the Late Woodland and visited only briefly for shellfishing forays? Was it heavily populated and marked by substantial villages and large and prosperous farms? Or was it something else entirely? Is it possible for a group of people to be tethered to the land without farming it? These questions, in turn, lead to important philosophical and political ones: Can land that is not used or shaped in ways that follow familiar European patterns of land use truly "belong" to an indigenous people? Is it their land, or is it a "wilderness" to be claimed by others?

The answers to some of these questions can be found in sites scattered throughout the city. But like most of the sites that chronicle the deeper past, many Late Woodland sites were dug at the beginning of the twentieth century with what, by today's standards, are woefully inadequate techniques. Also, because many of these sites were occupied by succeeding groups of people from Archaic times on, it is difficult to map out those areas that were associated specifically with Late Woodland peoples. This makes it hard to estimate the sizes of their settlements or make inferences about population size.[7]

Surprisingly, many of the best clues we have to reconstruct those years come from burials. Over the past century, archaeologists working in the city have found and recorded more burials dating to this period than to any earlier era. It is not clear whether this is the result of better preservation (given that these burials are relatively recent), greater population size, or other factors. Discoveries of burials have always particularly stirred the imaginations of archaeologists and the public. Archaeologists are well aware of the unique ability that burials have for recreating the past. The analysis of human remains provides an unparalleled opportunity to learn about issues like health, disease, and nutrition. And such analyses can also help recreate ancient philosophical and social systems.

Unfortunately, Native American burials in New York (and elsewhere in the nation) have been treated with astonishing disrespect. Over the past 150 years in New York, for example, Indian burials have been bulldozed with shocking casualness by construction projects. They have also been wantonly vandalized by looters looking for skulls and bones to sell or to add to their trophy collections.[8]

For Native Americans throughout the country, burial grounds are sacred, and any disturbance, including scientific excavation, is offensive and sacrilegious. This strongly held belief now has some legislative support. It has also challenged archaeologists, in recent years, to confront the ethical issues involved in excavating human burials and to consider the wishes of the concerned Native American communities (fig. 7.2).[9]

7.2. A sunrise ceremony in Central Park on October 10, 1992, sponsored by the American Indian Ritual Object Repatriation Foundation. Native American spiritual leaders from many parts of the country gathered in New York to conduct religious ceremonies and to educate the general public about the importance of the return of sacred objects to American Indian communities.

The burials that we discuss here were dug in earlier eras, between forty and one hundred years ago. What they clearly show us today are strong bonds between the living Late Woodland peoples and the dead members of their communities as well as equally strong connections between the peoples and their land—bonds that are important in many Indian communities throughout North America to this day.

There is still much to be learned about the area in those years. Yet even with the limited evidence currently available—evidence that includes not only human burials, but also an unusual pattern of dog burials—a wide range of Late Woodland beliefs about family, community, territory, the animal world, health, disease, diet, and economic change begins to emerge.

In reconstructing that Late Woodland world, we start with the evidence that will help us imagine some of the social and metaphysical aspects of the people's lives. This evidence, largely from burials, gives us some of the strongest clues that we have for understanding the Late Woodland peoples themselves and their concepts of community and land. With those in mind, we can reexamine the relationship between farming and sedentary life and explore the intriguing economic decisions that men and women living in coastal New York made during those centuries. When the results of these two approaches are combined, a panorama of a Late Woodland landscape comes into focus.

Protected from the Wild Beasts

You find these burial places everywhere in the woods, but especially along the banks of rivers or streams where they live or have lived. Sometimes you also see near these graves some markers hanging in a tree, such as a child's carrying plank or board. . . . And it signifies that there lies or sits buried there a woman with a small child or a pregnant woman.—Jasper Danckaerts, seventeenth century

Every day, thousands of cars, buses, and trucks race, or crawl in heavy traffic, past what was once a Late Woodland settlement in Queens. That site, known today as the Aqueduct site (see fig. 1.1), lies between the Aqueduct Race Track and Kennedy International Airport. The area surrounding the site is now crisscrossed by major highways, including the Southern State Parkway and the Van Wyck Expressway. But in Late Woodland times, the site was at the head of a creek, near the edge of a marshy area teeming with wildlife.[10]

The Aqueduct site was discovered in 1939 by Ralph Solecki and a group of fellow enthusiasts. (Years later, Solecki was the senior archaeologist at the initial Stadt Huys Block negotiations.) Although he was a young man, his distinguished career yet ahead of him, he was far from an archaeological novice. Since his early teens, he, along with a group of young men equally determined to save their city's past, had been excavating sites all over the city. When they discovered the Aqueduct site, Robert Moses, that quintessential architect of New York's modern landscape, was getting ready to push through the roadways that now encircle not only the Aqueduct site but much of the rest of the city as well. Discussing those days fifty years later, Solecki described Moses as the "one man who can be blamed for more single handed destruction of archaeological sites in the New York City area" than any other person.[11]

In the spring of 1939, Solecki and his group were working at the site, excavating refuse pits filled with debris from meals, discarded Late Woodland stone tools, and sherds from broken pottery vessels, when they found the grave of an adult woman. She was lying on her left side with her knees drawn up to her chin in a "flexed" position. Close to her knees they found another burial, this one of a four-month-old infant lying on its back. The grave pit itself was covered with an overlying layer of shell mixed with a large amount of charcoal.

We don't know what family tragedy brought these two individuals into their shared grave. But we do know a little about the woman's life and a little more about the funeral held for her and the child. A physical anthropologist examined her remains at the time of discovery and suggested that she was between fifty-six and seventy-five years of age when she died. She must have suffered from toothaches during her lifetime; her teeth were very worn down, and at some point at least four of them had been abscessed. Although we don't know her exact relationship with the infant buried beside her, we do know that the Munsee people in the seventeenth century lived in extended family groups, and it seems likely that these two were members of the same family and had lived in the community at the head of the creek.[12]

As the archaeologists continued digging near the grave, they discovered a series of postholes. Postholes look, to the uninitiated, simply like dark stains in the soil. But in cross section these stains have a characteristic tapering shape, showing where the sharpened end of a post had once stood before it either was pulled out of the ground or decomposed in place. Posts can be used in all sorts of architectural features: as parts of a house or another building, in a drying rack, a fence, a palisade, a grave marker, or any number of things. When archaeologists find postholes, they look to see if these traces of old architectural features form a pattern that hints at their function. At Aqueduct fourteen postholes surrounded the grave. Someone, centuries ago, had built a structure that encircled and maybe even covered the grave.

Solecki and his crew had found something that had not been recognized before in the city. He began searching early colonial documents for clues to interpret these encir-cling postholes. One seventeenth-century colonist noted that the people "fence their graves with a hedge, and cover the tops with mats, to shelter them from the rain." An-other was even more specific: "They make a large grave, and line it inside with boughs of trees, in which they lay the corpse, so that no earth can touch it. They then cover this with clay, and form the grave, seven or eight feet, in the shape of a sugar loaf, and place palisades around it. I have frequently seen the wife of the deceased come daily to the grave, weeping and crying, creeping over it with extended body, and grieving for the death of her husband."[13]

Other accounts describe "palisades resembling a small dwelling" or timbers set about a grave "so as to secure it from the approach of wild beasts." What Solecki had found, then, was probably all that was left of an enclosure that had once housed the dead woman and child and that had, like all houses, protected them from the elements and the wild animals.[14]

Many Late Woodland burials found at sites throughout the city are similar to this one: the body is in a flexed position, the grave is covered with charcoal and shell (per-haps the remains of a funerary feast given for the mourners and the dead), and there are few grave goods. The location of this grave at Aqueduct is also typical for its time. Unlike the earlier Orient period, when the dead were buried in special sacred precincts —or, for that matter, modern times, when many of the dead are buried in enclosed cemeteries on the city's outskirts—the Late Woodland families buried their dead close to where they had lived.[15]

The Twice Buried

The burial at Aqueduct is what archaeologists call a primary burial, that is, an inter-ment made at the time of death, with no subsequent handling of the human remains. Although this was the most common type of burial in Late Woodland times, there were also other burial practices. These practices, called secondary burials or, more sim-ply, bone or bundle burials, are more complex and involve several distinct stages. The first occurs at the time of death, when the body is placed in a temporary grave, in a charnel house, or on an above-ground scaffold. Then, at a later date, usually after the flesh has decomposed and the bones are dry, the bones are recovered from their tem-porary resting place and cleaned, bundled, wrapped, and prepared for their second burial.[16]

When archaeologists first found instances of these secondary burials in the early twentieth century, they didn't quite know what to make of them. Some archaeologists resorted to wild and sometimes lurid speculations involving tales of massacres and human sacrifices. Today, when we know more about such practices, which are common throughout the world, we argue that these secondary burials both reflected and helped create powerful concepts of society and territory in Late Woodland coastal New York.

The individual bundle burials found in the city are similar to other Late Woodland burials; they are located in a settlement and have few grave goods. The only difference is that for these individuals, this is their second burial.[17]

Early accounts suggest reasons for these ceremonies. Gabriel Thomas, a seventeenth-century observer of the Delaware, noted that "if a Person of Note dies very far from the Place of his own Residence they will carry his Bones home some considerable time after, to be buried there."[18] In this brief description we probably have the explanation for many of the individual bundle burials that have been found throughout the city. These may well be the remains of individuals who died away from home and whose bones were brought back for reburial. They may or may not have been persons of note, but they must have been members of a community living in coastal New York. In fact, the presence of all these individual bone burials seems to underscore a strong notion of place and community in Late Woodland times. These gathered bones were brought to these coastal communities because they had once lived there, their families still lived there, and therefore this area should be their final resting place. Such a strong idea of place seems decidedly at odds with the idea that the coast was largely vacant and visited only briefly, on a seasonal basis. By contrast, it does seem consistent with a notion of settled life.

These burials are similar to another form of secondary burial found in Late Woodland New York: the reburial of the bundled bones of a group of individuals in a common grave or ossuary. Reports mention that several Late Woodland ossuaries were discovered at the beginning of the twentieth century at Ward's Point and Throgs Neck, but almost nothing is known about them. Alanson Skinner reports finding an ossuary at the Bowmans Brook site in his native Staten Island. He discovered it in the first decade of the twentieth century, when a railroad cut was being widened for the steel plant that would eventually cover and destroy the site. Skinner notes that there were nearly one hundred large storage and trash pits at the site. The contents of these pits were either destroyed or otherwise lost—at least one complete pottery vessel was sold by a construction worker—and he managed to salvage very little from what appears to have been a substantial settlement. He did uncover, however, a number of individual primary burials, several individual bone burials, and an ossuary containing the bundled bones of up to half a dozen individuals.[19] Half a century after his salvage operations, another, much more complex ossuary was found in a heavily used city park in the Bronx.

This particular site, Archery Range (see fig. 1.1), was discovered in Pelham Bay Park by Edward Kaeser, who excavated it with the help of his brother. Kaeser had long hoped to find the Indian settlement that had been in that area when the Munsees sold the land to Thomas Pell, after whose estate the park is named, on November 14, 1654.[20] He thought that he had found a likely spot near a modern-day archery range. As it turned out, he unearthed something entirely different.

While excavating a pit about ten feet by eight feet in area, Kaeser realized that he was coming down upon "a continuous spread of skull surfaces." Careful excavation revealed a group of nine individual bundle burials, arranged in a roughly circular fashion around a white boulder. These bone bundles were well separated from each other as they circled the central boulder, and Kaeser speculated that each bundle might have originally been wrapped in a bark or hide covering that had long since disintegrated. In the eastern end of the pit, Kaeser discovered two additional bundles, each made up of the bones of a dog.[21]

After Kaeser mapped and recorded the burials, he removed them and continued digging through the orange clay layer on which they had rested. He then came to at least twelve additional human bundle burials. These burials were less complete than those in the upper layer. In some cases, an individual was apparently represented only by a skull or a few other skeletal parts. Because the bones in the lower grave were commingled, Kaeser speculated that they might all have been emptied into the grave at the same time from a common basket or other container. Under two of these skulls, Kaeser found the fully articulated skeleton of a dog. He also found a posthole, the remains of a post that had once stood in the northeastern corner of this common grave, perhaps marking its location or identifying its members (fig. 7.3).

The ages of the individuals buried there ranged from infancy to old age. Of the twenty-one skulls found, ten were filled with vertebrae and other small bones. In some cases we know that these small bones were from other individuals; Kaeser found children's bones in three of the adult skulls and an adult vertebra in one of the children's skulls. Although we don't know whether this was done as a symbolic expression of collective identity or simply for ease of transport, we know that this was not an uncommon practice in eastern North America. In fact, Thomas Jefferson had noted it, two hundred years earlier, when he was excavating a mound not far from his home, Monticello.[22]

Although parts of the site had already been destroyed by looters, Kaeser did discover some trash pits and midden mate-

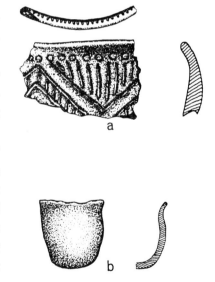

7.3. Artifacts recovered from the Archery Range ossuary: (a) *a rimsherd from a pottery vessel, and* (b) *an intact miniature pot, 1½ inches high, that had been placed near the remains of an infant.*

rial, as well as a primary burial and a bone burial, all dating to the same general time period. He thus argued that the ossuary was part of a settlement and not an isolated burial ground. As at Aqueduct and other Late Woodland sites in the city, the people at Archery Range had incorporated their dead into the place where they themselves lived.

Late Woodland ossuaries, like those at Archery Range and Bowmans Brook (see fig. 1.1), have also been discovered at sites along the coasts of Delaware, Maryland, and Cape Cod. We know little about these ossuaries because many of them were poorly documented at the time of their discovery. A number of them have been found in land associated with the Nanticoke people, who lived just to the south of the Lenape. Their reburial practices continued into modern times, and descriptions of them often found their way into eighteenth-century colonial records. Some of these narratives describe the Nanticoke bringing their dead relatives or friends along with them when they moved their villages into new areas. One of the most vivid eyewitness accounts of this practice comes from a Moravian missionary, John Heckewelder, then living in Pennsylvania: "These Nanticokes had the singular custom of removing the bones of their deceased friends from the burial place to a place of deposit in the country they dwell in. In earlier times, they were known to go . . . to fetch the bones of their dead from the Eastern Shore of Maryland even when the bodies were in a putrid state, so that they had to take off the flesh and scrape the bones clean, before they could carry them along. I well remember having seen them between the years 1750 and 1760, loaded with such bones, which, being fresh, caused a disagreeable stench, as they passed through the town of Bethlehem."[23]

What Heckewelder saw passing through Bethlehem in the mid-eighteenth century was a displaced people moving north because their lives and homes had been disrupted by expanding European settlements. Despite these upheavals, the Nanticoke were unwilling to abandon their dead. Instead, they disinterred the bones and brought them along to be reburied in their new homeland.

These and other historic accounts illustrate how peoples in the Northeast maintained themselves as a community and laid claim to a territory by reburying the bones of their dead there. In building their ossuaries, they apparently were also creating a collective unity; these group burials honor the community of the dead, not any one individual member.[24]

In some ways, the ossuaries at Archery Range and Bowmans Brook are similar to the great mortuary pits built by the Orient peoples several thousand years earlier. In both cases, it is the collective dead who are being honored. But the earlier Orient cemeteries, unlike these later ossuaries, were not built in habitation sites; they were dug into prominent features of the landscape in what appear to have been sacred precincts, away from the places where people lived and worked. Those hilltop cemeteries were the focus of a great deal of ritual activity, including the offering of many gifts to the honored dead. They were built at a time when small, scattered populations were settling down within fixed territories through which they moved on their seasonal rounds. These prominent burial structures would have been highly visible markers to them and to their neighbors, indicating that these people not only honored their ancestors but also proclaimed this land their territory. The cemetery's construction and all the accompanying rituals would also have united them as a people.

By Late Woodland times, we argue, there was far less seasonal mobility. The people had become increasingly tethered to the land and lived in communities scattered throughout the lush estuarine environment. These communities were both larger and more permanent than the earlier ones. And it was important to the people living there to integrate their dead into these communities even if it meant that in some cases the bones had to be brought there.[25]

Although we can suggest a number of reasonable scenarios for these group burials, the actual motivation behind them remains a mystery. There may have been a small group of people moving into the coastal area who brought the bones of their dead relatives and friends along with them to rebury in their new home. Or these ossuaries may have been built by families already living in the area who decided to move their homes to a new spot in their territory. They may have set up their new households for any number of reasons: their original settlements may have grown too large for comfort, they may have wanted to join another kin group, they may have found a location they liked better, or they may have wished to avoid social tensions. Some families may even have been practicing slash-and-burn gardening, which exhausts the soil after eight or ten years, and they may have moved to be near more-fertile soil. But whatever may have prompted their moves, these families brought the bones of their dead along with them to their new home.[26]

Alternatively, these rituals may have had nothing whatsoever to do with movements of people or households. Instead, they may have been triggered by spiritual, social, or political concerns that left no imprint in the archaeological record. Yet even if the impetus for these reburials eludes us, the fact that they, along with the other burials, were incorporated into the settlements of the living, seems to reveal the very real power that the bones of their ancestors held for the people living in coastal New York at that time. But more than suggesting such strong emotional and spiritual bonds, we think that this establishment of the community of the living and the dead together, in one place, also reflects a sense of permanency, of settlement. As archaeologists writing about a similar ossuary on Cape Cod have argued, these burial practices "tip the balance of evidence away from scenarios in which the coast saw no more than occasional visits or seasonal camps and toward a picture of permanent coastal habitation."[27]

He was out walking one Sunday morning looking for artifacts in the area along the Harlem River near what today is part of the city's vast subway yards. At that time, the whole area was covered with numerous shell deposits that had long intrigued him. As he walked along, he kept checking the road cut through a knoll where city workers were grading the newly established Ninth Avenue and 209th Street section of the growing city's grid.

Calver spotted bones in the dirt the workmen had dug up and, with his cane, began poking around a shell pocket in the embankment looking for the bones' source. What he uncovered was the burial of a fully articulated dog. Shortly thereafter he found a second dog burial, covered like the first with oyster shells and pottery sherds. Calver was elated with his discoveries and, in an article he wrote for a local newspaper, claimed that "these two latest finds have in them something which appeals strongly to the imagination of even those who take no special interest in the past, and have heretofore had no desire to know anything of the manners and customs of the native Manhattans."[30]

Soon after Calver discovered these dog burials, he and Bolton began exploring an adjacent area where construction crews were exposing remnants of what we now know to be a Late Woodland settlement (fig. 7.6). Over the next few years, Bolton and Calver excavated a number of human burials (both primary and secondary), many large storage and trash pits, midden material, hearths, and a total of eleven dog burials, each buried curled up, as Bolton described it, "nose to tail." With the exception of two puppies who shared a common grave, each dog was buried in its own grave, its body covered with a layer of shell. In other words, these dogs were buried as many humans were. Over the years, similar dog burials were found in other parts of the city.[31]

Not all Late Woodland dogs had ceremonial burials; in some cases, their disarticulated bones were found scattered in the general midden. Bolton suggested that "the Indian dog shared the meal, but sometimes he was the meal itself." Yet it is not clear what role, if any, dogs may have played in the local diet. The dog bones were never examined for butchering marks, and it may be that people disposed of most dead dogs by simply throwing them away with the household trash.[32]

Even if dogs were sometimes eaten, they would certainly have been much more than walking larders for the peoples whose lives they shared. Dogs, after all, are commensal with humans, not merely consumed by them. They live in human settlements, sometimes competing for food with humans, but they are also scavengers, keeping the settlement clean. They may work alongside humans as hunting aides or as beasts of burden. They may serve as extra warmth on a cold night, as watchdogs in unsettled times, and as beloved companions.[33]

7.6. An early-twentieth-century photograph of the outline of a shell pit at a Late Woodland settlement in the Washington Heights–Inwood area in Manhattan.

Yet dogs, for all their value, their proximity to human life, and the affection they give or receive, are animals and not full members of human society. Like the humans to whom they have attached themselves, they travel between the worlds of the forest and the settlement, but they really belong to neither world. Perhaps, then, because of this ambiguous relationship it isn't surprising that dogs are found in what appear to be ritual contexts.

We can find some clues of the significance of dogs from the descendants of these Late Woodland peoples, the modern Delaware. In their traditions, dogs appear frequently as animals with unique powers, guardians of both human health and the gates of the next world. These modern traditions suggest that the symbolic roles the Late Woodland dogs played may have been as powerful as their practical ones. The dogs may have been the links to that part of the spiritual world that controls death and the afterlife and disease and health.

In the twentieth century, Delaware families living in Oklahoma traditionally gave a child a dog that served not only as a pet but also as the child's guardian; it was hoped that the animal would attract any sickness that was about, thus sparing the child. A guardian dog was, in fact, believed to think "I am only a dog, the child is more precious." If the dog died, it was buried with loving care, and the child was then given another guardian. If the child died, then the dog was sometimes kept in the household to guard the child's spirit.[34]

Dogs were also believed to help adults, as Nora Thompson Dean (fig. 7.7) pointed out. Dean, also known by her Delaware name, Touching Leaves, was one of the most respected Delaware traditionalists of the twentieth century and was frequently consulted by scholars about traditional beliefs. In one such interview at her Oklahoma home, she recalled: "One of our dogs got cancer and we had to take him to the local vet to get his cancer cut out, but I guess they didn't get all of that cancer because the dog finally died. We called him *Sektun* which means 'black mouth.' I smoke a lot and maybe he foresaw something that might happen to me with my throat. That's the way I look at it. Later I was given another little dog, part beagle; I called him *Skinu* which meant 'young man,' and I didn't have him too long, and this little dog finally developed black tongue. We took him to the vet and he was given lots of shots but they were of no use. They finally cut his tongue off but he finally died too." When Dean was asked if she thought that the dog had taken diseases that had been meant for her, she replied, "That's what I think. I really feel that way and I always feel like what the old people say is true."[35]

These beliefs may be of long standing, going back to at least the Late Woodland. If so, then what Bolton, Calver, and other archaeologists found were the burials of dogs who had once served as guardians for the humans whose lives they had shared and whose diseases they were believed to have taken.

The rituals surrounding the placement of dogs in human graves—as opposed to those involving dogs buried in their own graves—may be of a different nature. Yet one hypothesis, which holds that these animals were buried to serve as hunting companions in the afterworld, is probably not correct. When dogs were found in either primary or secondary human graves, they were not associated with other parts of a hunting kit—that is, no spear points, arrowheads, knives, or other typical hunting gear was buried with them. In general, the dogs were the only grave offering.[36]

Modern Delaware beliefs again suggest a possible spiritual role for these dogs. In describing Delaware funerary customs, Nora Thompson Dean reported a belief that "our real soul, the *lenapeokan,* goes to where the Creator lives. The Milky Way is the path along which it travels. But before the soul gets to where the Creator is, there is a bridge to cross. This bridge is guarded by all of the dead dogs." A number of seventeenth-century European descriptions of Northeastern Indian peoples also relate similar beliefs concerning dogs guarding the gates to the next world or being sacrificed to serve as "forerunners in the other world." It is tempting to think that the dogs found in the Archery Range ossuary and in other human graves had been sacrificed and buried with humans to serve as their guides, or psychopomps, to help their souls gain entry into the afterworld.[37]

Ethnographic analogies and historical data such as these cannot definitively explain the archaeological past. But oral tradition has long been an important part of Indian history. And in this case, because of the historical continuity between modern Delaware peoples and those of the Late Woodland, there is strong evidence of a ritual relationship between dogs and humans, one that has persisted over the centuries. Delaware traditions suggest that dogs had far more than economic roles in coastal New York during the Late Woodland. Their burials in local coastal communities may have been the settings for rituals in which the Late Woodland peoples tried, as all peoples do, to understand and tame the uncontrollable and the unknowable forces of sickness and death. They may have used dogs in these ceremonies because they saw these domesticated animals as somehow standing at that terrifying frontier between life and death.

7.7. Nora Thompson Dean (also known as Touching Leaves), Lenape herbalist and traditionalist, photographed in 1972.

On the Eve of the European Incursions

The archaeological evidence we have discussed so far—the many large storage and trash pits at residential sites, some up to six feet in diameter and as many feet deep; the large and heavy ceramic vessels that could hold up to two and a half gallons of food; and especially the careful placement of the dead, both human and canine, near settlements, and the building of ossuaries that bound them together as a people—argues strongly for a sense of permanence, community, and territory in coastal New York on the eve of the European incursions. The area bears little resemblance to nineteenth-century mythic images of early America—the "forest primeval" or the "domain of Nature." Nevertheless, the one thing for which there is no clear archaeological evidence is full-scale farming. This is troubling because so much of conventional wisdom argues for a necessary link between the adoption of maize agriculture and the development of sedentary village life.[38]

Maize is a tropical crop that was gradually adopted over the centuries by northern societies in what is now the United States. By the end of the first millennium A.D., maize, along with beans and squash, had become an important part of the economies of the peoples living in the towns and cities along the great Midwestern and South-eastern river valleys. Maize makes its first appearance in the Northeast at least a thousand years ago, and possibly even earlier. Beans and some squashes probably arrived around that time, although one variety of squash may have a longer history in New England. Over the succeeding centuries, many of the peoples in the inland river valleys of New York and New England increasingly relied on this new triad of vegetable foods and were settling down in large permanent villages that spread over many acres and contained hundreds of people. But along the coast, there is remarkably little evidence for a reliance on maize, beans, and squash and equally little evidence for such large villages.[39]

One of the most cherished beliefs held by archaeologists is that the materials recovered from an excavation can be analyzed over and over again by archaeologists who come along generations later with new questions to ask and new techniques to answer them. This is why archaeologists are so insistent about the proper long-term curation of artifacts and all the records that every excavation produces. It was to such old collections that Lynn Ceci, an archaeologist at Queens College, turned to answer questions about maize and village life in coastal New York. When she first examined the problem for her doctoral dissertation in the late 1970s, she proposed that Native American sedentary farming villages were recent phenomena along the coast, spurred by contact with the newly arrived Europeans and the trading opportunities they offered. Before then, she suggested, there may have been only small scattered seasonal work camps.[40] Her provocative theory revitalized Late Woodland studies throughout the Northeast. But her argument was a theoretical one, based on the limited information available at the time. Years later, she began looking for hard data to test her original ideas.

Ceci knew that although small amounts of maize had been reported from coastal sites, the sites themselves had been dug a century ago, long before precise dating techniques, such as radiocarbon dating, had been developed. And so she turned her attention to archaeological collections that had been stored for a century at the American Museum of Natural History. She began searching through these old collections for such organic materials as charcoal, shell, or animal bone, which could be radiocarbon-dated. Not only did she find them, she also found some carefully stored fragments of charred maize—one from Bowmans Brook and the other from the nearby Sebonac site on Long Island. When the dates on the maize came back from the lab, they were unexpectedly early: A.D. 1270–1410 for Bowmans Brook and A.D. 1260–1485 for Sebonac. Ceci, excited by the implications of these dates, began a major reanalysis of the whole question of farming and village life in coastal New York. Unfortunately, she died before she could complete her project.[41]

Nevertheless, her work clearly shows that by at least the fifteenth century, and maybe even as early as the thirteenth, maize had in fact entered households in coastal New York. These dates raise a host of new questions: Did the coastal peoples grow the maize themselves or simply trade for it? How important was it in their economy? How quickly did it spread? How did it affect other aspects of their lives?[42]

In recent years, some of the most exciting ways of reconstructing ancient diets have come from the analysis of the bone chemistry of the human skeleton. An individual's skeleton is the material record of that person's past diet, diseases, nutritional stresses, and overall health. And that record can be read hundreds or even thousands of years later by physical anthropologists.

Scientists have discovered that different groups of plants follow very different pathways in their photosynthesis. Temperate plants, such as those native to the Northeast, follow what is known as a C3 pathway, while tropical plants like maize, which is an introduced plant in the Northeast, follow a C4 pathway. Because of these different pathways, each group of plants has a different ratio of the stable isotopes carbon 13 and carbon 12. Further, animals (including humans) who eat these plants will reflect these carbon isotopic ratios in their skeletons. Physical anthropologists can analyze small samples of bone collagen, determine its stable carbon ratios, and then go on to make inferences about the roles of both native and introduced tropical plants, such as maize, in human diets.[43]

This is what Patricia Bridges, who was a colleague of Ceci's at Queens College, did. She analyzed the bone chemistry and the skeletons of some of the individuals whose remains George Pepper had excavated at Ward's Point back in 1895. She was looking for evidence of diet and general health conditions. But because these excavations were done long before radiocarbon dating was even developed, Bridges had dates for only four of the burials—those that Ceci had dated from associated wood charcoal. These four were Pepper's most spectacular finds, the Middle Woodland child discussed earlier and a Late Woodland multiple burial of three adult men who had met violent deaths—at least twenty-three spear or arrow points were found either still embedded in their bones or lying among them—and had been buried together in a common grave. Bridges was also able to study a dog that Ceci had dated as Late Woodland.[44]

Bridges' study showed that the isotope values for the three Late Woodland men were "completely within the range expected for individuals eating terrestrial C3 (non-maize) plants."[45] But because the ratios were in the upper ranges for C3 plant eaters, the evidence could reflect either a limited reliance on maize or a reliance on marine foods in their diet. The uncertainty came about because eating marine foods—fish, shellfish, mammal, or even marine plants—can also bring about elevated stable carbon isotope values. Because of the extensive marine resources in the area, the question was an important one.

The bones of people who favor marine-based diets have higher stable nitrogen isotope values than those whose diets are based on terrestrial foods. Bridges' next round of tests, then, was aimed at measuring stable nitrogen levels in the bones. When the new results came in, Bridges discovered that, overall, the nitrogen values were above what would be expected for peoples basing their diets predominantly on *any* terrestrial plants, be they C3 or C4 or even on animals that eat terrestrial plants. In fact, the combined results of the two tests suggested a mixed diet based on both marine and terrestrial foods. She concluded that the individuals from Ward's Point whose bones she studied were exploiting marine food resources and that although terrestrial foods, both plants and animals, were also important, "maize was not a major component of their diet."[46] Although this is, admittedly, a very small sample to use to generalize about the diet of the much larger Late Woodland community, the results are suggestive. Intriguingly, the tests on the bone collagen from the Late Woodland dog at Ward's Point fell within the human range, suggesting that this particular dog, at least, ate as the humans did, perhaps scavenging from their garbage.

Bridges found that the overall health and diet of these Late Woodland men were good. They had suffered in varying degrees from osteoarthritis, both age related and the result of trauma.[47] But she found no signs of severe nutritional stress. In addition, although their teeth were worn down and several were chipped, and although some had gum disease or had lost teeth, they had relatively few dental cavities. Their lack of cavities, combined with their overall good health, is further evidence that maize was probably not a major part of their diet.

Contrary to common assumptions, diets that rely heavily on maize—or, for that matter, any cereal grains—are not necessarily more nutritious than those consumed by hunters, fishers, and gatherers. In fact, when cultivated cereal grains become an important part of the diet, overall health in a population usually deteriorates. In looking at skeletal populations from sites all over the world, archaeologists have discovered a pattern of nutritional stress following the adoption of agriculture. In the United States, for example, they have found that when maize (a crop poor in iron, zinc, and protein) was adopted as a food staple, the consequences included reduction in stature, increased dental cavities, iron-deficiency anemia, and malnutrition. These conditions can, in turn, make populations more vulnerable to bacterial infections. And populations that live in the crowded villages that are sometimes associated with a heavy reliance on agriculture suffer from the sanitation problems and infectious diseases that arise from such crowding.[48]

The pattern emerging from this combined paleobiological and archaeological evidence challenges the conventional wisdom that a heavy reliance on agriculture is a necessary precondition for living in permanent communities. These two Late Woodland innovations are clearly not linked. In fact, one of the most intriguing conclusions is the realization that although the *idea* of agriculture might be known in a region, such as coastal New York, its *practice* would not necessarily be embraced by everyone who learned about it. Such an important innovation might be adopted with varying degrees of intensity by different groups, depending on their needs at the time. But it might also be ignored. The evidence suggests that for those living in coastal New York, maize, beans, and squash apparently never dominated the traditional economy in the same way that they did elsewhere in the Northeast.[49]

Woodland peoples in tidewater New York were living in an extraordinarily rich environment. To them, the benefits of horticulture—a reliable food supply that could be stored for distribution in lean times; used to feed an increasingly large population; traded for goods, prestige, or peace with other groups; or even used to free some individuals from food-producing activities in favor of other kinds of work—were apparently not sufficiently impressive to compel them to assume the added burdens of intensive farming. In normal times, there would have been an abundance of wild plant and animal foods, much of which could be dried and stored to even out food shortages.[50] This was not the case for some of the inland groups, who lived in very different environments with fewer and less abundant natural resources. For them, a larger and more reliable food supply was important, and their economies increasingly relied on maize, beans, and squash.

If Late Woodland peoples in coastal New York did not rely heavily on agriculture, it was not because they were backward. They apparently knew about it and practiced it as they saw fit. Instead, they chose not to depend on farming because they could afford not to. As we saw with the Middle Woodland, modern values and expectations can sometimes blind us to the ways that other populations perceive and act on their opportunities. For many archaeologists today, the most provocative question is not *when* farming began, but rather *why*.[51]

Farming is, after all, a lot of work. To switch to full-time farming means a reorganization of the division of labor and a break with traditional food-collecting systems that had already proved to be successful. This is not something that people would do recklessly. We know from early European accounts that much of the farming in coastal New York was done by women. For these women to take on the added work of intensive farming—not only of planting, fertilizing, tending, and harvesting, but also of pounding and processing the crops—would have meant less time for them to spend on other customary economic activities, such as collecting and processing nuts, seeds, and other wild plant foods, as well as fish and shellfish. The same would hold true for men, who would have had to take time away from important fishing and hunting activities to clear and burn the land for gardens.[52] Major changes like these would not have been made lightly.

The evidence we have, then, suggests that although there may have been small gardens, agricultural foods were not a major part of the diet during the Late Woodland in coastal New York. But as is always the case, we need properly dug and analyzed sites, preferably ones with well-preserved plant and animal remains, to advance the argument.

As for the landscape, coastal New York may not have looked like the interior Northeastern river valleys, with their large fortified villages, scores of multifamily houses, extensive farmlands, and hundreds of people. But there was sedentary life nonetheless. On the eve of the European incursions, it was far from being the New York that a commentator dismissed as recently as 1987 as a "virgin place . . . lightly used . . . with a rich and almost empty coast."[53] Instead, we picture the landscape dotted with small communities like those at Archery Range, Ward's Point, Washington Heights–Inwood, Clasons Point, Bowmans Brook, and Aqueduct (see fig. 1.1). These and other sites were located along the coast's bays, inlets, and coves, near fresh water, and frequently within easy walking distance of a variety of available wild foods. These communities appear to have been made up of clusters of houses from which people went to other work sites during the year. There were large storage pits filled with foods for leaner days; drying racks for meat, fish, and shellfish; workshop areas for making pottery, stone tools, clothing, and other necessities; and, by the end of the Late Woodland, small gardens. Paths and trails crisscrossed the area, connecting these communities with each other.

These communities were the focus for ritual and social life at that time. They were places where people gathered, where smoking rituals united them with the spiritual world (fig. 7.8), where lineage members met to make important decisions, and where children were educated to become responsible adults. There were small sweat lodges for men to purify themselves, small houses where women went to give birth or stay during their menstrual periods, and burial grounds for family members and friends, some of whom had their bones brought from some distant place for a second burial. These were also places where dogs were incorporated into rituals surrounding disease and death. And as people began to garden, they may have added new rituals to coincide with the planting and harvesting of their crops. This was their sacred landscape.

Most important were the Late Woodland peoples themselves, the men, women and children who lived there. They may have gone off to fishing stations, migratory bird-hunting sites, or winter hunting camps, or moved their households from one spot to another. They may have journeyed inland to trade, make alliances, or attend ceremonies with relatives and friends. But coastal New York was their home. It was the place from which they set forth and the place to which they returned.[54]

The archaeological record, fragmentary though it is, conveys a strong sense of place, community, and local identity during Late Woodland times. The land was an integral part not only of the people's economic lives but of their social and spiritual ones as well. The archaeological finds discovered beneath the modern city firmly rebut the powerful and enticing myth that, as William Cronon put it, "when the Europeans arrived in the New World they confronted Virgin Land, the Forest Primeval, a wilderness which had existed for eons uninfluenced by human hands."[55] That wilderness is an invention. But it is one deeply ingrained in so many different aspects of the national consciousness that it is hard, even today, to relinquish.

7.8. These Late Woodland smoking pipes, found at sites in upper Manhattan, were probably used in rituals.

In the nineteenth century, a vision of a pristine land occupied only by "savages," with both land and inhabitants ripe for the benefits of "civilization," became a stirring one for people who saw themselves or their ancestors as colonists, pioneers, or builders of a new nation. This vision was particularly powerful for the millions who, fleeing poverty and persecution, came to the United States looking for a fresh start in a New World. But this romantic and self-congratulatory origin myth has a dark side. Over the years, its "crusader ideology" has, in the words of historian Colin Calloway, legitimized and "rationalized dispossession and conquest on the premise that America was virgin wilderness and that the few Indians living there 'wandered' the land but made no good use of it."[56] As it denied Native Americans their history and homelands, it also entailed staggering human costs. Cloaked beneath this mythical vision of a primeval American past is an equally compelling—but much more complex and morally ambiguous—shared history. As for New York, although the land was both beautiful and bountiful, it was certainly not a wilderness. Ever since it was first revealed to human eyes at the end of the Ice Ages, it has had a profoundly human cast.

When Giovanni da Verrazano sailed *La Dauphine* into New York Harbor on April 17, 1524, he wrote that he entered "a very agreeable place." In his brief stop off the coast of Aquehonga Manacknong, now known as Staten Island, he saw people "dressed in bird's feathers of various colors, and they came toward us joyfully, uttering loud cries of wonderment. . . . About [thirty] of their small boats ran to and fro . . . with innumerable people aboard who were crossing from one side to the other to see us."

Because a storm came up, he and his crew didn't land but instead went back to sea, leaving behind what he described as a land of "favorable conditions and beauty."[57]

The people exclaiming with "loud cries of wonderment" were the Late Woodland peoples, and the land of "favorable conditions and beauty" was their home, the land whose human history we have been following. Both their lives and their home were about to be transformed.

PART 3

The Recent Past

CHAPTER EIGHT

A Tumultuous Encounter:
"Some Monster of the Sea"

In 1649 a Dutch settler in New Amsterdam noted that "those natives of the country who are so old as to recollect when the Dutch ships first came here, declare that when they saw them, they did not know what to make of them, and could not comprehend whether they came down from Heaven, or were of the Devil. Some among them, when the first one arrived, even imagined it to be a fish, or some monster of the sea, and accordingly a strange report of it spread over the whole land."[1]

That "monster of the sea" almost certainly refers to the *Halve Maen*, the ship that Henry Hudson sailed into New York Harbor in 1609. Hudson's journey up the river that now bears his name—a voyage made in September, the Munsee month of the Commencing Cold Moon—was marked by exchanges of goods and violence, heralds of both the trade and the bloodshed that would mark the relationships between these peoples in the century ahead. His accounts and those of others alerted the Dutch to the area's commercial potential for the burgeoning fur trade. By 1624 the Dutch West India Company had set up fur-trading operations at Fort Orange, today's Albany, and by the following year the first European settlers had established themselves at the tip of Manhattan Island in a small Dutch outpost they christened New Amsterdam. As historian Gregory Dowd put it, there were now "new people in an old world."[2]

When Hudson, and Verrazano before him, sailed into New York Bay, the people who stood on its shores and paddled in their dugout canoes to see them were the Munsees. They and their ancestors, the Late Woodland peoples whose lives we followed in the preceding chapter, were part of a larger group of people, known as the Delaware, united by similar Algonquian languages and cultures. They are sometimes also known as Lenape (The People), and their territory is known as Lenapehoking (The Land of the People).

Those Delaware who lived in the New York region spoke a dialect called Munsee and had social and economic ties with similar-speaking peoples across a territory stretching from the lower Hudson Valley and western Long Island to northern New Jersey and then across to northeastern Pennsylvania. Although we collectively call these seventeenth-century peoples Munsee, after their dialect, there was no single Munsee political unit at that time; instead, there were a number of autonomous groups. The Munsee speakers in coastal New York lived in loosely organized communities that were often named after a particular place or a leader of proven ability. Their leaders, or sachems, led by persuasion, and individuals moved freely from one group to another. The names of some of these groups—Canarsee, Hackensack, Massapequa—still resonate in the place names of the modern metropolitan area, while others—Rechgawawank, Siwanoy, Wiechquaeskeck—are all but lost to the modern ear (fig. 8.1).[3]

Most European accounts of the Munsee peoples at this time are marked by the bias of the day. One Dutch pastor described the Munsees as "entirely savage and wild, strangers to all decency, yea, uncivil and stupid as garden poles, proficient in all wickedness and godlessness; devilish men who serve nobody but the Devil. . . . They are as thievish and treacherous as they are tall; and in cruelty they are altogether inhuman, more than barbarous, far exceeding the Africans." Other colonists appear to have tried, with varying degrees of success, for a more balanced view. One noted that the Munsees "are all properly formed and well proportioned persons," adding that although "nature has not given them abundant wisdom, still they exercise their talents with discretion. . . . It is true that they appear singular and strange to our nation, because their complexion, speech and dress are so different, but this on acquaintance, is disregarded. Their women are well favored and fascinating . . . and if they were instructed as our women are, there then would be little or no difference in their qualifications." Revealingly, most Dutch referred to the Munsees as *wilden,* or wild people.[4]

As for the Munsees' views of the Europeans, what little we know suggests that they quickly realized that their visitors were neither "from Heaven" nor "Devils." They soon called them *Swannekens* ("the salty people"), either because the Europeans came across the salty ocean or because their actions left a bitter taste. Years later, they described the Europeans as "not like themselves . . . an Original People, a race of men that has existed unchanged from the beginning of time; but . . . a mixed race, and therefore a troublesome one."[5]

The time of the European invasions and settlement of North America is usually called the Contact period by archaeologists and historians who focus on Native American life, and the early Colonial period by those who focus on the European and African experiences. By whatever name, this was a time when resident Indians and newcoming

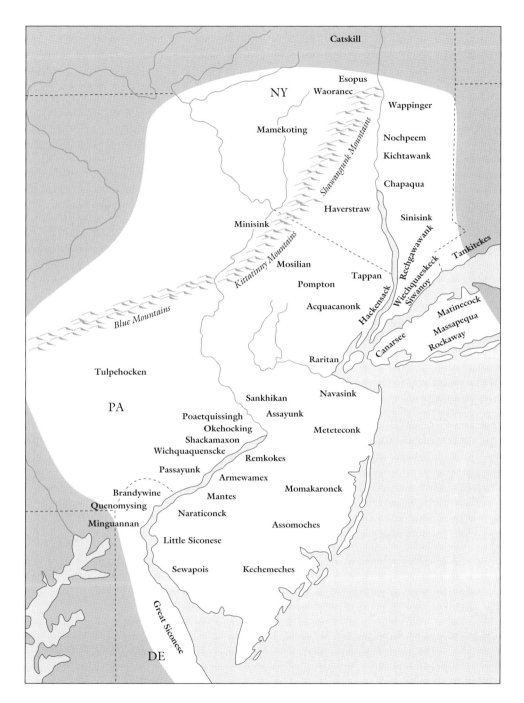

8.1. Lenapehoking, showing the names and approximate locations of some of the seventeenth-century Native American societies living there.

Europeans joined in trade and created a new history for this piece of land whose story we have been tracing.[6]

During the period of coexistence in the seventeenth century, the Munsees were a vital part of fledgling Dutch New Amsterdam, just as the traders and colonists were a vital part of Lenapehoking. The actual nature of the contact between these two groups, the residents and the newcomers, is poorly understood. We have few Munsee accounts from this period to tell their side of the story. The European documents that we have were written with prejudice and focus on the Europeans themselves and their interests. But the fragmentary written, oral, and archaeological records that we do have sketch a picture of Munsee life that is quite different from what is often portrayed as the grand story of European colonization. In fact, the Munsees were in no way marginal during those early decades of contact and colonization. They were not simply a backdrop for great events, a footnote in history, nor were they wilden, a part of the natural world. On the contrary, they were center stage. This was their home. They looked after the first settlers, shared meals with them, traded with them, worked on construction projects with them, fought with them, and signed treaties with them. The Munsees, like the Europeans, were actors making choices to deal with their changing world, adapting quickly and creatively to their new circumstances.

Archaeologists are keenly aware of the importance of studying the encounter between the disparate peoples who met on New York's shores. But many obstacles stand in the way of understanding the Munsee experiences at that time. During the sixteenth century and the earliest part of the seventeenth, when contact was sporadic, the Munsees' material culture, their household objects or weaponry, for example—the very things that archaeologists recover—were for the most part the same as those of the Late Woodland peoples. They were, after all, the same people. The only difference is that during the Contact period there were some Europeans and European goods and animals around. This can make it very difficult to tell if a site is a terminal Late Woodland or an early Contact one (figs. 8.2 and 8.3).[7]

Archaeologically, the way to date Munsee sites to before or after the European incursions is by the presence of European goods or bones of European domestic animals in their settlements. Unfortunately, these "signatures of contact" are rare in the city. Certainly, many Munsee settlements existed during the early years of contact between the two groups—the European documents are filled with references to them. But even when the first archaeologists were digging at the beginning of the twentieth century, they discovered very

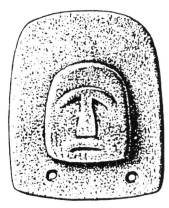

8.2. A Late Woodland or Contact stone pendant found at the Inwood site in upper Manhattan. These pendants were worn upside down so that the face on the pendant looked up at the wearer.

few European goods, hardly more than a bucketful, at Munsee sites in the city. And although these pioneering archaeologists were working with cruder excavation and dating techniques than modern professionals have, they were also working during a time when more sites in New York were available for study. An added problem for researchers studying this period is that as trade and contact increased through time, Munsee material goods become increasingly indistinguishable from those of their European neighbors.[8]

It is also difficult to establish a chronology for this critical period. The seventeenth century began with contact, but soon thereafter these disparate peoples with vastly different technologies and views of the world had joined each others' economies. This period of mutual discovery and trade became marked by a number of different but interrelated agents of change often occurring simultaneously. The entangled effects of trade, war, increasing European colonization, land dispossession, and changing ecosystems were only part of the turmoil. The most catastrophic and irrevocable agents of change were biological ones, the European diseases that killed countless Munsees and other Indian peoples throughout what is now the United States. By the end of the century, the Munsees were largely gone from the area that is the modern city of New York. By the middle of the following century, they were largely gone from Lenapehoking itself; their diaspora into the interior of the continent was well under way.[9]

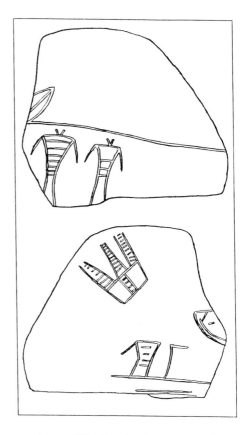

8.3. A Late Woodland or Contact sandstone fragment found on the surface of the Ward's Point site. Alanson Skinner (1925) speculated that the incised figures represent the Thunderbird, a patron of warriors and a powerful being who can create thunder and protect humans from horned serpents.

In the brief span of that one volatile century, the thousands of years of Indian guardianship of the land ended, and alien peoples began to build the modern city of New York. During that time, the early city, as Colin Calloway noted, "was a cloth woven from many threads, but the Indian strands that ran through it have often been ignored, forgotten, and allowed to fade."[10] In trying to retrieve those lost Indian strands and restore the Munsee experience to the forefront of the narrative of those times, we rely on oral traditions, colonial documents, and some sparse archaeological finds made within the territories of three of the most prominent Munsee leaders of the day, Penhawitz, Tackapausha, and Wampage. These finds prompt us to consider the importance of traditional concepts of spiritual power during the war years, the Munsee role in the burgeoning global economy, and finally, the irrevocable changes in the land itself. We see the Munsees actively involved in shaping their own history during these years and, as a consequence, in shaping the lives of the European traders and colonists as well as the development of the young city.

"The Nations Are Warring with Each Other"

On March 4, 1643, the mood among the European citizenry in New Amsterdam was a mixture of fear and recrimination.[11] Barely a week earlier, Governor Willem Kieft, ignoring the pleas of some of the colony's leading citizens, had ordered a brutal massacre of Munsee men, women, and children. In the midst of this tense atmosphere, three Munsee men arrived at the fort waving a white flag. Their leader, Penhawitz, had sent them to find out why the Dutch had killed some of his people when he had done "nothing but favors" to the Dutch.[12]

David Pietersz De Vries, a patroon from Staten Island and opponent of the controversial Kieft, along with Jacob Olfersz, another colonist, agreed to go back with the three Munsee ambassadors to Rechqua Akie, near today's Far Rockaway in Queens, to meet with Penhawitz and a number of other prominent Munsee leaders. Penhawitz was a well-known figure in New Amsterdam, a powerful leader from a powerful family. This peace conference was one of many held during the long years of the war that has come to be known as Kieft's War. At the time of this meeting, Rechqua Akie was a Munsee community made up of several hundred residents, many of them refugees from the ongoing conflicts with the Dutch and English.[13]

De Vries and Olfersz were given dinner and lodging when they reached Penhawitz's settlement, and the next morning they met with him and fifteen other prominent Munsee leaders. One sachem, the spokesman for the group, detailed their grievances against the Dutch. He began by describing how quickly their relationship had, in the few decades since the Dutch arrival, deteriorated from friendship to hostility. According to De Vries' account, the sachem told them "how we first came upon their coast; that we sometimes had no victuals; they gave us their Turkish beans and Turkish wheat, they helped us with oysters and fish to eat, and now for a reward we had killed their people. . . . He related also that at the beginning of our voyaging there, we left our people behind with the goods to trade, until the ships should come back; they had preserved these people like the apple of their eye; yea, they had given them their daughters to sleep with, by whom they had begotten children, and there roved many an Indian who was begotten by a Swanneken [European], but our people had become so villainous as to kill their own blood."[14]

This Munsee leader, whose name was not recorded, then gave De Vries and Olfersz ten fathoms of wampum each as a sign of friendship and peace, and they all went to Fort Amsterdam to see if they could prevent the conflict from escalating. But any peace was short lived. Some colonists, like Kieft and the colony's secretary, Cornelis van Tienhoven, had reportedly argued that the Indian peoples should be exterminated.[15]

At the beginning of the Contact era, as the Munsee sachem had told De Vries, by and large there were peaceful and cordial relations between the European settlers and traders and their Indian hosts. The Munsees had incorporated the Dutch into their traditional economic and social systems of reciprocity and sharing. But by this point, twenty years later, the Europeans were more self-sufficient, their settlements and trading operations were expanding, their own economy was dominant, and their dependence on local Indian peoples had declined.

Conflict was probably inevitable given the contradictory views of the world held by the two societies. As the European settlements expanded in the seventeenth century, a string of conflicts and catastrophes quickly followed. Some conflicts were related to the many and unavoidable daily cultural misunderstandings, others to more complex problems stimulated by the European arrivals and expansions, and by the introduction of a trans-Atlantic economy. In addition, there were internecine conflicts among various Indian groups over access to the highly desirable European trade goods, over hunting territories that would provide the peltries to use in trade, over the wampum trade, and over access to trade routes.

Indian peoples soon found themselves involved in an entirely new form of warfare, in which Europeans massacred entire communities and destroyed villages. In these wars, traditional weapons like bows and arrows, war clubs (fig. 8.4), and wooden shields were no longer effective. During these conflicts, traditional decision making, by consensus rather than by command, put the Indians at a decided disadvantage, at least initially.[16]

The most infamous of the conflicts was Kieft's War (1640–45), one incident of which was the massacre that led to the peace conference between De Vries and Penhawitz. The events leading up to this slaughter of Munsee families are complex and reveal the senseless, spiraling, retaliatory quality of so many of these conflicts. Many earlier troubles involved the different concepts of land and animals that the Dutch and the Munsees had. Dutch pigs, cattle, and other farm animals wandered freely, sometimes destroying crops in the Indians' unfenced gardens. In turn, Indian dogs bothered European free-ranging livestock. Instances of cheating, drunkenness, and theft on all sides led to arguments and sometimes violent resolutions.

8.4. A ball-headed club made of wood with shell inlay, of unknown provenience. This weapon could have been used by either the Delaware or the neighboring Susquehannock people.

The first sign that things were spinning out of control appeared in 1640, when Dutch troops, sent by Kieft to look for hog thieves, launched an unprovoked attack on a Raritan group of Munsees on Staten Island. The Indians responded the next year by burning Dutch farmsteads and taking captives. Kieft broadened the scope of the conflict by forming alliances with the English and with other Indian groups, and the attacks on Munsee settlements increased. The Munsees were soon attacked on two fronts: on one side by Dutch settlers, and on the other by Mahicans and Mohawks. To make things worse, Kieft then levied a tax to be paid by the Munsees in wampum, corn, or furs, to help pay for the costs of building new forts. The Indians protested that the tax was unfair, one complaining to De Vries that Kieft "must be a very mean fellow to come to this country without being invited by them, and now wish to compel them to give him their corn for nothing."[17]

Much of what we know of the deadliest phase of this war comes from the writings of De Vries, who both witnessed the events in February 1643 and served as an ambassador to Penhawitz's peace conference the following week. At the end of February, the Month of the Frog Moon, hundreds of terrified Munsees began streaming into New Amsterdam looking for asylum. They had fled for many miles in freezing temperatures through deep snows to escape Mahican attacks on their settlements to the north of New Amsterdam, in what is now Westchester. In that conflict, some of their relatives had been killed and others taken captive. The Munsee families moved into refugee camps near other relatives, one at Nechtanc (the modern Corlear's Hook) to the northeast of the Dutch fort and the other just across the Hudson at Pavonia in what is now Jersey City. When the refugees first arrived in New Amsterdam, the Dutch helped them with food and shelter. But then everything changed. Kieft had long been determined "to make the savages wipe their chops," and with the arrival of the refugees he saw his opportunity. Not all colonists wanted to go along with his plans. Many urged patience and humanity in dealing with these frightened people who had arrived in the dead of a fierce winter. But Kieft and his allies ignored their counsel and ordered his men to attack the two refugee groups at midnight, when he knew they would be sleeping.[18]

De Vries, who had opposed the attacks, later described that night's horror at the Pavonia refugee camp:

> I went that night at the Governor's, sitting up. I went and sat by the kitchen fire, when about midnight I heard a great shrieking, and I ran to the ramparts of the fort, and looked over to Pavonia. Saw nothing but firing, and heard the shrieks of the savages murdered in their sleep. . . . When it was day; the soldiers returned to the fort, having massacred or murdered eighty Indians, and considering they had done a deed of Roman valor, in murdering so many in their sleep; where infants were torn from

their mother's breasts, and hacked to pieces in the presence of the parents, and the pieces thrown into the fire and in the water, and other sucklings, being bound to small boards [cradle boards or carriers], were cut, stuck, and pierced, and miserably massacred in a manner to move a heart of stone. Some were thrown into the river, and when the fathers and mothers endeavored to save them, the soldiers would not let them come on land but made both parents and children drown—children from five to six years of age, and also some old and decrepit persons. Those who fled from this onslaught, and concealed themselves in the neighboring sedge, and when it was morning, came out to beg a piece of bread, and to be permitted to warm themselves, were murdered in cold blood and tossed into the fire or the water. Some came to our people in the country with their hands, some with their legs cut off, and some holding their entrails in their arms, and others had such horrible cuts and gashes, that worse than they were could never happen.[19]

All told, more than 120 Munsees had been butchered that night. Those who carried out the slaughter returned to Fort Amsterdam with thirty prisoners as well as the heads of some of the Munsee refugees who had been killed in the attack. Amid the protests of a number of the Dutch colonists, Kieft congratulated the soldiers and freebooters. As for the imprisoned Munsees who had survived that dreadful night, some were enslaved and either handed over as rewards to the soldiers who had captured them or sent to Bermuda as gifts to the governor of that island.[20]

Vengeance was now in the air. Despite the attempts of De Vries and Penhawitz, the massacres set in motion a series of raids and counterraids in which, as in all such situations, everyone lost. A number of different Munsee groups united and began attacking colonists, destroying their settlements, and taking captives. The war raged on and off for two more long years.

One of the casualties of the war was Anne Hutchinson, one of the most notorious women in Colonial America. Banished in 1638 from the Massachusetts Bay Colony for her antinomian doctrines, she first moved to Rhode Island and then, in 1642, in the middle of Kieft's War, she came to New Netherland along with her family and several followers and established a plantation, known as Anne's Hoeck ("Anne's Neck"), in what is now Pelham Bay Park in the Bronx.[21] In the September following the refugee killings at Pavonia and Corlear's Hook, Hutchinson was killed, along with most of her family and followers. A young Munsee patriot, Wampage, reportedly took credit for Hutchinson's death and, following tradition, took a variant of her name as his own. And that name, An hoock, placed with his mark "AH" (fig. 8.5), appears on a number of subsequent deeds and treaties. In the years that followed, the river near Hutchinson's house also took her name, as did the road, the Hutchinson River Parkway, that crosses it today.[22]

8.5. The mark of An hoock, a prominent Munsee leader who was also known as Wampage.

The final peace treaty was signed, according to contemporary accounts, "under the blue canopy of heaven in [the] presence of the Council of New Netherland and the whole community," as well as a number of Indian sachems, on August 30, 1645, at Fort Amsterdam. During this war 1,600 Indians had died, and much of the land had been laid to waste. The Munsees never recovered from these population losses. As for the Europeans, although many died and many others returned home, their populations began expanding rapidly after the war, when Peter Stuyvesant came to New Amsterdam and replaced Kieft. But not even the Dutch administration remained stable. In 1664 the English captured the colony, and that part of Lenapehoking was renamed New York.[23]

Archaeology is hard-pressed to tell us much about Munsee life during these difficult years in their history. In studying the fragmentary results of nearly century-old excavations, we can come up with barely a handful of references to finds relating to this period, arguably one of the most violent in the city's history. Although colonial documents mention a number of fortified Munsee settlements throughout the modern city, none have yet been found.

Two tantalizing reports of nineteenth-century finds, which may be apocryphal, claim to relate directly to the fate of some of the Munsees caught up in Kieft's War. One of these finds was made in the spring of 1886 by construction workers in Pavonia, close to the site of Kieft's midnight massacre. They uncovered a number of skeletons that local residents were sure were the remains of the hastily buried Munsee refugees killed on that cold February night. The nineteenth-century newspaper account of this discovery states that crowds "gathered around the place . . . while the excavating was going on and looked at the skulls and bones. The number of bodies can only be determined by means of the skulls, as the bones are all mixed together and many of them crumble at the touch into fine dust." Nothing more is known of these human remains that crumbled into dust, so we have no way of ascertaining if they were in fact those of the victims whose screams De Vries heard that night.[24]

The other find was made earlier, at the beginning of the nineteenth century, by local antiquarians exploring in what is now Pelham Bay Park (see fig. 1.1). They were digging in several mounds near the water's edge in what, according to local tradition, was a favorite Munsee burial ground. One of the largest mounds was popularly known as the place where An hoock had been buried a century earlier. When the antiquarians opened this mound, they discovered "a large sized skeleton, by the side of which lay the stone axe and flint spear of the tenant of the grave."[25]

Intrigued by the report of the discovery of what could be An hoock's grave, archaeologists working much later, at the beginning of the twentieth century, went back to the area looking for more evidence of the burial of one of the best-known figures in seventeenth-century Lenapehoking. They found nothing left of the site, and much of the knoll itself had long since been carried off by the relentless coastal tides. But if the antiquarians and local legends are right, Wampage had been buried in a traditional way, among his people, and in his ancestral homeland.[26]

Some reports of century-old excavations briefly mention that European gunflints and musket balls were found at a few Munsee sites, but there is no clear context for them. A few fragments of rum bottles were also found, mute testimony to the havoc that this trade beverage wrought on the resident population. And these old site reports, with their hodgepodge lists of discoveries, also contain references to some other seemingly insignificant finds, arrowheads made from European metals, which can tell us about the continuing role of traditional spiritual beliefs for the Munsee people in these turbulent years. These weapons were found at Ward's Point and the nearby Bloomfield and Old Place sites in Staten Island and at two other sites, Ryders Pond in Brooklyn and Throgs Neck in the Bronx (see fig. 1.1).[27]

The Throgs Neck site was discovered by Alanson Skinner in the first decades of the twentieth century, when he was looking for Contact sites in the Throgs Neck and Clasons Point sections of the Bronx. Today these areas are a mix of public housing and single-family bungalows, but they were still relatively open parts of the city when he was digging there. Skinner concluded that Clasons Point was once the site of Snakapins, a substantial settlement of the Siwanoy branch of the Munsee, the group to which An hoock belonged, and that Throgs Neck was where they had stayed briefly after leaving Snakapins. Both sites, however, had been occupied in the distant past by a number of different populations (this is where Skinner was digging when he dismissed the Orient peoples as a poor lot), and the contexts of many of the artifacts, including the few European trade goods, are uncertain. Although there is no evidence sufficient by modern archaeological standards to confirm Skinner's *specific* identifications of these sites, the odds are that these were certainly Siwanoy settlements. They are in Siwanoy territory, and colonial documents mention Snakapins as well as a number of other Siwanoy-Munsee settlements in that general area. In fact, in 1619, a ship's captain described one near Throgs Neck from which a "great multitude of Indians let fly at us from the bank, but it pleased God to make us victors." And among the few artifacts at Throgs Neck that Skinner identified with the short-term Siwanoy-Munsee stay there were a few gunflints and, significantly, a brass arrowhead.[28]

Similar weapons made from European metals were also found at the Ryders Pond site in Marine Park in Brooklyn. Ryders Pond is in an area the Munsee called Shanscomacocke and has been identified as one of the principal settlements of the Canarsee branch of the Munsee, the group that Penhawitz represented. Canarsees were among the refugees massacred that February night at the height of Kieft's War. Unfortunately, we know very little about Ryders Pond, the largest known Native American site in Brooklyn. Vague reports from the beginning of the twentieth century indicate that burials were also found there. At that time, a local collector and his family dug at the site but left no records of their work. Years later, in the 1950s and 1960s, avocational archaeologists Julius Lopez and Stanley Wisniewski analyzed the Ryders Pond artifact collection but, because of the way the artifacts were collected and because Indian peoples had lived at the site for thousands of years, all they could do was classify the artifacts. Among them, they list a few signatures of contact with Europeans: trade goods—rum-bottle fragments, spoons, and European pipes—and arrowheads made from European metals.[29]

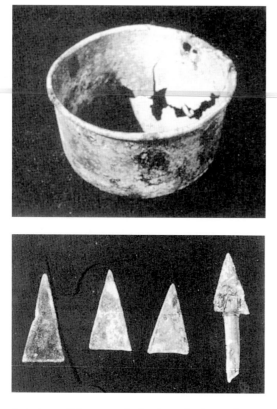

8.6. A small brass trade kettle and triangular brass arrowheads found in the Northeast. The point on the far right still has part of its wooden shaft. These are similar to items used in the New York City area.

For archaeologists frustrated by the cavalier destruction of the city's sites, this bare handful of metal gives us one of the few opportunities we have to understand Munsee life during a critical time in the city's history. Although we certainly can't tell the specific uses of these particular weapons, the materials they were made from tell us something about the Munsee response to the European presence.

These copper and brass points were not trade items in their own right. They, and other weapons like them, were carefully crafted by Indian armorers throughout the Northeast, from metals recycled from worn-out trade kettles (fig. 8.6). Although European guns and metal trade goods like knives, kettles, and axes were highly valued by Indians for practical reasons and as signs of prestige, anthropologist George Hamell argues that the metals themselves, especially copper and brass, were important not only because of their utilitarian qualities but also because they fit into traditional value systems. Native copper had been important in Eastern North America for thousands of years. It had mythical origins, was associated with exchanges with powerful spiritual beings, and was important for health and well-being. It seems likely that the supernatural powers long associated with native metals were transferred to the newly acquired European metals they resembled. In cutting up copper or brass trade kettles and making these points from the scraps, the Munsees at sites like Throgs Neck, Ward's Point, and Ryders Pond may have been appealing to the metals' spiritual qualities, as well as their utilitarian and prestigious ones, for help in hunting and in war—both vital concerns in those years. These new objects may have been deeply imbued with old meanings.[30]

These metal points, then, may be the material evidence of the continuing importance of traditional concepts of spiritual power in the daily lives of the Munsees in New York. And the points are also a powerful reminder that European commodities held multiple meanings for Indian peoples. These objects were not necessarily valuable because they were seen as somehow superior to traditional goods. In fact, they may sometimes have been sought out because they resembled objects that were already important in the Munsees' social and cultural lives long before the Europeans arrived.[31]

"Facing down the Stream . . . into Uncertainty"

When Penhawitz called his peace conference at Rechqua Akie within days of the brutal attack on the Munsee refugees, it is likely that one of the men there was his son Tackapausha. Tackapausha was a witness "under the blue canopy of heaven" at the signing of the treaty that ended that war, and he went on to become one of the most influential Indian leaders of the seventeenth century. In the ensuing centuries, rumors have surrounded some ancient earthworks that lie within his territory just outside the city limits. These embankments are in the quiet suburban town of Massapequa, not far from Jones Beach, a popular attraction for New Yorkers on hot summer days. According to some local legends this was once the site of a grisly massacre of more than a hundred Munsees by the notorious seventeenth-century mercenary Captain John Underhill. One of the more lurid accounts maintains that the Europeans "collected the bodies of the dead Indians and piled them up on a heap on the brow of a hill to keep off the cold wind while the English sat down on the leeward side to eat their breakfast." The ground was said to have a reddish tinge "caused by the free flow of Indian blood." Tamer local accounts saw the site, known as Fort Massapeag, as simply a fort or fortified village built by the Massapequa branch of the Munsee during the troubled seventeenth century.[32]

Recent archaeological studies suggest that these barely visible embankment lines and the shell midden that lies just outside them are instead mute testimony to the often uneasy trade that linked the peoples of North America and Europe. Together, they document the major role that the Munsees played in two momentous events: the forging of the global economy and the establishment of the city of New Amsterdam. But

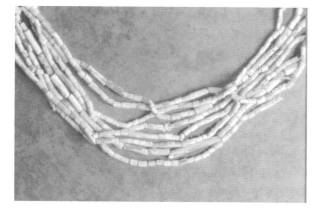

8.9. White wampum beads discovered at a New York State site.

large quantities of wampum to exchange with Iroquoian fur traders at Fort Orange. And by offering wampum among their trade items, the Dutch were able to lure other Indian traders down from what is now Canada and away from the French who, because of their geographical position, had no access to the highly prized wampum.[39]

Wampum became common currency for Europeans settling in New Netherland and parts of New England. When European colonists increasingly found themselves short of coins in European currencies, colonial governments responded by fixing prices in wampum. In New Amsterdam, Europeans used the beads not only to buy tobacco and furs, but also to buy grains and property, to pay rents, mortgages, and fines, and to put in church collection plates. When Jasper Danckaerts and Peter Sluyter came to New York in 1679, they quickly found that they needed wampum to have their baggage moved and for ferry rides between Manhattan and Brooklyn. In fact, they noticed throughout their visit that the currency most frequently used by Dutch, English, and Indian alike was wampum. No wonder, then, that wampum soon became part of the tribute that the Europeans demanded from the resident peoples.[40]

Certainly, wampum in many ways made an ideal currency. It was portable, nonperishable, and, when strung, came in easily measurable units. The standard measure was a fathom, that is, a six-foot-long string made up of approximately 288 beads, each of which was about a quarter of an inch long. In 1636 alone, coastal Indians handed over nearly 2 million wampum beads to Europeans. Local indigenous economies were revolutionized around the manufacture of this new commodity. Wampum making was so important that when one Munsee, nicknamed Hans, guided the Danckaerts party on a trip to northern New Jersey, he complained that in so doing, he had lost time that would have been better spent making wampum.[41]

For Hans and other coastal peoples, their chief entry into the new economy came from the shell beads. Wampum was in great demand by Indians and Europeans alike, although its value was increasingly determined by the Europeans. The Munsees and neighboring New England Indian coastal peoples were now, for the first time, part of a money economy. Their innovative response to the need for money was, quite literally, to make it. By substituting the new metal drills, or muxes, that they acquired from the Europeans for their old stone drills, they could vastly increase their rate of production for this new market. And so, for a brief period in the seventeenth century, coastal Algonquian peoples became the minters for everyone. Just as the tribes in the interior refocused their economies to trap furs for the European market, the ones along the coasts reorganized theirs to make wampum for that same market.

Out of these reorganized economies developed a curious triangular trade in which the Native American coastal peoples made wampum, which they exchanged with the Dutch for trade goods. The Dutch then sent the wampum, along with other trade goods, north to exchange with the tribes in the interior for furs. Finally, the Dutch brought the furs back down to New Amsterdam to ship to European markets.[42]

The best evidence for the coastal leg of that odd triangular trade and the entry of the Indians into the European market comes from archaeology. At a number of sites along the city's surviving shoreline (including Clasons Point and Throgs Neck in the Bronx, Clearview in Queens, and Ryders Pond in Brooklyn [see fig. 1.1]), early twentieth-century archaeologists found signs of wampum making.[43] But the most vivid picture of the shell bead trade and the role the Munsee peoples played in the new trans-Atlantic economy comes from Massapequa.

Because of its local fame and the rumors surrounding it, Fort Massapeag had been heavily looted over the years by pothunters, many of whom clawed through the site with potato and clam rakes looking for souvenirs to take home or sell. Then, in the 1930s, the site was further threatened by the construction of the housing development that now surrounds it. Although local preservationists were able to save the fort, construction activities destroyed the much larger Harbor Green site, an Indian village and burial ground some five hundred yards to the north of the fort. Amid the ongoing destruction, several concerned local archaeologists struggled to salvage what they could.[44]

Among the people working briefly at the site in the 1930s was Ralph Solecki, who, along with some of the archaeologists who had dug with him at the Aqueduct site, did the only systematic excavation and mapping ever done at Massapeag (fig. 8.10). Then, in the 1990s, Solecki turned his attention back to this site where he and his friends had worked together more than fifty years earlier. He managed to track down some of the avocational archaeologists who had dug there in the 1930s, talked to the surviving relatives of others, and interviewed people who had seen what the bulldozers had torn up in the village and the burial ground. Then he studied his own old field notes, Dutch colonial records, old photographs and maps of the area, and the salvaged artifacts he managed to track down, and he analyzed the way the fort had been built.

After examining all the evidence, Solecki quickly discounted the massacre theory; horrible massacres had certainly taken place, but they had occurred elsewhere in the area. The fort's European style and size both suggested that it was not a fortified Indian village (fig. 8.11). The earthworks were quadrangular with two corner bastions, the

8.10. Ralph Solecki digging at Fort Massapeag in 1938.

whole surrounded by a six-foot-wide ditch or moat. Sharply pointed wooden posts, six to ten inches in diameter, had been driven into the embankment to form the stockade whose main entrance faced the shore (fig. 8.12). Massapeag is smaller than the well-known fortified Indian villages in southern New England or those out on the eastern tip of Long Island in areas that the English claimed. In fact, its size, only one hundred feet to a side, would have made it much too small to shelter a typical Munsee village—many of their settlements at that time were made up of a number of multifamily long-houses, each averaging sixty by fifteen feet in size. In addition, the fort's location was an un-likely one for a village. It was not, as most In-dian palisaded villages were, on high ground. Instead, it stood on a lobe of land jutting out into a thirty-five-mile-long sheltered bay in an area easily accessible to coastal traffic from New York Harbor all the way to Block Island. Further, when Solecki dug several test pits inside the fort, he didn't find any of the domestic debris typically associated with Munsee settlements. And, in any case, there was a contemporary village close by.[45]

Nevertheless, the fort's palisades certainly suggested that they had been built for se-curity and defense. The people living in the nearby village may well have sought shelter within the fort's walls from time to time during those troubled years. But the accumu-lated evidence that Solecki managed to track down suggests that the fort was more than simply a temporary refuge. In fact, because of his efforts, the site is now a Na-tional Historic Landmark for its contribution to the understanding of the relationships between Indian people and colonists in the mid-seventeenth century.[46]

Although the rescue team found Indian pottery and stone tools at the site, they also found a number of mid-seventeenth-century European goods that hint at the nature of the Indian-European trade in those years. Mixed in among the Indian artifacts were Dutch smoking pipes, a brass mouth harp, handwrought nails, glass beads, fragments of European ceramic jars, an iron knife, and a brass needle. The archaeologists did re-cover several arrowheads crafted from European metals, similar to those found at Throgs Neck and Ryders Pond, but they did not find any European military hardware like gunflints, gun parts, or musket balls (fig. 8.13).[47]

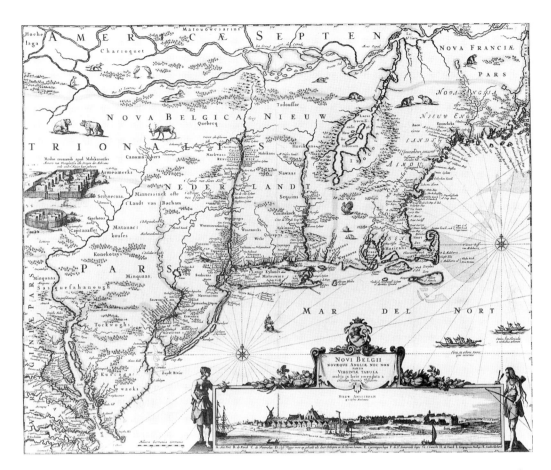

8.11. The Visscher map, showing New Netherland, New England, and Virginia ca. 1650. Note the size of Native American palisaded villages shown to the left. The Hudson River is the westernmost of the two rivers at the center of the map. Collection of the New-York Historical Society, negative number 44436.

Some of the strongest evidence for the economic role the fort played in regional history came from the midden area near the fort's entrance. In the 1930s, when avocational archaeologist James Burgraff heard about the site's possible destruction, he tested some shell heaps that he knew had already been ransacked by treasure hunters. He was hoping to find and save anything they might have missed. What he found was something the looters would have neither recognized nor appreciated—that the middens were made up mainly of quahog and whelk shells in various stages of being transformed into wampum. He also found quartz flake knives for cutting the shells into sections and sandstone abraders for the final shaping of the shell beads. Building

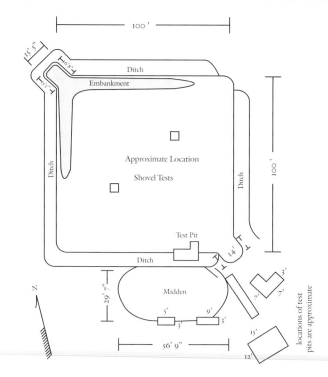

Ditch
Embankment
Ditch
Ditch
Approximate Location
Shovel Tests
100 '
100 '
Test Pit
Ditch
Midden
N
locations of test pits are approximate
56' 9"

8.12. *Site map of Fort Massapeag, showing the ditch, bastions, and locations of test excavations both inside the palisade embankment and in the shell midden area.*

on Burgraff's discoveries, Solecki argues that Fort Massapeag was also a wampum manufactory, a place where the Massapequas, probably those living in the nearby village, gathered to make the money that joined their economy with those of Europeans and Iroquoian peoples in the interior.[48]

Because of the fort's size, European-style construction, mid-century trade goods, wampum manufacture, and location along a coastal route in Tackapausha's territory, Solecki proposes that Massapeag might have been the legendary Indian-Dutch fortified post, which, despite repeated searches over the years, had never been found. No one was even sure that it had ever been built. Solecki's search through colonial records had revealed that on March 12, 1656, Peter Stuyvesant signed a treaty with Tackapausha agreeing that the events of Kieft's War would "be forgiven" and "never be remembered" and that Tackapausha would be recognized as "ye chiefe Sachem" of the western Long Island Indians. At that time, Stuyvesant promised that within six months he would "build A howse or A forte" that would be "furnished with Indian trade or Commodities. And the Sachem doth promise, that in this place Such people as shall thereon be placed by the Governor shall live in safety from him or any of his Indians."[49]

Trading posts, such as this promised one, would have been new and relatively short-lived phenomena in the region, and we know little about them. Fort Massapeag is the only known mid-seventeenth-century archaeological site within Tackapausha's territory that comes anywhere close to being a frontier post. Its small palisaded enclosure would have provided a secure place to store wampum and the equally important Dutch trade goods. And it would have given safe haven to Tackapausha's people and to Dutch traders from attacks by other European or Indian groups.[50]

The long-term patterns of looting, site destruction, and scanty evidence acquired years ago make it easier to raise questions than reach conclusions. Because of these difficulties, we cannot be certain whether this is Stuyvesant's promised trading post, an unrecorded one, or simply a refuge and wampum manufactory. If we take the most narrowly constructed, parsimonious of these interpretations—that Fort Massapeag was a refuge and wampum workshop—what can the site tell us today? Because of Solecki's superb detective work in tracking down and piecing together what fragmented evidence remains, Fort Massapeag provides the clearest and most compelling tangible evidence in the metropolitan area for the vital roles the Munsees played in the trans-Atlantic trade and the local colonial economy during that critical period in the formation of the modern city. The standing earthworks evoke, as nothing else in the area does, that brief moment when Indians, despite the wars and the epidemics, still had power and autonomy. One of their leaders, Tackapausha, had just signed an important treaty with their Dutch trading partners, and they were making the shell beads that had become the currency for everyone in New Amsterdam.[51]

Today, Fort Massapeag is surrounded on three sides by comfortable-looking houses set in large landscaped lawns. On the fourth side is the entrance, which now faces a community recreation area. But three and a half centuries ago, when the fort was built, the setting was very different. Those standing at the fort's entrance would have seen not teenagers playing baseball but instead a salt meadow with the Great South Bay beyond. Traditional dugout canoes of allies and relatives coming to trade and visit may have been lined up along the shores of the two inlets that led into the bay, and there may also have been Dutch coastal sloops and yachts eager to trade their goods for the finished wampum.[52]

Many of the Munsee men and women making wampum outside the post, and living in the nearby village and neighboring areas, no longer dressed as they had thirty years

8.13. Some of the artifacts found at Fort Massapeag. Top row, left to right: *four Native American pottery sherds, a stone drill, a stone projectile point, a piece of shell in the process of being transformed into wampum, and an abrading stone possibly used in wampum manufacture.* Bottom row, left to right: *a glass bottle fragment, a fragment of European pottery, a brass mouth harp, a brass tube, and three fragments of European smoking pipes.*

earlier, when the first Europeans arrived. Now, those who could afford it wore lengths of duffle, a coarsely woven woollen cloth that they obtained from Dutch traders in exchange for wampum or corn. It was as warm as traditional hides, lighter, and easier to convert into clothing. Both men and women wore dark hues, for black, blue, and gray were the preferred colors in this part of New Netherland. They still wore traditional face paint and tattoos, but these days more were wearing only black paint, the color of mourning, in honor of their relatives and friends lost in the wars and epidemics.[53]

Wampum making was serious business for them. Shell beads were needed for much more than getting duffle cloth or other popular personal items like shirts, stockings, fishhooks, axes, knives, hoes, copper or iron kettles, spoons, or liquor. Europeans were now not only trading for wampum, they were also demanding large quantities of it as tribute. In addition, powerful sachems like Tackapausha increasingly needed wampum belts, each made of thousands of beads, to use in this highly competitive new world of trade and diplomacy.[54]

By the 1650s, making wampum had become a prime winter activity for those Indian communities with access to valuable shellfishing stations, and many local economies were now reorganized around its manufacture. Initially, it may have been made by individual entrepreneurs, but the millions of beads needed for trade, tribute, and diplomacy soon involved the energies of large numbers of the population at coastal settlements throughout the region. After all, few intergroup activities took place without the exchange of wampum.[55]

As for Fort Massapeag's fate, Solecki speculates that with the English takeover of the area in 1664, it "became obsolete and fell into disuse" and that "the timbers of the palisade would have reached an advanced stage of deterioration."[56] When a surveyor mapped the area in 1687, he drew in seven "Indian Houses," but there is no sign of the fort itself, although the area is labeled Fort Neck (fig. 8.14). Following the English takeover, Tackapausha and some of his followers moved to the north shore, and the final sale of Fort Neck lands took place at the end of the century.

The remains of the earthworks and the few bits of shell still visible on this small plot of land bring home the important role the Munsees played in the emerging global economy and provoke us to reflect on the complex nature of their social interactions with the Dutch newcomers. Massapeag was a mint, a place where wampum was made and where, along with other valuables, it could be safely stored, a place where traders might have come to collect wampum, and a place where refuge might have been sought by Indians or Europeans in times of danger. It may also have been a trading post, built with Indian and Dutch cooperation. As such, it could have provided opportunities where social relationships could be formed, where pipes and gossip could be shared, and where these two very different peoples could get to know each other, learn

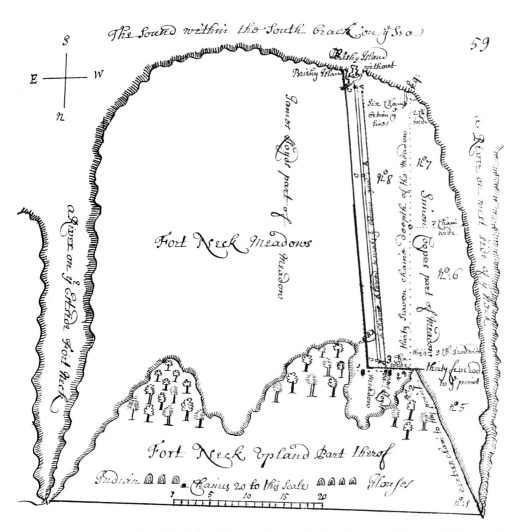

8.14. *Surveyor's map of Fort Neck (1687). Note the seven Indian houses at bottom of the map just above the scale. Collection of the New-York Historical Society, negative number 58381.*

each other's languages, consider alliances, attempt to reach compromises, and make agreements.[57]

More vividly and poignantly, what Massapeag evokes is that moment at mid-century when, in spite of the wars and epidemics, the Munsee response to the European arrivals had given them some prosperity, and both sides may have felt that they might somehow manage to live and work together. After all, Tackapausha and Stuyvesant had just signed an agreement that stated that "ye Sachem shall live in peace with All ye Dutch & English within this Jurisdiction of the New-netherlands . . . [and the]

Governor doth promise for himselfe and All his people within the Jurisdiction to live in Peace with the said Sachem and All his People."[58]

Although neither side knew it, that co-existence was not to be. As historian James Axtell remarked, for us today studying those critical years, "one of the hardest things . . . to remember is that events now long in the past were once in the future. Although history is lived forwards, facing down the stream of time into uncertainty, it is understood and written only in retrospect." Today we know how the seventeenth century ended. But those making wampum at the fort, and those coming to collect it, could not. They were still "facing down the stream . . . into uncertainty."[59]

What they could not have foreseen was that by the end of the century, wampum would be made by Europeans in places like Albany, New York, and Bergen County, New Jersey. Colonial women, many of them farmers' wives, were among the new minters at these commercial "factories," using lathes and imported conch shells from the Caribbean. These larger and thicker shells yielded more and longer beads, while the lathes could do it all much faster and more efficiently than the most industrious Munsee working by hand. Also ahead were more wars, the English takeover of New Netherland, increasing waves of European immigration, and the unimaginable further impact of the diseases that were sweeping across Lenapehoking.[60]

"Some Raging Mortal Disease"

War was not the only ordeal the Munsees had to face. Had it been, it is possible that some balance between the opposing forces might have been struck and that this story of the land and its people might have taken a very different turn than it did. But the Munsees had to confront far more deadly enemies than those they faced in battle: the host of European diseases that repeatedly struck down Munsees of all ages in seventeen separate epidemics.[61]

These diseases, "the enemy no one saw," affected Indians not only in the Northeast but throughout the entire Western Hemisphere, with horrifying results. As one scholar pointed out, when the smallpox virus arrived in the Americas it "found ideal conditions —millions of completely susceptible human hosts. . . . [who were, in effect] 'virgin soil' in which the smallpox flourished." The consequences were catastrophic. Here in the Northeast, these deadly new viruses and bacteria spread quickly, often in advance of the Europeans themselves. They traveled invisibly along trade routes, on blankets and other trade goods and from person to person through communities where people gathered to trade, fight, marry, bury their dead, or conduct rituals for the afflicted, and through longhouses where related families lived together in close quarters.[62]

It is difficult to estimate the exact number of Indian people who died along the coast during these epidemics. In 1656 New Netherlander Adriaen Van der Donck reported that his Indian neighbors told him "that before the arrival of the Christians, and before the small pox broke out amongst them, they were ten times as numerous as they now are, and their population had been melted down by this disease, whereof nine-tenths of them have died." In 1670, Daniel Denton piously recounted, "To say something of the Indians, there is now but few upon the Island, and those few no ways hurtful but rather serviceable to the English, and it is to be admired, how strangely they have decreast by the Hand of God, since the English first setling of those parts; for since my time, where there were six towns, they are reduced to two small Villages, and it hath been generally observed, that where the English come to settle, a Divine Hand makes way for them, by removing or cutting off the Indians, either by Wars one with the other, or by some raging mortal Disease."[63]

Modern estimates of Munsee deaths from these diseases range from 50 percent to as high as 91 percent of the population. Whatever the actual numbers, this was an enormous demographic and personal catastrophe with profound social and economic consequences. This was a time when everyone was dying—children, traditional healers, leaders, kin-group members, friends, and neighbors. Those who managed to survive those dark years often had to rebuild their communities without elders, traditional leaders, or family members to help them.[64]

It is because of the horrifying effect of these pathogens that historian Francis Jennings sees the Americas as "more like a widow than a virgin. Europeans," he argued, "did not find a wilderness here; rather however involuntarily, they made one. . . . The so-called settlement of America was a *re*settlement, a reoccupation of a land made waste by the diseases . . . introduced by newcomers."[65] And with the horrendous effects of disease, combined with those of the wars and the increasing numbers of new colonists, the way was paved for the loss of Lenapehoking.

"They Have Bought the Island of Manhates from the Wild Men"

One of the most popular American myths, repeated generation after generation, is the tale of how the Dutch bought the island of Manhattan from the Indians for twenty-four dollars' worth of baubles. A less well known version of New York City's origin myth, one from the sellers' point of view, was told to the Moravian missionary Heckewelder by a Delaware man when they were both living in Bethlehem, Pennsylvania, in the late eighteenth century:

As the whites became daily more familiar with the Indians, they at last proposed to stay with them, and asked only for so much ground for a garden spot as, they said, the hide of a bullock would cover or encompass, which hide was spread before them. The Indians readily granted this apparently reasonable request; but the whites then took a knife, and beginning at one end of the hide, cut it up to a long rope, not thicker than a child's finger, so that by the time the whole was cut up, it made a great heap; they then took the rope at one end, and drew it gently along, carefully avoiding its breaking. It was drawn out into a circular form, and being closed at its ends, encompassed a large piece of ground. The Indians were surprised at the superior wit of the whites, but they did not wish to contend with them about a little land, as they had still enough themselves. The white and red men lived contentedly together for a long time, though the former from time to time asked for more land, which was readily obtained, and thus they gradually proceeded higher up the Mahicannittuck [the Hudson River], until the Indians began to believe they would soon want all their country, which in the end proved true.[66]

A closer look at the events leading to the founding of the city shows that, as a letter back to Holland in November, the Month of the Snowy Moon, 1626, somewhat offhandedly comments, the Dutch "bought the island of Manhates from the Wild Men for the value of sixty guilders." We don't know what was given to the Munsees for the "value of sixty guilders" (or who gave it), but it is highly likely that in accepting these objects, they believed not that they were actually selling their land in the European sense—that is, permanently alienating themselves from it—but rather that they were allowing the visitors to use it for a while. Hunting or planting rights might be *transferred* to someone, but that meant neither a permanent transfer of the land nor exclusive use of it. Land was seen as something that was held in trust for the Creator, Kishelemulong, and as such could not be sold or even owned.[67]

Heckewelder describes an encounter with two of his Lenape neighbors that illustrates some of these points. One night, after these two men put their horses in the missionary's meadow, the horses ate the grass that Heckewelder had planned to mow. When he complained the next day, one of the men responded:

> My friend, it seems you lay claim to the grass my horses have eaten, because you had enclosed it with a fence: now tell me, who caused the grass to grow? Can *you* make the grass grow? I think not, and no body can except the great Mannitto. He it is who causes it to grow both for my horses and for yours! See friend! the grass which grows out of the earth is common to all; the game in the woods is common to all. Say, did you never eat venison and bear's meat?—"Yes, very often."—Well, and did you ever hear me or any other Indian complain about that? No; then be not disturbed at my horses having eaten only once, of what you call *your* grass, though the grass my horses did eat, in like manner as the meat you did eat, was given to the Indians by the Great Spirit.

Besides if you will but consider, you will find that my horses did not eat *all* your grass. For friendship's sake, however, I shall never put my horses in your meadow again.[68]

Heckewelder's experience shows that for many Munsee, land ownership meant that whoever "owned" the land could certainly use it by planting it, mowing the grass on it, or even hunting on it, but that the land itself never belonged to that person in perpetuity.

However differently the Munsees and the Europeans may have viewed land and other kinds of property at first, both sides soon became aware of the differences, and the Munsees were not credulous for long. Anthropologist Robert Grumet, who has examined the surviving records of land transactions between the Munsees and the Dutch and English, argues that Munsee leaders in fact were playing a delicate game in these land sales, sometimes accepting prices for less than the land was actually worth, hoping that it would "obligate givers to reciprocate in other ways." They were selling their land carefully in an attempt "to buy time and protection."[69]

But these land sales, no matter how carefully crafted, were taking place against a backdrop of other events, not only the ongoing wars and epidemics, but also the influx of large numbers of strangers into the area. By the end of the seventeenth century, the settlers outnumbered the Munsees by a ratio of roughly 100 to 1. As one Lenape sadly noted about his people, "two of them die to every one Christian that comes in here." These newcomers were eager for land, and the Munsee who were left found themselves selling it.[70]

In the years between 1630 and 1758, many Munsees, including Tackapausha, Penhawitz, and An hoock, put their marks on nearly eight hundred deeds as they sold their lands piece by piece, first to the Dutch and later to the English (see fig. 8.5). The land that makes up the five boroughs of the modern city was essentially all sold by the beginning of the eighteenth century. And so, beginning with that famous transaction in November 1626, the land of the Munsees increasingly passed into the hands of strangers until the Munsees themselves became strangers in their own land.[71]

Yet the changes in name and guardianship were only the least of the changes affecting the land. A few scattered archaeological finds hint at the enormity of those changes.

The Land Is Transformed

When Skinner was digging at Throgs Neck and Clasons Point, he found pig and cattle bones, clear evidence of contact with Europeans. Pig bones were also found at a site in Pelham Bay Park not far from Wampage's reported grave. And reports indicate that cracked sheep and cattle bones were found in a Munsee site on Staten Island. Like the metal arrowpoints, these bones are apparently insignificant finds, which can nonetheless pry open a small window into Munsee life in the seventeenth century.[72]

We don't know how the bones of these particular European domesticated animals wound up mingled with other more traditional Munsee household refuse at the sites. The meat could have been given, bought, or stolen, or the livestock could have been raised by the community; conflicting accounts suggest all these possibilities. No matter how the meat got to these settlements, its presence brings home the profound and irrevocable economic and ecological changes taking place in seventeenth-century coastal New York.[73]

These changes were many, varied, and, as always, interconnected. As the colonial settlements grew, Dutch farms began expanding more and more into areas traditionally used by the Munsees. The colonists cut down forests for lumber, cleared fields, and then planted European crops and grazed European domesticated animals, both alien to the area. These practices radically altered local ecosystems and destroyed the habitats of many of the animals that the Munsees had traditionally hunted and the plant communities on which they had depended. The Munsees had to find new strategies to get food and to deal with their rapidly changing natural world.

Compounding these ecological problems was the tense climate of war. Not only did the fighting frequently take energies away from customary activities, but both Munsee and Dutch crops were sometimes destroyed as part of the mutually punitive nature of these conflicts. Other economic stresses came from the manufacture of the increasingly essential wampum. Because this had become a post-harvest winter activity, wampum making conflicted with the traditional deer-hunting season. Some families now no longer went to their winter hunting territories in the interior, choosing instead to stay along the coast by the source of wampum's raw materials. Increasingly, many families could no longer rely on their usual foodstuffs or familiar annual work cycles. By default, they were becoming more and more dependent on the colonists.

These pig and cattle bones suggest that acquiring European animals and perhaps other foods, by whatever means, may have become one way of replacing traditional foods. We don't know how quickly or to what extent the Munsees became dependent on these alien foods—we simply have no properly dug sites to give us that information. But these few bones are the tangible clues suggesting the enormity of some of the upheavals and the resulting conflicts that the Munsees faced—the demands of tribute and trade, the causes and consequences of war, the competition over land, the destruction of traditional ecosystems and economies, the increasing size of settlements along the shore, the encroaching Dutch farms, the temptation to seize European animals as they would game, and the increasing dependence on colonists whose own interests and economies were totally incompatible with theirs.

What William Cronon writes of neighboring New England applies to New York as well: "[A] distant world and its inhabitants gradually [became] part of another people's ecosystem, so that it is becoming increasingly difficult to know which ecosystem is interacting with which culture. . . . They [Indian and European] rapidly came to inhabit a single world, but in the process the landscape . . . was so transformed that the Indian's earlier way of interacting with their environment became impossible."[74]

The Diaspora

By the beginning of the eighteenth century, the thousands of years of Indian stewardship of the land that makes up the modern city were over. A few Munsees lived on in the area, working as tenant farmers, laborers, field hands, sailors, and servants, or sell-

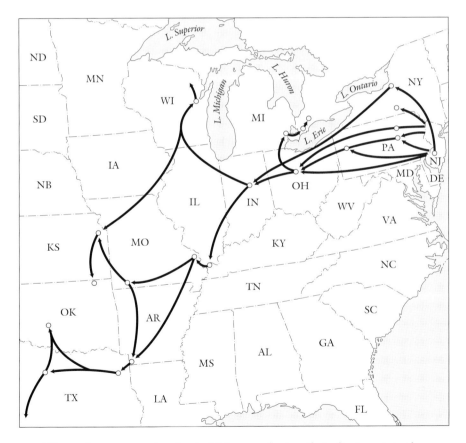

8.15. The various routes taken by the Delaware during their diaspora into the interior of the continent.

ing baskets, straw brooms, mats, and herbal medicines. Many others moved to isolated parts of New Jersey or New York or joined other Munsees in settlements along the Delaware River. Although some of the descendants of these groups are still living in the greater metropolitan area today, the Munsee language itself had died out by the beginning of the nineteenth century and could no longer be heard on the city's streets.[75]

For most of the surviving Munsees in greater Lenapehoking, the end of the Seven Years' War in 1763 marked the beginning of their diaspora, and they began heading west. We see traces of their voyages in town names across the American heartland, in places such as Delaware, Ohio; Muncie, Indiana; Lenapah, Oklahoma; and Muncey-town, Ontario. Their modern histories are found in other parts of the continent (fig. 8.15). In New York, they are largely forgotten, and the traces of their long presence there are found mainly in a few artifacts stored in museum drawers, in a few place names (such as Manhattan), and in some rare and threatened archaeological sites.[76]

In the centuries that followed, their homeland was increasingly filled with newcomers, many of whom claimed it as their own, ignored its past, and began building one of the modern world's greatest cities. The traces of these newcomers' lives, like those of the earlier inhabitants, inevitably became part of the city's archaeological record, and our narrative now becomes their story.

CHAPTER NINE

The Arrival of the Global Economy

Henry Hudson's arrival in Lenapehoking ushered in the global economy there and led to the eventual transformation of the New York area into one of the world's greatest economic capitals. But the story of that transformation begins on another continent, in Europe. In the early seventeenth century, the Protestant Netherlands threw off the yoke of Catholic Spain and emerged as a major European power. With a strong economy based on transporting European cargoes and controlled by its merchants, the country entered its Golden Age. The Dutch economy remained the strongest in Europe for much of the century. But the Dutch, like their competitors elsewhere in Europe, wanted to extend their trade beyond Europe. Merchants financed commercial voyages to various parts of the world, and once they found an area that looked promising, they formed chartered companies to which the Dutch government granted monopolies for Dutch trade there. Company investors provided capital and shared in the losses and profits of the trade. The most famous and successful of these companies was the Dutch East India Company, which had a monopoly for Dutch trade in the enormous area extending east from the Cape of Good Hope.[1]

It was in this mercantile context that the Dutch East India Company hired Henry Hudson to look for a northeast passage around Norway and across the Arctic Ocean to East Asia. Turned back by the ice, Hudson changed course and crossed the Atlantic to look for a northwest passage instead. In September 1609, he and his crew sailed the *Halve Maen* into New York Bay and up today's Hudson River to what is now Albany, a trip that ultimately had tragic consequences for the Munsees and other Indian peoples. Along the way, he traded for furs and other products. Although Hudson considered his expedition a failure because he did not find a passage to the East, the furs he brought back showed that there was another kind of profit to be made in North America.

The potential of the fur trade was the reason behind the Dutch settlement of New Netherland. But in spite of its early entry into the global economy, the area remained the backwater it had been for almost two additional centuries, although with one big difference: instead of being provincial in comparison with the territories of the Native American groups of the interior, as it had been during the Woodland centuries, the area was now peripheral to Europe. It was only in the nineteenth century, after the American Revolution, that New York was transformed, first from an economic and cultural backwater into a core economic area, and finally, in the twentieth century, into the economic and information superpower that it is today.

Archaeologists have found many sites documenting the city's growing role in the global economy. These discoveries span much of the city's history, beginning in the early seventeenth century, even before the Dutch settlement, and extending through the nineteenth century.

Before the European Settlements: The *Tijger*

For a dozen years after Hudson's voyage in 1609, Dutch merchants financed numerous expeditions to Lenapehoking to profit from the fur trade. In the fall of 1613, three ships —the *Tijger*, captained by Adrian Block (after whom Block Island, in Long Island Sound, was named); the *Fortuyn,* captained by Hendrick Christiaensen; and the *Nachtegael,* captained by Thijs Mossel—met in New York Bay and set into motion the earliest archaeologically documented event associated with the European presence in the New York area. As the captains of the ships wrangled over their respective shares of the furs they had acquired from their Native American trading partners, fall turned to winter and ice began to form on the Hudson. In January, disaster struck: the *Tijger* caught fire and burned to the waterline. Block, refusing offers to divide his crew between the two remaining ships in exchange for a share of the furs, began building a small yacht, the *Onrust* (Restless). While he was on shore supervising the vessel's construction, some of his crew joined in mutiny with some of the crew from the two other ships, seized the *Nachtegael,* and set sail, abandoning the captains and the rest of the crews to their fate.

The stranded men were in serious trouble—they had at their disposal only the *Fortuyn* and the *Onrust,* both too small to carry them all back to the Netherlands (the *Onrust* was too small even to weather an ocean crossing). The men had to spend the winter on Manhattan Island, and they are thought to be the first Europeans to winter there. But they were not without friends. Because the captains had made earlier trading trips to Lenapehoking, they already knew some of the Munsees. Furthermore, Block is reputed to have brought two young Indian brothers, sons of a sachem, back to Holland on an earlier voyage; the boys could well have been Munsee. The brothers, called Orson and Valentine by the Dutch (their real names are not known), had stayed in the Netherlands for more than a year and returned to Lenapehoking with Christiaensen on the *Fortuyn*.[2]

The Munsees helped the sailors survive the harsh winter by supplying them "with food and all kinds of necessaries . . . until the [*Onrust*] was finished." This was probably one of the episodes that the Indian sachem referred to during Kieft's War three decades later, in 1643 (see chapter 8): "He told how we first came upon their coast; that we sometimes had no victuals; they gave us their Turkish beans and Turkish wheat, they helped us with oysters and fish to eat."[3]

Although they did not have enough ships to cross the Atlantic, the Europeans were not idle. Block took the *Onrust* and explored Long Island Sound and the New England coast north to Cape Cod. Christiaensen sailed up the Hudson and built a trading post and fort on an island near modern-day Albany. This fort established a permanent base of operations for the Dutch fur trade, something that was badly needed to protect Dutch interests from European competitors. The seafarers were saved in the spring by the arrival of two other ships; their captains agreed to transport the remaining crew back to Holland in exchange for shares in the furs. The stranded had no choice but to agree, and the ships set sail, arriving in the Netherlands in July 1614.[4]

The next chapter in the story of the *Tijger* took place more than three hundred years after the rescue, in 1916, when excavations began for the new Interborough Rapid Transit subway tunnel at the corner of Greenwich and Dey Streets, by today's World Trade Center (see fig. 1.2). The alignment of Greenwich Street formed the seventeenth-century shoreline of the Hudson River, before landfilling moved the shore four blocks further to the west. There, twenty feet below ground, workmen discovered a heavily charred keel and three ribs from a ship. Fortunately, the supervising foreman for the project, James Kelly, was also an amateur historian (he later became the official Brooklyn County historian). He knew the *Tijger's* history and was soon convinced that that was the ship they had found. He and others who saw the remains in situ noted that they lay in a layer of charcoal along with a Dutch double-headed axe, a length of chain, a cannonball, trade beads, clay pipes, and some blue-and-white pottery sherds. This layer was buried under eleven feet of river silt and nine feet of landfill.[5]

Kelly arranged for the eight and a half feet of the ship's hull that intruded into the subway tunnel to be removed and brought to the old Aquarium at Manhattan's Battery, where it was submerged in the sea-lion tank so the wood would not disintegrate. Decades later, in 1943, when the Aquarium was about to be demolished, he arranged for the ship to be brought to a local museum. Amazingly for the time, not only was the ship photographed in situ but its removal was captured on film, which still exists today (fig. 9.1).[6]

Unfortunately, Kelly and his colleagues found no evidence that conclusively identified the ship as the *Tijger,* and some people question his identification. The *Tijger's* partisans, however, point out that all lines of evidence used to date the remains point to its being that ship. Radiocarbon dating of the ship's wood indicates that it came from a tree that was cut down probably some time between 1450 and 1610. The later end of this period is a reasonable one for the wood used to build the *Tijger.* In addition, the analysis of an iron bolt from the ship suggested that it was made in a manner typical of the period around 1600. Finally, marine historians analyzing the techniques used in the ship's construction have identified them as early Dutch in style. So we know that the ship from the subway tunnel was probably Dutch and built in the sixteenth or early seventeenth centuries. We have no record of another ship burning in the Hudson River

9.1. The remains of what may be the Tijger, *before it was removed from the ground to make way for a subway station. (The dendritic lines are cracks in the glass plate from which this photograph was made.) © Museum of the City of New York.*

during this time. Although we will probably never know for certain, the odds are strong that these are the remains of Block's *Tijger*.

The story of the putative *Tijger* resumes yet another half-century later, in 1968. Then, right next to the spot where the ship's remains had been found in 1916, construction was beginning for the World Trade Center. The newly created South Street Seaport Museum joined with Henry Druding (one of the Trade Center engineers and a marine enthusiast) and James Kelly to save the rest of the ship before it was destroyed by the construction of the 110-story twin towers. They recruited archaeologists Ralph Solecki and Bert Salwen to find the ship and direct its excavation.[7]

When construction excavations began to approach the depth where the ship had been found in 1916, Solecki and Salwen went to the site. But even though they explored the area all the way down to glacial sands, well below where the *Tijger* should have been, they found no traces of the ship at all. There are several possible explanations for their failure. One is that there may have been a mistake in the original measurements recording the ship's location in 1916 and that therefore the archaeologists were looking in the wrong place. If that is true, then all of its remains were destroyed in the 1960s, when the World Trade Center was built.

But Druding has proposed a more provocative explanation. He suggests that the archaeologists did not find the rest of the ship because only the front part of the *Tijger* had been scuttled in the first place. Instead, he argues, Block salvaged wood from the *Tijger* when he built the *Onrust*. Following his scenario, most of the ship's remains were removed by the subway workmen in 1916. All of this is just speculation, however; we will probably never be sure of the fate of this seventeenth-century Dutch ship.

Commercial Life in Dutch New Amsterdam and English New York

In 1621 the Dutch government created the Dutch West India Company and awarded it a monopoly for trade in the Americas and along the west coast of Africa. In order to develop the trade in furs, company proprietors claimed the colony of New Netherland, which extended from the Connecticut to the Delaware Rivers and included much of today's states of New York, New Jersey, and Connecticut (see fig. 8.11). Initially, in 1624, they placed settlements up the Hudson at Fort Orange near today's Albany (at the heart of the fur trade), on the colony's borders at the Connecticut and Delaware Rivers (for defense against the English in New England and Virginia), and on Nutten (today Governors) Island in New York Harbor. A year later they established New Amsterdam, which soon became the colony's principal town.[8]

New Amsterdam was placed in a strategic location: from there, the Dutch could protect the Hudson River and the fur trade. It also had one of the finest natural harbors in all North America. The landmass of Manhattan Island protected the East River port—and the small wooden seventeenth-century ships that moored there—from the prevailing westerly winds. Because the salty waters of the East River rarely froze over, the port could be used year-round. Furthermore, the settlement was located on an island, thus making it easy to defend. New Amsterdam served as an entrepôt, where the Dutch transferred goods from riverboats to ocean-going ships for the long Atlantic crossing.[9]

When Joel Grossman and his crew excavated at the Broad Financial Center site on Pearl Street in downtown Manhattan (see fig. 1.2), they discovered the remains of a building dating to the 1640s that epitomized the commercial nature of the Dutch colony: Augustine Heermans' warehouse. Heermans, a Bohemian born in Prague, had arrived in New Amsterdam by 1643 as the agent for a Dutch mercantile firm. He was renowned for his learning and for his forceful personality, and he soon became one of the wealthiest merchants in New Amsterdam. He dealt in Hudson River furs, Virginia tobacco, wines, and provisions. He was also active in the trade in enslaved Africans. His family connections probably helped him in his career; in 1651 he married a Dutch woman, Janneken Verlet, who was related to the Dutch West India Company's director-general, Peter Stuyvesant.[10]

In the late 1640s Heermans built a warehouse along the East River shore, overlooking the port, where he stored his merchandise while he arranged for its transport or resale. His was one of two private warehouses flanking the large Dutch West India Company warehouse, or Pach Huys. Together the three warehouses dominated the block's skyline in the mid-seventeenth century (see fig. 2.2). Heermans owned his Pearl Street warehouse for only a few years, however. Facing financial difficulties in 1653, he sold it to the Amsterdam company he worked for, Peter Gabry & Sons, which continued to own it until the British confiscated it (along with the two adjacent warehouses) in 1665, shortly after their conquest of New Netherland.

It did not take Grossman's crew long to realize that they had found the remains of the warehouse Heermans had built more than 350 years earlier. First they discovered the footings from three walls and a large section of floor, which was paved over with river cobbles. They could see that the building was located on land that their research showed had been granted to Heermans. Second, although they found only a few ceramic sherds in the builders' trenches in which the walls were laid, these sherds were all consistent with a dating of the late 1640s, the period when, according to historical documents, Heermans had built the warehouse. In addition, the width of the building (the only dimension that they could infer from the three remaining wall footings) matched that given for the warehouse in written records: both indicated a building twenty-six feet wide. Views from the period show that the building was three stories tall with a loft under its sloping gable roof (see fig. 2.2).[11]

Although the archaeologists found very few artifacts on the warehouse floor, one is the oldest datable European artifact that has ever been found in New York: a coin that was privately issued by Prince Maurice of the House of Orange to commemorate his election as a Stadtholder of the City of Utrecht in 1590 (fig. 9.2). The excavators also found a slate pencil, which warehouse workmen might have used to keep track of inventory, and several pieces of seventeenth-century clay tobacco pipes. Some of the pipe bowls were charred inside, showing that they had been smoked, perhaps by warehouse workmen, while others showed no signs of charring and therefore may have come from a shipment of pipes that had broken in transit. All in all, the artifacts and the structural remains of the warehouse provide the earliest concrete evidence that we have attesting to the city's commercial beginnings.

The fur trade was still the backbone of the colony's economy at the time of the English conquest in 1664, but trade in agricultural products soon surpassed it in importance. Although trade suffered because of economic depressions and a series of European wars, New York underwent commercial growth during times of peace, particularly in the early eighteenth century. Then colonial merchants began to develop a series of trade relationships that became known as the "triangular trade," a network that was very important to the eighteenth-century English colonists in North America. As part of this network, colonial merchants exported furs, whale oil, and tobacco to England, agricultural products to the plantations in the British West Indies, and flour to the Mediterranean and the other English colonies in North America. They transported enslaved people from Africa to the West Indies and to the North American colonies. And they also imported finished goods from England and rum and molasses from the West Indies for trade with the colonists and the Native Americans. But New York was not the economic leader of the eighteenth-century English colonial cities in North America; that distinction belonged first to Boston and later to Philadelphia.

During the colonial period, taverns were the largest secular

9.2. Both sides of the coin found on the floor of Heermans' warehouse. The coin was issued in 1590 by Prince Maurice of the House of Orange in honor of his election as a Stadtholder of the City of Utrecht.

buildings in their communities. They provided accommodation for travelers and served as gathering places for people who lived nearby. It was there that people stopped by to hear the news. Taverns also played an important role in economic life: merchants met at them to cut the deals that directed the commercial life of the town. Before the Merchant's Exchange was built in 1827, New York's merchants met in the taverns and coffeehouses that were close to the East River port.

On January 25, 1670, Captain Matthias Nicolls, secretary of the Province of New York, told the mayor's court that Governor Francis Lovelace, the second English governor of the province, intended "to build a howse uppon the lott, adjoining next unto the State-howse, and to make sd. howse to be an Inn or Ordinary." The tavern that Lovelace built was indeed next to the State House, with its broad side facing Pearl Street (see fig. 2.4). Governor Thomas Dongan in his 1686 charter confirmed the tavern as "reserved for the Crown along with the Governor's Garden and the King's Farm beyond the gate." In addition to being a gathering place for merchants and other city residents, the tavern was used for municipal meetings, particularly after the State House was deemed unsafe in 1697, when the City's Common Council resolved to "sitt att the House . . . Adjoyning ye Citty Hall untill the 13th day of October, Next." The names of some of the tavern's proprietors have come down to us: Edward Buckmaster ran it in 1695–96, George Rescarrick in 1696–98, Joseph Davids in 1699, William Davis in 1703, and John Sheppard in 1703–6.[12]

We have already described the discovery of the remains from the King's House Tavern at the Stadt Huys Block, the project that ushered contract archaeology into the city (see chapter 2). During that excavation, the archaeologists dug a total of twenty-seven test cuts inside the tavern's walls. They found the charred wooden basement floor of the tavern, making it clear that the building had burned down. This was the first hint that archaeologists, or anyone else, had of the fate of the building; historical records simply showed the tavern lot empty in 1706.[13]

The archaeologists delineated what remained of the tavern's stone foundation walls so that they could determine the building's shape and size. It was twenty-five feet wide and forty-four feet deep, including a small ell extension at its rear. The extension was probably a kitchen; the floor was slightly higher here than in the rest of the building. Under the ell's floor they discovered a barrel containing around twenty whole or almost-whole bottles (some of the bottles were stolen by pothunters who invaded the site one night after the archaeologists had left for the day). They also found some clay tobacco pipes inside the barrel, including one that was intact. In fact, this was the only whole pipe found at the Stadt Huys Block; because pipe stems are so fragile, archaeologists rarely find unbroken pipes.[14]

Inside the tavern walls, the archaeologists found more than four thousand pieces of clay tobacco pipes and almost two thousand fragments of bottles and drinking glasses (see fig. 2.9). However, they found few ceramic sherds—no more than four hundred were discovered in the whole area. This surprised archaeologists Nan Rothschild and Diana Wall, because they thought that colonial taverns provided travelers with accommodations and meals (some of which would have been prepared and served on ceramic dishes) in addition to serving as gathering places for socializing and conducting business (which would be reflected in the archaeological record by the pipe fragments). To resolve this mystery, they decided to compare the breakdown of the artifacts from the King's House with those found in the excavations of contemporary taverns located in more rural parts of the colonies. They wanted to see if there were significant differences between urban taverns and their rural counterparts.

The archaeologists located reports on excavations at three other late seventeenth- and early eighteenth-century English colonial taverns, roughly contemporary with the King's House. One was in Jamestown, Virginia's capital until 1699, and another was John Earthy's Tavern in Pemaquid, a fishing community on the coast of Maine, both dating to the last quarter of the seventeenth century. The third was the Wellfleet Tavern. Today this tavern is located on a peninsula on Cape Cod, but in the late seventeenth and early eighteenth centuries the peninsula was a separate island in Wellfleet Harbor. This tavern was not located in a town but had been used as a station by whalers waiting to sight their prey in the harbor. Together with the King's House, the archaeologists saw that these taverns could be viewed as four points along a continuum ranging from urban to rural: the King's House was located in a city, the Jamestown Tavern in a town, John Earthy's Tavern in a village, and the Wellfleet Tavern in a completely rural area.

Rothschild and Wall then chose two different kinds of artifacts—clay tobacco pipes and ceramic dishes—to serve as signatures for making inferences about the activities that took place at taverns. They argued that the number of tobacco pipes would correlate with the importance of socializing and attending meetings at the taverns—times when people smoke—while the number of ceramic sherds would indicate the importance of providing food and accommodation for guests (be they whalers or travelers).

Rothschild and Wall suspected that taverns in urban areas might tend to be more specialized and devoted to socializing, while those in rural areas might tend to be multipurpose, providing accommodation for travelers as well. If that were true, the artifacts from the four taverns would show proportionately more tobacco pipes at the urban sites and proportionately more ceramics at the rural sites. In fact, there should be regular differences in the proportions of pipes and ceramics among the four sites as they moved across the continuum from the most urban site (the King's House) to the town site (the Jamestown Tavern) to the village site (John Earthy's Tavern) to the rural tavern (the Wellfleet Tavern). And that is exactly what they found (fig. 9.3).[15]

In early English colonial life, then, taverns meant different things to different people. To rural folk they were multipurpose, providing room and board for travelers as well as meeting places for local residents, while for urbanites like those gathered at the King's House, they were not only used for socializing but also served a more specialized purpose: they were meeting places for merchants who were conducting business.

Unfortunately, archaeologists usually find only indirect evidence for trade in such important goods as furs, cloth, and agricultural products because these commodities are biodegradable. But they have uncovered direct evidence for the trade in nonperishable goods in New York throughout its history. The most common of these artifacts are the ceramic dishes and tobacco pipes imported from overseas. As whole objects, these artifacts are very fragile—they are likely to break, and once broken, the fragments are soon discarded. But these fragments are virtually indestructible and are therefore ubiquitous at archaeological sites. They tell us what kinds of dishes and pipes merchants sold and people bought and used in their homes. They also raise questions about the nature of the trade relations between the colonists and manufacturers in the mother country.

9.3. The percentages of the tobacco pipes and ceramics from the four tavern sites. The more rural the site, the higher the percentage of ceramic sherds; the more urban the site, the higher the percentage of tobacco pipe fragments.

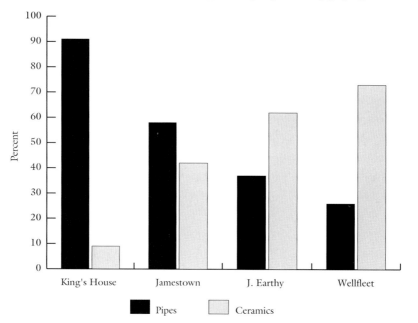

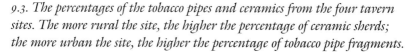

Joel Grossman and his crew made an odd discovery that raised such questions at the Broad Financial Center site in the Wall Street district. They uncovered the footings of a small outbuilding or shed (nine by five feet) in a backyard next to the lot where they had found Heermans' warehouse. When they began to dig inside the outbuilding, they found thousands of clay tobacco pipe fragments buried in layers of silty soil. All in all, they found more than seven thousand fragments from almost nine hundred pipes, the largest sample of tobacco pipes of that period that has ever been uncovered from a single feature in New York and one of the largest samples of early eighteenth-century pipes found anywhere.[16]

As they uncovered these artifacts, the excavators realized that these were not ordinary pipes. They included a large number of slightly defective pipes and some pipes that must have been rejects—they could never even have been smoked at all. Some bowls were squashed, some had holes in them, some holes had been clumsily patched with clay, some stems had clay obstructions in their bores, others had two boreholes running through them. Some of the pipes had been impressed with the marks of their makers, but the marks were illegible, or backward, or repeated many times. These were clearly not fine-quality pipes.

Among the many questions this find raised were how such peculiar pipes had come to New York in the first place and why they had ended up in the outbuilding. Diane Dallal, the pipe expert who analyzed them, noticed that many of the pipes had maker's marks. The marks on all but four of the pipes bore the initials RT, suggesting that they had been made by Robert Tippet, the name shared by several of the successive heads of an extremely productive pipe-making family that was active from around 1660 until 1722 in Bristol, England, the center of the English pipe-making craft at the time. Eighteenth-century pipes found in the English colonies in North America bear the Tippet mark more often than that of any other workshop.

Despite the maker's marks, Dallal was not convinced that these pipes had actually been made by the Tippets. She knew that part of the pipe-manufacturing process included sorting the pipes after they were removed from the kiln and inspecting them individually for flaws. Pipes that had broken in firing were thrown away, and those with slight defects were sold as "seconds." Although it was possible that the Tippets had dumped these seconds on the American colonial market, it was not likely, for two reasons. First, none of the other thousands of Tippet pipes found in the colonies showed these defects. Second, all the pipes' malformations occurred in the molding stage, not the firing stage, of pipe manufacture, and it was not likely that a professional shop like the Tippets' would have bothered to take up precious space in their kiln to fire such aberrations.

Dallal then explored the possibility that the pipes had not been made at the Tippet shop in Bristol but in New York by someone who either coincidentally had the initials RT or had simply copied the Tippet mark. She discovered the names of four "pyp-makers" who worked in the city during this period. None of them had the initials RT, but one of them was Thomas Worden, who began to work in New York in 1702. His name stood out because all of the four marked pipes from the dump that did not have the Tippet mark were marked with the initials TW. She also discovered that a Thomas Worden was listed as a pipe maker working in London in the 1690s. She further noted that the only complete pipe bowl stamped with TW in the dump was shaped in the London style, which can easily be distinguished from the Bristol style. This suggests that the Thomas Worden who had made pipes in London in the 1690s may have emigrated to New York, where he began to manufacture pipes that he made in the London style and marked with his own initials.

In this case, the pipes from the dump could be "wasters" from pipe-making kiln sites in New York—pipes that had been rejected after kiln firing either because they were broken or because they were of poor quality. But again, the fact that the pipes' malformations had been made in the molding stage and not the firing stage made this unlikely. And in addition, the excavators did not find pieces of "kiln furniture"—the supports used for stacking the pipes in the kiln—with the pipes that would indicate that they had been dumped just after firing. So the origin of the malformed pipes is still a mystery today.

The question of who dumped the pipes in the outbuilding also remains unanswered. Unfortunately, the early decades of the eighteenth century (when the pipes were made) are a period in the city's history that can be extremely difficult to research. Despite all her efforts, Dallal could not discover the names of any of the people who lived or worked on the property when the pipes were thrown in the outbuilding. It is possible that someone culled substandard and broken pipes from shipments over a period of years and threw them into the building. The clay pipe fragments that were found may simply have been recycled and placed intentionally in the outbuilding to form a paving or the bedding for a floor. Pieces of ceramic like these are good for pavements and pavement beddings because they promote drainage and reduce flooding, a real plus on the low-lying ground at the Broad Financial Center site.[17]

Trade Center of the New Nation

After the Revolutionary War, New York became the premier American city, a position that was based on its new economic role. After their trade ties with the British were broken by the Revolution, the city's merchants created new ones in other parts of the world. Later, as the United States became a major source of the raw materials needed by industrializing Britain and an important market for British goods, much of that trade passed through the port of New York. Trade continued to grow astronomically, especially after the War of 1812 and the opening of the Erie Canal in 1825, which formed the final link in a water route providing the city's merchants with access to the enormous Midwestern hinterland. By the middle of the nineteenth century, the city had become not only the country's foremost manufacturing center but its center of banking and finance as well. New York continued to be the premier American port until the mid-twentieth century. Many of the goods that passed through the port were important in the everyday life of New Yorkers. Such goods included the cloth they used to make their clothes and to furnish their homes and the dishes they used to set their tables.

In the eighteenth and early nineteenth centuries, most New Yorkers used English earthenware vessels for serving meals and Chinese porcelains for serving tea. Merchants imported these dishes and then sold their stock either directly to the consumer or to a local retailer. Archaeologists working in New York have often found broken dishes from china merchants' stock. Merchants' clerks often disposed of broken crockery by dumping it in a nearby landfill or into a backyard privy pit.

There are two ways to tell if ceramic sherds came from a china dealer's stock rather than from a home. First, an abundance of ceramic sherds in a layer of soil where other kinds of artifacts are almost completely absent clearly proclaims the discovery of goods from a china store. Second, archaeologists can identify china-stock dishes upon close examination because they see none of the signs of wear, such as the scratch marks made by knives in cutting food, that they commonly see on dishes from domestic sites.

During the eighteenth and early nineteenth centuries, several crockeries were located on Water Street near today's South Street Seaport area. When Joan Geismar and her crew excavated the site at 175 Water Street (near John Street; see fig. 1.2) in 1981, they found broken crockery from china stores in several backyards. Two of the pottery collections that Geismar and her crew unearthed date to the beginning of the nineteenth century. These dishes may have been discarded from the businesses of a father and son, Garret and William Kettletas, who had crockery shops on that block in the first decade of the nineteenth century. In the backyard behind the father's shop, the excavators found some sherds discarded in a wood-lined privy pit and others in a barrel that may have served as an underground cistern for storing rainwater. Regardless of where they had been dumped, the ceramics were in matching patterns, showing they had all been broken and thrown away at around the same time.

Garret Kettletas' son, William, ran a crockery store on the block from 1800 to 1809 and was joined by his father there for several years, from 1804 to 1808, before the senior Kettletas set up his own business next door. On the younger Kettletas' property, the archaeologists discovered a large stone privy containing literally thousands of ceramic and glass sherds. After analysts had carefully pieced them together, they had a collection of more than four hundred dishes, including painted and printed teawares and plain white plates and platters, all made in England and imported to New York. There was also a nest of mixing bowls with spouts for pouring batter, clearly stamped with the name of Wedgwood, the famous English potter, on the bases.[18]

Archaeologists usually find the remains of only the nonperishable goods (like ceramics) that stocked the city's warehouses. But otherwise perishable organic items can be preserved in the ground if they are charred by fire. One of the worst fires ever to hit New York was the Great Fire of 1835. It began on December 16 and spread rapidly throughout the city, destroying almost seven hundred buildings before it was extinguished. The fire, in which thousands of people lost their fortunes, changed the face of the city irrevocably, as the older federal and Dutch-style buildings that burned were rebuilt in the more modern, Greek Revival style.

When Roselle Henn and Diana Wall and their crew began the excavations at the Assay site on Front Street just south of Wall Street (see fig. 1.2) in 1984, they knew that the Great Fire had swept through the block almost a century and a half earlier. They also knew, however, that several excavations had already taken place on nearby blocks, which had also been devastated by that fire. Although the archaeologists digging those sites had occasionally found charred basement floors, for the most part the evidence of the fire's destruction had already been destroyed by subsequent redevelopment. So after they removed the demolition debris from the recent buildings on the Assay site and began testing to see what was there, they were thrilled to uncover a basement floor blackened by fire and covered with burned artifacts dating to the 1830s, showing that the floor was left from a building that had burned in the 1835 fire. Furthermore, the thickness of the charred layer indicated that a large sample of the goods from a business that had been wiped out by the Great Fire might still be preserved on the floor.

The archaeologists gridded out the lot in five-by-five-foot squares. Their plan was to excavate every other square in the grid so that they would have a 50 percent sample of the objects on the wooden basement floor. As the excavations began, the archaeologists referred to the history of the Front Street property to see what kind of business had been on the lot when the fire broke out. They knew that before the Revolutionary War, most merchants in New York were "general merchants" who dealt in many different kinds of goods. But in the early nineteenth century many began to specialize in particular kinds of merchandise, such as hardware, dry goods, or china.

They learned that before the fire, Anthony Winans had had his grocery on the property. He had moved his business there in 1822, and there it stayed until he was wiped out by the fire thirteen years later. The archaeologists knew that a merchant like Winans, who described himself as a grocer during this period and who worked close to the East River port in the city's commercial district, was probably not a shopkeeper serving a neighborhood clientele but an importer of exotic groceries. They also discovered that the lot was the site of Winans' countinghouse and warehouse, but that he did not live at the Front Street address. Instead, he and his family lived away from the docks, on Cliff Street.[19]

As they dug, the archaeologists realized that they had made a spectacular find. They discovered the lower portions of the barrels, baskets, and crates in which Winans stored his stock in his basement at the moment the fire destroyed his business (fig. 9.4). They realized that the excavations would allow them not only to discover the stock of a particular importer at the moment the fire broke out, but also to learn more generally, from Winans' example, about the different kinds of goods that grocers were importing into New York in the second quarter of the nineteenth century, when the city affirmed its position as the primary port of the nation after the Erie Canal opened in 1825.

As they proceeded with the excavations, the archaeologists continued to uncover more and more of Winans' stock. Although the fire had burned some of it to congealed lumps, it had only lightly charred the rest. They discovered that he was importing a variety of fruits, vegetables, nuts, and spices from all over the world. Most common were coffee, grapes, and black pepper. The peppercorns, found embedded in the cloth bags they had been stored in for their long voyage from Sumatra, were found toward the front of the warehouse, close to Front Street. The grapes and coffee beans were found together along one of the side walls of the basement. The grapes were discovered lying amid fragments of the wide-mouthed, double-handled baskets they had been stored in, while the coffee beans, probably from Turkey or Central or South America, were found still in the barrels in which they had been shipped to New York.[20]

9.4. A crate of bottles that had been stored on the Winans' basement floor.

The excavations revealed that Winans was dealing in far more than what we think of as groceries today. The excavators discovered amid the charred ruins of the shop a large number of bottles, some packed in a crate that they uncovered along the northern basement wall. The shapes of the bottles told them not only that Winans was dealing in wine, beer, and porter or ale, but that he was importing these beverages from England. Still other wine bottles had the sloping shoulders showing that both they and the wine they contained had come from France. Some of these wine bottles bore glass seals embossed with the word LEOVILLE and a bunch of grapes, advertising that the wine came from Léoville, the St. Julien estate of the Marquis de Las Cases in Bordeaux. Winans was also importing tobacco pipes. The excavators found the fragments from almost 1,500 pipes clustered in the middle of the floor. Made in six different styles, these pipes were charred on the outside from the fire but showed no evidence of the charring inside their bowls that would show they had been smoked.[21]

As for the fate of Winans' business, the documentary record shows that the fire did not wipe him out completely. The archaeologists discovered that by the next year he had reopened his grocery business in the same neighborhood where he had worked before the disaster.

Exploring Trade Networks

One of the questions that archaeologists who are interested in tracing the development of the global market need to answer is where the commodities that they excavate were actually made. Sometimes it is easy to tell where an artifact was manufactured. For example, a tobacco pipe made in the mid-seventeenth-century Dutch style and embellished with the impressed mark of EB on its heel can be assumed to have been made in the Amsterdam shop of Edward Bird, a British pipe maker who practiced his craft in the Netherlands from 1630 until 1665. Similarly, it's not hard to recognize a stoneware tankard that was made in the Rhineland in the seventeenth century, or an early nineteenth-century porcelain teacup that was made in China for the European or American trade. And some dishes bear marks that tell the name of the company that manufactured them. Bottles, too, sometimes have marks that show where they were made or where they were filled. The seals on the wine bottles from Winans' grocery, for example, allowed archaeologists to discover that the wine in the bottles came from a particular vineyard in Bordeaux. Drugs were sometimes sold in bottles bearing the embossed name and address of the drugstore where they were purchased or the name of the product the bottles contained. All these clues help in tracing the larger commercial world of early New Yorkers.

Most artifacts, however, do not bear the names of the people who made them or the places where they were made. Furthermore, most are not made in styles that are specific to a particular country. And even when we can see that a three-legged red earthenware pot, for example, is a *grape* or pipkin made in the Dutch style, we cannot tell whether it was imported from the Netherlands or whether it was made by a potter working in the Dutch tradition in New Amsterdam or New York.

Allan Gilbert, an archaeologist at Fordham University, has been working for more than a decade on a technique for deciphering where ceramics were made. Gilbert's goal is to identify the places of origin of the clays used in the manufacture of bricks and ceramic dishes that have been found by archaeologists in the New York area. He began his monumental project by compiling an archive of samples taken from the ceramics from archaeological sites and from clays native both to the New York area and to the Netherlands. He then analyzed the chemical composition of the clays. The principle behind his study is that the chemical compositions of clays from the same clay source are more similar to each other than they are to clays mined from other clay sources.[22]

So far, Gilbert has discovered that the bricks and ceramics used in New Amsterdam and New York found their way there from several different points of origin. The so-called Dutch yellow bricks found at Fort Orange and New Amsterdam are very similar in their chemistry, suggesting that they came from the same source. He can tell that some of the red-earthenware pots had been imported from the Netherlands because the proportions of the elements in their clays are most similar to those found in clays from Bergen-op-Zoom, a Dutch town that was a center for the production of red-earthenware dishes. He also discovered that an early eighteenth-century red-earthenware mug that looks English in style was made of a clay whose composition is very similar to clays from New Jersey, indicating that it was probably locally made. Some matching earthenware bottles found at the King's House Tavern are very similar in shape to some German stoneware and Dutch faience bottles. But Gilbert's analysis shows that the bottles' clay is similar to the clay used to make some red-earthenware roofing tiles found at both Fort Orange in Albany and at the New Amsterdam sites. And we know that some potters were making these tiles in the New York area as early as the seventeenth century.[23]

The potential of the New Netherland and New York clay archive for the archaeological study of the trade in ceramics and bricks is enormous. Because of their durability, ceramic sherds are the most common artifacts found in sites everywhere. This kind of study is particularly valuable for places like colonial New York, where clay objects might have been made in the Netherlands, in England, in the greater New York area, or in other parts of the world. The ongoing development of the clay archive and the chemical analysis of the ceramic artifacts found in the city will allow archaeologists to trace the trade in these goods and to understand how they came to play their roles in the lives of New Yorkers.

CHAPTER TEN

Daily Life in New Amsterdam and Early New York

In settling New Netherland, the Dutch West India Company was not interested in colonization for its own sake. It had only one goal: to make money for its investors. But it realized that settlers were important both to make the colony self-supporting and to provide the critical mass of population needed to protect its interests from both local Native Americans and European competitors. One of the recurring themes in the history of the colonial city, however, is the difficulty that first the Dutch and then the English had in attracting settlers to the area. For the Dutch, the seventeenth century was a time of unprecedented prosperity at home; few wanted to settle in what they saw as the wilderness, in one of the Netherlands' more obscure and least lucrative colonies. To lure settlers, the company opened the colony to other Europeans and gradually relaxed its restrictions on the private trade in furs. It also began to import enslaved Africans to provide labor.

New Amsterdam's first European settlers (the Swannekens, as their Indian hosts called them) were a few Walloon families—French-speaking Protestants from today's Belgium who wanted to escape the oppression of Catholic Spain, which then controlled their homeland. First arriving in New Netherland in 1624, they soon built their houses around the fort that the company was building at the tip of Manhattan Island (fig. 10.1). The Walloons were soon followed by a number of men who were company employees. Mostly from northern Europe, they planned to make their fortunes in New Netherland and then move on. It was only in the mid-1640s, after the end of Kieft's War and when the company relaxed its trade restrictions, that significant numbers of Dutch families began to emigrate to New Netherland and the size of New Amsterdam began to grow substantially. Between the 1640s and 1650s the European population doubled from 400 or 500 to 1,000 people, and by 1664 it had reached 1,500.[1]

Overall, the population of New Amsterdam was extremely diverse. In fact, one of the most often-quoted descriptions of the people of New Amsterdam is that of Father Isaac Jogues, a Jesuit missionary, who reported hearing when he visited the settlement in 1643 that "there were men of eighteen different languages" there. All in all, probably no more than half the European settlers of New Netherland came from today's Netherlands. The rest were mostly Protestants from other parts of Europe and from other Dutch colonies. There were also enslaved Africans, most of whom are thought to have come from West and West Central Africa. West Central African origins particularly are reflected in some of the names of the earliest of these involuntary immigrants: Anthony Van Angola, Domingo Angola, and Lucie d'Angola. It is estimated that Africans made up from as much as a fifth to almost half of the city's non-indigenous population in the 1660s. And of course there were the Indians, some of whom were also enslaved. They

10.1. The Hartgers View of New Amsterdam, showing the Walloon farmhouses surrounding the fort on the southern tip of Manhattan in the late 1620s. This view was reversed before it was printed originally; because it is shown oriented correctly here, the writing is backward. The Native American canoes were probably included as a convention; Indians in the Northeast did not make their canoes in this style. Collection of the New-York Historical Society, negative number 58785.

included not only the Munsees who lived there but also the members of other groups who either were brought there in bondage or came there to trade. So the cultural heterogeneity and ethnic tensions that characterize modern-day New York City have roots deep in the city's past.[2]

By the 1660s the settlement had become a small, fortified, European-like medieval city at the tip of Manhattan Island. The long palisade that stretched from river to river at the city's northern border (commemorated by today's Wall Street) had been built in the 1650s as protection against Indian and English attack (see fig. 2.3). The city, made up of structures built in the Dutch style with stepped gables facing the street, focused on the East River port, the colony's commercial hub, which provided its link to both the source of the furs and the market across the Atlantic.

The Dutch ruled New Netherland for less than half a century. In 1664 the English conquered the colony in a skirmish that was part of the Anglo-Dutch Wars fought by the Dutch and English for European hegemony in the seventeenth century. The English ruled the colony, which they renamed New York (for its proprietor, the Duke of York), for more than a century, until the American Revolutionary War.

Although people often assume that documents tell all that is needed to be known about life in the recent past, in fact records are quite reticent about everyday life—the things that people took for granted. As historian Daniel Boorstin points out, "We know more about some aspects of daily life in the ancient Babylon of 3,000 B.C. than we do about daily life in parts of Europe or America a hundred years ago."[3] This is because people rarely recorded the details of their daily rituals, such as the food they ate for dinner or the kinds of plates they used to set their tables.

The records are mute on daily life in Dutch New Amsterdam. But archaeologists can do much to re-create it by studying the artifacts they find in an old backyard or on an old basement floor. Then they can turn to historical records to identify the people who lived or worked on the archaeological site at the time the artifacts were deposited in the ground. Combining the information from the artifacts and the written records, they can construct a micro-history providing a glimpse into the everyday life of a particular home or workplace at a particular moment in time.

Although these micro-histories are invaluable in their own right in bringing the past to life, archaeologists can also use them to investigate larger issues about the daily lives of groups of people at particular moments in time. These questions might involve the complex meanings attached to the most mundane events, such as daily meals. Using this method, archaeologists first identify the foods and the cooking and serving dishes that people used; then they explore what the foods and dishes may have meant to the people who ate or used them. Finally, they can begin to answer how and why the meanings of the meals and other aspects of domestic life changed through time. So just as archaeologists have uncovered daily life in Babylon or in the deeper past of what later became New York City, they are now uncovering it for the early city itself.

In this chapter, we present glimpses into two households whose members lived in New Amsterdam and early New York. We use the information learned from the artifacts and the histories of these households and others like them to discuss two larger questions related to the Dutch presence there: How did the Dutch adapt their traditional way of life to what was for them the completely new environment of New Netherland, in the middle of Munsee territory? And for how long did the Dutch in New York maintain their ethnic identity after the English conquest?

Before we begin, however, a word of caution: the households in New Amsterdam and early New York could be very complex. Living together under the same roof might be a householder and his family members, who were usually of European descent; employees who worked in the family's business, who might also be of European descent; and enslaved people, some of whom were Indians but most of whom were of African descent (40 percent of the households in New York in 1703 included enslaved Africans). What this means for archaeologists studying the colonial city is that we do not know exactly who may have actually owned or used any particular artifact found in a household's refuse. Although we may speak of artifacts from a Dutch house, the artifacts may in fact have belonged to the African occupants of that house. For the case studies that follow, we do know that members of the two families were slaveholders, but we do not know whether enslaved people lived in either household during the periods when the artifacts were deposited in the ground.[4]

Daily Life in the Dutch and Early English Colony

In 1983 Joel Grossman and his crew, while excavating the Broad Financial Center site on Pearl Street (see fig. 1.2), discovered several backyard privy pits from Dutch outhouses filled with discarded household trash. Four of these privies had been used at various times by the households of two European American families who lived on the properties in the seventeenth century. The household trash that had been thrown into the privies allowed the archaeologists to examine daily life in these homes at different points in the city's early history.

The archaeologists found two privy pits on a parcel that Cornelis van Tienhoven bought in 1653. Van Tienhoven, a native of Holland who had arrived in New Amsterdam in the 1630s, served as the Dutch West India Company's secretary and held other offices as well. He had married Rachel Vinje (or Vigne), whose parents had immigrated to New Amsterdam from France; the couple had two children. Van Tienhoven was a controversial figure in the small colony. Although he had learned Indian languages and reputedly had had a number of liaisons with Indian women, he was known for his cruelty to his Indian neighbors. In fact, in 1656 the company fired him, as it was said that there could not be peace with the Indians as long as he remained in the colony. Later that year he disappeared. It still is not clear whether he absconded or committed suicide by drowning; although his hat and cane were found floating in the river, they could have been part of a ruse. But before he vanished, van Tienhoven had improved his Pearl Street parcel by tearing down the small house that had been on it when he bought it (see fig. 2.2) and building a larger one there. His wife continued to live in the new house until her death in 1663, and their son, Lucas van Tienhoven, a doctor, was still living there in 1679 (see fig. 2.4).[5]

The two privy pits that the archaeologists found on the old van Tienhoven property dated to different periods in the seventeenth century. One of the privies had been placed in a builder's trench containing ceramics, pipes, and glass that showed it had been built relatively early. The artifact that could be documented as having been made most recently was a ceramic sherd with a thick tin glaze, a kind of pottery that potters first began to make around 1640. The archaeologists knew, then, that the privy had to have been built during or after that year. The artifacts they found inside the privy's fill all confirmed that it had been abandoned not long after 1650. These artifacts included a piece of Westerwald—a Rhenish stoneware first manufactured around 1650—and delft tiles with ox-head motifs at their corners—a style of decoration that was introduced around the same year (fig. 10.2). The early dates of these artifacts told the archaeologists that this, then, was the privy that went with the original house on the parcel, the privy that van Tienhoven abandoned and filled in when he redeveloped the property around 1655. Supporting evidence that the privy was abandoned at the time the first house was torn down comes from the architectural debris found inside it. The debris, including Dutch yellow brick and delft tiles, presumably came from the older, smaller house and showed that it had been built and furnished in the Dutch manner.[6]

The archaeologists also found other artifacts among the trash in this early privy, including some glass beads and parts of a *roemer*, a Dutch hollow-stemmed goblet with a flared base. This roemer still had some intact prunts—small lumps of glass the size and shape of raspberries, which were applied to the outside of glasses both to decorate them and to make them easier

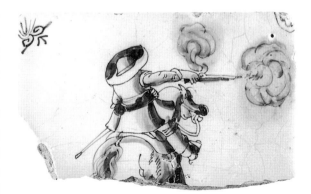

10.2. A delft tile from the earlier privy on the van Tienhoven property. Ox-head motifs appear at the corners of the tile.

to grip. Also in the privy were a bone handle from a knife or fork and fragments from several Dutch-made tobacco pipes. One of the pipe fragments had a small, fat, belly-shaped bowl and bore on its heel the impressed mark EB, for Edward Bird or his son, Evert.[7] Together, the artifacts from this privy on van Tienhoven's property make up the oldest collection of materials that we have from a home in Dutch New Amsterdam.

The fill in the other privy pit on the van Tienhoven property dated to shortly after 1680, the period when van Tienhoven's son, Lucas, and his wife were living on the property with their children. The fill contained ceramic sherds from more than twenty-two dishes, many of which were typically Dutch in style. These included pieces from *steelpanen,* or skillets with distinctively Dutch handles shaped like celery stalks, which the Dutch used for making pancakes, and sherds from a colander, easily recognizable by its glaze-lined perforations. There were also fragments from eight delft plates, popular dishes in seventeenth-century Dutch homes. Many of these plates were decorated in a blue-on-white Chinese style. Someone had also tossed in a pair of broken Chinese porcelain saucers decorated with matching painted blue floral motifs, a wig curler, a louse comb, a glass bead, a knife or fork handle made of antler, and a lead fishing sinker (fig. 10.3).[8]

More than 140 fragments of tobacco pipes had also been thrown into the privy. All but one had been made in England. The exception was a Dutch pipe from Gouda. The large numbers of English pipes show that by the 1680s, two decades after the English takeover, the people who lived in the van Tienhoven household had made the switch from Dutch to English pipes, even though the household was still using Dutch dishes.[9]

On the same site, down the block from the van Tienhoven house, archaeologists found the pits from two other privies on a lot that belonged to the Kierstede family from the late 1640s until the early eighteenth century. Hans Kierstede had been born in the city of Magdeburg in Saxony, Germany; at the age of twenty-six, in 1638, he came to New Amsterdam as the Dutch West India Company's surgeon. Two years later he left the company's service to set up a practice of his own. In 1642 he married

10.3. *Some of the artifacts from the later privy on the van Tienhoven property* (clockwise from top left): *sherds from a Chinese porcelain saucer, a red earthenware colander, and a delft plate; a knife or fork handle made from antler; and a lead fishing sinker.*

Sara Roelofs, who as a child had emigrated with her family from Amsterdam. Before settling in New Amsterdam, her family lived in Rensselaerswyck near Fort Orange in today's Albany, where her father was a farmer. There Sara and her sister became friendly with the Indians who lived nearby and fluent in their languages. After her father's death, her mother, Anneke Jans, married Domine Everardus Bogardus, a minister in the Dutch Reformed Church and a powerful figure in the colony, in 1638.

In 1647 the company granted Kierstede a parcel of land at the corner of today's Whitehall and Pearl Streets, overlooking the East River (see figs. 2.2 and 2.4). There he built the house in which he and his wife raised their family. The Kierstedes were known as friends of their Indian neighbors; it was in front of their house that in 1661 the city built one of its two markets for trade with the Indians. And Sara is said to have built a shed in the Kierstedes' backyard where Native American women made craft goods to sell at the market. Hans Kierstede died in 1666, and Sara subsequently remarried. Kierstede descendants continued to live in the Pearl Street house for more than six decades, until 1710.[10]

10.4. A candleholder and a candlesnuffer from the Bayard privy, ca. 1680.

One of the backyard privies that the archaeologists found on the Kierstede lot had probably been built at around the time the property was first developed in 1647. The trash inside this privy contained tobacco pipes and ceramics that allow us to date its abandonment to the 1680s or 1690s, well after the doctor had died and his wife had remarried. Records show that around that time, the Kierstedes' daughter, Blandina, was living in the house with her husband, Peter Bayard. Bayard had been born in Holland; his mother, Anna Stuyvesant, came to New Amsterdam with her children as a widow when her brother, Peter Stuyvesant, replaced Kieft as director general of the Dutch West India Company in New Netherland. Bayard later joined the Labadist community in Maryland that Jaspar Danckaerts and Peter Sluyter had founded (see chapter 3). The artifacts found in the privy were probably used in the Bayard household, by either the Bayards or their enslaved workers.[11]

Some of the more interesting items the archaeologists found in this privy were metal objects: a candleholder, a candlesnuffer, the "pull" from a drawer, the bowl of a spoon, and part of a pewter plate (fig. 10.4). There were also a number of tobacco pipe frag-

10.5. Pieces of a large buff earthenware vessel (right) *and of a Dutch-style red earthenware* grape, *or three-legged pot.*

ments. Most of the pipes had been imported from the Netherlands—several were marked with EB, for Edward Bird (like the pipes found in the early van Tienhoven privy), and one was marked with "HG," for the Dutch pipe maker Hendrik Gerdes, whom Anna Maria Van de Heijden, Bird's widow, married in 1668.[12] Unlike the members of the van Tienhoven household, the people in the Bayard household apparently continued to smoke Dutch pipes well after the English conquest.

The archaeologists also found two small ceramic discs that had been ground into shape from sherds of clear-glazed red earthenware; these discs were probably gambling tokens used in games of chance. Similar gaming pieces have been found in excavating the slave quarters at several plantations in the South and in Jamaica in the West Indies as well as at the Almshouse in Albany.[13] There was also a large piece of a delft charger (or plate) decorated in the Chinese Wan-li pattern (a form of decoration that became popular in the Netherlands around 1670) as well as part of a *grape,* or three-legged pot, a typically Dutch, all-purpose vessel used for cooking, eating, and holding hot coals for warming one's feet (fig. 10.5).

Grossman's team also discovered another privy on the old Kierstede property. This privy was presumably installed at the time the earlier privy on the property was abandoned, in the 1680s or 1690s. The fill inside it included a distinctive Silesian wineglass with a teardrop-shaped air bubble in its stem, a style first introduced in the early eighteenth century. The archaeologists argued that this privy, which was made of brick, must have been abandoned around 1710, when the last Kierstede descendants moved away from the lot.[14]

Thrown in this privy were more metal objects, including a hand guard from a small sword, a pewter plate, and a tankard. There was also a large piece of a whistle that had been carved out of an old clay tobacco pipe stem; whistles like these are thought to have been traded with Native Americans for furs. In addition, more than eight hundred tobacco pipe fragments were found in the privy; those with their makers' initials on them showed that by about 1710, the people living in the Kierstede house had finally made the switch from Dutch to English pipes. The archaeologists also found fragments of broken dishes and a bottle (fig. 10.6) as well as some personal items, in-

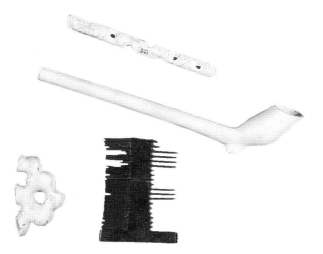

10.6. Artifacts from the later Kierstede privy: a tobacco pipe stem made into a whistle, a tobacco pipe, a handle or "ear" from a delft porringer, a bone comb, a green-glazed buff earthenware dish, and a glass wine or liquor bottle.

cluding an ivory comb with two rows of teeth—one row of coarser teeth for dressing hair, and another of finer teeth for combing out lice—two ceramic haircurlers (probably used for grooming the wigs that were popular at that time), two straight pins, and a thimble.[15]

The artifacts from these privies provide wonderful detail about the fabric of everyday life in these households, but even more important, they provide information that archaeologists can use to address larger issues about life in the past.

Adaptations in Dutch New Netherland/Lenapehoking

One of the most absorbing questions for archaeologists studying daily life in colonial times is, How did the newcomers, who came from many different cultural traditions in the Old World of Africa and Europe, adapt their traditional ways of life to the varied physical and social environments they encountered in what was for them a New World? This world was, after all, already populated with peoples who had their own well-established cultural traditions and adaptations to the land. Unfortunately, so far we have no information on the ways Africans adapted to what for them must have been a cold and cruel environment. But we do have data about the Europeans. In fact, archaeologists have studied the adaptations of many different European groups to many new environments in North America.[16] In studying these adaptations, they ask, Which cultural traditions did the colonizers appropriate or modify from the indigenous peoples, which of their own traditions did they retain, and which did they create anew? They have discovered that although most European colonists initially tried to perpetuate the traditions they brought with them from home, they soon found out that they had to modify or even replace some of them once they settled in North America.

Each group of European colonists had to reconcile the European practices they knew with the conditions they found in their new home, and the nature of that reconciliation differed from area to area and from group to group. The English colonists in New England, for example, tended to immigrate in family groups and attempted to re-create all aspects of English rural domestic life in their new home. Archaeologists working there can see these attempts expressed in ceramic dishes made in the English style. The Spanish colonists of St. Augustine, Florida, by contrast, were mostly single men; many of them married local Timucua Indian women. Together these Spanish men and Indian women created a new *mestizo* culture, which can be clearly seen in the archaeological record; household refuse from mestizo homes shows large numbers of dishes made in the local Timucua style, clear evidence of the important role of Native American women in shaping Spanish colonial domestic life in Florida.[17]

New Netherland is unique because it is the only colony in North America to be claimed and administered by the Dutch. Even though for much of the earlier period of Dutch rule European immigrants consisted disproportionately of men, these men (unlike their Spanish contemporaries) did not tend to marry Native American women. Instead, most men of New Netherland either married European women or did not marry in the colony at all.[18]

Unfortunately, archaeologists know little about the earliest Dutch adaptations to New Netherland. All three of the Dutch colonial sites excavated to date—the Broad Financial Center and Stadt Huys Block sites in New Amsterdam and part of Fort

Orange in Albany—were settled only in the 1640s, two decades after the initial Dutch settlement, and are therefore fairly late in the new colony's history. This means that no information is available on the earliest European settlers—the Walloon families who arrived at the frontier outpost of New Amsterdam in the 1620s—or on the next population wave, which arrived in the 1630s and was dominated by the men working for the Dutch West India Company. But there are artifacts from the third period, from the 1640s onward, when the settlement was characterized by families like the van Tienhovens and Kierstedes and when New Amsterdam was transformed from a European outpost into a small city. Several archaeologists have looked at Dutch adaptations to New Netherland in the mid- and late seventeenth century.[19]

Paul Huey analyzed Dutch life at Fort Orange during and after the 1640s. He was particularly struck by the extent to which the Dutch at that frontier outpost on the Hudson River used household furnishings imported from Europe to try to replicate the life they had known in the Netherlands. As Huey put it, "no effort was spared in the importation of the rich material culture of this period and in reestablishing the comfort and sophistication of everyday life in the Netherlands." The same can be said of life in New Amsterdam. Archaeologists have discovered all sorts of evidence showing the strength of Dutch influence on the architecture of New Netherland: pieces of lead glass from casement windows, yellow and red brick from houses built in the Dutch style, and terra-cotta tiles (known as pantiles) to make roofs fire resistant. Artifacts from inside these houses show that early colonists made an effort to decorate their homes comfortably and in the Dutch way: archaeologists have found countless pieces of blue-on-white delft tiles (like those found in the earlier van Tienhoven privy) used for hearths, stairs, and baseboards, and green- and rust-glazed terra-cotta floor tiles. All these artifacts show that by mid-century the Dutch were quite successful in their attempts to create comfortable Dutch bourgeois homes in what was for them a new land.[20]

Archaeologists have also studied Dutch foodways in New Netherland in order to understand more about Dutch adaptations there. The term *foodways* refers to the broad range of activities that people undertake to obtain, distribute, prepare, and consume their food. Foodways thus reveal the interface between a people and their habitat and are at the heart of understanding how people adapt to their environment.[21]

Archaeologists approach the study of the foodways of European settlers by looking at evidence from a variety of sources, including the dishes in which people prepared and served their meals, and the bones, seeds, shells, and other remains of the food that people actually ate. Meta Janowitz, an archaeologist who started working with Dutch material at the Stadt Huys Block laboratory in 1979 (see chapter 2), completed a major study of the foodways practiced by European settlers in New Amsterdam. Although

11.2. The "Plan of the City of New York," 1789 (redrafted by Hayward for D. T. Valentine's Manual, *1851). The area that would become the Assay site block is two blocks south of Wall Street on the river side of Front Street.*

No matter where they work, archaeologists are interested in how people organize their space—how they create their landscape and why they construct it in the way they do. In doing "settlement studies," archaeologists take a large area as their research unit and, within that area, study the relationships among several sites from the same time period within a single culture.[3] The area they study—the "site" in the larger sense— might be a river drainage or an ancient city, or even New York City, and within that larger site they excavate a number of smaller ones. For the pre-colonial past in coastal New York, the data are so poor that we can only speculate about settlement systems. But archaeologists studying the settlement systems of New York and other modern cities are in a much more fortunate position: they can reconstruct the city at any point in its modern history almost entirely by studying maps and other historical documents. In studying the settlement system of a modern city, they often do not have to excavate at all.

Since modern archaeology came to New York City, two archaeologists—Nan Roths-child and Diana Wall—have studied the changing patterns of settlement within the early city. They wanted to be able to place the individual sites that they had studied so intensively in their excavations into the larger context of the city as a whole. By examin-ing the changing use of space through time, they aimed to gain insight into the city's changing culture. They knew that although people created the urban landscape, the urban landscape in turn structured the social relations of the people who lived in the city. They wanted to be able to study that landscape so that they could better under-stand the social dynamics of the city at different points in its past.[4]

Rothschild and Wall, working independently on separate projects, used historical

11.3. New York in 1840, as shown by the Society for the Diffusion of Useful Knowledge.

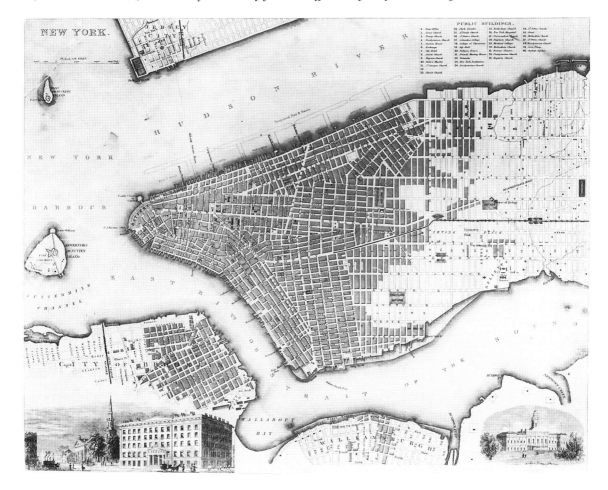

records to reconstruct the city at various points in its history. Rothschild focused on the eighteenth-century city, while Wall concentrated on the city in the early nineteenth century. Together, their work covers the spatial metamorphosis of the city over a century and a half, at a time when it was undergoing a dramatic transformation.

Eighteenth-Century Neighborhoods

Although the eighteenth-century city has long been known for its heterogeneity and integration, this does not mean that all the land in the city was used in the same way. Rather, there were definite neighborhoods in colonial New York: people with a common bond tended to live and work in clusters on the same street, although they might be joined there by others who did not share that bond.[5]

Nan Rothschild wanted to explore how wealth and ethnicity influenced the formation of New York's neighborhoods at different points in the eighteenth century. Historians studying the colonial period in New York (and in the other American seaboard cities) have noted that as time went by, fewer and fewer people controlled more and more of the wealth. In 1701, for example, the wealthiest 10 percent of the city's population owned about 45 percent of the land in the city, while by 1796 the wealthiest 10 percent of the people owned more than 60 percent of the land. Rothschild wanted to see if the increasing imbalance in wealth was expressed in the city's social geography.[6]

New York has always been known for its ethnic heterogeneity; at any point in its history it can provide a laboratory for studying the importance of ethnic identity in the formation of neighborhoods. After the Munsees and other Indian peoples, the city's oldest ethnic groups included the Dutch (among the most tolerant of their contemporaries) and the enslaved Africans. They were joined by a small group of Jews who first arrived in New Amsterdam in the 1650s.[7] After the English conquest in 1664, more and more English settled in the city, and exiled Huguenots also moved there after the 1685 Revocation of the Edict of Nantes threatened their rights in France. A half-century later, the Scots and Germans began to make their presence felt in the city.

Rothschild knew that ethnicity—that part of social identity that is based on the perception of a shared common cultural or geographical or biological origin—could be an important factor in creating neighborhoods in the city. Both today and in the past, recent immigrants tend to move into areas that have already been settled by people from their home communities. Ethnic ties can be important in finding jobs and places to live in a new country, as well as in creating a comfortable cultural milieu. As migrants become acclimated to the ways of their adopted city, some move away from their original neighborhoods to communities that are based on factors other than ethnicity.[8]

Although, as Rothschild pointed out, ethnic identity can be rigid and used as the basis for discrimination against some groups (such as Native Americans and African and Jewish Americans in both colonial and modern times), for other groups it can be extremely fluid. Under some circumstances, for example, individuals can choose to emphasize their ethnicity or to neutralize it (by "assimilation") in constructing their social identities. They can even switch from one ethnic group to another. One of the residents of New Amsterdam provides a classic example of this fluidity. Charles Bridges had been born in Canterbury, England, but when he emigrated to the Dutch colony of Curaçao, he changed his name to Carel Van Brugge. In 1647 Van Brugge accompanied Peter Stuyvesant to New Amsterdam, where he continued to be Van Brugge until the English conquest, when he changed his name back to Charles Bridges.[9]

Rothschild wanted to compare the relative importance of ethnicity and wealth in structuring urban space at the beginning and end of the eighteenth century. Choosing 1703 and 1789 as target years for examining neighborhood formation in the city, she began by compiling a directory of the people who lived in New York in each of these years. Her directories included peoples' names, ethnic affiliations, levels of wealth, occupations, and, of course, addresses. She obtained this information from a broad variety of historical records: tax and church records, census returns, city directories, and even the records from a German fraternal organization. All told, her directories listed about one thousand people for each of the two years. She then plotted the locations of their homes on a set of maps that indicated their ethnic affiliations and levels of wealth for each of the study years.

What Rothschild discovered was intriguing. At the beginning of the eighteenth century, when the city was relatively young, ethnic identity was a very important factor in structuring the city's neighborhoods, especially for those of Dutch, English, and French Huguenot descent: they tended to live in definite residential clusters. The Dutch were heavily concentrated on several streets in the southern and central parts of the island, while the English were most heavily clustered on the east side. The French Huguenots tended to live in a separate cluster to the north of one of the Dutch enclaves, as well as on the east side, alongside the English. In fact, Broadway on the west side was the only street that had approximately equal numbers of English, Huguenot, and Dutch families living side by side.[10]

Furthermore, Rothschild noted that in the city of 1703, the members of the different ethnic groups appear to have used several principles in deciding where to live. First of all, the Dutch for the most part lived separately from both the English and the French Huguenots. Second, churches seemed to play an important role in forming and maintaining ethnic neighborhoods. The Dutch Reformed Church was just adjacent to the Dutch enclaves in the central part of the city, the old Anglican church at the foot of Manhattan Island was close to an English enclave there, and the newly built Trinity

Church (on Broadway at the head of Wall Street) was just down the street from the English homes on Broadway. The Huguenot cluster was just adjacent to their church, L'Eglise François de Nouvelle York, which had been established in 1688.

The presence of a church was not the only attraction that lured residents to a particular part of the city. Members of all three groups lived near the East River, the port at the hub of the city's economy. When Rothschild looked at the spatial distribution of the city's residents by wealth, she saw that in 1703 in general, rich people of all ethnic groups tended to live on the east side, near the East River port, and poorer people tended to live in the western and northern parts of the city. But she was surprised to find that she could identify only four residential clusters that were based on wealth. One street near the East River port was the site of a cluster of homes belonging to many of the city's richer merchant families and to artisans who made luxury goods. These craftsmen presumably located their shops to be near their rich customers who lived nearby. The southern end of the city, which was heavily occupied by Dutch families, and two streets in the center of the city were inhabited almost exclusively by lower-income New Yorkers. But most of the city's streets were economically heterogeneous, with wealthy, middle-income, and poor people living side by side. It seems, then, that at the beginning of the eighteenth century in New York City, people paid more attention to ethnicity than to wealth or class in deciding where to live.[11]

When Rothschild looked at the distribution of the city's residents by ethnicity and wealth in 1789, she was struck by several changes. First of all, for the members of some of the city's older ethnic groups, ethnicity no longer seemed to be a factor in deciding where to live. She found that Dutch, English, and French families were spread fairly evenly throughout the whole city, although there were still slight concentrations of both English and Dutch residents on the streets where their ancestors had lived in 1703. For the most part, however, she noted that the city's "major early ethnic concentrations had broken down."[12]

Rothschild discovered that although the Dutch and English no longer lived in ethnic enclaves, the members of other ethnic groups did. Some of these were groups whose members had first arrived in the city well over a century before but who had always faced discrimination from other New Yorkers, while others were made up of more recent immigrants. Africans, for example, were among the earliest arrivals after the Dutch founded New Amsterdam. After the Revolution, although most of the city's residents of African descent were still enslaved and forced to live in the homes of their owners, those who were free established their own community in the northeastern part of the city. Jews, who had been in the city for almost a century and a half, were most heavily clustered in the lower city, around the corner from their Mill Street synagogue.[13]

The other ethnic neighborhoods in the 1789 city were made up of more recent immigrants: the Germans and Scots who had begun to arrive in numbers in the middle of the century. Most Germans lived in clusters on Broadway and Chatham Street, two streets that together made up one of the city's main inland thoroughfares. Scots lived all over the city (except at its southern end) but formed three clusters: one on the west side, one on the east side, and one, on a street that they shared with the free African community, in the northern part of the city.[14]

Whereas ethnicity was apparently an important factor for some groups in the shaping of the 1789 city, money was now more important than it had been earlier in the century. The city's wealthier residents—its merchants—tended to live on the east side, close (but not too close) to the East River port. And although the city's poorer inhabitants tended to live throughout the city, they formed clusters at the city's southern end and on the streets overlooking the docks. The rich and poor were not the only ones to cluster, however—members of the emerging middle class were concentrated on two streets running parallel to the East River and on several other streets as well.[15]

Although both ethnicity and wealth, then, were important factors in organizing the spatial structure of the city at both the beginning and end of the eighteenth century, Rothschild was able to show how their relative importance had changed for different groups during that time. At the beginning of the century, when the English conquest of the Dutch colony was only a generation old, many English and Dutch families marked their social distance from each other by living apart, but by the end of the century, ethnicity was no longer important to them in deciding where to live. For other groups, ethnicity remained important in structuring the city's space: newly arrived Scots and Germans and members of those older immigrant groups that faced discrimination— the free people of color and the Jews—all tended to live in ethnic enclaves. As for economic factors, although they were important at the beginning of the eighteenth century, they became much more important as the century progressed. As Rothschild put it, "Even given economic constraints on residential choice, it is clear that people did exercise options in choosing their living place and that, as the century wore on, more of these choices were linked to economic factors than to ethnic ones."[16] These economic factors became only more important as time went by. In fact, by the mid-nineteenth century, they had become paramount.

Nevertheless, it is misleading to assume that Dutch ethnicity ceased to be important in the post-Revolutionary city or that assimilation was an irreversible process. After the Revolutionary War, well over a century after the English conquest, some New York Freemasons of Dutch extraction claimed that they were "not well acquainted with the English language" and successfully petitioned the Masonic Grand Lodge to form their own Holland Lodge, where they could perform "their labours in the Low Dutch language." Many of the early members of the Holland Lodge were prominent New

people who lived in the city in the late eighteenth and early nineteenth centuries. She consulted sources similar to those that Rothschild used: city directories and tax and census records. She ended up with six samples of people who were living in the city at ten-year intervals, from 1790 to 1840 (the samples totaled more than two thousand people). The samples showed where people lived and whether they lived in combined or separate homes and workplaces. They also indicated the values of their real estate and personal property so that she could place them into rough socioeconomic groups. In looking at her data, she saw that most of the city's elite had separated their homes and workplaces during the first decade of the century, before 1810, while most members of its middle class waited until the 1830s, a full generation later.[21]

Wall plotted the locations of the city's separate workplaces and the homes of its poor, middle-class, and wealthy families for three different years. She used 1790 as a base year, to show the structure of the city before any of the changes that she was exploring had occurred. She also chose 1810 and 1840, the years following the periods when most of the wealthy and middle class (respectively) had moved their homes away from their workplaces.

The 1790 city was relatively integrated; there were very few separate workplaces. Wall could see that class, as Rothschild's study had shown, was an important factor in deciding where to live. Wealthier families clustered their homes and workplaces in a core area near the East River port and on the west side near Broadway, although there were poorer and middling families (like the Van Voorhis family) living and working in these areas as well. Significantly, the rich did not live outside this central urban core. Instead, they stayed close to the source of their wealth: the warehouses and wharves of the rapidly growing commercial city. Only the poor and middling lived on the periphery, beyond the urban core.

Twenty years later, in 1810, the social geography of the city had changed. It now had a "downtown"—a commercial district made up predominately of merchants' counting-houses—in the area where the city's wealthy families had once lived, along Wall Street and near the East River port. Most of these wealthy families had separated their homes from their workplaces and now lived in new residential areas clustered around the commercial core. The men from these households could still walk to work and come home for their midday dinners. But these new neighborhoods were not only residential, for mixed among the homes of the city's leading citizens were the combined homes and workplaces of the city's poor and middle class (like the Robsons' houses, first on Roosevelt Street and then on East Broadway).

Many of the men of these more modest households either worked in their homes or walked to work in the new commercial heart of the city. Middle-class artisans and shopkeepers continued to board their male employees in their homes. Their combined homes and workplaces formed clusters around the commercial core, while the area with the heaviest density of poorer residents was located to the north, near the Collect Pond.

By 1840 most members of the middle class had joined the city's rich in establishing separate homes. For all but the poorest New Yorkers, the city of integrated homes and workplaces was gone. Most remarkable was the increasing specialization in the use of urban space: the city now consisted of a number of neighborhoods that were much more consistent than ever before in terms of function and socioeconomic group. There was now a commercial district focused on the Wall Street area that was almost strictly devoted to business; only the poor lived there. In addition, the rest of the city was beginning to become segregated by class. While some wealthy families still lived downtown, close to the business district, many others succumbed to the exorbitant sums they were offered for their downtown homes, which had become prime commercial real estate, and moved out to the new exclusive elite "suburbs" that were developing at the city's edge, in the area of the old village of Greenwich—the area that had attracted the Robsons—and in Brooklyn. In 1836 the diarist Philip Hone accepted what he considered to be an outrageous offer for his home on lower Broadway and moved with his family out to Greenwich. As he explained in his diary, "I have turned myself out of doors; but $60,000 is a great deal of money." He added: "All the dwelling houses are to be converted into stores. We are tempted with prices so high that none can resist, and the old downtown burgomasters, who have fixed to one spot all their lives, will be seen during the next summer in flocks, marching reluctantly north to pitch their tents in places which, in their time, were orchards, cornfields, or morasses a pretty smart distance from town, and a journey to which was formerly an affair of some moment, and required preparation before hand, but which constitute at this time the most fashionable quarter of New York."[22]

The elite Greenwich Village neighborhood focused on Washington Square, which had been developed in the late 1820s on the site of a potter's field. The men in these wealthy suburban families (like Francis Sage) commuted to work, traveling on the omnibuses and ferries that began commuter service to serve them. For these families, New York was no longer a walking city.

The city of 1840 also contained middle-class and working-class residential enclaves. Most middle-class men commuted to work, while many members of poorer families continued to work at home as part of the "out-work" system, where whole families living in tenement apartments performed piecework for local manufacturers (fig. 11.7). Working-class neighborhoods had to be close to the commercial core—these workers could not afford to use public transportation to get to and from work. Omnibus fares of eight to twelve and a half cents were too high for a laborer who made only a dollar a day. Many other members of the poor worked in the service industries. Some, like the Irish women who worked as domestics, still lived in the homes of their employers, while others, including men and women of African descent, lived in enclaves close to the homes of their clients. Both provided services to the residents of the new suburb at Greenwich.

The spatial separation of homes and workplaces among the members of the city's middle class and elite changed the social geography of the city in another significant way. For these groups (although not for the poor), the city's commercial district had been transformed into a world of men, and the middle-class and wealthy residential neighborhoods became during the day a world of women and children. These worlds were so separate that on August 31, 1839, a local newspaper, the *Mirror,* asked its readers: "Did you ever see a female in Wall-street, dear reader? . . . The sight of a female in that isolated quarter is so extraordinary, that, the moment a petticoat appears, the groups of brokers, intent on calculating the value of stocks, break suddenly off, and gaze at the phenomenon."

11.7. View of the Five Points, ca. 1827, lithograph from Valentine's Manual, *1855. This working-class neighborhood was a few blocks to the north of City Hall. Collection of the New-York Historical Society, negative number 44668.*

In addition to having a significant effect on the use of space in the city, the separation of the home and workplace was also associated with profound changes that took place in family life, inside the homes of middle-class New Yorkers. We use their dishes, cups, and glasses from the archaeological record to examine some of these changes in domestic life in the next chapter.

CHAPTER TWELVE

Daily Life in the Nineteenth-Century City

During the century that followed the Revolutionary War, broad changes swept through New York and the other American seaboard cities as the impersonal relations of the market economy replaced the old kinship ties and face-to-face relations of the colonial economy. We have already examined the effect that this transition had on the social geography of New York, where middle-class and elite families separated their homes from their workplaces, thus creating a new commercial district in the Wall Street area as well as a new set of residential neighborhoods. At the same time, immigrants were pouring into the city and creating working-class neighborhoods that were within walking distance from their workplaces. In this chapter, we first explore how this urban transformation was expressed in the family life of the native-born middle class. Then we look at one of the city's poorer immigrant neighborhoods—the Five Points district—and examine aspects of home life there.

The Great Transformation and Middle-Class Family Life

When the homes and workplaces of the middle class and wealthy were still combined under the same roofs, men like silversmith Daniel Van Voorhis and physician Benjamin Robson produced goods for market and sold goods and services out of their homes. Yet these heads of households were not only in charge of economic life—they were also responsible for the moral and physical well-being of their families. Artisans' wives like Catherine Van Voorhis were primarily responsible for running the household and caring for small children, but they also helped their husbands in the family business. Older children worked alongside their parents, with daughters helping their mothers and sons helping their fathers in the family trade. And like the Van Voorhis household—which in 1790 was made up of sixteen people, half of whom were not members of the immediate family—many colonial and late eighteenth-century homes included a number of people who were not family members. Employees, including journeymen, apprentices, and clerks as well as young women who helped with the housework, all tended to live with their employers. And many New York City households (as many as one in five in 1790) also included enslaved Africans. For the most part, these households were tightly knit corporate units, made up of people who, whether through choice or coercion, lived and worked together.[1]

By the middle of the nineteenth century, the structure of the middle-class household had changed, and a stricter division of labor governed the activities of family members. The Robson and Sage households on Washington Square were typical of the times. Benjamin Robson and his son-in-law and next-door neighbor, Francis Sage, worked downtown and were away from home all day. Their primary domestic responsibility was for the household's economic well-being, a responsibility that they fulfilled in the separate, public sphere of the marketplace.

Children no longer learned their adult roles by working alongside their parents at home. Instead, like the Sage children of Washington Square, they went off to school and, like their fathers, were away from home for much of the day. For the first time, toys and other things were made and marketed for middle-class children, with the thought that these objects would help teach them appropriate adult roles. It is from this period that archaeologists first find a profusion of children's toys and other items: mugs and plates inscribed with adages to inspire morality and good work habits, dolls and toy china tea and dinner sets to teach girls to be nurturers and hostesses, and pieces from competitive games like marbles, dominoes, and chess to instill the entrepreneurial spirit into boys (figs. 12.1 and 12.2).

Middle-class women like Eliza Robson and her grown daughter Mary Sage were home during the day, tending to the house and children. They had become the full-time caretakers of the moral, physical, and emotional well-being of the members of their households. Historians have referred to this new emphasis in the role of middle-class women as the "cult of domesticity," which was marked by the elaboration of domestic life, or "women's sphere." Women's roles now revolved around several inter-related goals of domestic duty: raising responsible citizens for the good of the nation, being the moral guardians of the family and the larger society, and projecting an image of refined gentility to reinforce their families' position in the class structure. Women bolstered their families' status by entertaining in their new double parlors that replaced the work spaces that had once occupied the first floor of the old combined homes and workplaces. These housewives now supervised "servants" or "domestics" (as opposed to the "help" and enslaved of the earlier era) who actually did the work that enhanced

12.1. A doll, pieces from a doll's tea set, and a doll's baking dish, from a middle-class home in Greenwich Village, 1860s.

the quality of domestic life. The servants tended to be young and unmarried, and were usually, like two young women who worked in the Robson home, recent immigrants from Ireland. They slept on the top floors of their employers' homes, in spaces that were unheated in winter and sweltering in summer.

By contrast, male employees—like the journeymen and apprentices who had worked in the Van Voorhis shop—no longer boarded with their employers' families. Instead, they lived in the new lower-middle- and working-class neighborhoods that were developing in other parts of the city, like the Five Points and the Lower East Side. Free people of color lived in their own homes, too. The middle-class home, instead of being the "little commonwealth" of the colonial period, had become a "haven in [the] heartless world" of the marketplace, with its appurtenances serving as symbols of respectability.[2]

Diana Wall wanted to find out how this change in gender roles and the emergence of the related cult of domesticity had occurred among the city's middle class. Scholars are divided in their views of who actually instigated this change. Some regard women simply as victims whose roles were redefined not by themselves but by men and the larger society. Others look on women as actors in their own right who, along with men, contributed to this restructuring of gender relations. But which of these interpretations is correct?

Wall thought that she might be able to answer this question by combining the study of changes in the composition of the people who lived in these households (information she could glean from the historical record) with the study of changes in the kinds of dishes women bought and used in their homes (information she could get from the archaeological record). If, on the one hand, she could show that middle-class women had already begun to enhance domestic life *before* the spatial separation of the home and workplace, then women, as well as men, could be seen as actors in the development of a separate sphere that ultimately led to the transformation of gender relations. On the other hand, if she could see evidence that women began to enhance home life only *after* homes separated from workplaces, then it would seem that they were reacting, or adapting, to economic changes that had already been initiated by men and the larger society.

In order to find out about the changing composition of the city's middle-class households, Wall used census records to discover more about the people she had used for her study of the city's changing social geography. And she used the ceramic sherds from sites dating to that period to see what kinds of dishes women were using to set their tables. Focusing on the half-century that followed the Revolutionary War, she chose 1840 as a cutoff date because she knew that by then this new domestic role for women had already become the ideal: during the 1830s a whole new literature had begun to appear promoting this new definition of womanhood.

Wall realized that if women's roles were changing inside the city's combined homes and workplaces, she would see changes in the makeup of the people who were living in these integrated households.[3] First, there would be a decrease in the average number of children, as children were no longer looked on as helpful "little hands" but instead were regarded as responsibilities who had to be educated to become the citizens of the future. There would also be an increase in the number of women working as domestic servants in each household because the enhancement of domestic life entailed a great deal more

12.2. Mugs that probably belonged to the Sage children on Washington Square. These mugs were found in the backyard privies behind the Robson and Sage homes.

ARRANGEMENT
OF A DINNER OR SUPPER TABLE,
CONSISTING OF NINE DISHES.

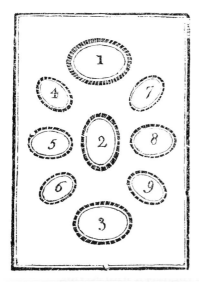

12.4. A plan for arranging serving dishes on the table, ca. 1802, from Susannah Carter's The Frugal Housewife *(1802).*

no longer on the food (which was now mostly out of sight in covered serving dishes) but on a centerpiece, which might be a castor or condiment stand, a celery glass, or even a vase of inedible flowers (fig.12.5). The appurtenances of middle-class domesticity and respectability had replaced the food as the center of the meal.

Although household help (now called servants or domestics) were much more common than they had been before, they no longer ate with the family but instead waited on them at meals. The mistress ladled out the soup (the dish that began the meal), stressing her role as family nurturer, while the master carved and served what Americans then (as now) considered the most important dish of the meal—the meat—thus stressing his role as the family provider. The servant handed round the dishes considered to be relatively unimportant—the vegetables and starches.

Throughout the same period, "tea" was also an important meal but one with a very different meaning: it was a social event. Because families entertained their guests at tea, this meal provided an opportunity for displaying social status while trying to enhance the family's position in society and arrange marriages and careers for the children. The tea ceremony was held after dinner, first in the late afternoon during the period when dinner took place at noon, and later at night after dinner shifted to the evening. Hostesses served tea and, sometimes, wine at these parties and (in the evening) often supper or desserts. When the parties shifted to the evening, another ritual appeared: afternoon tea, which became a female social event, indulged in by both middle-class and wealthy women.[8]

Women put a great deal of thought into choosing the dishes they used for serving meals, as is evident from the diary of Elizabeth Bleecker, a broker's daughter. After her marriage in 1800, Bleecker and her husband, Alexander MacDonald, lived with her family while they set up their household. Bleecker recorded some of the purchases that she made for her new home, including the dishes she chose. She and her mother went shopping on Broad Street, where her mother bought her some "Cups and Saucers," presumably for tea. She also went alone on several separate occasions to shop for "Plates and Dishes." In August, just before the couple moved into their new house, she and her sister Mary went shopping to "look for Tea Pots." They evidently did not find any that suited, because she continued to shop for them. She finally reported in early September that she had bought "a Tea-Pot, Sugar Pot, and Milk Pot at Mr. Peter's," a china and glass dealer who had his shop in Maiden Lane.[9]

Bleecker's diary entries show that women were very selective when shopping for dishes to grace their tables. Wall regretted that Bleecker and her contemporaries did not describe their purchases in greater detail. But she knew she could use the ceramic sherds from archaeological collections to find out about the kinds of ceramics these women were actually buying.

Wall looked at the dishes from New York households dating to the late eighteenth and early nineteenth centuries. The dishes, recovered from the privies and basement floors of eleven middle-class homes (including the Van Voorhis and the old Robson homes), were used at family meals and social teas in combined homes and workplaces in lower Manhattan that dated from the 1780s to the 1830s. Based on the dates of manufacture for the dishes that made up the assemblages, which reflected the time when the dishes were bought, she placed the households in three groups, dating to the 1780s, around 1805, and the 1820s. She then looked at two different aspects of the dishes: their decorative motifs and their cost.[10]

Wall was interested in examining the decorative motifs on these dishes to see what they might reveal about the changing importance of dinner for early New York families. Archaeologists know that people use style to mark the different social contexts in which objects might be used. For example, clothing is a common marker in American culture—many people wear one style of clothes for work and another for leisure so that they and others will know whether they are at work or at play. Archaeologists also know that changes in the styles of objects through time can reflect changes in the meaning of the context in which the objects were used. Women's fashions, for example, change as the meaning of womanhood changes.

With this in mind, Wall began to look at the decorative motifs on the china from the eleven households. She expected that the motifs used for tea dishes would be quite different from those used for dinner dishes, because the social

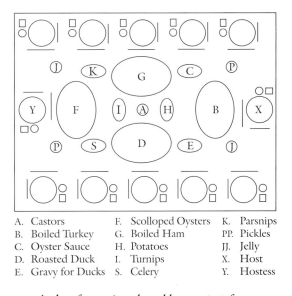

A.	Castors	F.	Scolloped Oysters	K.	Parsnips
B.	Boiled Turkey	G.	Boiled Ham	PP.	Pickles
C.	Oyster Sauce	H.	Potatoes	JJ.	Jelly
D.	Roasted Duck	I.	Turnips	X.	Host
E.	Gravy for Ducks	S.	Celery	Y.	Hostess

12.5. A plan for setting the table, ca. 1846, from Catharine Beecher's Domestic Receipt-Book *(1846).*

meanings of these meals were very different throughout the period. Tea was a public meal, for outsiders, while dinner was always a private meal, for household members. Furthermore, if the social meaning of these meals changed through time, with tea becoming more feminized and dinner becoming more ritualized, she expected to see these changes expressed in the motifs on the dishes used in presenting these meals.

Wall found that the decorative motifs on most of the teawares and the tablewares from the households fell into four broad groups for all three periods: all-white dishes, dishes with shell-edged decoration, dishes with Chinese landscapes, and dishes with floral motifs. She also saw that the motifs on the teawares and the tablewares were different for each of the three periods, and that the popularity of these motifs changed through time. All the households in the early group (which included the Van Voorhis household and dated to the 1780s) showed a preference for "royal" plates that were plain white with simple, classically molded rims, like those used in the Van Voorhis household (fig.12.6, left). The early teawares, by contrast, were evenly divided between Chinese landscapes and floral patterns. All the households in the middle group (c. 1805) had sets of plates with blue- or green-painted shell-edged decorations around their rims (fig. 12.6, middle) along with sets of plain white dishes. The tea vessels from the households in the middle group showed that floral motifs were now more popular than Chinese landscapes. Finally, for the latest group, dating to the 1820s, there was a marked change in both plate and teacup patterns. Just as in the Robsons' old home, most of the tablewares from these households were decorated with Chinese landscapes (fig. 12.6, right), while most of the teawares were embellished with floral motifs.

The changes in the popularity of the various styles—from plain white to shell-edged to chinoiserie for the plates and from chinoiserie to floral motifs for the teacups—showed that the social meaning of these meals had already begun to change inside the combined homes and workplaces of the city's middle class, before families moved to the suburbs.[11]

Next, Wall looked at the amounts of money that middle-class women were willing to spend on their dishes. She wanted to find out if they were beginning to spend more money on the dishes used for serving family meals while they were still living in their integrated homes and workplaces. If they were, it would suggest that women were already making more elaborate meals, and hence enhancing domestic life, before the shift into separate homes. She assigned values to the dishes by using information both from the price lists of the English potters who made the earthenware dishes that were popular in the United States at this time and from the records of local merchants who imported Chinese porcelain from Canton.[12]

She saw that for the three chronological groups, the relative costs of the tablewares

12.6. Left to right: *a creamware plate in the royal pattern from the Van Voorhis household, 1780s; a pearlware plate in the shell-edged pattern, ca. 1810; a pearlware plate in the willow pattern from the Robsons' old home, 1820s.*

were quite different from those of the teawares (fig. 12.7). Those for the teawares were relatively high for the early group and stayed relatively high, with only a slight increase in value through time. This suggests that the goal of the mistress of the house was always to have an expensive, showy tea set for entertaining her friends.

The relative costs of the tablewares, by contrast, were quite low for the earliest group. But during the first three decades of the century, middle-class New York women were willing to spend ever-increasing amounts of money on the dishes that they used for family meals. In fact, by the 1820s, the mistresses of these households were willing to spend almost as much for their plates, which were usually seen and used only by household members, as for their cups and saucers, which were used to entertain their guests. This decision suggests that the meanings of family meals and hence of family life were changing as well: they were becoming more important inside the combined homes and workplaces of the city's middle class.

The data from the census records and from the fragments of dishes from the city's archaeological sites thus allowed Wall to show that middle-class women were redefining domestic life, and their role within it, well before the separation of the home and workplace took place. This suggests that women, along with men, actively contributed to the separation of men's and women's spheres and the development of the cult of domesticity. If true, this interpretation has ironic implications: if this structural transformation was a consequence—albeit unintended—of changing social practices on the part of both men *and* women, then middle-class women were at least partly responsible for their ultimate isolation in the home. And it is this very isolation that many middle-class American women have been protesting off and on ever since.[13]

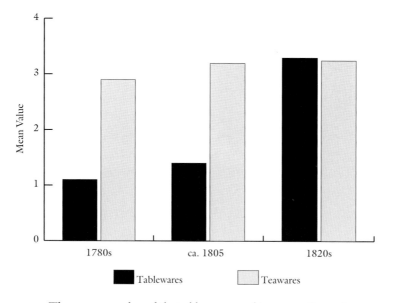

12.7. The average value of the tablewares and teawares from the eleven households, by chronological group.

Life in a Working-Class Immigrant Neighborhood

New York City's working class had invented itself twice by the middle of the nineteenth century. The earlier working class, which dated to before the 1840s, was a heterogeneous group of predominately native-born people who worked with their hands and who had inherited the republican ideology of the Revolutionary War. But their children did not become the working class of mid-century. Instead, their place was taken by immigrants who began arriving in New York in waves in the 1840s. Between 1840 and 1855, the city's population doubled, with immigration playing a major role in its growth: in 1855 more than half its population of almost 630,000 was foreign-born. And most of these immigrants were manual workers; in that year almost 85 percent of the city's manual workforce had been born overseas. It was the immigrants and their children who transformed the city's working class by drawing on cultural roots developed in Europe. Since then, immigrants have for the most part dominated the city's workforce and shaped its working class.[14]

At the middle of the nineteenth century, most of the city's immigrants were Irish and German. The Germans immigrated for a number of economic, religious, and political reasons, while the Irish were fleeing the potato famines that repeatedly ravaged their country beginning in the mid-1840s. By 1855, when there were almost twice as many

Irish as Germans in the city, these two groups together made up almost 45 percent of the city's population. Irish men tended to work as laborers, bricklayers, and stone-cutters, while German men worked as cabinetmakers, tailors, cigar makers, bakers, and shoemakers. Because a workingman's wage was usually not enough to support a family in the nineteenth century, the women of the working class, unlike their middle-class counterparts, helped make ends meet by using various economic strategies both inside and outside their homes. The work of working-class women, like that of working-class men, tended to follow ethnic lines. Many young unmarried Irish women (most of whom had emigrated on their own) worked as servants, living in the homes of the middle- and upper-class women who were their employers. In fact, census records indicate that more women in New York worked in domestic service than in any other sphere: in 1855, more than 31,000 women were employed as servants in the city. Irish women, both married and single, also worked in their own homes, often as seam-stresses or laundresses, while German women tended to work alongside their husbands and children in family-organized shops in the tailoring business and other trades. Women of many ethnic groups also provided accommodations for boarders, many of whom were themselves recent arrivals from the home country.[15]

Under the strictures of contract archaeology, the vagaries of modern development determine the locations of archaeological excavations. It just so happens that only a few modern development projects have taken place in neighborhoods where the poor lived in the nineteenth century. Therefore, although contract archaeologists have exca-vated many sites associated with the city's middle and upper-middle classes, they have dug only a few sites associated with the city's working class. One of these excavations, at the Courthouse site, took place in the city's most famous working-class area, the Five Points district (see fig. 11.7).[16]

The Five Points, named for the space created by the intersections of three streets, lay to the northeast of City Hall Park on the edge of today's Chinatown. Although the nineteenth-century neighborhood was associated with crime and iniquity, today it is devoted to the city's criminal justice system—the prison popularly known as the Tombs and many of the city's courthouses are located there. In fact, the site was excavated in preparation for the construction of a new federal courthouse. The site consisted of fourteen building lots located at one end of a block bounded by Pearl and Baxter Streets (see fig. 1.2); the other end of the block fronted on the Five Points intersection. Before the nineteenth century, the area was outside the city's edge, near the Collect Pond, where Dutch colonists had noted the presence of Native American shell mid-dens. For Dutch and English colonists, the pond was the focus for many industries that either needed fresh water or were so noxious or dangerous that they were inappro-priate for the densely settled city, including slaughterhouses, potteries, tanneries, and breweries. During the first decade of the nineteenth century, the city began to fill in the pond, which had become heavily polluted, as well as the surrounding low-lying area. The neighborhood first became home to many African Americans and other members of the native-born working class, but they were soon joined by Irish and other immigrants. By the 1830s the neighborhood had achieved its status as the city's most notorious slum. When Charles Dickens came to the city in 1842, he made a point of visiting the neighborhood and wrote: "Poverty, wretchedness, and vice, are rife enough where we are going now. This is the place: these narrow ways, diverging to the right and left, and reeking everywhere with dirt and filth. . . . Debauchery has made the very houses prematurely old."[17] The Five Points owed much of its notoriety to its location: it was the slum that was closest to the city's political and commercial center, and therefore it was the slum that was most visible to the city's middle class and foreign visitors.[18]

Over the past few decades, historians have argued that contemporary stereotypes of slums belied communities that, though often beleaguered and dangerous, could also be sustaining and even nurturing for many of their residents. Their studies document the importance of kinship and neighborhood ties in alleviating the hardships of tenement life. In addition, although most of those who lived in the tenements were extremely poor immigrants, they had not necessarily been among the poorest in their home countries. Instead, the immigrants were those who could afford to emigrate. The standard of living for most of the poor in New York was higher than for their counterparts in the home country—many were able to furnish their apartments relatively comfortably and had access to better clothes and food, including, as immigrants often bragged to their relatives back home, meat two or even three times a day.[19]

What Rebecca Yamin, the director of the interpretive phase of the Courthouse project, and her research team found in looking at the records and artifacts from the tenements on the Courthouse site adds an important dimension to this picture. Their work underlines the dissonance between the stereotypes portrayed in contemporary descriptions of life in the Five Points and what life was actually like for many of the people who lived there. Although some of the artifacts support the stereotypical view of the slum, other discoveries repudiate that stereotype and instead suggest that at least some of the residents had a vision of home life that would not have been completely foreign to members of the city's middle class. The artifacts from one privy, for example, "included matching dishes and serving pieces, as many as six tea sets, including three imported from Staffordshire, one of bone china, and one of Chinese porcelain, and extensive glassware including an unusual lacy pressed square bowl manufactured in New England, and numerous cut decanters. The tenants ate imported condiments, cured their ailments with prescribed medicines, and saved their pennies in a redware bank."[20] Their study supports the view that the term *slum* as applied to working-class neighborhoods in New York is an oversimplification; the city's poorer communities were complex places. This becomes clearer in looking at the records and artifacts from one of the tenements in the Five Points district.

Heather Griggs, one of the archaeologists working on the Courthouse project, took a close look at a predominately Irish tenement on Pearl Street. Using a combination of historical and archaeological data, she discovered enormous diversity among that building's residents. Although many of the tenement's occupants were unskilled laborers and seamstresses, some artisans and entrepreneurs who owned their own businesses also lived there. Griggs was able to study the financial dealings of some of these entrepreneurs by examining their banking records at the Emigrant Savings Bank. She discovered, for example, that Timothy Lynch, a tinsmith who lived with his family in the tenement in the 1850s, moved as much as six hundred dollars in and out of his bank account every month over a four-year period. This is the same amount of money that the *New York Times,* in 1853, estimated a workingman's family needed to survive for a whole year. Lynch was certainly doing better than most of his fellow tinsmiths; although there is no record of illegal doings, he may have been making his money in the underground economy. Lynch's neighbor Michael McLoughlin, the brother of the Pearl Street tenement's owner, kept more than two thousand dollars in his bank account over a three-year period in the mid-1850s.[21]

The artifacts found in the backyard cesspool were not at all what the archaeologists had expected to find in one of the poorest sections of the city. They found dishes in a variety of brightly colored printed and molded white patterns, a few gilded porcelains, elegant stemmed glasses, and a cruet of imported Irish glass. They did not find many serving dishes, suggesting that American middle-class standards for respectable dining were not followed by Irish immigrant families. But they did find decorative figurines and flowerpots, showing that the residents had definite visions of what constituted proper home life. The artifacts included a teacup printed with the image of Father Theobold Mathew, the founder of Ireland's temperance movement (fig. 12.8), suggesting that temperance may have been highly valued in at least one tenement home. The archaeologists also found children's things—cups printed with names and didactic sayings, toy tea sets, porcelain dolls, dominoes, and marbles—that were identical to those found in middle-class neighborhoods. Conventional wisdom had held that the children of the tenements had to spend their time scavenging for things they could sell in order to contribute to their families' finances. But, as Griggs notes, these toys suggest that "some children . . . may not have been required to work . . . to supplement the family income" but instead "were being raised with a set of [middle-class] values that emphasized . . . individual and private property, values that would allow them to succeed in American society."[22]

The study of the Pearl Street tenement suggests that for many, the support of the local immigrant community was so important that it overrode distinctions of money and class. Successful members of the immigrant communities in New York do not seem to have attempted to conform to nineteenth-century American protocol by moving to middle-class neighborhoods, where they probably would not have been welcomed anyway. Instead, they, like the immigrants who preceded and succeeded them, continued to live among their relatives and friends of the same ethnic group in the neighborhoods where they owned property, and where their children prepared for entry into the middle class. But these successful members of the community were unusual. For most of the residents, life was much harder.

The artifacts found in one backyard privy at the Courthouse site were very different from those found in other features on the block: there were some very ornate ceramics; an unusually high number of chamber pots (thirty-seven in all); three glass urinals, all designed for women (fig. 12.9); and a ceramic pot inscribed with the words "AMAILLE, s.d. Vinaigrier." The privy also contained the skeletons of three infants—two newborns and a fetus. Taken together, these objects suggested to Yamin that at least some of the privy's contents may have come from a brothel. At first, Yamin was not sure she could prove it—illegal businesses like brothels tend not to be listed in such records as city directories. But she had a stroke of luck when she consulted Timothy Gilfoyle, a historian who studies prostitution in nineteenth-century New York. His research had discovered that a John Donohue had been indicted for running a "common, ill-governed, and disorderly house" in the cellar of 12 Orange Street (one of the buildings on the lot where the privy was found) in 1843—right around the time that the artifacts had been discarded. This fact provided a convincing link for Yamin's argument that many of the artifacts in the privy had come from a brothel and indicated that they had been thrown away when the brothel was closed down.[23]

In the nineteenth century, prostitution was the most lucrative occupation open to a working-class woman. Most prostitutes came from working-class families where a parent had died or where there were problems at home. Although many young women worked at prostitution full-time, others worked in other trades and occasionally used prostitution to supplement their incomes. Most left "the life" by the time they were thirty or so and went on either to marriage or to another profession. Many others died young, from venereal diseases, from violence directly related to their occupation, or from the complications of

12.8. A teacup, printed with the image of Father Theobold Mathew (the founder of Ireland's temperance movement), from the Courthouse site.

drug or alcohol addiction. A few stayed in the business and went on to own and run their own brothels as madams. In the mid-nineteenth century, being a madam was the only way that a woman could hold a managerial position and even be an entrepreneur. In other words, although prostitution posed serious risks to all of its practitioners and often had tragic consequences, it had a strong economic allure: it could not only provide a good income for young women (for a short period of time); it also offered a few women substantial financial opportunities that they had in no other line of work.[24]

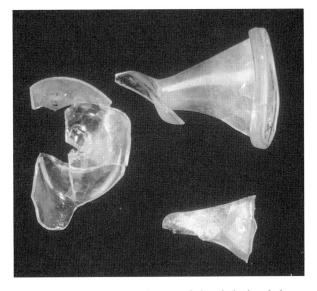

12.9. Glass urinals from the privy behind the brothel at the Courthouse site.

Although historians know a great deal about what middle-class reformers thought about prostitutes and brothels, they know very little about brothels from the points of view of the women who worked in them or the men who were their customers. When Yamin examined the objects from the privy, they provided her with a new perspective that underlined the duality between the private lives of the young women and their public lives at work. The more ornate ceramics that came from the privy were almost consistently the kind that were used among the middle class at that time for entertaining; in this case, they were presumably used for entertaining their middle-class male customers, who would expect such amenities. There was an old-fashioned tea set made of Chinese export porcelain, which included chocolate cups as well as tea cups, and other showy tea cups as well. Punch cups and the ninety-nine wine bottles found in the privy suggest that drinking played an important role in brothel life. The wine was probably served in tumblers—there were sixty-six tumblers but just a few wineglasses. There was also a large number of small plates, brightly decorated in printed patterns, which might have been used for serving snacks. These snacks probably included brandied fruits, olives, or capers (evidenced by wide-mouthed bottles, used for storing these foods), veal (evidenced by the bones from calves), soft-shell clams (evidenced by their distinctive shells), and coffee (evidenced by coffee beans). All these foods were not found in other features at the Courthouse site. The archaeologists also uncovered three glass bird feeders—objects that otherwise have been found in New York only at sites associated with middle-class families.[25]

The archaeologists found many personal items that the young women may have used for their public performances—perfume bottles, a miniature flask, combs, a hair brush, mirror fragments, and the ribs from a folding fan. They also recovered sewing materials—not only the hooks and eyes and straight pins that archaeologists often find, but also more elaborate sewing equipment, including a folding ruler, a carved bone stiletto for making decorative holes in embroidery, a delicate thimble, and some bobbins for making lace. A contemporary account describes prostitutes as sewing or knitting in the brothels as they waited for customers; this equipment might have been used by the young women as props when they were on display.

There were also poignant reminders of the hidden, dangerous, and tragic side of prostitution. The three women's urinals presumably were used when the young women were sick in bed, perhaps from the venereal disease that was one of their occupational hazards—a contemporary study shows that almost half the prostitutes practicing in the city at mid-century suffered from syphilis. In addition to a syringe, thirty-nine medicine bottles were found in the privy, one—embossed BRISTOL'S EXTRACT OF SARSAPARILLA—prescribed specifically for venereal disease, others for general stomach ailments. But most tragic of all were the remains of the three infants. Two of the infants had come to term; it is not known if they died of natural causes or were the victims of infanticide. The third, who had not reached term, had been aborted, either deliberately or spontaneously. But none of these infants had been buried; instead, their deaths had been hidden. All in all, Yamin's study presents a complex picture of the women of the brothel.[26]

Faunal experts Pamela Crabtree and Claudia Milne studied animal bones and shell from the Courthouse site in order to find out about the diet of the people who lived there. Faunal experts are well aware of the pitfalls involved in making inferences about diet from such remains. They have evidence only for the parts of people's diets that included meat from the bones or shells that people disposed of at home. By contrast, butcher-bought boneless cuts of meat (such as Italian and German sausages, stewing meats, or hamburger) and shucked shellfish (such as preserved oysters) are invisible in the archaeological record.[27]

This limitation notwithstanding, Crabtree and Milne's study of the animal bones from the features at the Courthouse site revealed that different ethnic groups showed definite preferences for different kinds of meat. One building was occupied by several northern European families. Two were German—headed by Samuel Stone, who ran a secondhand clothing store, and Samuel Lubra, a tailor—while the third—headed by Lambert Blower, also a tailor—was Dutch. The bones found in the backyard cistern that these three families shared included a preponderance of those from sheep—in fact, more sheep bones were found there than in any other feature from the site. Because the bones were from older sheep and not lambs, it was clear that at least one of the families ate a lot of mutton. The bones also showed that the mutton was usually bought by the leg. Germans are not known for eating mutton, but it was relatively cheap in New York City at the time, and that could well have been the important factor.[28]

Around the corner was the Irish Pearl Street tenement that we discussed above. For at least some of the families in this building, the meat of choice was pork, which was one of the cheaper meats available in the city but by no means the cheapest. The large number of foot bones from pigs showed a preference for pigs' feet. They may have been simmered in wine and spices to make crubeen, a traditional Irish favorite. Also found among the pig bones were fragments of bottles that had held Lea and Perrins Worcestershire Sauce and pepper sauce, showing that, as Heather Griggs put it, the residents were following "their cultural tastes, even if this were more costly than . . . alternatives."[29]

The meat preferences of the immigrant groups were not only different from each others' but were also very different from the Robsons', the native-born, upper-middle-class family who lived on Washington Square. The animal bones from their privy (and from those of other middle-class New Yorkers) showed a definite preference for beef; bones from cattle were much more prevalent than those from sheep, pigs, or fish.[30]

Down the street from the German families was a tenement where several Italian and Polish families lived. The faunal remains found in the privy they shared included not only the food bones that the analysts expected (this group seems to have shown a strong preference for fish, particularly cod, suggesting that many of the tenants were Catholics who ate fish on meatless days) and the bones of the cats and rats that also lived in the tenement, but also the bones from a small male monkey. Italian organ grinders traditionally used monkeys from Central and South America to pass around the cup for tips, and census records listed many organ grinders on the Courthouse block in the last half of the century. The monkey's bones provide a vivid reminder of this way of making a living, one that persisted well into the twentieth century. Further research showed the analysts that organ grinders usually hired, rather than bought, not only their instruments but also the monkeys (which were often worth twenty or thirty dollars).[31]

The Five Points and Washington Square are neighborhoods that were built on landfill—they had both been low-lying land before the beginning of the nineteenth century. Landfilling by claiming land from rivers and marshes has been one of the major themes of New York's growth from the seventeenth through the twentieth centuries; it has been used to create some of the most valuable real estate in the city. In the next chapter we investigate what archaeologists have learned about claiming land from the rivers.

CHAPTER THIRTEEN

Building the City: The Waterfront

Although the goods that passed through the port of New York formed the city's economic base throughout most of its history, an important component of the city's economy was, and still is, its real estate. In fact, a real estate deal forms the central event in the popular myth that describes the birth of the city: Peter Minuit's purchase of the entire island of Manhattan from the Munsee Indians in 1626 for a mere twenty-four dollars' worth of trinkets (see chapter 8 for the Munsee perspective on this deal).[1] In fact, a large part of the story of the physical growth of the city (as well the private fortunes of many of its residents) is the story of the growth of the city's real estate market. Over and over again, as the city grew northward from the tip of Manhattan Island, speculators bought up huge tracts of land just beyond its edge and then, as the city continued to grow, subdivided these parcels into urban lots that they sold at enormous profits.

As part of this commodification of land, the Europeans altered the city's terrain on an unprecedented scale. They leveled hills, drained marshes, and filled in ravines to make the land suitable for their needs. They even made new land by claiming it from the rivers. People tend to think of the process of adding landfill along the city's shores as a modern phenomenon, one that was made feasible only after the introduction of modern earth-moving equipment like front-end loaders and backhoes. But in fact, the city's residents began making new land well over three hundred years ago, soon after the first European settlement. They focused this activity on that part of the outpost that contained its most valuable real estate—along the shore adjacent to the East River port. In the intervening centuries, New Yorkers conducted landfilling operations in all five boroughs, including much of the shoreline of the modern city. And during the past few decades, archaeologists have been able to study the early transformation of Manhattan's waterfront.

Views and old maps of the city provide an overall picture of the development of the waterfront and the landfill process in New York. Because the East River port was the city's economic focus until the mid-nineteenth century, it was a popular subject for the artists who portrayed the settlement. They drew views from ships anchored in the river, from Governors Island in the city's harbor, or from Brooklyn, then a separate town across the river. By comparing the views and maps from different periods, we can trace the development of the waterfront and the landfilling process from the time of the first Dutch settlement.

The appearance of the port in the mid-seventeenth century was amazingly different from its aspect even fifty years later. A view depicting New Amsterdam at the southern tip of Manhattan Island around 1650 shows the East River shoreline before most alterations had begun (see fig. 2.2). With the exception of a small wharf, the riverfront then was untouched, with a narrow beach extending down from the low-lying island to the river. The Dutch called this area along the shore the Strand, which means "beach" in their language as well as in English.

Beginning in the 1650s, New Amsterdammers began to develop the waterfront, and within a decade its configuration had changed completely (see fig. 2.3). First, to counteract the continual erosion of the shore in front of the Stadt Huys, the municipal government ordered the building of a seawall. By the 1660s, this wall extended all along the East River shore and linked up with the city's defensive palisade at today's Wall Street. Second, the New Amsterdammers, following Dutch tradition, dug a canal, or Gracht, on the line of today's Broad Street to drain the low-lying swampy ground there. Three bridges crossed the canal, which small craft could enter at high tide. Throughout this period, ships anchored in the East River, where small boats loaded and unloaded them, as the water was too shallow for dockage along the shore.

After the English conquered New Amsterdam and rechristened it New York, they continued to develop the waterfront. By the 1670s they had filled in the Gracht and had built the Great Dock, which extended out into the East River, enclosing a marina where boats could moor (see fig. 2.4). But the innovation that was to have the most profound impact on the changing shoreline was the Dongan Charter (1680), which set the precedent of allowing the city government to raise revenue by selling "water lots," or the right to build wharves and "make land" out in the rivers between the low and high watermarks. And its successor, the Montgomerie Charter (1731), granted the city the additional power to sell water lots extending *beyond* the low watermark, four hundred feet out into the water. Under these charters, those who bought water lots were required to fill them in at their own expense. At the time that the Dongan Charter was adopted, the East River shoreline was still located at today's Pearl Street, three blocks inland from South Street, which forms the shoreline today, while the Hudson shore was located near today's Greenwich Street, four blocks east of the modern shore. Beginning in the 1680s, the city began to sell the water lots that would eventually form the land between the seventeenth-century shoreline and the shoreline of today.

The making of land accomplished two goals for early New Yorkers. First of all, it extended the city's shoreline beyond the shallow water near the natural shore so that eventually ships could tie up at landside wharves instead of having to anchor out in the river. Second, the "made land" provided more of the city's most valuable real estate—the low-lying area adjacent to the harbor—which merchants could develop to accommodate the warehouses and stores they needed to handle the goods entering and leaving the port. By the eighteenth century, these newly made waterfront parcels had become the bases of operations for some of the city's richest mercantile families, such as the Schermerhorns and Van Cortlandts, who often acquired the right to make land through their political connections with the city's government.[2]

Old maps provide us with an overview of the landfilling process, which occurred on a lot-by-lot basis. These lots eventually formed block-wide ribbons of new land running parallel to the shore. By the late 1720s (see fig. 11.1) land had been claimed up to today's Water Street, and by the end of the century (see fig. 11.2) the next ribbon of land, between Water and Front Streets on the east side, was completed and landfilling had begun on the west side as well.

New York's waterfront during the colonial period is unusual among the British American colonial cities in that New Yorkers did not build many piers that projected out into the harbor; they built slips instead. As blocks of landfill were added along the East River waterfront, fill was added out into the water on either side of the ends of the larger streets that ran perpendicular to the shore, forming slips or inlets where small boats could moor (see fig. 11.1). Later, as a subsequent block of landfill was added, the original slip was filled in and converted into a dry street and a new slip took its place (see fig. 11.2). These filled-in slips provided large pieces of public land that were often the sites of markets, as they were located conveniently close to landings where farmers could moor their boats and unload livestock and produce for sale.[3]

The landfill process continued in the early nineteenth century, and the ribbons of land between Front and South Streets on the east side and between Washington and West Streets on the west side were gradually completed (see fig. 11.3). By 1840, lower Manhattan had achieved the silhouette that would characterize it for more than a century, until the 1960s. Then New Yorkers once more began to claim and build the new blocks of land in the Hudson River that resulted in Battery Park City, just to the west of the World Trade Center. Today, well over a third of Manhattan south of City Hall is land claimed from the rivers.

During the past few decades, archaeologists have conducted excavations on many landfill blocks in the city. Most of the sites, which date from the seventeenth through the early nineteenth centuries, are located along Manhattan's East River waterfront. The excavations in the landfill have allowed archaeologists to flesh out the story of how early urban dwellers first made the land and then built upon it. They have pinpointed the sources of the material used to make up the landfill and they have documented how early builders held the landfill in place so that it would not be washed away by tides and currents. Furthermore, they have delineated techniques that early New Yorkers developed for building on newly made land so that buildings did not crack and crumble as the fill continued to settle beneath them. Finally, they have discovered the presence of archaeological sites that were created *before* the landfill was installed and that have been preserved beneath it.

The Archaeology of Landfill

Archaeologists have discovered that early New Yorkers obtained their fill from almost any place where they could find a supply of appropriate material. Digging in lower Manhattan, archaeologists have found dark gray silty deposits in some landfills, indicating that the soil had been dredged up from nearby slips that had silted up so much that it was difficult to sail boats into them. They have found trash in some landfills, showing that the landfill had been used as a dumping ground by both local residents and the workers who picked up garbage around the city. They have also found remarkably clean fill, suggesting that it had come from razing a hill or excavating a cellar hole. More surprisingly, they have found fill made up of "exotic" materials, which presumably entered the harbor as ship ballast before being dumped in the landfill. In fact, the fill can sometimes help trace the voyages of some of the ships that anchored in the harbor. At several sites, archaeologists have found coralline sand and large pieces of coral from the Caribbean, brought in on ships plying the Caribbean trade. They have also found large pieces of English flint, testimony to the trans-Atlantic trade.

Artifacts that archaeologists find in the landfill can date to any period before the fill was used to make land. When they excavate seventeenth-century landfill, for example, all the artifacts they find date to the seventeenth century or earlier. These early artifacts are invaluable because so few traces exist of the brief four decades of Dutch rule and the long eleven-thousand-year presence of Native Americans in what became the city. The artifacts from one seventeenth-century landfill include fragments of dishes and tobacco pipes and even the soles and heels from seventeenth-century shoes, all reminders of the European presence (fig. 13.1). At another seventeenth-century landfill site, archaeologists found several Native American artifacts, including spear points, Late Woodland arrowheads, and even a weight used to sink a fishing net.[4]

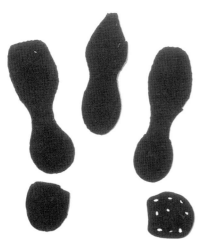

13.1. Fragments of seventeenth-century shoes from the landfill at 7 Hanover Square.

Archaeologists working in landfill can learn about important concerns of the day, some of which were matters of life and death to the city's inhabitants. During the summers of the 1790s and early 1800s, the city was swept by a series of yellow-fever epidemics. At that time doctors did not agree about the causes of yellow fever or how this disease spread (it was not until the beginning of the twentieth century that it was confirmed that yellow fever is transmitted by mosquitoes). One common hypothesis was that yellow fever was spread through the vapors or miasmas given off by decaying organic material, and one place that such miasmas could be found was in landfill, which was often made up of garbage. Physician Richard Bayley graphically described the garbage and other objects that he saw being used for landfill in 1796: "Carts were employed to collect such dirt and filth as all large and populous cities furnish in abundance; and with materials of this description [it] was filled up, and to give greater salubrity to the mass, there were occasionally added, dead horses, dogs, cats, hogs, &c. &c."[5] That same year, in response to the yellow-fever epidemics, the city created the Department of Health and made Bayley its first health commissioner. Soon after, the city enacted regulations demanding that clean sand be used to fill in the water lots and bring them up to grade.

But ordinances, of course, are not always followed. This became clear when archaeologist Joan Geismar, working with the data from two sites she had excavated, compared the garbage content of the landfill to determine how effective these ordinances were. One site, 175 Water Street on the East River, was created in the mid-eighteenth century, long before yellow fever had become a serious issue in the city. The other, located on the Hudson River on the west side, was filled between 1797 and 1817, after the ordinance had been issued and while yellow fever was still a concern.

Geismar discovered that the ordinances prescribing clean fill *were* taken seriously during the period when the epidemics raged. In comparing the amounts of artifacts or garbage from the landfill from the two areas, she discovered that garbage was more than five times as dense in the landfill at the East River site than at the west side site. The earlier landfill had especially large quantities of leather scraps and animal bone in it —exactly the organic material to create the miasmas that later became of such concern. Yet the later fill, which was deposited during the period of the epidemics, was by no means completely clean. Geismar found a large cache of bones, including the skulls and jaws of cattle, suggesting that the area may have been used for illegal dumping by butchers from a nearby market. So although the fears of yellow fever and the city regulations to improve the city's sanitation certainly had an effect on the behavior of most people, some New Yorkers flouted these rules.[6]

Obtaining material to use for landfill is only one of the problems involved in making land. Another is figuring out how to hold the landfill in place so that it is not washed away by tides and currents. Before the nineteenth century, these techniques were not documented in written records. Instead, they formed part of a vernacular tradition, passed down orally from master craftsman to apprentice, that has since been lost. But archaeologists working in New York have rediscovered some of these traditions.

Wooden-plank bulkheads provide the simplest solution to this problem, archaeologists have found. But they have seen other solutions as well. They have uncovered sections of large wooden wharves, known as cobb wharves, which are made of log frames filled with large stones or cobbles (hence the term *cobb*) and then sunk in place in the river. These are much stronger than plank bulkheads and were used not only to retain landfill but to provide dockage for boats and support for waterfront buildings. Contemporary views (see, for example, the lower right corner of fig. 10.8) and written accounts give us some information about these wharves. Hector St. John de Crevecoeur, a Frenchman who lived in the British American colonies in the late eighteenth century, wrote: "I have seen them made in forty feet of water. This is done with the trunks of pine attached together which they gradually sink, fill in with stone and cover the surface with earth." But these contemporary descriptions are not detailed enough to reveal how these wharves were actually made.[7]

Archaeologists interested in studying waterfront structures like wharves face two problems. The first, of course, is finding a wharf in their project area. If an entire set of water lots was filled in at around the same time, there may be no large fill-retaining structures inside the archaeological site, which in lower Manhattan is almost inevitably confined inside the borders of a modern city block. The larger and more permanent retaining structures are instead located at the river end of the original water lots, which are now under the modern sidewalk or street. The other problem is that these structures extend well below the water table, down to the bottom of the river. Archaeologists usually have access to pumps during their excavations, but these pumps can remove the water only from small areas because of the rate at which the water flows back in.

Before 1984, archaeologists had discovered several cobb wharves at the East River landfill sites; however, because of pumping problems, they could only partially uncover and document them. But owing to a fortuitous set of circumstances, archaeologists Roselle Henn and Diana Wall and their crew were able to uncover and record more than one hundred feet of one of these wharf systems, all the way down to the old river bottom, at the Assay site. This site, located between Front and South Streets just north of Old Slip, in the shadow of the East River Drive on the modern shore (see fig. 1.2), was claimed from the river at the beginning of the nineteenth century and in 1984 was about to be turned into Financial Square, a modern office tower.[8]

As is usually the case, before going into the field the archaeologists had studied the property's history, which old maps showed was both complex and provocative. One map (see fig. 11.2), which documented the block in the 1780s, before any landfill had been added to it, showed several piers extending from Front Street out into the river, through the area that would later become the block. Another showed that less than a decade later (fig. 13.2), the block had been partially filled in in an L-shaped configuration: land had been made in the southern half and northwest quarter of the block while a small basin was still unfilled on the northeast quarter of the site. Finally, by 1803, the block was completely filled in—the basin was gone.

The maps showed, then, that the block had been filled in at least two episodes: three-quarters of it had been made between 1789 and 1797, while the fill in the fourth quarter had been added later, after 1797. Because the archaeologists would be digging in the northern half of the block, they realized that they had a good chance of uncovering both the north-south wharf that supported the fill deposited on the west, or landward, side of the little basin in the 1790s and the wharf along its southern boundary.

13.2. A detail of the Taylor-Roberts Plan, showing New York in 1796. The partially filled Assay site block is shown two blocks to the left of Wall Street, on the river side of Front Street.

When the archaeologists explored the locations of the wharves shown on the map of 1797, they discovered the tops of both the north-south wharves and the pier that had once extended out into the river. Although Henn and Wall were thrilled that they had found the wharves, they were also disheartened. The water table at the site was so high that they knew that all they could do was record the uppermost parts of the structures.

But here the archaeologists had a stroke of luck. Throughout the earlier part of the project, construction workers had been building a slurry wall around the edge of the southern part of the site, south of the area where the archaeologists were working. The slurry wall, which was made by pouring concrete into a narrow trench dug down to bedrock, would eventually form a wall enclosing the entire site, sealing it off from groundwater. After its completion, water could

13.3. The wharves that made up the seawall on the Assay site in the 1790s. The block-and-bridge wharf is on the left.

be pumped out of the block and would not seep back in. The construction workers had finished the slurry wall on the southern part of the block and now wanted to continue their work around the northern edge of the site, in the area where the archaeologists were working. The archaeologists realized that if they had access to the wharves after the slurry wall was completed, they could do the unprecedented: record the construction of the wharves all the way down to the bottom of the river.

The archaeologists and the Landmarks Preservation Commission began a series of negotiations with the developer, the Howard Ronson Organization. The compromise they reached represented a win for both sides: construction could begin immediately on the slurry wall in the northern part of the site, but the archaeologists would have access to the wharves after the slurry wall was finished.

Throughout July 1984, the archaeological crew worked on recording the wharves. First the backhoe removed all the landfill alongside the wharves in the area where the marina had been in the 1790s (fig. 13.3). Then the crew began to make scale drawings and take photographs of the wharves. They even excavated inside them in several places. By the end of July, they had recorded the construction of the wharves in their entirety, a feat that might never be accomplished again.

They discovered that the landfill on the west side of the marina was held in place by two separate north-south wharves that were made in a similar manner and that abutted each other. Each wharf was about forty-five feet long and fifteen feet high and consisted of a framework of heavy timbers, each well over a foot in diameter, and a

floor of split timbers that rested on the lowermost logs. The framework formed a series of four- to eight-foot-long cells (fig. 13.4). Each cell was filled with ballast, made up of field stones and large pieces of coral, that rested on the floor; the weight of the ballast sank the wharf and anchored it in place. Cross-ties fastened with dovetailed joints were used to reinforce the structure. Above the floors, toward the tops of the wharves, was a series of semi-platforms made up of smaller logs that did not extend all the way through the wharf. The semi-platforms served to redistribute the weight of the ballast so that its pressure would not cause the outer wall to collapse. All the logs were attached to each other through various forms of wood joinery; there was no metal hardware in the structure. The only metal fasteners found were used to connect upright braces extending from the bottom to the top of the wharves at each end, to prevent them from shimmying.[9]

The third wharf at the site, the one that formed the southern seawall of the 1790s marina, was very different—it was made up of two different kinds of structures (see fig. 13.3). One consisted of a series of square "blocks," about twenty feet on a side and set about forty feet apart, that were built in a manner similar to the north-south wharves. Between the blocks were simple wooden bulkheads, which together with the blocks formed a solid seawall to hold back the landfill. But why were there two different seawall structures? After rechecking their old maps and studying later views of the shoreline, the archaeologists realized that the different structures had been built at different times. One set—the blocks—had been built before the 1780s, long before any landfill had been added to the area, as part of the pier that extended out into the river; this is the pier shown on the map of 1789. While the pier was in use, the blocks were spanned by "bridges" of planks, providing a road-like surface so that carts could roll out along the pier (fig. 13.5). The block-and-bridge style was preferred for building piers out into the river because currents could run freely between the blocks and prevent the buildup of silt and filth resulting from more solid constructions. In fact, in 1798 (long after this particular pier was built) the city required this kind of pier construction to help fight yellow fever.[10] But the excavations at the Assay site showed that block-and-bridge piers were in use well before the epidemics. After the decision had been made to fill the area south of the pier, the plank bridges were removed and the spaces between the blocks were filled with simple bulkheads to

13.4. A view inside the wharves. Most of the ballast that had formerly been between the logs has been removed, although some rocks are visible under the central log.

13.5. View of a block-and-bridge wharf on the Hudson River, ca. 1807. From Valentine's Manual, *1859. Collection of the New-York Historical Society, negative number 74145.*

hold back the landfill. The complete uncovering of the north-south wharves and of the faces of several of the blocks from the block-and-bridge pier at the Assay site allowed us to understand the fabric of New York's waterfront as it existed in the eighteenth and early nineteenth centuries.[11]

Although by no means as ubiquitous as the wooden bulkheads and wharves, the most dramatic examples of structures used to hold back the fill are the derelict ships that have been discovered in Manhattan's landfill. The hulls of the ships provided the physical support needed to hold the fill in place, so that it would not be washed away by tides. Ships discovered in archaeological contexts are extremely important in that they offer concrete examples of how these vessels were built throughout the past, during periods when shipbuilding was still largely a vernacular tradition; for example, there are neither plans nor models showing how ships were made in the colonial period.

When excavations began at the 175 Water Street site in 1981, Joan Geismar was directing her first large-scale urban project. The site was being dug before its development by the Howard Ronson Organization for the American headquarters of the National Westminster Bank. Before fieldwork began, background research showed that this site was made up of landfill that had been deposited in the mid-eighteenth century. Geismar focused the excavations primarily on the site's old backyards so that she and her crew could discover the artifacts that had been left by the people who had lived and

worked on the block after the landfill was in place; her aim was to address issues of trade and economics. The archaeologists planned to confine their exploration of the landfill to four "deep tests," or large holes that would be dug by the backhoe.[12]

Excavations began in late October. By the first of the year, the field season was drawing to a close. The excavation of the backyards, which had been very productive, was almost finished, and only one deep test in the landfill remained to be dug. On January 6, as the backhoe excavated this fourth and final deep test, which was located near Front Street, close to the middle of the block, the earth fell away, revealing a wooden structure. At first the archaeologists assumed that it was a plank bulkhead, like those that had been found at other landfill sites in the area. But as the backhoe exposed more of the structure, its curved shape and outer sheathing of pitch and horsehair indicated that they had found a ship. The discovery of the ship was not completely unexpected. A few years earlier, part of a ship had been discovered in the landfill under 207–209 Water Street at the South Street Seaport Museum. Archaeologist Robert Schuyler and his students had been able to uncover only a small part of the ship because it was under a standing building.[13]

After the identification of the ship at 175 Water Street was confirmed, nautical archaeologists Warren Riess and Sheli Smith were called in, and for the next thirty-four days they supervised the crew, who worked overtime to uncover the ship and record how it was made. Almost all of the ship was inside the site block and accessible to the archaeologists. She proved to be a ninety-two-foot-long, twenty-five-foot-wide merchant vessel, built with a blunt bow to carry more cargo. The tropical shipworms, or *teredos,* embedded in her pitch-and-horsehair sheathing testified that the ship had played a role in the triangular trade; she had probably transported agricultural produce from New York to feed the enslaved on the plantations in the British West Indies and carried rum, sugar, and molasses back to New York.[14]

The ship had been stripped of all of the hardware that could possibly be reused, floated out to the river side of the water lots that were about to be filled at what would later become Front Street, and tied into a wooden bulkhead line. Her hull was then loaded with a ballast of coralline sand, granite cobbles, and yellow brick clinkers, and she was sunk in place. The ship formed the boundary for the eastern ends of the four water lots belonging to five merchants who had obviously worked cooperatively in organizing the sinking of the ship, which would help in the filling and stabilizing of their newly made land (fig. 13.6).[15]

The excavation of the ship (dubbed the *Ronson,* after the developer who paid for the excavations) generated enormous excitement even among that most jaded of audiences, resident New Yorkers. On a freezing cold Sunday in February, more than eleven thousand of them waited on line to file past the site so they could see the ship. Some

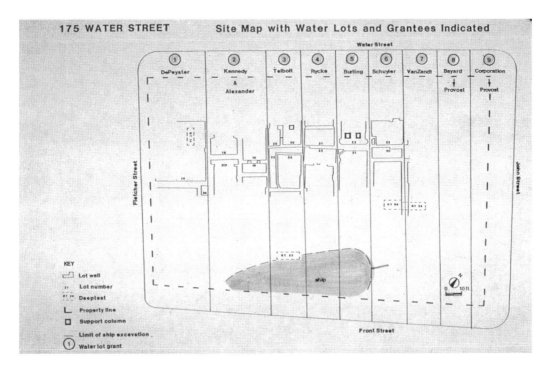

13.6. Map of the 175 Water Street site, showing the water lots, the names of their owners, and the location of the ship that was sunk to hold the landfill in place.

New Yorkers wanted the whole vessel to be excavated, conserved, and reconstructed so that it could go on display in the city where it had been scuttled. However, the wooden ship owed its preservation to the fact that it had been buried under the ground and below the water table for more than two hundred years. Once taken out of that environment, the wood from the ship would begin to deteriorate quickly and would need to be conserved. Estimates for removing, conserving, and then exhibiting such an enormous artifact ran to $6 million, a hefty price tag. As a compromise, a twenty-foot section of the ship's bow was removed and sent away for conservation at the developer's expense; the rest of the ship's timbers were measured, photographed, and destroyed (fig. 13.7).

Almost three years after the initial discovery, a new quest began. The $350,000 pledged by the developer to conserve and store the ship's bow was running out and the bow was ready for a permanent home, but it was proving hard to find one. New York's mayor, Ed Koch, called a news conference to announce that unless a museum in New York came forward to take responsibility for the *Ronson,* she would go to the Maritime Museum in Newport News, Virginia, which had pledged $400,000 to house

13.7. Archaeologists recording the structure of the Ronson.

and display the bow. Unfortunately, no New York museum could match this offer. So the bow of a New York eighteenth-century merchant ship now makes its home in Virginia. As of this writing, however, the ship is expected to be returned to New York as a permanent exhibit at the South Street Seaport Museum.[16]

After landfill is put into place, it takes a long time to settle, and any buildings that rest on it while it is settling soon begin to crack. Ever since people first began making land, builders have been coming up with engineering solutions to this problem. Today, structures built on landfill usually rest on steel pilings that are driven through the landfill and the underlying natural soil to bedrock, which supports the weight of the building. Archaeologists have discovered that in the past, New Yorkers have used several solutions to this problem.

The oldest of these solutions was first discovered in 1981 at 7 Hanover Square (see fig. 1.2), where an office tower was being built just a block north of the Stadt Huys Block and the Fraunces Tavern Museum. This was the first large-scale excavation of a landfill site in the city. Before fieldwork began, the site's background study showed that the fill here was extremely old: it had been deposited on the block, which was just next to the Pearl Street shore, in the 1680s and 1690s. Nan Rothschild, Arnold Pickman, and Diana Wall, the project's directors, were interested in exploring the nature of the landfill and the underlying shore deposits, as well as looking for fill-retaining structures.

The crew began the excavations by placing several test cuts on different parts of the site to sample the landfill. But as they dug, they kept finding deeply buried stone walls. The archaeologists decided to follow these maze-like walls through the site to see where they went and what they were. Much to their amazement, they soon discovered that the stone walls were the foundation walls of the earliest buildings that had been built on the Pearl Street side of the block, dating from the 1690s. Furthermore, they realized that these walls extended all the way down through the landfill and rested on the original shore. The walls had not been destroyed when later buildings were built on top of them only because the walls extended to such great depths.

Ultimately, the archaeologists realized that what they were dealing with at 7 Hanover Square was a seventeenth-century solution to the structural problem of building on unstable landfill in an intertidal zone, and perhaps it was a method to hold the fill in place as well. This technique allowed the load of each building to rest on its foundation walls, which in turn rested on the original river shore beneath the fill. In other words, the stable natural shore, instead of the unstable landfill, bore the weight of the building.[17]

Because the seventeenth-century builders had come up with this solution to the problem of building on fill, the archaeologists were able to uncover the foundation walls of seven of the houses that had been built on the landward, or Pearl Street, side of the block in the 1680s and 1690s (fig. 13.8). They uncovered the walls of the English-style mansion belonging to Robert Livingston on the large water lot that he had acquired from Captain William Kidd, the famous privateer, in 1693. They also found the walls of six more-modest houses that a contemporary view shows had been built in the Dutch stepped-gable style for Livingston's ethnically Dutch neighbors to the north. Like the landowners on the 175 Water Street site, who had arranged cooperatively to scuttle the ship to hold the landfill, these six landowners at 7 Hanover Square also cooperated in building the back wall for their houses—the three-foot-wide wall formed a continuous back building line for all six houses. These buildings were still standing in 1717, when they were incorporated into a view of the New York shore from the East River (see fig. 10.8).[18]

Laying deep stone walls that rested on original land would work only when building on landfill blocks that were in the intertidal zone and close to the original shore. When new land was made further out, in deeper parts of the river, this technique was impractical—the stone walls would have had to have been laid under water. Instead, archaeologists have discovered two other solutions that early builders devised for building on this deeper landfill. One is extremely common and has been recorded at site after site; the other has been found at only one site. These two solutions follow two different principles.

Most commonly, early builders rested a building's

13.8. The seventeenth-century stone walls at the 7 Hanover Square site. The Livingston house, which takes up two lots, is in the lower left corner of the view; the Dutch houses are the smaller ones toward the top of the image.

13.9. A spread-footer complex from the Assay site.

stone foundation wall on top of a wooden complex called a spread-footer (fig. 13.9). To make a spread-footer, builders first laid a series of heavy wooden planks side by side, perpendicular to the line of the foundation wall that they were building. These planks formed a platform about five feet wide running the entire length of the wall. Then the builders laid one or two large wooden beams, with square cross-sections of up to a foot on a side, down the middle of the plank platform in line with the foundation wall. Finally, they laid the building's stone foundation wall on top of the wooden beams. This construction technique spreads the load of the building over the wider area covered by the underlying plank platform, so that in effect the building floats on top of the landfill. Builders' guides from the early nineteenth century mention these spread-footers and stress that they should be placed below the water table, so that the wood will remain constantly wet and therefore will not decay. In all the cases where archaeologists have found spread-footers in Manhattan, they have found them below the water table.

The builders who constructed the first series of buildings in what had been the open basin or marina at the Assay site came up with a solution for building on landfill that has not been found anywhere else in the city. The structures, which were built right after the marina was filled in, rested on pilings. These were made of logs about ten inches in diameter; one end of each log had been hewn to a point that was reinforced with an iron strap. The logs were then driven, pointed ends first, down through the landfill into the gray silts of the old river bottom, so that they formed a double row along the line of the wall that was to be built (fig. 13.10). Heavy wooden beams (similar to those used in spread-footers) were then laid across the tops of the pilings, and the stone foundation wall of the building was laid on top of these beams. Again, as with the spread-footers, both the pilings and the overlying beams were placed below the water table. In choosing this solution, the builders ensured that the load of the building passed from the foundation wall through the wooden beams to the underlying pilings and finally came to a rest on the original river bottom into which the pilings had been driven. But the reason why builders chose this solution is not clear. This technique, which was used at the Assay site before the invention of the steam-driven pile driver, was obviously much more labor intensive and expensive (in terms of the consumption of wood) than the spread-footers. Perhaps the landfill in the basin had not been filled up to grade at the time the buildings were built, and the pilings in effect were stilts supporting the buildings, which were probably warehouses.[19]

Buried Ground Surfaces

One of the most important lessons that excavations in the landfill have taught archaeologists is that the landfill can serve as a blanket, protecting and preserving an older ground surface buried beneath it from the ravages of later development. Thus, by examining the ground under the landfill, we can, for example, discern the original slope of the shore of the East River, retrieve artifacts that had been dropped (either accidentally or intentionally) on the natural river bottom, and even discover earlier archaeological sites located beneath the old ground surface.

13.10. The tops of the pilings, upon which were laid the wooden beams holding the stone footings of the buildings.

When the archaeologists were excavating at 7 Hanover Square, they wanted to explore the natural seventeenth-century shoreline—the one that had been seen by Henry Hudson, Tackapausha, Sara Roelofs, and Anthony Van Angola. As their backhoe excavated from west to east across the block, the wall of the trench that it exposed showed the layers of soil that made up both the landfill and the underlying topography of the old shore, allowing them to see for the first time in three centuries the old natural beach that had been hidden from view under the landfill (see fig. 2.2). They discovered that the "beach" was a layer of reddish-brown sand deposited by the outwash of an early glacier that had melted forty thousand years ago; these sands at the time of the filling were in the process of being eroded by the tidal action of the East River. The slope of this sandy shore was quite steep near land but became more gradual further out in the river. About forty feet out from shore, the archaeologists discovered a layer of gray silt overlying the reddish-brown sand and extending further out into the river; the silt layer had been deposited by the river. The reddish-brown sand of the beach marked the area above low tide, where tidal action did not allow the gray silt to accumulate.[20]

The archaeologists discovered a number of seventeenth-century artifacts on top of this ancient shore, showing that New Amsterdammers and early New Yorkers some-times dumped their trash in the river. The broken edges of some of these fragments of pottery and tobacco pipes had been dulled by being rolled around by the waves.

Archaeologists working at excavations on landfill blocks further out in the East River have found artifacts on the old river bottom, buried under the landfill. Unlike the discarded trash that archaeologists usually find, some of these items were probably dropped accidentally into the river, either overboard from a boat or off the side of a wharf that had formed an earlier shoreline. Many of the artifacts were made of metal, a material that seldom ends up in the archaeological record because in the past it was usually sold for scrap and recycled. But on the river bottom, archaeologists have found pewter plates and spoons, utensils that we know from estate inventories were ubiqui-tous in colonial homes but which are rarely found in the ground, as well as personal items like shoe buckles, probably lost from the shoes of passersby (fig. 13.11).

One of the spoons found on the river bottom at the Assay site may have been placed there intentionally. As archaeologists worked to uncover the large wooden wharf com-plex at this site, they found a number of objects embedded in the river-bottom silts next to the wharves. The river bottom in this area had been sealed by the early nine-teenth century, when landfilling moved the shoreline further to the east. One of the artifacts discovered in the buried silt was a spoon with several x's or +'s scratched on the inside of its bowl. In 1984, when the find was made, the archaeologists did not even notice the +'s, and if they had, they might have assumed that they had been scratched there accidentally. However, more recent work by Leland Ferguson, an archaeologist who studies the enslaved in the South, suggests another interpretation.[21]

Ferguson was the first archaeologist to notice the presence of incised +'s on the bases of some hand-built, unglazed red earthenware (or "colonoware") bowls from the Caro-lina low country. Similar motifs have also been found on the bowls of spoons found on plantations in Virginia. Ferguson argues that these marks are cosmograms derived from the Bakongo people who live in today's Angola and Congo in West Africa, one of the places where the enslaved who were brought to North America were captured. The Bakongo use this cosmo-gram to depict the relationship between the earth and the water and the living and the dead: the horizontal line in the + rep-resents the water that serves as the bound-

13.11. Two spoons found under the landfill, on the bottom of the eighteenth-century East River. The lower spoon shows the x's or +'s scratched in its bowl.

ary between the living and their ancestors, while the vertical line represents the path of power across the boundary, from below (the land of the ancestors) to above (the land of the living). Ferguson thinks that the bowls were used as containers for sacred medicines (or *minkisi*), which "control the cosmos connecting the living with the powers of the dead" and which were used in curing rituals. It is possible that the incised spoons found in Virginia played a similar role.[22]

Most of the colonoware bowls marked with such crosses were found on the bottoms of rivers and streams, supporting the interpretation that the enslaved used them in rituals involving the waters that separate the living from the dead. So far, these bowls have not been found in the North. But the discovery of the spoon with its inscribed +'s on the buried bottom of the East River suggests that some of the enslaved Africans in New York may have practiced a similar ritual there. And if so, the evidence of that ritual was preserved for almost two centuries by the protective layer of landfill above it.

Landfill preserves inland sites as well as those located on the shore. The eighteenth-century African Burial Ground was preserved from the ravages of development until the late twentieth century because of a thick layer of landfill that was placed on top of it in the early nineteenth century. And much of the Late Woodland Aqueduct site is still preserved under fill that was laid in the 1930s. But whether inland or on the shore, after the landfill is put into place, it becomes land where people build their homes and workplaces and lay out their backyards.[23]

Building in the City: Early Urban Backyards

Just as today some city dwellers use their backyards as settings for barbecues or gardening while others use theirs for dumping trash, throughout the city's history people have used backyards for many purposes. Although some backyards had kitchen or decorative gardens, backyards were also work areas where people hung out their clothes to dry and performed tasks that were messy or that took up too much space to do indoors.[1] Some people worked in their backyards when it was too warm to work inside; others kept their pigs there (when they were not roaming the city's streets). Most significantly from the archaeological perspective, throughout much of the city's history backyards were the sites of basic utilities—the outhouses or privies that held human waste and the rain barrels and cisterns that held rainwater.

When archaeologists dig in the backyards of early New Amsterdam and New York, they do not find the remains of the old outhouses or rain barrels that once stood there. Features like these were located at or above the old ground surface and have usually been erased by the development and redevelopment that characterize urban life. They also have few opportunities to trace the layouts of old garden plots. But archaeologists often find the remains of those backyard features that were originally built underground—the shafts or pits from wells, privies, dry wells, and cisterns.

These deep features are interesting for two reasons. First of all, because many early New Yorkers used them for rubbish disposal, archaeologists often find them filled with trash. And archaeologists love trash because it can provide many insights into the details of everyday life and the cultures of the past. Second, these features are artifacts in their own right. The construction techniques that New Yorkers used to build these features—like the wharves we described in the previous chapter—formed part of vernacular traditions that had been lost until archaeologists rediscovered them.

Privies

The study of privies and of the deposits found inside their shafts is an important theme in the archaeology of the modern period. Just as discussion of the excretion of human bodily wastes is taboo in polite modern American culture (today Americans use euphemisms like "going to the bathroom" or "going to the john" to avoid direct reference to excretion), it was also taboo in the recent past. Historical documents are almost completely mute on this subject. People who lived in early urban North America had two different places for eliminating bodily wastes: the backyard outhouse or, when the trip to the outhouse was unappealing on cold or rainy nights or when someone was sick, the chamber pot. Chamber pots were kept in commodes or under beds and after use were emptied into the backyard privy. Archaeologists have found an enormous array of ceramic chamber pots, dating from the seventeenth through the nineteenth centuries, that were used by New Yorkers (fig. 14.1).

The backyard outhouse sat on top of a shaft or pit. Underground privy shafts in a city like New York are different from many of those found in rural areas. Country shafts often consist of a simple hole dug in the ground and topped by an outhouse. After the pit was filled, it was capped off with clean soil. Then a new one was dug and the outhouse was moved and placed on top of it. But in urban backyards, space was at a premium; privy pits were permanent structures, carefully lined with wood, brick, or stone. When the pits filled up, they were cleaned out. Privies were rarely moved from one spot to another.

Archaeologists have learned a great deal from studying privies, which often contain two distinct kinds of deposits: a lower one, made up of "night soil" or human waste, and an upper one, made up of the trash and debris thrown in to fill up the pit after people had stopped using it. Archaeologists can study the materials in both layers of fill to find out about the lives of the people who used the privy and abandoned it.[2] In fact, the artifacts found in privies provide the data for many of the chapters in this book. By dating the artifacts in the upper fill of a privy, archaeologists can learn when the people who lived or worked on the property stopped using it and even (for nineteenth-century privies) when residents acquired access to indoor plumbing. By studying the structure of the shafts, they can see how construction techniques for building these hidden features changed through time and can even make inferences as to why they may have changed. So far

14.1. A white earthenware chamber pot, dating from the mid-nineteenth century, from a New York City site.

in New York, archaeologists have recorded four different kinds of privy shafts, each characteristic of a particular phase of the city's history.

Archaeologists working in the area of New Amsterdam in today's Wall Street district found some distinctive seventeenth-century barrel features in several old backyards. At first they couldn't figure out what these features were. But after analyzing their structure and contents, they realized that they had uncovered the vaults or pits from privies. Each vault consisted of two barrels, two to three feet in diameter, with their tops and bottoms removed. They had been set into the ground, one on top of the other, so that the bottom of the uppermost barrel fit inside the top of the lower one (fig. 14.2). Encased in clay, the barrels formed sleeves lining the pits in which they were placed to depths of more than five feet. Soil was then packed around the clay-sheathed barrels to hold them in place, and a layer of shell was strewn across the dirt floor of the vault.[3]

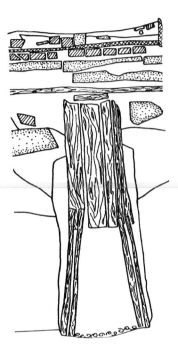

14.2. Section drawing of fragments of a seventeenth-century privy shaft lined with wooden barrels, from the Stadt Huys Block site. Note how the bottom of the upper barrel sits inside the top of the lower one. The lines around the barrels demarcate differences in soil types, and the areas above the barrels indicate layers of later flooring.

The archaeologists studying the barrel features saw that they were well suited for serving as the vaults for privies. The clay around the barrels provided an impermeable barrier, preventing the pit's contents from escaping through its sides; the contents could leach out only through the bottom of the lower barrel, where uric acid would be neutralized by the lime in the shell. The excavators noted that some of the barrels contained a layer of dark organic soil at the bottom, resting on top of the shell layer. This layer was night soil, deposited while the privy was in use. In some of the features, the soil packed around the barrels to hold them in place contained datable artifacts, such as ceramic sherds and tile fragments. These showed that the vaults had been made in the mid-seventeenth century. The artifacts found in the fill inside the privies showed that they had all been abandoned by the beginning of the eighteenth century.[4]

Although archaeologists found several Dutch seventeenth-century privies, they did not find the foundation walls of any of the houses associated with them. But they know from early pictures of the city that most Dutch colonists built houses with their facades flush with the streets (see fig. 2.3). Therefore, we can use the privy vaults' locations in backyards to make inferences about where seventeenth-century Dutch New Amsterdammers thought it was appropriate to place their privies relative to houses and work areas. Each privy was located slightly more than halfway to the rear of the property, at the

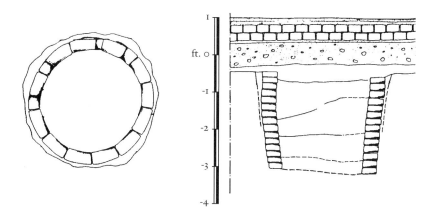

14.3. Top and side views of a late seventeenth- or early eighteenth-century brick-lined privy shaft from the Broad Financial Center site. The lines around the bricks demarcate differences in soil types; those above the bricks indicate a more recent brick floor.

side of the lot, so that it was conveniently close to the house but somewhat secluded. In later years, New Yorkers organized their backyard spaces differently.

Archaeologists have found more-elaborate late seventeenth-century privy vaults that replaced the earlier barrel-lined pits. These newer vaults were lined with dry-laid, arc-shaped bricks designed so that the bricks, when laid end to end, formed a circle about three feet in diameter (fig. 14.3). Like the barrel vault, the brick-lined pit had a dirt floor; it was designed so that its contents could leach out into the underlying soil. These privies, abandoned and filled in during the early eighteenth century, were placed about two-thirds of the way toward the back of the lot (slightly to the rear of the earlier Dutch barrel privies) and, like the barrel privies, off to the side of the yard.[5]

Archaeologists digging at eighteenth- and early nineteenth-century residential sites have discovered more than a dozen square or rectangular wooden boxes buried in back-yards. These boxes, which had dirt floors, contained the dark organic silty deposits that constitute night soil as well as the heavy density of artifacts that is associated with privy vaults. Although they were all made of wooden boards, their construction was not uni-form. The boards of some were set vertically, while those of others were set horizon-tally. Some were found on landfill blocks that had old abandoned cobb wharves run-ning through them. Often the vault builders on these blocks used the side of the wharf as one side for the vault. One box privy at the Assay site was nestled into the corner where two wharves intersected, with the logs from the wharves forming two sides of the vault, while horizontally laid boards formed the other two sides. The lack of standardization in wooden vault construction shows that these were ad hoc structures built with only one goal—to line the privy pit and hold back the surrounding soil as cheaply as possible; the method used was not important.[6]

In 1833 the city's Board of Health stipulated that privy vaults built in the older part of the city (the area south of Spring Street, in today's Soho) be constructed only of brick or of stone.[7] But by then many of the wooden box privies had already been replaced. The datable artifacts found inside the box vaults show that these privies had been abandoned by around 1820. These box privies were placed nearer the back of the yards than the earlier brick or barrel privies and either to the side or in the middle of the yard.

A large majority of the privy vaults that archaeologists have excavated in New York —more than fifty of them to date—were lined with dry-laid, rough stone. These pits were installed during the late eighteenth and early nineteenth centuries (fig. 14.4). Measuring about five feet in cross section, they extend down to depths of up to thirteen feet. Builders constructed them in the same way as the earlier brick privies: they dug a hole the same shape but slightly larger than the privy vault and then laid the courses of stone that would serve as the pit's lining. Some of these stone-lined pits were square, and others were round. All the privy pits excavated so far in Brooklyn and Greenwich Village, parts of the city developed relatively late (after about 1820), are round, suggesting that this shape may have been preferred by then.[8]

In some cases where a single landlord owned two adjacent houses, the occupants of both houses shared a single stone-lined privy that straddled the property line (fig. 14.5).[9] These shared privies were abandoned and filled by around 1820, when individual privies with stone-lined pits were built on each of the lots. The introduction of the custom of one privy per building was presumably related to changes in the meaning of privacy in the early nineteenth century.

Archaeologists have discovered that the introduction of privies with standardized, stone-lined pits was accompanied by the introduction of their standardized placement. In yards that did not contain other backyard buildings, the privies were just inside the rear property line of the yard, either at the corner or in the center of the lot. There, the privy, though close enough

14.4. *A brick cistern* (lower left), *a stone privy* (upper right), *and two dry wells at the Sullivan Street site, seen from above, showing their arrangement in a backyard.*

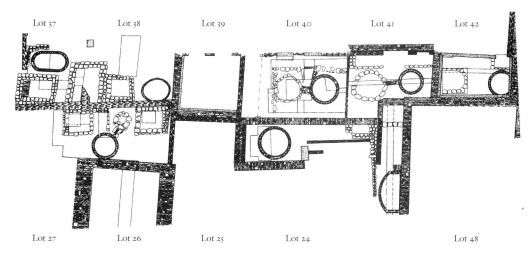

14.5. Detail of the site map of the Telco Block, showing the narrow backyards with cisterns and privies placed side by side. Lots 37–38 and 26–27 each had an early single privy that straddled the property line. Troughs linking cisterns to dry wells or privies are evident in lots 26, 40, and 41.

to the house for convenience, was far enough away to keep the smell at bay and prevent the privy's contents from seeping into the basement. But properties in working-class neighborhoods often had two tenements on them, one facing the street and one to its rear, with the yard in between them. In these lots, outhouses were placed between the tenements.[10]

Cisterns and Dry Wells

An ample supply of fresh, clean water was a continual problem for early New Yorkers. In the seventeenth century, residents obtained their drinking water from natural springs located north of what was then the city, near the Collect Pond at today's Foley Square. Vendors filled their casks at the springs and loaded them onto carts, which they drove into the city where they sold the water. Later New Yorkers drew water from public and private wells located throughout the city. Residents had to haul the water to their homes (often up many flights of stairs) and then haul slops out again. But the city's ever-increasing population put a strain on this system, as the water table became more and more contaminated by human waste and industrial activities. At the beginning of the nineteenth century, politician Aaron Burr helped establish the Manhattan Company, the city's first water supply system. This company laid twenty-five miles of water pipes made of hollowed-out pine logs under the city's streets. But this system, which pumped water from the springs that were by then just at the city's outskirts and stored it in a reservoir near today's City Hall Park, only partially solved the problem. It was run by a private company, and water was not cheap; only two thousand households were able to afford subscriptions to the piped water. There were also continual problems with water flow. Furthermore, as the city continued to grow, the water table that fed the springs that filled the company's reservoir became more and more polluted. It was only with the completion of the Croton Aqueduct in 1842 that the installation of indoor plumbing became feasible for a large number of New Yorkers.[11]

Before piped water was readily available, many New Yorkers had cisterns in their backyards. These receptacles stored rainwater that could be used for cooking, bathing, and washing clothes. Some cisterns were made of wood or brick and placed underground in the yard, next to the house so that they were close to the roof gutters that supplied them with rainwater and to the kitchens where the water would be used.

The construction of cisterns, like the construction of privies, is not recorded in historical documents. In fact, when archaeologists first found some large wooden-box features in backyards on the late seventeenth-century landfill sites along the East River, these boxes were complete mysteries to them. Now, however, they generally accept that the boxes, which range from three and a half to five feet in width and from five and a half to more than six feet in length, were cisterns. We do not know their heights because they were truncated by later construction, but unlike the wooden box features that proved to be privies, they were built with a great deal of care and according to a standardized plan (fig. 14.6).[12]

The artifacts found in the refilled trenches around the boxes showed they had been built at the beginning of the eighteenth century. This was around the same time that the landfill was installed and the properties were first developed. The artifacts found inside the boxes indicated they had all been abandoned and filled in the mid- to late eighteenth century. Each box was located in a backyard and placed next to the kitchen ell extension of the earliest house that had been built on the lot.

At first, archaeologists thought that the boxes might have been used for cold storage or for storing ice. But archaeologist Ed Morin convincingly argued that they were cisterns. He based his theory on several lines of evidence. First was the way the boxes were made: they were built to withstand enormous pressure on the inside walls as well as on the floor—a real concern for storing a liquid like water but not for storing solids like ice or root crops. Second was their location: they were placed right next to the houses whose roofs served as catchments for rainwater and the kitchens where the water would eventually be used. Third was the evidence from the layer of fine, dark silt that covered the bottom of one of the boxes. This silt looked like the dark silt layers found on the bottoms of nineteenth-century cisterns; it came from fine particles suspended in the water that gradually settled to the bottom of the cistern. Fourth was the clay casing surrounding the boxes that helped seal the cistern, preventing the fresh water it contained from seeping out and keeping the brackish water in the surrounding landfill from seeping in. Finally, this interpretation was supported by an advertisement for the sale of one of the Barclays Bank site lots, which appeared in a newspaper in the 1750s:

> TO BE SOLD, the house in Hanover Square belonging to the estate of Bartholemew Skaats, deceased, new [*sic*] in possession of Hugh Gaine: "tis" 3 story high, has two rooms on a floor, with a good kitchen, cellar and cellar kitchen, *a cistern and pump in yard,* with priviledge of passage to the dock.[13]

Archaeologists have discovered that by the early nineteenth century, brick cisterns were ubiquitous in the city's backyards (see fig. 14.4). They were large (one is reported to have had the capacity to hold ten thousand gallons of water) and usually cylindrical in shape. Their brick floors rested on stone platforms for stabilization. Inside, the cisterns were lined with mortar to help make them watertight. Builders sometimes placed a slab of stone on the cistern floor; the slab served as the resting place for the nozzle of the pump's hose so that it would not draw in the silty sediments that had collected on the cistern's floor.[14] Like their wooden-box predecessors, these structures were placed underground, just outside the back kitchens of the houses they served.

Archaeologists have found a number of dry wells—which look like very small, round privy shafts and are lined with dry-laid stone— in nineteenth-century backyards (see fig. 14.4). Early New Yorkers used these features to drain the excess water that accumulated in their backyards. Sometimes they placed a dry well close to the backyard cistern to catch the cistern's overflow. Often, brick troughs or drains channeled the water from the cistern to the dry well (see fig. 14.5).[15]

Privies, Cisterns, and Health

By the early nineteenth century, the arrangement of cisterns and privies in most of the city's backyards had become standardized. Builders placed stone-lined privies just inside the back property line in either a back corner or in the

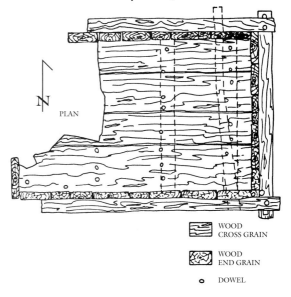

WOOD
CROSS GRAIN

WOOD
END GRAIN

o   DOWEL

14.6. A plan of a wooden-box cistern from 7 Hanover Square.

middle of the lot, and they placed brick cisterns just outside the back walls of adjacent houses. Although this arrangement was fine in many parts of the early nineteenth-century city—such as the developing suburbs of Brooklyn Heights and Greenwich Village, where properties consisted of relatively small single-family homes placed on relatively deep lots—it could have disturbing ramifications in parts of the city where people used land more intensively.

As property became more valuable, landowners in working-class neighborhoods began to build two tenements on a single parcel, with the privy in the yard between them. The privy's placement had the alarming consequence that the contents of the privy vault could seep into adjacent basements, where families were often living.[16] And property owners in the downtown business district tended to enlarge their buildings by extending them further and further into the backyards. The Telco Block site on Fulton Street near today's South Street Seaport provides a glimpse of what this meant in terms of the sanitation on these properties.

Fire swept through the Telco Block in 1816 and destroyed most of the buildings there. After the fire, the landowners on the block redeveloped their properties. In order to get as much value from their land as possible, they extended their new buildings as far back as they could, leaving only narrow strips of backyard behind these structures. What this meant was that the brick cisterns, which builders placed (according to standard procedure) just outside the back wall of the structure, and the stone-lined privies, which builders placed (also according to standard procedure) just inside the back property line, were positioned side by side on those narrow strips of land (see fig. 14.5). The contents of the privies could leach out not only into the adjacent basements but also, if the cisterns' mortar seals were broken, into the cisterns, contaminating the water stored there.

With the enormous population increase in the city in the nineteenth century, human waste began to contaminate the groundwater, the source of the city's drinking water. One result of the city's poor sanitation facilities was the series of cholera epidemics that struck New York in the nineteenth century: the epidemic of 1832 killed more than three thousand city residents, and that of 1849, more than five thousand. The situation was so serious that it finally prompted the city government to initiate the construction of a modern water and sewage system.[17]

In 1842 New York City celebrated, with enormous fanfare, the completion of the Croton Aqueduct. The system consisted of forty miles of pipes and aqueducts that brought a virtual river of water from the Croton Reservoir in Westchester County down into the city. Most people thought that the system would have a profound impact on the lives of New Yorkers; some even thought that its pure water would replace alcohol as the beverage of choice in the city and would thus prove a force for morality and public order.[18]

Archaeologist Jean Howson has explored the impact of Croton water on the lives of the city's residents. She discovered that although access to public water solved one set of problems, it also created a new set. As New Yorkers installed indoor plumbing, they began to pump water in unprecedented amounts into their homes. Of course, they needed a way to dispose of the waste water. Some laid waste pipes from their houses to their old brick cisterns, punched holes in the cistern floors for drainage, and thus converted their cisterns into cesspools. Others hooked up their privy shafts as cesspools. But, given the enormous quantity of water that began to flood the city, this was not a permanent solution—it urgently needed a system of public sewers, a project the city began in the late 1840s.[19]

Howson was struck by her discovery that the completion of the water and sewer system by no means guaranteed the introduction of indoor plumbing into every home; members of different socioeconomic classes had very different experiences in obtaining access to municipal sanitation facilities. Before water could be introduced into homes, the city had to lay hundreds of miles of water pipes under its streets, and individual houses had to be hooked up to these pipes. Although the city began to lay water pipes fairly quickly, the decision to hook a particular building up to the pipes and to install plumbing fixtures in the house rested with the owner of the building, who had to pay a one-time hookup fee and an annual ten-dollar fee for using the water. Members of the city's wealthier families (who usually owned their own homes) tended to hook up their homes to the water pipes first, whereas the poor (whose homes were usually owned by absentee landlords) often had to wait for this amenity.[20] And the laying of sewers throughout the city was a long-term, piecemeal process. The city laid sewers in wealthier neighborhoods long before they laid them in poorer neighborhoods, and owners had to pay a hookup fee as well as a sewer tax. The appearance of a sewer line under a street did not guarantee that the street's inhabitants had access to this amenity.

No records reveal when most buildings were hooked up to Croton water and the city's sewer lines, so it is hard to document exactly when people acquired indoor plumbing. Howson used the dates of the artifacts found in the cisterns and privies at the Sullivan Street site in Greenwich Village to explore this issue. The mid-nineteenth-century residents of the site, which is now part of the law school library at New York University, consisted of two groups of people. "Respectable" upper-middle-class families such as Dr. Benjamin Robson and his wife, Eliza, lived in the houses on Fourth Street, on the northern side of the block overlooking fashionable Washington Square (see chapters 11 and 12). Poorer families faced Amity (now called Third) Street, on the southern side of the block. In the 1830s the Amity Street homes were occupied by middle-class artisans, but as the century progressed many of these buildings were converted into multi-family tenements. Water pipes had been laid under both Amity and Fourth Streets by 1848, and sewers had been laid under Fourth Street by 1845 and under Amity Street by 1857.

By looking at the artifacts from the privies, Howson showed that the wealthier residents of the Sullivan Street site acquired indoor plumbing long before their poorer neighbors. The Robsons on Fourth Street, who owned their own home, abandoned their privy in favor of indoor plumbing as early as 1850, while the people who lived in the tenement across their backyard fence were not able to abandon theirs for another twenty years. Into the late nineteenth century, women and children of the tenement, who unlike their wealthier neighbors had no household help, continued to haul water from corner pumps or backyard cisterns into their homes and up many flights of stairs, and to carry their waste and slops down again.[21]

Deciphering a Nineteenth-Century Backyard

In most cases where archaeologists have the chance to explore backyards in densely populated areas like New York, they find only the underground parts of backyard features. All evidence of the historic landscape—the paved areas and planting beds, the cistern pumps and outhouses—was usually destroyed by later construction on the property. In one case, however, an archaeologist working in New York did have the opportunity to explore the landscape of a relatively untouched urban backyard. This yard is located behind the Merchant's House, a house built in the 1830s that is now a museum on Fourth Street in the East Village (see fig. 1.1), in a neighborhood that today is a mosaic of trendy clubs and Bowery flophouses.

The Merchant's House project began in 1990, when Diana Wall received a call from a historic architect whose firm was doing an architectural study of the Merchant's House. He asked if she would be interested in doing an archaeological study of the backyard. Wall knew the property and was enthusiastic about the project because of its history.[22]

In some ways the history of the Merchant's House is typical of properties in Greenwich Village. Its small urban lot was once part of a larger farm that was located outside the city before urbanization began to encroach on the area in the early nineteenth century. The farm was subdivided repeatedly as the Village was developed as a residential suburb on the city's edge. Joseph Brewster, a hatter, bought the lot and the one next door in 1831. Brewster, like many small-scale developers of his day, built two identical houses on the adjacent parcels in the area, which was quickly becoming one of the city's most fashionable residential neighborhoods. The row houses were built in a style that he thought would appeal to the city's wealthier families, who were now moving their homes out to Greenwich. Brewster sold one of the houses and moved into the other himself (the one that would later become the Merchant's House). But he and his family lived there for only a few years; in 1835 he sold the property to Seabury Tredwell, a successful hardware merchant.[23]

It is with the arrival of the Tredwells that the history of the Merchant's House becomes unusual. Most of the existing houses in New York that were built in the early nineteenth century have complex histories. Though built as single-family homes, they were renovated into multifamily dwellings in the late nineteenth century; subsequently, some of them were re-renovated back into single-family homes. This, however, was not the case with the Merchant's House. From the time the Tredwells moved there in 1835, family members continued to live in the house for almost a century, until the death of their youngest daughter, Gertrude, in 1933. As the family lived there, their fortunes waned, so they did not continually renovate their house to keep up with the times but left it relatively untouched for almost a century. After the death of Gertrude Tredwell, family members led the effort to have the house converted into a museum because they realized that it provided a rare glimpse of upper-middle-class home life in the nineteenth-century city.

Wall jumped at the chance to excavate in the yard behind the house because she thought that it, like the house, might be relatively undisturbed and could provide a rare opportunity for archaeologists to explore the nineteenth-century landscape of an urban garden. She arranged to teach a field course at the City College of New York, and the following spring she and the students began the first of three field seasons in the backyard.

The little that is known about the landscaping of the yards behind middle-class row houses in nineteenth-century New York comes from a handful of architectural plans and real estate advertisements from contemporary newspapers (fig. 14.7). They indicate that these were simple, classical spaces, made up of symmetrical planting beds and pathways that provided both pleasant views from house windows and sites for the outhouse or privy that was placed near the rear garden wall and the underground cistern that was close to the back wall of the house. Central garden beds were planted with grass, while those along the edges of the backyard contained flowers, shrubs, and climbing vines.[24]

When the excavations began, the layout of the yard behind the Merchant's House appeared similar in feeling to the gardens shown in the architectural plans, with two large central planting beds and narrow flower beds along the sides of the garden separated from each other by stone pathways (fig. 14.8). The old outhouse was gone; a raised planting bed in its place at the rear of the garden was a recent addition that the museum had installed in the 1960s.

Wall and her students had one main goal for their project: to decipher the layout of the garden during the period when the Brewsters and Tredwells lived in the house in the mid-nineteenth century. As they excavated, they discovered in many parts of the garden a layer of reddish-brown sand that lay just under the layer of tan sand that was the bedding for the modern stone paths. They analyzed the artifacts in the reddish-brown sand and saw that they all dated to the late eighteenth or early nineteenth centuries. They realized that this layer of reddish-brown sand was the bedding for the paths of the mid-nineteenth century garden and that they could use the sand layer as a signature to show them where these nineteenth-century paths had been.

As they plotted the presence and absence of the layer of reddish brown sand from test cut to test cut, the team discovered that although the modern layout of the yard was quite similar to that of the nineteenth-century garden, it differed in some details (fig. 14.9). The reddish-brown sand under the modern side paths showed that these

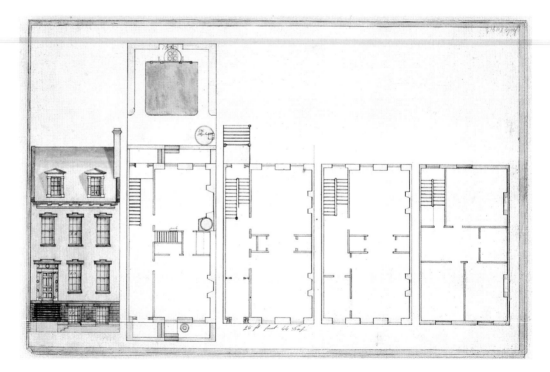

14.7. Calvin Pollard's architectural drawing of an early nineteenth-century brownstone, showing its facade, a plan of each floor, and the backyard (on the ground-floor plan). Collection of the New-York Historical Society, negative number 74146.

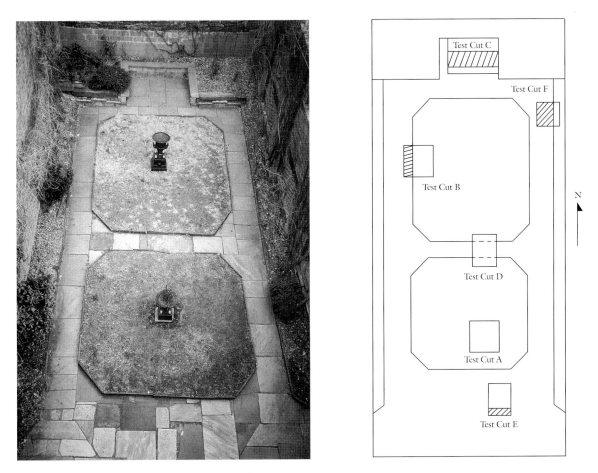

14.8. The backyard behind the Merchant's House Museum, 1993.

14.9. Detail of the site map of the backyard behind the Merchant's House. The hatching indicates areas where the archaeologists found the layer of reddish-brown sand.

paths remained roughly where they had been in the nineteenth century. However, the central planting area was much larger in the nineteenth-century garden than it is today. And the absence of the sand layer under the path dividing the two central beds showed that there was no path there when the garden was laid out in the 1830s. In the original garden, there may have been one large central planting bed (like the one in the contemporary architectural plan) or the path may have been located elsewhere, further to the north, dividing the original, longer planting area into two planting beds of roughly the same size.

Below the layer of reddish-brown sand, the students found eighteenth-century artifacts—ceramic sherds from teacups and plates and fragments of tobacco pipe stems—that had been left behind by the families who had lived there when the property was still a farm. Those artifacts served as reminders that until recently, much of today's city was country—an issue we explore in the next chapter.

CHAPTER FIFTEEN

Beyond the City's Edge

The city of New York began in the early seventeenth century as a small settlement at the foot of Manhattan Island, and from there it grew "uptown." At first its growth was very slow. It was only in the nineteenth century, when its economy was booming, that the city grew radically: between 1790 and 1890, its population multiplied almost fiftyfold, from 33,000 to 1.5 million. And in 1898, with the incorporation of the modern boroughs of Brooklyn, Queens, Staten Island, and the Bronx into New York City, the city assumed its modern political boundaries—the boundaries of the archaeological site we discuss in this book. But because of its gradual early growth, for much of its history there were thousands of acres of rural land within the 325 square miles that make up the city today (fig. 15.1).

This land—which only a century and a half ago was farmland interspersed by towns and villages—plays an important role in our study of the city as a site. In the eighteenth century, New York started building institutions at the city's edge to serve its poor. During the Revolutionary War, the land was dotted with fortifications and camps for the soldiers who defended the city from attack. In the nineteenth and into the twentieth centuries, much of the land at the city's periphery was transformed from farmland into residential suburbs for middle-class and wealthy families.

Archaeologists have uncovered many traces of the city's rural past in northern Manhattan, the Bronx, Queens, Brooklyn, and Staten Island. They have brought to light ways of life that were common there before the areas were swallowed by urban sprawl—ways of life that most modern Americans tend to overlook when they think about New York's history.

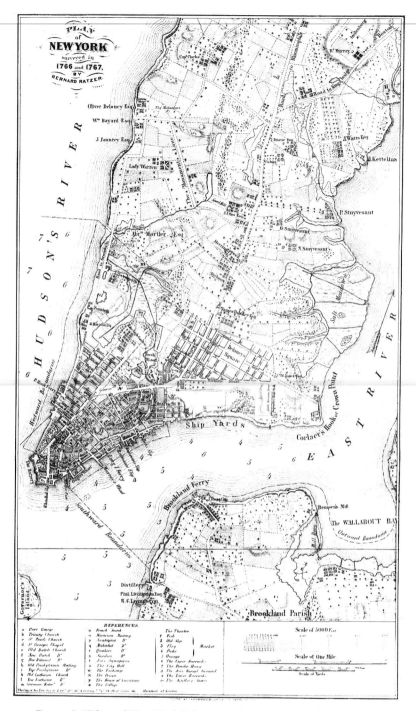

15.1. Ratzer's "Plan of New York," showing the southern half of Manhattan and parts of Brooklyn in 1766–67. The city is confined to Manhattan's southern tip, and the rest of the area that later became the city is rural in nature. Collection of the New-York Historical Society, negative number 56838.

Farms, Estates, and Plantations

Several kinds of farms encircled the early city. Some farmers lived on isolated farmsteads, others in nucleated farm villages, and still others on large estates run as plantations. During the late seventeenth and eighteenth centuries, most farmers grew grains like wheat, corn, and oats for export; raised livestock, both for export and to sell locally; and grew produce for sale in the city. Merchants shipped most of the grain and livestock to the British West Indies to feed the enslaved laborers on the sugar plantations there. Toward the end of the eighteenth century, grain production shifted further up the Hudson Valley as farmers closer to the city began specializing in the perishable but more valuable produce and dairy products for the city's growing population. Before emancipation in 1827, many of the nearby farms and plantations depended on enslaved labor for agricultural production. At the end of the eighteenth century, around 40 percent of the white households within a dozen miles of the city included enslaved workers—a higher proportion than in any southern state.[1]

Colonial farmhouses survive today in every borough. Most are owned by the city and protected as historic structures; one is a farm museum. But all that is left of the farmland—which in the past could total hundreds and even thousands of acres—are small plots surrounding the houses. The woodlands, orchards, vineyards, fields, marshes, meadows, and pastures that made up these farms have been sacrificed to urban development. People today know little about the city's agrarian past. Archaeologists have tested areas around many of these houses in places where modern construction was about to take place; in one case they even got the chance to dig in some old agricultural fields.[2]

Although the excavations have been small in scale, they have revealed some interesting information concerning the structural history of several old farmhouses. At the early eighteenth-century Wyckoff House in East Flatbush, Brooklyn (see fig. 1.1), for example, Arthur Bankoff and his Brooklyn College field school discovered the original bed of Canarsie Lane. The excavations showed the road's alignment as it was from about 1650 until the late nineteenth century, when it was shifted to the other side of the house. The orientation of the farmhouse was also reversed when the road was moved —what had once been the back of the house became its front—so that the house continued to look out on the road (fig. 15.2).[3]

Archaeologists Arnold Pickman and Eugene Boesch, while digging at the late eighteenth-century Adriance Farmhouse in Bellerose, Queens (now the Queens County Farm Museum; see fig. 1.1), found the eighteenth-century farm road under the modern driveway. They discovered that the old road had begun as a dirt track, which became heavily rutted with use. Then the Adriances laid a new roadbed over it, made up of a

15.2. The Wyckoff House in the 1990s.

cobble bedding (for good drainage) covered by earth. Preservationists had thought that the orientation of this house, like that of the Wyckoff House, had been reversed at some point in its history. But the discovery of the farm road's original alignment under the modern driveway, combined with the fact that the house today looks out on the old farm road, revealed that its orientation had not changed.[4]

Excavations have also been conducted at the eighteenth-century Rufus King House in Jamaica, Queens (see fig. 1.1). King was a key figure in early American history. In addition to being a framer of the Constitution, he also served as the new nation's ambassador to England after the Revolutionary War. In 1805 he bought the house that is now named after him and began expanding it. Written sources indicate that among the additions he made was a summer kitchen—a separate building designed to keep both the main house and the cooks cool in hot weather. Archaeologist Linda Stone discovered that a building standing on the property today, which preservationists had interpreted as the kitchen that King had built, in fact was not that addition. She found the remains of King's original summer kitchen, which she dated with the help of a British gambling token inscribed with the year 1793. The token may have been a souvenir from

King's ambassadorship. Stone found that the original kitchen, which had had a dirt floor, had burned down and was replaced by the present, more substantial kitchen building during the tenure of the family of King's oldest son, John, who served as governor of New York in the 1850s. Stone's discovery has enabled the historical association that runs the house-museum to interpret the history of the house more accurately.[5]

Archaeologists have also uncovered remnants of eighteenth- and early nineteenth-century farmland. In 1982 Anne-Marie Cantwell, Arnold Pickman, and Diana Wall led an excavation at Sheridan Square in the heart of Greenwich Village (see fig. 1.1), where community groups and the New York City Department of Transportation were planning a viewing garden. This excavation was a volunteer dig, with community members and archaeologists contributing their time and labor.[6] The archaeologists were intrigued by the site because there was no record of there ever having been any buildings on it. And they did make some remarkable discoveries related to the city's early farm history. They uncovered traces of late eighteenth- and early nineteenth-century topsoil that was underlaid by scars left by an early plow, a tangible reminder that before Sheridan Square became the hub of the trendy West Village—and even before the Robsons moved to the fashionable suburb at Washington Square—Greenwich had been a rural farming community. They also found holes left from a line of posts that had once cut across the site. These were aligned with an old property line; the posts could well have been from the fence that divided two substantial eighteenth-century farms that were owned by the Herring and Warren families, neighbors who were active on opposing sides during the Revolutionary War.

If we look farther north, we see that during the seventeenth and eighteenth centuries, much of today's Bronx was partitioned into a few large landholdings, which were controlled by some of New York's richest and most powerful families. Although most were gradually subdivided into smaller properties, several remain quite large to this day. Archaeologists have conducted long-term projects at two of these sites: Rose Hill Manor and Van Cortlandt Mansion.

For more than a decade and a half, Allan Gilbert of Fordham University has worked with Fordham historian Roger Wines in researching and excavating Fordham's campus, which was part of the seventeenth-century Fordham Manor (see fig. 1.1), which spanned 3,900 acres. Shortly after the British government granted the manor to John Archer in 1671, Archer sold off parts of the land to pay his debts. In 1694 Reyer Michielsen, a Dutchman, bought some of the land (the parcel that encompasses most of the modern campus) and built a farmhouse there. Benjamin Corsa, who had married into the Michielsen family, bought the farm in 1737. His family continued to live in the house until after the Revolution.[7]

In 1787 a wealthy New York mercantile family named Watts acquired the farm and turned it into a country estate, which they christened Rose Hill. The Wattses continued to farm the land until they sold it in 1823. Then the land changed hands several times before the Roman Catholic Diocese of New York acquired it in 1839 for the site of St. John's, a Catholic men's college and seminary. In 1846 the Jesuit order took over the college, which was incorporated as Fordham University in 1907.

Gilbert's excavations have focused on both the ruins of the original farmhouse and the daily life of the boys who lived at the college in the nineteenth century. His careful reading of both the historical and the archaeological records has revealed details about the building's structural history. The house, which was built around 1694 and torn down in 1896, began as a small, one-and-a-half story Dutch-style wooden farmhouse. The Wattses enlarged it by adding two wings, and it was probably they who added the

15.3. A watercolor by Archibald Robertson showing Rose Hill in 1815.

full second story and made it look more up to date by adding a Georgian-like facade when they transformed it into Rose Hill Manor after the Revolution (fig. 15.3). The diocese and the Jesuits altered it again so it would better suit its new, institutional roles—at various points in the nineteenth century it served as a novitiate, an infirmary, a dairy, and a residence hall for various groups, including members of the Sisters of Charity, priests, and workmen.

As Gilbert points out, because he has been able to unravel the history of the house's renovations, he is in a position to use the architectural materials from the house to develop a comparative collection of mortar, brick, and window glass dating from the late seventeenth through the nineteenth centuries. Although these materials are the most commonly found artifacts at modern sites, archaeologists usually ignore them in their analyses because they do not know how to study them. Gilbert hopes that this collection will allow archaeologists to use these materials to date old ruins, particularly those that do not have other artifacts associated with them.

In 1986, when workers building new dormitories on the Fordham campus uncovered several trash dumps, Gilbert's crew shifted their attention from the old farmhouse to the dump sites. They found enormous quantities of broken mid- to late nineteenth-century plain white ironstone dishes (fig. 15.4), which had probably been used by the generations of students and faculty who ate the pork and beef whose bones were also found. Fragments of paneled tumblers and of bottles that had held wine, sarsaparilla, and ginger ale (including one marked "CANTRELL & COCHRANE/BELFAST & DUBLIN") showed something about drinking habits at the college. The wine bottles probably contained the wine that was produced in the college's vineyards. The archaeologists also found marbles (made from marble, clay, and glass), bone dominoes, and dice—evidence of the students' games, some of which may have involved gambling.[8]

Less than two miles northwest of Fordham lies Van Cortlandt Park, site of the Van Cortlandt Mansion (see fig. 1.1), a historic house that was the heart of a colonial wheat plantation. In 1990–92, Brooklyn College's field school, directed by Arthur Bankoff and Frederick Winter, excavated in areas around the house, which had been built on land that had been occupied by Late Woodland people. In 1646 Adrian Van der Donck acquired the property as part of an enormous tract with sixteen miles of Hudson River waterfront, which extended north from Spuyten Duyvil at the southern edge of the Bronx to Yonkers, just across today's Westchester border, and east to the Bronx River. Van der Donck acquired the estate as a patroonship, under a land tenure policy established by the Dutch to encourage settlement. The Dutch West India Company granted the patroon a large tract of land on the condition that he guarantee its settlement, clearance, and cultivation. It is not clear if Van der Donck kept his side of the bargain, because he abandoned the property after an Indian attack in 1655 and died in Holland

15.4. Dishes from St. John's, the Catholic men's college that became Fordham University.

soon thereafter. The property was then subdivided.[9]

In 1694 Jacobus Van Cortlandt began to acquire the land that would become today's Van Cortlandt Park. His father, Oloff Stevense Van Cortlandt, had arrived in New Amsterdam in 1638 as a soldier working for the Dutch West India Company and soon became one of the richest merchants in the colony. After his death the family continued to expand its mercantile fortune; its ships were important carriers in the triangular trade. By the 1730s, Jacobus Van Cortlandt had acquired all of the original Van der Donck holdings, which he turned into a plantation where the family grew wheat and milled it into flour before shipping it to the West Indies. When he died in 1739, his son Frederick inherited the land and in 1748 began to build the large, vernacular Georgian stone house that is today's Van Cortlandt Mansion (fig. 15.5). For the rest of the eighteenth and most of the nineteenth centuries, the house and land were owned by a succession of Van Cortlandt heirs. The wheat plantation included such industrial components as mills and forges as well as extensive farmlands. The family sold the land that became the park to the city in 1889.

During the Revolutionary period, the Van Cortlandt Mansion played several roles. It was George Washington's headquarters after his defeat at the Battle of Brooklyn in 1776, and it was from the mansion that he set out to repossess the city after the British defeat in 1783. Earlier, during the long British occupation of the city, the property's proximity to the British lines made it a convenient spot for General William Howe to have his headquarters. But before the British took over the plantation, its owner, Augustus Van Cortlandt, who was the New York City clerk, hid the city's records in the family's burial vault, which was located nearby. There they remained for the duration of the war, under the noses of the British.

The archaeologists were interested in learning about land use throughout the site's history, from Native American times through the end of the Van Cortlandt era.[10] More than seven feet below the modern ground surface, they found a buried foundation wall that appeared to be from a seventeenth-century building, probably from Adrian Van der Donck's home. Unfortunately, in 1910 the city had run a sewer line right through the area and gutted much of the foundation; the archaeologists could find no undisturbed layers of soil with artifacts that they could use to date the wall.

Using old photographs to guide them, the team next excavated in an area where a large barn had once stood. Although they did not find the barn's foundation, they did discover two underground dry-laid stone features set side by side, ten feet apart. The features were square, measuring slightly more than five feet on a side and, as subsequent excavation showed, had dirt floors at depths of around ten feet. To this day archaeologists do not agree about what these features were. Although they resemble the privy vaults found in the city, these are too far from the house to have been convenient for its residents. Some archaeologists have suggested that they were privies that had been built for farm workers, whereas others have proposed that they were root cellars or underground silage pits used for storing grain (although getting grain or root vegetables in and out of the pits might have been awkward). Whatever their original function, they were later filled up with trash that has proved to be an archaeological bonanza.

Inside these mystery structures, the team found fragments of what ultimately proved to be more than six hundred dishes, glasses, and bottles, including sixty-four plates,

15.5. The Van Cortlandt Mansion in the 1990s.

fifty soup bowls, almost thirty serving dishes and platters, twenty-seven cups and saucers, and eleven pitchers. Although most of the dishes were in patterns popular in the early nineteenth century, mixed in among these were embossed bottles that had been made much later, after 1880, suggesting that both the dishes and the bottles had been dumped in the pits soon after that date. Because this was around the time that the Van Cortlandts sold the property to the city, it seems likely that either Parks Department personnel or family members dumped old, unwanted family dishes that had been stored in the house into these features, both to get rid of the dishes and to fill the pits up to grade.[11]

Assuming that the dishes and tableware had been used in the mansion between 1810 and 1840 (the period when dishes like these were fashionable), they were probably used by Augustus Van Cortlandt (a widower whose wife had died in 1808) or his grandson, Augustus White. When his grandfather died in 1823, White inherited the estate on the condition that he change his name to Van Cortlandt. Augustus White Van Cortlandt, who never married, died in 1839.[12]

Alyssa Loorya, who began working on the collection as a Brooklyn College undergraduate, went on to do a study of the dishes in graduate school. What struck her most about the collection was that the people who were living in the house in the 1820s and 1830s were using dishes that were very similar in pattern to those used by contemporary middle-class New Yorkers, like the Robsons on Washington Square. Both families had plates in two different blue-on-white chinoiserie patterns: a more expensive Canton Chinese porcelain and a more modest English willow-patterned earthenware. But there were also enormous differences between the collections from the Van Cortlandt and Robson homes. Proportionately, the Robsons had far more cups and saucers than plates, while the Van Cortlandts had many more plates than cups and saucers. In addition, in absolute numbers the Van Cortlandts had many more plates than the Robsons (or than any other middle-class family in the city whose dishes have been excavated), and many more of the Van Cortlandts' plates were in the more expensive Canton pattern rather than in the cheaper willow pattern.[13] The question, of course, was why.

It seems most likely that the disparity in the numbers of different kinds of dishes used by the two families is related both to their positions in the city's class structure and to the locations of their homes. The Van Cortlandts were one of the richest families in the state, while the Robsons were merely members of the city's growing upper-middle class. During the early nineteenth century, the city's wealthiest families entertained each other at dinner parties as well as at after-dinner tea parties, while the middle class usually entertained their friends only at tea. The Van Cortlandt Mansion was located about twenty miles north of the city, a fair distance to travel in the early nineteenth century, while the Robsons lived in the new suburb at Greenwich, just at the city's edge—close enough to be convenient for daily commuting. What this may have meant for the Van Cortlandts is that when they were at their Bronx estate, they did not entertain guests at evening tea parties but only for longer, overnight visits. Tea was just one of many different meals the Van Cortlandts offered to their guests at their country house, and the many ornate plates and relatively few teacups found among their dishes underline this way of entertaining. By contrast, most of the Robsons' guests arrived after dinner and were served a cup of tea along with a light refreshment. The high number of teacups that were used in their home highlights their different mode of entertaining and the different role they played in the social life of the city.[14]

Villages and Towns

Many early towns and villages—often located at transportation nodes like boat and ferry landings, the intersections of roads, and, later on, at railroad stations—served as entrepôts for transporting farm produce to the city. In the seventeenth century, the Dutch established a number of towns, including Harlem in northern Manhattan; Brooklyn or Breuckelen, New Amersfoort or Flatlands, Midwout or Flatbush, New Utrecht, and Boswick or Bushwick, all in today's Brooklyn; and Oude Dorp or Old Dorp on Staten Island. English families also settled towns in New Netherland. They moved across Long Island Sound from New England, first to eastern Long Island and then further to the west, to today's Brooklyn and Queens. There they settled Gravesend; Maspeth; Flushing, which became a Quaker community; and Middleburgh (later known as both Newtown and Elmhurst). Other English families moved west from Connecticut to settle the town of Westchester in today's Bronx.

In the late 1970s, Winter and Bankoff conducted excavations with their Brooklyn College students at Gravesend (see fig. 1.1), which was settled in 1643 by the English Anabaptist Lady Deborah Moody and her followers. The Anabaptists had come to Dutch Long Island to escape the religious restrictions of Puritan New England. Gravesend was unusual in that it was a planned community; it was laid out in four contiguous squares divided by two intersecting roads. Each quadrant was designed to hold ten house lots arranged around a common, with supporting farmland radiating out from the village center.

The archaeologists, digging in the northwest and southwest quadrants of the town, located the seventeenth-century ground surface buried under modern debris. But they found no traces of house foundations anywhere, not even in the southwest quadrant, where the excavations were most extensive and where early records indicated that houses had stood. As Winter notes, the "excavations indicated that no houses had ever been built there. . . . In fact, it appears that the well ordered plans for the early Graves-

Northeast. Some worked as day laborers on oystering boats in an industry where they had once held prominent positions; others worked wherever they could. But by 1916, the waters had become so polluted that the Staten Island oystering industry collapsed completely.[20]

In 1971 and 1972, archaeologist Robert Schuyler brought archaeological field schools from City College to Sandy Ground. He was interested in locating trash dumps from both black and white homes so that he could use the artifacts to study this multi-ethnic community. His students found more than one hundred spots where Sandy Grounders had dumped their garbage. Schuyler chose several dumps, which the students then excavated. Later, William Askins, who as an undergraduate had dug at the site, used this material as part of the data for his dissertation.[21]

Askins was interested in exploring how expressions of class and ethnic identity might have changed among Sandy Grounders of African descent as their position in the community declined with the arrival of big business and the passage of Jim Crow laws toward the end of the nineteenth century. He argued that people might emphasize —through a combination of choice and coercion—different aspects of their social identity depending on their situation. He wanted to investigate the extent to which Sandy Grounders of African descent exercised their complementary identities as African Americans and as members of the working class as their economic and social positions changed.

Askins looked at two different kinds of artifacts to explore this issue: the houses in which Sandy Grounders lived and the dishes on which they ate their meals. He argued that because houses are so large and visible, they make clear statements about the identities of their residents to neighbors and outsiders. He discovered that during the earlier period of the settlement (before 1870), Sandy Grounders of African and European descent were living in houses built in different styles. White Sandy Grounders were living in the Dutch Colonial or Georgian houses typical of much of Staten Island, while black Sandy Grounders were living in I-houses, which are designed with a central hall and a room to each side (fig. 15.6). These houses were popular among both blacks and whites in the Chesapeake, where many of the Sandy Grounders of African descent had grown up. As Askins notes, the African Americans "may have built in the traditional English [I-house]

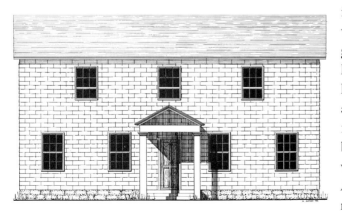

15.6. An I-house from Sandy Ground.

style of the eighteenth century Mid-Atlantic which their ancestors had learned in their acculturation to this dominant
culture."[22]

Askins discovered that black and white Sandy Grounders
who built houses later in the century seemed to be following a
different principle in choosing a style for their homes. Their
choice now seemed to depend not on regional or ethnic origin
but on class. Two different styles of houses were popular after
1870: the three-bay temple (fig. 15.7) and, again, the I-house. I-
houses were now built for the poorer residents of Sandy
Ground—the black and white farmers who were having
trouble making ends meet or who rented (rather than owned)
their homes. The three-bay temple houses, by contrast, were
built by relatively affluent members of the community, both
black and white—oystermen, small-business proprietors, or
those who were in prestigious occupations, such as ministers.

15.7. A three-bay temple house from
Sandy Ground.

As Askins argues, "a simple correlation of ethnicity and house style is not found
throughout Sandy Ground history. Though ethnicity, or regional culture, may have
been expressed in the earliest period of the community, during the later period the picture is much more complex. Instead of ethnicity, . . . relative class position is what was
expressed."[23]

When Askins turned his attention to the ceramics that the women of Sandy Ground
used, he discovered that all the women—whether of African or European descent—
used similar dishes from the late nineteenth through the early twentieth centuries. This
suggests that the African American and European American women of Sandy Ground,
during good times and bad, chose to underline their common ground with their
neighbors. These similarities in dish styles paralleled the mutual aid that crossed the
color line in the community. People from Sandy Ground who were interviewed in the
1930s talked nostalgically about the community's cohesion in the late nineteenth century; they recalled that black and white children played and went to school together,
that some black families attended white churches, that some white Sandy Grounders
attended cakewalks and ox roasts organized by black churches, and that some of the
sports teams were integrated. People of different ethnicities shared garden produce,
midwife services, and health remedies. The similarities in the dishes showed that this
form of solidarity continued in the community even after the bottom fell out of the
oystering industry and the economic status of the oystermen plummeted. However,
the similarity in the dishes did not mean that the meals eaten in all these houses were
the same—the dumps associated with white homes contained many more glass bottles

and jars used for storing condiments like pickles and sauces, showing that the cuisines in these homes were quite different. As Askins notes, these differences and similarities in styles of houses and dishes could also be related to different gender roles in the Sandy Ground community: "Women, the most important links in inter-household conviviality, may have expressed . . . a community identity, as modest rural Victorians. Men, who built the houses or chose the builders, expressed occupation or class in their very public symbolic domain."[24]

The Suburbs

New York has the oldest commuter suburbs of any city in the world. Their creation was directly related to the factors of urbanization that caused the separation of the home and workplace in the early nineteenth-century city (see chapter 11): the growth of the large, impersonal economy, the increasing numbers of immigrant poor, and the virulent diseases and epidemics that came to be associated with "the city." Those who could afford it moved their homes away from the downtown business district and out into the suburbs that were developing at the city's edge, in Greenwich Village, Jersey City, Hoboken, Brooklyn Heights, and, soon after, in other parts of Brooklyn.[25] There they lived in residential communities made up of almost identical single-family row houses. Technological innovations in transportation, including steam ferries and horse-drawn omnibuses, linked the new suburbs to the city so that men could commute from these communities to work in Manhattan.

At home in the suburbs, mid-nineteenth-century "how-to" books encouraged women to use home furnishings to further their agendas for their families. They were advised to shop for furniture in different styles for decorating different rooms in their suburban homes, as befitted the activities associated with each room. One style, Italianate, was deemed appropriate for the entertaining that took place in the parlor, where middle-class women tried to project the image of refined gentility to reinforce their families' position in the class structure. The Gothic style, with its ecclesiastical associations, was suitable for family dining rooms, where women inculcated moral values into their children during meals and thus encouraged them to become responsible citizens.

Archaeologists have uncovered traces of middle-class mid-nineteenth-century suburban life in Manhattan's Greenwich Village (including at the Robsons' home on Washington Square) and in Brooklyn's Boerum Hill and Fort Green.[26] In studying their finds from these different but contemporaneous communities, they have been struck by the almost rigid uniformity of the artifacts from all the sites, indicating that the ways of life inside these homes followed the same pattern. In spite of the profusion of china patterns that became available with the industrial revolution, the women in these homes used one kind of china to serve their families' meals and another to entertain friends at tea. Whether they were at the poorer or richer ends of the middle-class spectrum, they chose ironstone plates in the Gothic pattern, which were plain white with molded panels around their rims, for family use in their Gothic dining rooms. And for entertaining their friends in their Italianate parlors, they chose white porcelain cups and saucers, often with gold-painted decoration, in the more elaborate Italianate style (fig. 15.8).

15.8. A porcelain teacup and saucer in the Italianate style, from the Robsons' home, 1840s.

There was, however, one difference between the dishes from the Greenwich Village and Brooklyn households. The archaeologists working in Brooklyn found dinner plates and soup bowls in both the Gothic *and* Italianate patterns, showing that Brooklyn women entertained for dinner as well as for tea. But none of the Greenwich Village families had dishes in these Italianate forms: all of their large dinner plates and soup bowls were in plain Gothic ironstone. Because the trip to Brooklyn was a major expedition, perhaps when the Brooklyn families entertained their friends or relations from the city, they served them dinner instead of just after-dinner tea. So geography may have played a role in determining entertainment styles among the middle class, just as it did among the very rich, as we saw in looking at home life at the Van Cortlandts'.

Forts and Encampments

In August 1776 the British fleet, armed with 1,200 cannon and carrying 32,000 troops and 13,000 seamen, had massed in the Narrows off the coast of Staten Island.[27] Over the next two months, the British conquered the city. First, General William Howe led his troops to victory against Washington's men at what became known as the Battle of Brooklyn. Then, with the British in pursuit, the Americans retreated, first to Manhattan, then north to Harlem Heights (where they succeeded in turning back the British temporarily), and then to Westchester. The British controlled the city, which became a Tory stronghold, until the very end of the war, in 1783. New York was the only American city to be occupied by the British army for almost the entire duration of the Revolutionary War. As recently as the late nineteenth century, New Yorkers continued to commemorate November 25, 1783, the day the British left the city, by celebrating Evacuation Day each year.

Amazingly enough, extensive traces of the fortifications from the Revolution and from the War of 1812 survive today within the modern borders of the city. Avocational archaeologists have always been fascinated by these sites. Early in the twentieth century, William Calver and Reginald Bolton spent years salvaging traces of Fort Washington and of the British encampment around the Dyckman Farm in northern Manhattan. They excavated 50 of the 120 semi-subterranean huts where British and Hessian soldiers lived. Their work there produced an outstanding collection of military buttons and other accoutrements associated with eighteenth-century British soldiers in North America.[28]

More recently, avocational archaeologists have excavated at other Revolutionary War sites. One of the most important of these excavations was at Fort Independence (see fig. 1.1), which was built in 1775–76 as part of the network of fortifications the Americans prepared to protect the city from British attack. The fort safeguarded the King's Bridge, the city's link to the mainland across the Harlem River. The British seized Fort Independence in 1776 and continued to hold it until their offensive collapsed in 1779.

In 1958 the New York City Archaeological Group, led by Julius Lopez and including Stanley Wisniewski, Michael Cohn, and Harry Trowbridge, found the remains of Fort Independence. The details of the fort's construction are not known except for the fact that it was enclosed by earthworks. But the archaeologists found parts of the stone foundation walls of two buildings that had stood within it. The function of the smaller building, which was around fifteen by thirteen feet, remains a mystery, but the larger building, which measured about thirty-two by ten feet, seems to have served as officers' quarters during the British occupation. The archaeologists made this interpretation because amid the building's rubble they found relatively ornate artifacts, including buttons; cuff links, including one of pewter embossed with a lion; green, blue, and clear glass faux gems that had been lost from their settings; and small-caliber lead shot, presumably for use with officers' pistols. They also found artifacts that indicated the tedium of life at the fort: dice that someone had made from lead musket balls. The balls had been shaped into cubes, and the dots on each facet had been punched in with a nail or other sharp object. The officers had probably used these dice for gambling, to while away the hours as they guarded the fort. Making dice from musket balls seems to have been a fairly common practice during the War for Independence, because Calver and Bolton found similar lead dice at Revolutionary War sites in northern Manhattan.[29]

The archaeologists also found a number of brass and copper buckles from the clothing of officers and common soldiers. Some were from belts worn round the waist, others from straps worn at the knee, and others still were from shoes. They also found twenty-two coins (most of which were British pennies bearing the image of King

George II) and numerous buttons, including twenty-seven inscribed with one of the numbers of the seven different regiments that were posted at the fort.

Lopez suggested that the soldiers ate from wooden or pewter dishes because they did not find any sherds from ceramic plates; most of the sherds they found were from tea cups and saucers. These vessels were in patterns that were surprisingly fashionable considering that they were being used at a fort in a remote colonial outpost that was at war. Some sherds, those of creamware and of white salt-glazed stoneware, were English-made, while others were of imported Chinese porcelain. The artifacts provide an intimate look into the daily rituals at Fort Independence.

An Almshouse Kitchen

Traditionally, New Yorkers built institutions to serve the poor out at the city's edge, where land was cheap and where the inhabitants were out of sight. As the city grew over time and its borders advanced, these institutions had to move over and over again. During the eighteenth century, many of the city's institutions were located on the Commons, in today's City Hall Park, then an open area at the city's northern edge where local residents had pastured livestock in the seventeenth century. There the city housed its mentally ill in an asylum, its prisoners in a jail, and its poor in an almshouse. In later years, many of these institutions were moved to Blackwell's (later Welfare and now Roosevelt) Island in the East River, where they stood throughout much of the nineteenth century.

Today there are two buildings standing in the northern end of City Hall Park: the Tweed Courthouse, which was built on Chambers Street between 1862 and 1870, and City Hall, built between 1803 and 1812. In the late 1980s the city planned to install a utility line between the two buildings. Before they began their project, however, archaeologists excavated along the path of the utility line. They discovered the brownstone foundation and cellar hole of an eighteenth-century building as well as a buried layer of organic soil that was the ground surface of the Commons in the 1700s. The architectural materials they found included mortar and a lot of bricks, indicating that the building had been built of brick. One of the archaeologists, Sherene Baugher, argues that the building served as the kitchen for the city's first almshouse, which had been built in the 1730s.[30]

The artifacts included unusually high numbers of bone button backs—bone disks that would later be covered with cloth and that were pierced by a single hole—and "button blanks"—pieces of flat bone, often the ribs or shoulder blades of cattle, from which the disks had been cut (fig. 15.9). Baugher notes that the "residents were

15.9. Pins, buttons, and a button blank for making bone buttons, from the city's Almshouse, eighteenth century.

required to work in return for their food, lodging, and clothing."[31] The abundance of button backs and button blanks suggests that button making may have been one of the tasks required of Almshouse residents. They made the buttons either for their own clothing or for the city to sell.

The discovery of the Almshouse kitchen underlines the role that archaeology can play in revealing the ways of life of one of the many groups ignored in written documents—the very poor. Archaeology was also responsible for the discovery of a burial ground for another such group—the city's enslaved Africans.

CHAPTER SIXTEEN

"We Were Here": The African Presence
in Colonial New York

Enslavement was a common practice in both the urban and rural parts of what later became the city of New York. The Dutch turned to slave labor in 1626, only a year after they founded New Amsterdam, when the Dutch West India Company began to import enslaved Africans. The English continued the practice to make up for the colony's perennial labor shortage. Although the enslaved included both Indians and Africans, the large majority were of African descent. In fact, among all the British colonial cities in North America, eighteenth-century New York City had a population of enslaved Africans second in size only to Charleston, South Carolina. And in mid-eighteenth-century Brooklyn, which was largely rural, more than a third of the population was of African descent.[1] It was only in the late 1790s that New York State began its slow and faltering steps toward emancipation, which was completed on July 4, 1827.

The enslaved worked at a variety of jobs. In the city, some were unskilled laborers, hired out by their owners to work on public-works projects or as stevedores at the city's docks. Others were highly skilled craftsmen who worked side by side with their owners, producing goods for market. Still others (especially women) labored in domestic service, performing the onerous tasks that were involved in running colonial urban households, or worked as vendors and peddlers in the city's streets and markets. In rural areas, enslaved women worked as household help and men as farm labor.[2]

In New York, unlike in the plantation South, most of the enslaved men, women, and children did not have separate quarters but instead lived under the same roofs as their owners and formed part of the urban colonial household. Some lived in cellars, others in garrets, and others still in "Negro kitchens" in their owners' backyards. Although a large percentage of New York's colonial households—40 percent of the homes on Manhattan Island in 1703—included the enslaved, most of these homes had only two or three slaves: they were widely dispersed throughout the seventeenth- and eighteenth-century city. And this dispersal had a profound impact on the family and community life of Africans in early New York.[3]

The presence of the enslaved in colonial New York and its environs has always been known, but it did not form part of the historical consciousness of the city's modern residents. Ideas of enslavement and of people being worked to death, like ideas of conquest, would have challenged the myth of the colonial era as the Golden Age of the city's past. In the early 1990s, however, the long tradition of enslavement in New York City was brought dramatically into the public consciousness with the discovery of an archaeological site—the African Burial Ground, containing the remains of hundreds of the city's enslaved people—and the actions of a dedicated, concerned group of New Yorkers of African descent.

Researching and Excavating a Block on Broadway

The story of the African Burial Ground began much as any of the other recent archaeological projects we have discussed. In 1989 the General Services Administration (GSA) began plans to build a $276 million federal office complex at 290 Broadway in lower Manhattan, just a block north of City Hall Park (see fig. 1.2). The design for the L-shaped parcel of land called for a thirty-four-story office tower on Broadway and a four-story pavilion at the corner of Elk and Duane Streets. As a federal agency, the GSA had to comply with federal regulations to determine the impact of the proposed construction on various aspects of the natural and cultural environment. The agency hired an engineering firm, which in turn hired a small archaeological consulting firm, Historic Conservation and Interpretation (HCI), to study the potential for historical and archaeological resources in the project area. The head of this firm, Edward Rutsch, assembled a team to do the research and to write a report of their findings. Following standard practice, the team first researched the history of the site and then explored the likelihood that archaeological remains could have survived intact in the ground.[4]

The researchers soon discovered that in the late seventeenth and eighteenth centuries, a boundary line dividing two properties ran diagonally through the block. The property on the northern side of the line changed hands several times before becoming part of a huge estate that was owned by the Rutgers family in the eighteenth century. In 1673 the government had granted the property on the southern side of the line to Cornelis Van Borsum for his wife, Sara Roelofs (who had first been married to Hans Kierstede; see chapter 10), to compensate her for her services as an interpreter during peace negotiations with the Esopus Indians in upstate New York. This parcel of land, which extended roughly from today's Broadway to Centre Street and from Chambers to Duane Streets, had been part of the city's "Commons." These were public lands used first for such communal purposes as grazing cattle and later, in the eighteenth century, as the site of many of the city's public institutions, including its almshouse. When Roelofs died in 1693, she left the land to her eight surviving children. For a number of reasons, however, the ownership of the land was disputed both among her heirs and with the city for a century after her death. In the public mind, the land continued to be part of the Commons and available for public use throughout this long period.[5]

The researchers discovered that in the mid-eighteenth century, the property was used as a "Negros Burial Ground," as it was labeled on a contemporary map (fig. 16.1). Further research suggested that the burial ground was in use by 1712. It may have been used even earlier, however, because the city instituted a policy of racially segregating its dead in 1697, when it ordained that people of African descent, free or enslaved, could no longer be buried in the recently chartered Trinity Church's cemetery; the new churchyard had formerly served as the city's potter's field. The burial ground probably continued to be used until around 1795, when much of the original Roelofs property was divided into urban lots for later sale and the city created a new cemetery for those of African descent further uptown.[6]

The researchers could see that the cemetery had been located on undesirable, un-appropriated land that was literally "beyond the pale"—it was outside the palisade that protected the city from French or Indian attack for much of the eighteenth century. This led them to think that, given the isolated living conditions for those of African descent in the eighteenth-century city, a funeral at the secluded burial ground might have been one of the few occasions when the enslaved came together as a people, away from the watchful eyes of the dominant European community. They speculated that the burial ground had been important to the African community as both a sacred space and as a meeting ground. Hints of the importance of the burial ground and of the ritu-als that took place there can be found in this description that the New York City clerk wrote in 1865, more than two generations after the burial ground was abandoned:

> Beyond the Commons lay what in the earliest settlement of the town had been appro-priated as a burial place for negroes, slaves and free. It was a desolate, unappropriated spot, descending with a gentle declivity toward a ravine which led to the Kalkhook [Collect] pond. The negroes in this city were, both in the Dutch and English colonial times, a proscribed and detested race, having nothing in common with the whites. Many of them were native Africans, imported hither in slave ships, and retaining their native superstitions and burial customs, among which was that of burying by night, with various mummeries and outcries.[7]

In addition to its continuous use by the African community during this period, the

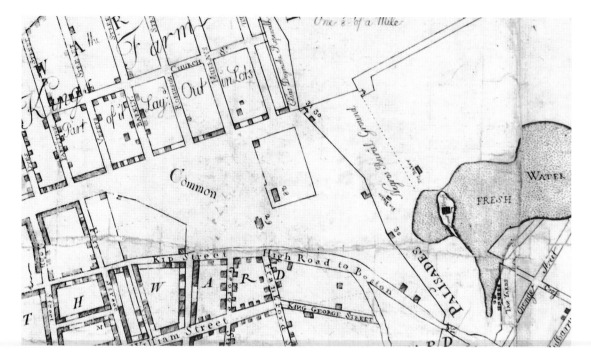

16.1. Detail of Maerschalck's "A Plan of the City of New York from an Actual Survey," 1755, showing the location of the "Negros Burial Ground" just to the north of the Common, between the palisade and the Fresh Water Pond, or Collect. Collection of the New-York Historical Society, negative number 2731.

researchers discovered that the burial ground may have played important roles in other events that shook the city in the eighteenth century. Africans made up from 14 to 21 percent of the city's population at that time, and fear of a slave revolt was ever present among its white inhabitants. In 1712 the city's slaves did revolt: a group of slaves set fire to an outbuilding and then ambushed and killed the white firefighters who responded to the alarm. As a result, six African conspirators committed suicide, and nineteen others were executed. A second revolt occurred in 1741. Though this incident was apparently not a formal conspiracy, the subsequent trials resulted in the execution of thirty-four people of African descent and four people of European descent. The executions following both events took place in the Commons, and it is likely that the adjacent burial ground served as final resting places for all those executed.[8]

The African Burial Ground may have been used for the interment of American soldiers of both African and European descent during the Revolutionary War. During their long occupation of New York City, the British reportedly used the burial ground for interring some of the American prisoners of war who had died in their custody.[9]

After the Revolution, the astronomical growth began that was to characterize New York City for the next century and a half. As the city grew, it spread uptown, with Broadway serving as a main artery for its development. In the 1790s the city reached the part of Broadway where the burial ground was located, and land there became valuable for the first time. The Roelofs heirs won their claim against the city and finally, a century after Sara Roelofs' death, reached agreement among themselves and divided their inheritance. The block was developed first for mixed residential and commercial use at the beginning of the nineteenth century, but as the century progressed, more and more of the block was redeveloped for offices, warehouses, and light industry. An L-shaped lane or alley extending from Reade to Elk Streets was laid out when the block was developed in the 1790s; this street was later named Republican Alley.[10]

The researchers saw that although the historical evidence was not as explicit as they could wish, it seemed clear that the property where the GSA wanted to build its office tower was the site of the burial ground that had served the city's African community throughout the eighteenth century. But their search of the city's building records suggested that the burial ground could not have survived the ravages of development: the block had been redeveloped in the nineteenth and early twentieth centuries, and many of the new buildings had subbasements that extended more than twenty feet into the ground. The only buildings with single basements were on the Duane Street side of the block, not on the Reade Street side where the African Burial Ground had been located. As the researchers stated in their report, "The construction of deep subbasements would have obliterated any remains within the lots that fall within the historic bounds of the cemetery, including all lots of Reade Street and Broadway." They recommended excavations within the confines of Republican Alley, which appeared to be undisturbed, to see if any remains of the burial ground had survived in this area.[11]

In May 1991, the archaeologists moved into the field, concentrating their efforts on the search for the burial ground in Republican Alley. Almost immediately the team began to find human skeletal material, although the bones were discovered in a "disturbed context," in soil that had already been dug up and then redeposited when nearby buildings were constructed. Off and on throughout the summer, working around the schedules of construction crews who first had to secure the archaeologists' deep excavations against cave-ins, the archaeologists continued their work. Soon they began discovering intact, undisturbed burials in the Republican Alley area. The Metropolitan Forensic Anthropology Team (MFAT), based at Lehman College in the Bronx, contacted Rutsch and arranged to come on board to analyze the human remains. In addition to their experience as a forensic team, these physical anthropologists had recently

tion; he was under such pressure that it was not possible for him to stop the excavations and write a research design. Its lack concerned everyone—the government agencies who were overseeing the GSA's handling of the project, local archaeological groups, and especially the descendant community. For the descendants, it symbolized once again that discrimination against the ancestors had persisted into the late twentieth century. Finally Rutsch, seeing that his firm was too small for the size the project had become, resigned, and the GSA replaced HCI with a much larger archaeological consulting firm, John Milner and Associates (JMA). JMA had the resources to handle the project, which had become enormous. It had also managed the excavations of two African American burial grounds in Philadelphia.[22]

As the spring progressed, members of New York's African American community began holding public meetings and ceremonies throughout the city to celebrate the burial ground and to protest the GSA's handling of the project. A town meeting was held, symbolically, at Trinity Church, the Episcopal church whose opening in 1697 was coincident with the ban of the burial of people of African descent in what then became the church's graveyard, and which thus may have caused the creation of the African Burial Ground. People of African descent, representing a wide range of religions, held rituals outside the archaeological site and at Lehman College, where the remains of the dead were being stored prior to analysis (fig. 16.4).[23]

As spring turned to summer, protests continued to grow. And it was becoming more and more apparent that although the GSA had heard the community's complaints, it would not respond to them. In late July 1992, when the excavators had found more than four hundred burials, Mayor Dinkins wrote a letter to Diamond formally requesting that the excavations cease. Among other issues, he pointed out that the GSA's "continuing actions . . . are deeply disturbing to many New Yorkers." A few days later, Diamond formally rejected the mayor's plea, saying that because his agency was in compliance with federal regulations, there was no reason to halt the excavations. Instead, it would continue with construction.[24]

Finally, after months of impasse from the descendant community's perspective, many of the issues surrounding the African Burial Ground were resolved very quickly by a means that, though completely unexpected to most observers at the time, in retrospect should have been

16.4. Alegba Egunfemi Adegbolola, a Yoruba spiritual leader, performing a ceremony at the African Burial Ground in 1992.

wholly predictable. The only entity that could be effective in stopping the excavations and the GSA's construction of the building was a congressional committee that could make it difficult for the agency to get funding. Less than a week after Dinkins received his reply from Diamond, Gus Savage, a congressman of African descent from Illinois and chairman of the Committee on Public Works and Transportation's Subcommittee on Public Buildings and Grounds, called a congressional hearing in New York, right across the street from the site. He heard testimony from Dinkins, the Landmarks Preservation Commission, members of the descendant community, and, of course, the GSA. At the end of the hearing, the enraged congressman shouted at the GSA representatives, "Don't waste your time asking this subcommittee for anything else as long as I'm chairman, unless you can figure out a way to go around me! I am not going to be part of your disrespect." He went on to accuse Diamond of arrogance in his dealings with the African American community.[25]

Three days later, the General Services Administration announced that it would permanently stop the archaeological excavations at the cemetery. Construction would continue on the site of the thirty-four-story office tower proposed for the Broadway side of the site (the burials had already been removed from this area), but the "pavilion," the four-story building proposed for the eastern side of the site, would not be built, and the graves of those still buried in that area (estimated at around two hundred) would not be disturbed. The archaeologists finished excavating the burials they were in the process of exhuming, packed up their equipment, and left the field. Following the advice of conservators, a layer of fill composed of clean sand was placed over the unexcavated part of the site, bringing its surface up to the surrounding grade, and a layer of sod was laid over the site.

The GSA established an advisory panel made up of historians, archaeologists, politicians, and members of the descendant community to resolve problems that remained. The panel ultimately decided that the analysis of the remains would be carried out by Michael Blakey's team at Howard University, with Blakey as scientific director (fig. 16.5).

For the African American community, the transfer of the bones to Howard symbolized their success in gaining control over the study of their ancestors. It was marked by a celebration at Howard University in November 1993. As reporter Emilyn Brown described it: "The 'official' transfer of the remains . . . proved to be a simple, yet highly effective gesture. Before a standing room only audience, a royal Kente covered box, containing the last of the transferred remains, was handed to Dr. Blakey by Mary Lacey Madison, a community activist chosen to participate for her long involvement with the African cemetery. Accompanied by prayers offered from a representative group of spiritual leaders . . . the ceremony began and concluded with libations to the ancestors."[26] In 1993 the site was designated a National Historic Landmark.

16.5. Michael L. Blakey (right), *the scientific director of the African Burial Ground Project, at the site in 1992.*

With their unwavering determination concerning the African Burial Ground, members of the city's African American community had successfully challenged anthropologists and an overseeing federal agency and seized control of an archaeological project. This was the first time in New York that anthropologists had come into direct conflict with another group that had powerful and legitimate, though very different, claims to the past. Although most archaeologists in New York ultimately supported the descendant community in their fight to stop the excavations, for many the controversy was a vivid lesson in how archaeology had changed over the years, since the days of the first professionals like Alanson Skinner and George Pepper. Today, archaeologists all over the world are learning that they are not working in a vacuum. As more and more groups become interested in their heritage, archaeologists are only one of a number of parties who are concerned with interpreting the past. Archaeological studies are being used by many modern ethnic groups and nation-states, and archaeologists may not always agree with these groups or with how their own work is being interpreted. Nonetheless, all these parties often have to work together to explore this unknown but shared world.[27]

"Irrefutable Testimony"

After the transfer of the remains to Howard, Blakey and his team began the long process of analysis. The team includes, as associate directors, archaeologist Warren Perry and historian Edna Medford, with urban anthropologist Sherrill Wilson (who had been actively involved in the community struggle since its inception) as director of public education. Although the analysis is still under way, the preliminary results are gripping as they detail the lives and deaths of the members of the African community in the eighteenth-century city.

The archaeologists' meticulous excavation records have revealed the enormous care with which people buried their dead. Almost all the graves were oriented east-west with heads to the west, so that if the dead were to arise, they would see the rising sun. Most people were buried in hexagonal coffins, although there were a few rectangular and tapered ones. Most people, too, were buried in shrouds. The analysts know this because, although the shrouds themselves did not survive the centuries of interment, the pins that held them in place did; shroud pins were among the most common artifacts that the excavators found in the graves (fig. 16.6). In several cases women were buried with children; presumably these were mothers and their children who had died at the same time, perhaps at childbirth (for newborns) or from epidemics (for older children). Sometimes infants were found cradled in the arms of their mothers (fig. 16.7).[28]

The archaeologists have discovered that some African customs were maintained in the culture that enslaved people of African descent constructed for themselves in New York. More than twenty people had had their front teeth filed into distinctive shapes, such as pointed and hourglass shapes, following a custom that is common among many groups in West Africa and West Central Africa (the area where it is thought that many of the enslaved were captured). Some anthropologists look on evidence of tooth filing as an indication that a person was born in Africa, because no contemporary written sources have been found describing this practice in North America.[29]

The presence of African cultural traits in New York is particularly apparent in looking at the grave of an individual known today only as Burial 101. These are the remains of a man in his early thirties who may have been born in Africa—he has filed teeth. In addition, his bones show evidence of treponemal infection, perhaps from yaws, prevalent in tropical America and Africa. An analysis of his DNA showed a close affinity to people living in West Africa today, implying that they all shared a female ancestor in the not-too-distant past.[30]

Burial 101 was buried in a hexagonal coffin that had on its lid an elaborate heart-shaped design formed by the heads of ninety-two iron

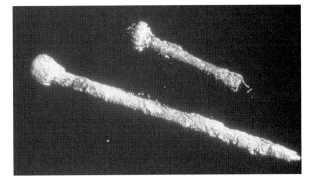

16.6. Shroud pins from the African Burial Ground.

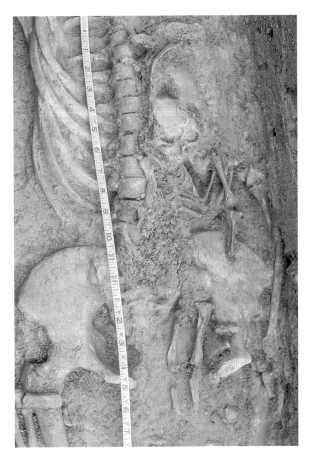

16.7. A detail of the burial of a woman, showing her hips and vertebrae. The tiny bones of an infant can be seen on her hip bone.

tacks. Excavators initially hypothesized that the design represented a heart that had been placed on the coffin lid, perhaps symbolizing the affection of the mourners for the deceased. But Blakey thought that he recognized the motif from another context, and he showed the symbol to African art expert Kweku Ofari-Ansa. Ofari-Ansa identified the design as the Sankofa symbol used by the Akan people of Ghana and the Ivory Coast (fig. 16.8): "The original figure was derived from the behavior of birds. . . . [which] characteristically turn their heads towards their tails to either scratch or groom themselves. This was interpreted to mean 'turning ones head toward the past,' . . . in order to build the future." An abstract heart-shaped version of the symbol, similar to that found on the coffin lid, was depicted on Akan ritual cloth, which "was used during important, highly spiritual ceremonies relating to ancestral remembrance, celebration of rites of passage into the realm of the ancestors, and reinforcement of a communion between humans and the spiritual world."[31]

Some archaeologists working on the project have seen the use of this motif as a prime example of the importance of multivalent symbols—symbols that have different meanings in different contexts—for oppressed groups forced to live in the shadow of their oppressors. The symbol could have meant "Sankofa" to the African funeral participants but "heart" to any casual European observer. Any subversive meaning the Sankofa symbol might have assumed for the enslaved Africans would not be apparent to European onlookers.[32]

The archaeologists also found grave goods included with some of the burials. A child, between five and seven years old, was buried with a silver ornament strung on a leather thong around the neck. A few people were buried with other kinds of objects, including pieces of coral, shells, a pocket knife, a tobacco pipe, a sherd of stoneware pottery decorated with a blue spiral, quartz crystals, cuff links, and a ring. Some of these adorned the body, others were included in the coffin, and still others were placed on top of the coffin lid. Perry and his archaeological team are researching these objects as well as other burial practices for parallels in African cultures and among African peoples in other parts of the world.[33]

16.8. The bird image (left) on which the stylized Sankofa image (right) is based.

Several people were buried with glass beads that had been strung into bracelets, necklaces, or waistbands. In many West African cultures, beads play an important role in rites of passage, including birth, puberty, marriage, death, and so on. In parts of Africa it was customary to bury the dead with such personal belongings as ornaments and beads. These accessories imparted spiritual power and status to those who wore them, and provided protection, particularly for children. Two of the infants interred at the burial ground were buried with strands of beads. In one case, the strand was placed around the waist, and in the other, around the neck.[34]

One of the most evocative burials found in the cemetery was that of a middle-aged woman. Like many others, she had been wrapped in a shroud and placed in a wooden coffin. But most unusually, a strand of more than one hundred beads encircled her hips (fig. 16.9). Most of the beads were glass, but two may have been made from cowrie shells, which had almost disintegrated in the centuries before they were excavated. Her front teeth had been filed into traditional African hourglass and pointed shapes. Although we will probably never know the story of this woman with certainty, her filed teeth suggest that she was born in Africa, and it is possible that she managed to bring the beaded girdle with her through the infamously cruel Middle Passage. The only other known burial from an African site in the Americas similar to hers was that of a man excavated at a plantation site in Barbados. This man has been identified as an Obeah, or folk doctor. Some think that the woman known today only as Burial 340 may also have been a healer or ritual leader in her community in eighteenth-century New York.[35]

By far the most striking aspect of the study of the dead in the African Burial Ground is the evidence of the enormous physical hardship that these people suffered during their lifetimes. Many appear to have been literally "worked to death."[36] This is made obvious through an examination of the skeletons of both children and adults.

The analysis of the bones of the children shows an extremely high incidence of malnutrition and disease. First of all, almost 50 percent of those buried in the burial ground are children, an unusually high percentage. And of those who died before they were twelve, 40 percent were infants—a very high infant mortality rate. Furthermore, the skeletons of both children and adults exhibit characteristics indicating malnutrition and other kinds of physiological stress. Many show enamel hypoplasia—horizontal lines visible on teeth—which indicate that growth was interrupted at some point while the tooth was growing, between the time of birth and around six years of age for the front teeth. There is also a high incidence of Harris lines—bands of greater bone density in arm and leg bones, which are visible on X rays. These also indicate stress, often from malnutrition, during the time of long-bone growth, between birth and approximately eighteen years of age. In addition, more than half the population shows signs of infectious disease, including yaws, pinta, syphilis, and infectious meningitis. And about half show evidence of porotic hyperostosis, resulting from severe anemia, which could be from malnutrition, infectious diseases, or from sickle-cell disease (most of the enslaved are thought to have come from tropical West Africa, whose population had a high frequency of the sickle-cell trait). Some skeletons exhibit bone deformations, indicating rickets and other conditions. Although many of these signs of stress

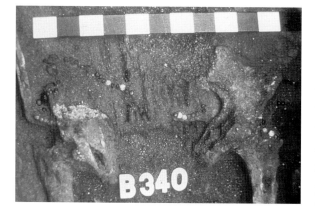

16.9. *A detail of the bead girdle that was found on Burial 340. Note the cowrie shells, which are badly decayed, on the left side. The black-and-white squares at the top of the image form a scale; each square equals one inch.*

appear during childhood, a time of growth, their effects are permanent, showing childhood stress in the teeth and bones of adults.[37]

Most revealingly, the teeth and bones of the children uncovered at the burial ground are on the whole marked by much more developmental stress than those of their elders. Blakey accounts for this phenomenon by noting that many of the adults interred in the burial ground, unlike the children buried there, spent their childhoods in freedom in Africa, where life was much more benign than in colonial New York. He estimates that as many as one-third of the enslaved people of African descent in eighteenth-century New York had been born in Africa and brought in bondage to the city.[38]

Although we know from historians' research that some of the enslaved worked in highly skilled trades, those who toiled in physical labor worked extremely hard, as their bones tell the Blakey team today. Most adults show signs of enlarged muscle attachments on their arm and leg bones and on their vertebrae. And the bones of many—both men and women—show lesions at the points of muscle attachment. Lesions such as these form where bone has been literally torn away from bone by excessive muscular strain.[39]

Traditionally, both women and men in West and Central Africa (and in other parts of the world) carry heavy objects by balancing them on their heads. Blakey maintains that many of those interred at the burial ground, particularly the women, show the physical evidence of this custom pushed to extremes: they have "ring fractures" at the base of their skulls—injuries from the strain of carrying loads on their heads that were too heavy for their necks to bear. In fact, one woman may have died from such an injury; her vertebrae seem to have been literally thrust into the base of her skull by the weight of the load on her head.[40]

Burial 101, the man interred in the coffin bearing the Sankofa symbol, illustrates the kind of information that scientists like Blakey can learn about peoples' lives from studying their skeletal remains. This man shows no evidence of enamel hypoplasia or Harris lines, suggesting that he enjoyed a childhood relatively free of physiological stress, perhaps in Africa (as the filing on his incisors suggests). But his vertebrae display fractures that are clearly visible to the naked eye, suggesting that after his capture and removal to the Americas as an adult "his forced labors were," as Blakey put it, "backbreaking in the most literal sense." Yet his burial in the coffin with the Sankofa symbol indicates that although he endured such hard work, he enjoyed considerable prestige in his community.[41]

Another burial has given the Howard team a unique glimpse into the violent death of a young woman. She was buried with a lead musket ball embedded in her chest. Her bones showed fractures from repeated blows to her face, and a twisting fracture on her lower arm. Both sets of fractures, as well as the wound from the musket, occurred at the time she died, and some members of the research team speculate that she may have been killed in punishment for an act of resistance.[42]

Blakey, in his position of scientific director of the African Burial Ground Project, sees himself as performing many roles. One is his role as a scientist. He also has a set of obligations to his business client, the GSA. This agency pays the bills, which are estimated to come to about $5.2 million before the project is completed. (This figure should be seen in the context of the cost of the construction project; the cost of the burial ground study is less than 2 percent of the cost of the building, which has been estimated at more than $270 million.) But Blakey firmly believes that he is equally obligated to what he refers to as his ethical client, the descendant community. He and other project members perform all the scholarly activities that their peers do: they present papers at professional meetings and publish in scientific journals. But they are also concerned with incorporating feedback from the modern-day African American community into their research and with getting information about results out to the general public. Sherrill Wilson's Office of Public Education and Interpretation (OPEI) for the project has presented thousands of programs on the burial ground to tens of thousands of people. OPEI also publishes *Update,* a widely distributed quarterly newsletter. By honoring all these sets of obligations, Blakey feels that the "scientific, cultural, spiritual, or religious treatments of the cemetery" complement rather than compete with each other.[43]

As would be expected, the symbolic importance of the burial ground has transcended not only the boundaries of the city but also those of the nation. In 1995 a group of chiefs from Ghana visited both the Howard Laboratory in Washington and the burial ground in New York as part of a "Tour of Fihankra," a pilgrimage of atonement and reunification "based on the historical reality that some of the ancestral traditional rulers helped sustain the Trans-Atlantic slave trade." In explaining the pouring of a libation at the cemetery as part of this pilgrimage, one participant said that they "all put on mourning clothes as if we were going to a funeral. . . . We felt that these were our people who have been buried here, they could be our sisters, brothers, our great-grandfathers and great-grandmothers. The libation that I poured was to ask for forgiveness from them, so that they should accept our pleading for forgiveness."[44]

The African Burial Ground has become an enormously important site for modern-day Africans, African Americans, and all New Yorkers. This sacred site underscores and commemorates the deep historical presence of Africans in New York and their contribution in building the nation. As David Dinkins eloquently put it: "Millions of Americans celebrate Ellis Island as the symbol of their communal identity in this land. Others celebrate Plymouth Rock. Until a few years ago, African-American New Yorkers had no site to call our own. There was no place which said, we were here, we contributed, we played a significant role in New York's history right from the beginning. Now we—their descendants—have the symbol of our heritage embodied in Lower Manhattan's African Burial Ground. The African Burial Ground is the irrefutable testimony to the contributions and suffering of our ancestors."[45]

PART **4**

Conclusion

We come and go, but the land is
always here. And the people who love
it and understand it are the people
who own it—for a little while.

—Willa Cather, *O Pioneers!*

CHAPTER SEVENTEEN

Common Ground

In looking at New York City as one vast archaeological site, we have wandered beyond its bright lights and into forgotten worlds long hidden beneath the modern city. Under this sprawling, congested, noisy capital of the modern world, archaeologists, lured by the buried past, have discovered a succession of landscapes and a panoramic view of many of the peoples who inhabited those landscapes over the past eleven thousand years.

The very land on which the modern city rests has changed enormously over the millennia. Because of the complex natural history of the area, many of the environments once seen by its earliest residents are difficult to imagine in modern times; they no longer exist anywhere in the world today and can be visualized only through archaeology. Furthermore, the land has been claimed and altered by all those who once lived on it. Some peoples made profound statements of place and community by burying their dead in traditional burying grounds or by bringing them home for reburial. Generations of fishermen, ancient and modern, returned to traditional fishing spots along the city's nearly six-hundred-mile coastline. Hunting and agricultural practices, both Native American and European, transformed the landscape. Landfilling and land leveling further altered the area. Forts were built to protect claims to the land; local industries polluted its waters. And its residents built their homes and work spaces all across the landscape, transforming it in the process.

New York's geographical position has offered its residents markedly different opportunities. In earliest times, when the coast was one hundred miles away, the people adapted to an inland area with a hunting-and-gathering economy. Around four thousand years ago, when rising sea levels stabilized, the coast reached its present familiar location. This marked the beginning of a long and successful adaptation to a rich estuarine environment. The coast's bounty made

297

possible a distinctive way of life in the Woodland centuries, one that remained essentially egalitarian even as local residents came into contact with more-complex societies living in the interior of the continent. New York's coastal resources were so abundant that even when some of the neighboring inland Woodland peoples began focusing their economies around maize, beans, and squash agriculture, those living along the coast were in no hurry to follow suit. Instead, they continued with their traditional hunting, fishing, and gathering activities and merely added farming to their already successful and diverse economy. In these Woodland times, Native Americans established trading routes connecting the coast with the interior—routes that were later adopted by European fur traders and colonists.

Throughout the thousands of years of their occupancy, the Indian peoples' attitude toward the land was essentially that of a collective guardianship. For them, the Atlantic coast remained a formidable barrier, albeit often a lush and bountiful one. Then, in the seventeenth century, Europeans and Africans arrived in Indian territory. The meetings of these peoples from three different continents, each with their own traditions, technologies, social orders, customs, diseases, religions, and economies, brought about dramatic changes that, for better and for worse, created the "New World" that in turn led to the establishment of New York City.

The labors of these three peoples, whose encounters were often tragic, were critical in the creation of the emerging trans-Atlantic economy. For the Africans, the coast was a cold and bitter land of enslavement. For the native Munsees, it became important in a new way—as the source of the shells that they transformed into wampum. These shell beads were both the money that ran the economy and a vital part of the fur trade. But the entangled effects of disease, war, ecological changes, and dispossession ended their long stewardship of the land, and most of the surviving Munsees were gradually displaced from their homeland into the interior of the continent. For the Europeans, the coast became a "new" land of economic opportunity.

The Europeans brought with them an economy in which almost everything could be bought and sold. For two long centuries, even human beings had a price. The market economy also molded people's attitudes toward the land. It had become something that could be "owned" by individuals and radically transformed by draining, leveling, and filling. New land could even be created along the shorefronts, a process that continues to this day.

For the Europeans, the coast was never a barrier. Instead, it was a gateway to and from the rest of the world. Its rivers led to the rich interior of the country, and its harbor became a link to other continents. In later centuries, millions of people from other parts of the world came looking for better lives and resettled the land. In time, the city became the site of Revolutionary War battlegrounds, the first capital of the United

States, the premier American maritime port, a major manufacturing center, a world financial center, an international media and information capital, and one of the modern world's greatest cities.

Because of all these varied natural and cultural histories, that great city became a major American archaeological site as it spread for 325 square miles over the traces of many of its earlier residents. Scores of smaller sites—cemeteries, inland encampments, forts, ossuaries, warehouses, shellfishing communities, wharves, dog burials, battlefields, workshops, scuttled ships, taverns, plantations, cornfields, landfills, almshouses, suburban backyards, hunting grounds, and towns and villages—make up the larger site that is the city itself.

In spite of the breadth of this archaeological panorama, the tangible nature of the archaeological finds gives an immediacy to the daily lives, and even the thoughts and actions, of these early inhabitants. Through archaeology, we catch glimpses of a wide range of individuals: the first pioneers who abandoned some of their tools before moving on to their next campsite, nineteenth-century housewives choosing dishes for their family tables, an enslaved African marking a coffin with a traditional African design, and Munsee families acquiring European domesticated animals while neighboring European and African women began cooking Indian foods in traditional Dutch pots.

With equal intimacy, these material remains evoke the countless ceremonies that gave meaning to the lives of those who once celebrated them on this common ground. There were smoking rituals that linked the inhabitants with the spiritual world, domestic rituals of family dinners and company teas, rites of health and death in which dogs played major roles, and, over and over again, the somber rituals of mourning, be they performed by relatives filling a six-year-old child's grave with wealth, families gathering the bones of their long-dead relatives for reburial, or enslaved families burying their dead at night outside the city's walls.

The study of an archaeological site like New York City is far from parochial. Because of the site's great time depth, size, complex human and natural history, and impact on the world outside its borders, the archaeology of New York reaches well beyond local history to address more universal aspects of the human experience. The meanings embedded in these artifacts, features, and human burials shed new light on the development of capitalism and the global economy, the social constructions of community and landscape, and the development of sedentary and urban ways of life. They unite the long-unfamiliar indigenous history with the more familiar recent history into one continuous narrative that creates a unique American past. These archaeological finds tell us of things we never knew, remind us of those we are proud to remember, and testify to those we prefer to forget.

In this chronicle of the ever-changing history of an American city, we have tried, as

17.1. Delaware spiritual leaders from Oklahoma and Canada gathered at Ellis Island in 1987 for a blessing ceremony honoring the remains of their ancestors. The bones had been discovered during renovations of the Great Hall of the Ellis Island Museum of Immigration. The island, now owned by the National Park Service and a national shrine to the American immigrant experience, is also part of Lenapehoking, the ancestral homeland of the Delaware. This blessing ceremony was arranged by the National Park Service and planned by the Delaware. Plans are currently under discussion for the final reburial of these and other ancestral Delaware remains.

one anthropologist put it, "to speak the past into being, to summon it with words and give it dramatic form . . . by forging ancestral worlds in which others can participate and readily lose themselves." New York's archaeological discoveries, its ancestral worlds, have, we believe, significance for the modern world. They are literally the stuff of meaningful history, easily transformed into local pride, a sense of place, and even legend, all of which are important in today's often rootless and restless world. In appreciating these discoveries, some people may simply find themselves agreeing with Mr. Sammler, Saul Bellow's protagonist, that "everyone needs his memories. They keep the wolf of insignificance from the door." For others, these ancestral worlds may take on added importance as they are recast into powerful cultural symbols (fig. 17.1; see also fig. 16.4).[1]

The present is so deeply rooted in the past that, as many have argued, it can be difficult to know where you are, let alone where you are going, unless you first know where you have been. We believe that the archaeological record bears singular witness to where we all once were. The finds unearthed beneath the modern city reveal the many and diverse routes that earlier peoples followed, each path leading, in its own way, to the creation of the modern city that is New York.

In writing this narrative, we have tried to build strong connections between all those who shared the land in the past and those who have now inherited it. We believe that we are all, as Abraham Lincoln said, "heirs to a great estate."[2] For us, that great estate is the past, which belongs to everyone. It is truly common ground.

Yet the archaeological record, like the land itself, is inherited from previous generations and is only temporarily owned by us. It will soon belong to our descendants. And so with this inheritance come responsibilities. We know from bitter experience just how fragile archaeological sites are and how easily they and all the information in them can be irrevocably lost. Sites that are destroyed are gone forever.

We hope that all the heirs will work together to protect and cherish the buried past so that it can be passed on to succeeding generations, who in their turn will also own it, value it, and love it. They are the ones who will build on that collective heritage, redefine it, and take pride in it. We hope that it will give as much meaning and pleasure to their lives as it has to ours.

Notes

Chapter 1: The Archaeology of New York City

1. This search for information distinguishes archaeologists from antiquarians, whose interest lies primarily in the object itself—its age, its aesthetic quality, its value. For antiquarians, the context in which the artifact was found and its associations are less important. A number of general introductory texts in archaeology discuss the significance of context as well as general archaeological methods and techniques. See, for example, D. H. Thomas 1998; Renfrew and Bahn 2000.
2. United Nations 1991:14.
3. Rothschild and Rockman [Wall] 1982:6.
4. The concept of a present-minded people sharing a future but not a past is adapted from Kammen 1993:41. Colden 1825:77–78 as cited in Lowenthal 1985:109.
5. Kammen 1993:538, 619. David Harvey makes a similar point. He writes that the "Roots phenomenon" and other preoccupations "with identity, with personal and collective roots, [have] become far more pervasive since the early 1970's because of widespread insecurity in labor markets, in technological mixes, credit systems, and the like" (1990:87). See also F. Jameson 1984.
6. See Cotter et al. 1992 for the story of archaeology in Philadelphia.
7. Vincent Scully as cited in Goldstone and Dalrymple 1974:223.
8. National Historic Preservation Act of 1966, title I, section 101.b.3; reprinted in King et al. 1977:206.
9. The federal legislation that supplements the Historic Preservation Act includes the National Environmental Policy Act (1969) and the Archaeological and Historic Preservation Act (1974), as well as Executive Order 11593 (1971) and various regulations. See King et al. 1977.
10. The dates are archaeological conventions and are approximate. In some cases they are based on radiocarbon dates; in others, on comparisons with similar sites that have been dated in adjacent areas. This ordering in no way suggests an evolutionary sequence, periods of millennia-long stasis, or dramatic changes in the ways of life of the early residents of the area. These arbitrary divisions simply reflect our current and imperfect knowledge of the archaeological record for that part of the past (see Snow 1980 and Dincauze 1990 for other timetables). By archaeological convention, in uncalibrated dates the "present" in B.P. is 1950. For a discussion of the complexities of radiocarbon dating, see D. H. Thomas 1998.

Chapter 2: Digging in New York

1. See Cantwell and Wall, n.d.
2. The phrase "creative destruction" is adapted from Harvey 1985, 1990.
3. 71 Pearl Street, LP-0041, file, NYC Landmarks Preservation Commission 1966, 1980.
4. Regina Kellerman and Joseph Shelley conducted the limited excavations at the Stadt Huys.

5. The loss of parts of the building's facade is recorded in an unsigned memo in the 71 Pearl Street file at the NYC Landmarks Preservation Commission.

6. The commission's staff members who were active in bringing archaeology to the city included Executive Director Lenore Norman, preservationist Kathryn Misch, and counsel Dorothy Miner; the commission's chairman at that time was Kent Barwick.

7. In the 1950s Salwen had been involved in the famous case of the Trenton Six; he also helped found the statewide New York Archaeological Council and worked with it in successfully suing several state and federal agencies that had not fulfilled the requirements of the National Historic Preservation Act. See Rothschild 1990b; Klein 1990.

8. This description of the history of the site is based on Rothschild et al. 1987.

9. Today, many projects are able to assign a staff person to interpreting the excavations to the public. The Stadt Huys Block excavations were memorialized in a painting by Hedi Pagremanski, an artist who specializes in New York City street scenes. The painting, called *The State House Block Dig* (1980), is owned by Goldman Sachs. She also did a painting called *The Telco Dig* (1983), which is in the Pagremanski-Page collection.

10. 71 Pearl Street, LP-0041, file, NYC Landmarks Preservation Commission 1966, 1980; see Baugher and Wall 1996.

11. The report, titled "The Archaeological Investigation of the Stadt Huys Block: A Final Report" (Rothschild et al. 1987), is on file with the NYC Landmarks Preservation Commission.

12. This project was directed by Joan Geismar (1989).

13. Joan Geismar did the background study of 17 State Street (1986).

14. Kaufman was quoted in Dunlap 1990; see Baugher and Wall 1996.

15. The 3 percent figure is from Pagano 1992. Under the current regulations, even land that is owned by the city is not protected from the destruction of archaeological sites. This is particularly serious when we consider that most of the undeveloped land in New York—areas where we might expect to find the fragile traces of the Native American past—

is owned by the city; much of this undeveloped land is administered by the Department of Parks. Other cities in the United States have enacted regulations similar to the federal legislation to cover development that occurs on city-owned land or with city funds. The Professional Archaeologists of New York City (PANYC), a local professional organization, has drafted legislation that would cover these situations, but it has yet to be adopted by the City Council.

Chapter 3: The Creation of the World

1. Danckaerts 1941:150–51. For other Delaware origin myths, see Bierhorst 1995 and Newcomb 1956.

2. The glacier's edges were marked by moraines, long ridges made up of the tons of soil and stone pushed by the glaciers as they moved south. These moraines are still prominent features of the city's landscape, running across Long Island and Staten Island. The most southerly moraine, the Ronkokoma, created almost twenty-two thousand years ago, underlies the Long Island Expressway. The boundaries of the vegetation zones cannot be defined with precision. See Sirkin 1986; Belknap and Kraft 1977; Edwards and Merrill 1977; J. Kraft 1985; Funk 1991; Dincauze 1988; and Gramly and Funk 1990. See Deloria 1995 for a Native American critique of the archaeology of this period. The depiction of Paleoindians as pioneers is adapted from Dincauze 1990.

3. To date, the earliest sites, such as Monte Verde in Chile (ca. 12,500 B.P. and possibly earlier), have been found in South America. The relationship, if any, of these early South Americans to the apparently later North American Paleoindians is unclear. For the peopling of the Americas, see Fagan 1987, 2000; Meltzer 1993; Meltzer and Dillehay 1999; and Wenke 1999.

4. For Clovis and later Paleoindians, see Fagan 1987, 2000; Meltzer 1993. In addition, for dating of Clovis sites see Meltzer and Dillehay 1999; Fiedel 1999; Curran 1996. The dates given here are in radiocarbon years, reflecting the limitations of carbon 14 dating, especially for this period. These dates are somewhat earlier, perhaps by as much as two thousand years, than calendar or "real-time" years. See Fiedel 1999 and Fagan 2000 for discussion of radiocarbon

calibrations for Paleoindian sites. For pre-Clovis sites, see Adovasio et al. 1990; Dincauze 1981; Fagan 2000; Goodyear et al. 1999; Meltzer 1993; Meltzer and Dillehay 1999; and Wenke 1999.

5. Fagan 2000:85; Meltzer and Dillehay 1999:61.

6. For an appreciation of early American achievements, see Meltzer and Dillehay 1999:61.

7. Paleoindians are assumed to have had a hunting, fishing, and gathering economy. This term covers a wide variety of economic strategies that are not based on domesticated plants or animals; see Fagan 2000 and Bettinger 1987.

8. For the function of fluting, see Meltzer 1993:123. See H. Kraft 1977 and Snow 1980 for detailed discussions of the variety of fluted points found at Port Mobil.

9. Conversation with Albert Anderson, September 12, 1990.

10. These three separate areas are referred to collectively as the Port Mobil site. The artifacts found on Charleston Beach may represent a separate Paleoindian encampment or may have eroded down from the higher ground at the tank farm. The points found at the northernmost site, North Beach, are somewhat larger than those at the other sites and may represent an earlier encampment (H. Kraft 1977). A Clovis point was found during World War I on a nearby property (Sainz 1962).

11. Conversation with Albert Anderson, September 12, 1990. Much of the discussion here is based on H. Kraft 1977, as well as discussions with Herbert Kraft and Albert Anderson in 1990 and 1991. See also Leonard Eisenberg 1978; Snow 1980; Funk 1991; Gramly and Funk 1990; and Moeller 1980. For a discussion of the variability in point size, see H. Kraft 1977. Avocationals Donald Sainz and Albert Anderson were interested in having a professional excavation at Port Mobil (Sainz 1962). Several test excavations were conducted in the general area by faculty and students from New York University and Columbia University, but no buried Paleoindian deposits were found (Salwen 1968a). Sainz and Anderson followed these excavations with great interest and were somewhat surprised to see women students as part of the crew. Until then, they had viewed archaeology as a male pursuit.

12. Archaeologists have long been intrigued by the possibility that some vestiges of Paleoindian life on the continental shelf might have survived the damages of the wave action of the rising seas (Emery and Edwards 1966; Edwards and Emery 1977:250–251). Some archaeologists are reconstructing paleoenvironments and geomorphology in the hope of using such data to find intact submerged sites. Archaeologist Arnold Pickman notes the significance of the development of barrier-lagoon systems in such searches: "Such systems involve the formation of lagoons behind offshore bars. Deposits of mud and marsh vegetation form during the process of siltation of the lagoon. As sea levels continue to rise, the waves eventually attack the offshore barrier and the lagoonal deposits. However, since the sea level would have risen since the formation of the initial lagoonal deposits, the zone of erosion may pass above any underlying archaeological data." Once such barrier-lagoon systems are identified, remote sensing and borings could then be used to locate buried sites (Pickman 1984:3; see also Pickman 1982a, 1982b; and Funk 1997).

13. See Callahan 1979 for a discussion of techniques used in making fluted points. Some points may have been used as hafted knives. On raw materials for making stone tools, see Ritchie and Funk 1973; Funk 1976; H. Kraft 1977; and Snow 1980.

14. For mastodon finds in New York City, see Calver 1948. For human interactions with extinct megafauna, see Snow 1980; Meltzer 1988; Tankersley 1998; and Dincauze 1988. Although some archaeologists have suggested that Paleoindians were responsible for the extinction of the megafauna—the so-called overkill theory—most archaeologists see the situation as more complex, and related to the constantly shifting post-glacial environment; see Fagan 1987; Grayson 1991; and Mead and Meltzer 1985.

15. See H. Kraft 1986:41; Snow 1980:133; and Funk 1991. For the nature of the Paleoindian diet in the Northeast, see Dincauze 1988; Gramly and Funk 1990; and McNett 1985.

16. In spite of their usefulness, ethnographic analogies are problematic in a number of ways (see Fagan 2000). No matter how carefully analogues are

chosen from modern hunting-and-gathering societies, the earlier societies may have been quite different from their modern counterparts.

17. Dincauze 1990:20.

Chapter 4: Settling Down in the Archaic

1. Although there is no consensus on how to define, date, or divide these post-glacial times, the subdivisions used here are commonly employed by a number of archaeologists. They are based on currently perceived differences in technology, environmental shifts, and human adaptations to the environment. See Snow 1980; Ritchie 1980; H. Kraft 1986; Funk 1997; Pfeiffer 1990; and Winters 1969 for discussions of these issues and, in some cases, alternate chronologies.

2. The environmental reconstructions are based on Funk 1991; Salwen 1975; Lavin 1988; Dincauze 1989; Nicholas 1987, 1988; and Robinson et al. 1992.

3. Newman 1977:566; Newman and Salwen 1977.

4. This hypothesis of a cultural hiatus, or "empty quarter," is sometimes referred to as the Ritchie-Fitting hypothesis, after two of its early proponents (Fitting 1968; Ritchie 1965). See Robinson et al. 1992 and Funk 1991, 1996.

5. Broyles 1971 and Coe 1964. See also Fagan 2000.

6. See Ritchie 1971 for a discussion of projectile points in the Northeast. See Snow 1980 on the dangers of defining temporal periods solely on the basis of projectile-point types.

7. See Ritchie and Funk 1971 for descriptions of these four sites and the radiocarbon dating.

8. In 1965, when Ritchie published his major synthetic survey, *The Archaeology of New York State,* the table of contents reflected this 4,500-year hiatus. It read "The Earliest Occupants—Paleo-Indian Hunters (c. 8,000 B.C.)," followed by "The Archaic or Hunting, Fishing, Gathering Stage (c. 3,500–1,300 B.C.)."

9. Ritchie and Funk 1971:45.

10. See Braun and Braun 1994 on techniques of stone boiling, hide preparation, and tool manufacture. Here, as earlier, descriptions of the sexual division of labor are assumptions, nothing more.

11. Celts are ground stone tools, usually made from hard igneous rock, which require considerable time and labor to manufacture (Robert Funk, pers. comm., July 1998).

12. Petersen and Putnam (1992:20) point out that this period may even have been more hospitable than some later colder and wetter ones. Reconstructing the environment in the Northeast is problematic. The few studies done indicate considerable regional diversity, and their results cannot necessarily be extrapolated to neighboring areas. Ritchie and Funk (1971) have suggested that the Staten Island area straddles the Carolinian and Canadian Biotic Provinces and may well have been more congenial than other places to the north. For more recent Early Archaic finds, see Funk 1991, 1996; Robinson et al. 1992; Nicholas 1987, 1988.

13. Cronon 1983:13.

14. See Funk 1991; Lavin 1988; Dincauze and Mulholland 1977; Dincauze 1989; and Snow 1980.

15. Some archaeologists prefer to use the term "shell matrix" in referring to shell middens, to leave open the actual use made of the shells at any one particular site (Claassen 1991).

16. The quotation is cited in Truex 1982:5. See also M. R. Harrington 1909; Schaper 1993. The shell heap near the Collect has long since disappeared from the city's landscape. If any of it remains today, it lies buried beneath the area bordered by the downtown federal and state courthouses and the neighboring restaurants and shops of Chinatown and Little Italy. Archaeological excavations at the Courthouse site may have uncovered a small part of that midden. Unfortunately, no artifacts were found in connection with the shell, so its date can not be determined (Leonard Bianchi, pers. comm., 1993).

17. The seminal studies on the effect of rising sea levels on our understanding of the Archaic were done by Bert Salwen (1962, 1965). He argued that we may be finding only that part of the seasonal round of the Archaic peoples that took place inland, and that many of their sites, located on the continental shelf, have since been drowned by the advancing seas. This would account for much of the spottiness of the archaeological record. See also Snow 1980; Funk 1991; and Braun 1974.

18. See Claassen 1995; Funk 1991, 1996. The Dogan

Point site was originally dug by Louis A. Brennan, a charismatic avocational archaeologist who worked in the Lower Hudson Valley (Brennan 1974, 1977). The site has recently been re-excavated by Cheryl Claassen (1995).

19. See Snow 1980:178 for a discussion of this point. Howard Winters (pers. comm., 1994) suggests that shellfish, in general, were a minor part of Archaic diets and may have been significant only when other, more important foods were scarce. Claassen (1991, 1995) outlines the difficulties of assessing the role and the nutritional value of shellfish in early societies and discusses of the role of shellfish middens and plant collecting (1995). See also Little and Schoeninger 1995.

20. Erlandson 1988.

21. Middle Archaic projectile points have been found at the Ward's Point, Chemical Lane, and Harik's Sandy Ground sites in Staten Island (Jacobson 1980; Rubertone 1974; and Lavin 1980). See also Dincauze 1976, 1993a; H. Kraft 1986; Braun and Braun 1994; Robinson et al. 1992; and Snow 1980.

22. For various interpretations of the Late Archaic and its variability in artifact styles and regional adaptations, see Snow 1980; Moeller 1990; Tuck 1975; Pfeiffer 1980, 1990; Ritchie 1980; and Funk 1976. Late Archaic points have been found at a number of sites in New York City; see Lavin 1980; Williams 1968; Weil 1971; Lenik 1989b; Leslie Eisenberg 1982; Silver 1984; Skinner 1919, 1920; Cohn and Apuzzo 1988; Smith 1950; and Wisniewski 1986. Because many soils in New York are highly acidic, making preservation of organic remains poor, and because many of these sites were dug before now-standard excavation techniques to recover plant or animal remains were used, we have little evidence of what foods were eaten. Based on studies in neighboring areas, we assume that deer, shellfish, and other animal foods were part of the diet, but we have no data to help interpret their relative significance.

23. A number of archaeologists started excavating these sites around the end of the nineteenth century, but the major excavations were done in 1919 by Alanson Skinner and Amos Oneroad (Skinner 1920).

24. Claassen 1995:139. See also B. Smith 1992 and Wat-

son 1988 for the implications of disturbed habitats and the development of horticulture.

25. The quotation is from Skinner 1909:221. See Haviland and Power 1994 for the results of modern experiments using weighted atlatls. Although this is the earliest clear evidence we have for these atlatl weights in New York, earlier Archaic peoples may also have used them, as did their contemporaries in parts of New England (Snow 1980:185). See Hall 1997 for possible ceremonial use of atlatls by more recent peoples.

26. Dincauze 1990 and Braun and Braun 1994 (especially fig. 35). For general discussions of the flexibility of, and variation in, hunting, fishing, and gathering societies, see Bettinger 1987 and Fagan 2000.

27. Many of the reported knives and spear points may also have served other functions during the Late Archaic (Moeller 1990). See Williams 1968 for a discussion of argillite tools found on Staten Island.

28. For mortuary ceremonialism in other parts of the Northeast, see Dincauze 1968, 1975; Pfeiffer 1990; Ritchie 1980; Robinson 1996; Snow 1980; and Tuck 1975.

29. Custer 1988; Lavin 1988; and Salwen 1975.

Chapter 5: Funerary Pyres on Long Island

1. Archaeologists have come to no real consensus concerning what to call the brief cultural period between the end of the Archaic and the beginning of the sequent Woodland period. Many archaeologists place these cultures in either a Transitional or a Terminal Archaic period or stage. The dates for these periods are both variable and approximate (see especially Snow 1980; Funk 1991, 1997; Pfeiffer 1990; and Ritchie 1980). We focus our discussion of the Transitional period on the Orient culture, which may be somewhat more recent than other regional Transitional cultures. For discussions of rituals and ways of life during this period, difficulties of classification, and other related issues, see Dincauze 1975; Funk 1976, 1991; Ritchie 1959, 1980; Robinson 1996; and Pfeiffer 1990.

2. This point type continued to be used by later Woodland peoples. Orient fishtails have been found at a number of sites, including the Tubby Hook site

in Manhattan, Bay Terrace Creek in Queens, Smoking Point and numerous other sites in Staten Island, and Throgs Neck in the Bronx (Skinner 1919, 1920; Silver 1984; Wisniewski 1986).

3. These vessels are usually called steatite or soapstone pots, but at least some were made from amphibole talc (Ritchie 1959). We do not know if Orient peoples went to the quarries or traded for finished pots.

4. Skinner 1919:72.

5. Booth 1982 and Latham 1953, 1978. Two of the sites, Orient I and Orient II, are in Orient on the North Fork. Sugar Loaf Hill is in the modern town of Southampton on the South Fork. It, like Jamesport, which is on the North Fork, overlooks Great Peconic Bay. There may have been a fifth cemetery in Cutchoque that was destroyed by bulldozing (Ritchie 1980:164).

6. Booth 1982:58. See Truex 1982:51–52 for a brief history of this group of avocationals.

7. See Dincauze 1975; Pfeiffer 1980; Robinson 1996; and Tuck 1975 on more recent related finds in neighboring regions.

8. Ritchie 1980:175.

9. Ritchie 1980:177. Much of this discussion is based on Ritchie 1944, 1959, and 1980. For other Orient sites in the area see Ritchie 1959, 1980; Salwen 1962; Boyd 1962; Ritchie and Funk 1973; and Snow 1980. See Ritchie 1959 for a reconstruction of the diet at the Stony Brook site and the radiocarbon dating of these Orient sites. Because both Stony Brook and Orient II yielded similar carbon 14 dates, Ritchie speculated that Orient II may have been the cemetery for the Stony Brook peoples, who had lived about forty-six miles away.

10. At Orient I, only individual graves, some twenty-five in number, were dug. Each of the other three sites had a mortuary pit as well as individual graves (Ritchie 1944, 1959; Booth 1982; and Latham 1953, 1978).

11. Ritchie 1959:71.

12. Ritchie 1959:77. Cremation was common during parts of the Archaic, as well as during the Transitional, throughout much of the Northeast. For fuller discussions of cremations and other Archaic burial practices see Dincauze 1968, 1975; Robinson 1996; Snow 1980; Pfeiffer 1980; and Ritchie 1980.

13. Ritchie 1980:177.

14. Other items were probably also consumed by the funerary fires but left no traces in the ashes. Despite Ritchie's assertions, Strong (1997:49) argues that there may have been one instance of a hearth in the pit at Orient II.

15. Many of these sherds were quite large, and reports indicate that one was used to cover a human skull. In one instance fragments from the same vessel were found in thirty-two separate grave lots. Although Latham and his cohort looked everywhere for the plugs, or punched-out pieces, from these bowls, they never found any (Latham 1953, 1978).

16. Ritchie (1959:51) notes that the iron pyrites found had decomposed to limonite.

17. Miller and Hamell 1986:325. See also Brown 1997: 473 and Haviland and Power 1994:81, 84. Reports suggest that some of the ocher was strewn in circles and that stone circles, some up to five feet in diameter, were associated with some of the caches. These circles may have had spiritual associations (Strong 1997:51–52).

18. Ritchie 1959:91. See Ritchie and Funk 1973 on the development of Orient and its possible ties with southern New England and the rest of the Northeast. The honored dead at these hilltop cemeteries apparently came from communities who lived at some distance from them (Ritchie 1959:75).

19. Ritchie notes that a cluster of small quartz pebbles had been recovered at Orient II. From other sites, we know that such clusters can be part of a ceremonial rattle made from a turtle shell filled with these pebbles. These pebbles might indicate that rattles were used by religious leaders during Orient mortuary ceremonies (Ritchie 1980:174–75).

20. Ritchie 1980:178.

21. See Charles 1985; Charles and Buikstra 1983; J. Brown 1995, 1997; and Goldstein 1989 for the role that secondary burials play in such representations. The quotation is from Flannery (1972:29), who was discussing early burials in the Near East.

22. See Fagan's discussion of Middle Archaic burial ceremonialism in the Midwest (1995:372).

Chapter 6: Tidewater Trade and Ritual

1. Most but not all archaeologists use the term *Woodland* to describe this temporal period in this region. See Snow 1980 and Dincauze 1990 for alternate classifications.

2. Braun and Braun 1994:62. See Fagan 2000; Braun and Braun 1994; Braun 1987; Buikstra et al. 1986, 1987; and Dincauze 1990 for the economic and social implications of the use of ceramics. The phrase "container revolution" is from B. Smith 1986.

3. Roy Latham and his crew found a few early Vinette pottery sherds at an Orient site, but pottery was not widespread at that time (Ritchie 1980:173). See Fagan 2000; B. Smith 1986; and Snow 1980 for the origins of pottery in the Northeast.

4. C. Smith 1950, 1987. For more recent changes in Smith's system, see Lavin 1986, 1987, 1995; Lavin et al. 1994; Lavin and Kra 1994; Custer 1987; Lopez 1961, 1982a, 1982b; and Salwen 1968b.

5. See C. Smith 1950 for descriptions and classifications of this pottery and the Early Woodland in general. See also Funk 1976; Heckenberger et al. 1990; H. Kraft 1986; Ritchie 1980; and Snow 1980. The North Beach site was excavated by Ralph Solecki in 1938 and is reported in C. Smith 1950. Lavin (pers. comm., 1998) has pointed out that because some spear-point styles from Late Archaic and Transitional times continued to be used into Early Woodland times, the paucity of Early Woodland sites may be illusory: any Early Woodland sites where pottery was not used may have been misclassified as earlier.

6. Fagan 2000; Brose et al. 1985; and Brose and Greber 1979.

7. For descriptions of Middle Woodland tool assemblages on the coast, see Kaeser 1963, 1968, 1972, 1974; Snow 1980; and C. Smith 1950 (especially for the pottery of this period). See Lavin 1995 and Snow 1980 for discussions of the continuity between Early and Middle Woodland. The quotation is from Dincauze 1980:29. The situation for western New York State is quite different (Ritchie 1980).

8. See Lavin et al. 1994 and Little 1987 for estimates of travel time. See Dincauze 1993b on the concept of marginality.

9. The Morris-Schurz site has sometimes been discussed as though it were two separate sites—the Morris Estate Club site and the Schurz site. Following Kaeser (1963), we consider it here as one site that is currently bifurcated by modern buildings. See also Lopez 1955 and R. P. Bolton 1976.

10. Kaeser 1963:41. Kaeser described the mica plates as approximately two inches in diameter. Silver (1991:232) reexamined twenty-five of them, which she described as ranging from clear to brown in color.

11. See Kaeser 1963 and Lopez 1955. For Fox Creek points see Kaeser 1968. See fig. 4.1 for other Middle Woodland point types. For dates see Funk 1976; H. Kraft 1986; and Silver 1991. For descriptions of this decorated pottery, see Cross 1956; Kaeser 1968, 1972; Lopez 1955, 1961; Silver 1991; and Stewart 1998. The work of avocational archaeologist Julius Lopez remains critical in defining the Abbott pottery in New York.

12. Lorraine Williams, Shirley Albright, and David Parris of the New Jersey State Museum developed techniques for identifying the sources of the argillite and the mica (Williams et al. 1982; Parris and Williams 1986). Silver (1991) applied their techniques in studying the materials from a number of Middle Woodland sites in the city. According to Williams (pers. comm., 1994), although there is some argillite in the Palisades area near New York, it is likely—in terms of workability, quality, and availability—that the argillite discussed here is from the Delaware Valley. Not all of that argillite is of the reddish-purple variety. See also Silver 1991. For Abbott Farm, see Cross 1956; Stewart 1998; Williams et al. 1982; and R. Wall et al. 1996.

13. For interregional networks, see Silver 1991; Kaeser 1968; and Stewart 1989.

14. The phrase "sumptuary implement" is taken from Brose et al. 1985:152.

15. Stewart 1998:273.

16. Parris and Williams 1986. For mica in the mid-continent, see Seeman 1979.

17. Kaeser 1968:43. Tobacco has been found at Middle woodland sites in the Midwest dating to A.D. 160. It is not native to the eastern woodlands and may

dred by three hundred feet, and had been adjacent to a marsh. In the end, this part of the expressway was never built, and the site, eligible for the National Register of Historic Places, is still preserved under these roadways (Rothschild and Pickman 1978; Pickman 1980).

12. Solecki 1947.

13. The first quotation is from Denton 1902:9; the second is from De Vries [1642] in J. F. Jameson 1909:223. Solecki (1947:48) notes that Theodore Kazimiroff, an avocational archaeologist and Bronx historian, had uncovered Late Woodland burials surrounded by postholes at Ferris Point in the Bronx. Unfortunately, these finds have not been published.

14. The quotations are from Van der Donck 1968:86–87 and Heckewelder 1876:274.

15. Similar burials have been found at a number of sites, including Bowmans Brook and Ward's Point in Staten Island, Washington Heights–Inwood in Manhattan, and Van Cortlandt Park and Clasons Point in the Bronx (C. Smith 1950; Skinner 1909, 1919; R. P. Bolton 1909; and James 1896, 1897).

16. Cantwell 1990, 1994; Goldstein 1989; and Hertz 1907.

17. See R. P. Bolton 1924; Jacobson 1980; and Skinner 1909, 1919 for reports of other secondary burials.

18. G. Thomas 1912:340.

19. See Skinner 1909, 1919; and Ritchie 1980. See Ceci 1990 for dating of this site.

20. One of the sellers was Wampage, also known as An hoock (Kaeser 1970:20), who is discussed in the next chapter.

21. Kaeser (1970:13). This discussion of the Archery Range site is adapted from Kaeser 1970.

22. Kaeser 1970; Jefferson 1788. See also Bushnell 1920: 124 and Curry 1999.

23. Heckewelder 1876:92. See also Curry 1999; Weslager 1942, 1983; Jirikowic 1990; and Bradley 1989.

24. Weslager 1983; Zeisberger 1910; and Lindestrom 1925. Such expressions of a collective unity have a long history throughout eastern North America (J. Brown 1997).

25. See Bernstein 1999.

26. See Bernstein et al. 1994 and McManamon and Bradley 1988. There is no archaeological consensus on the movements of people or ideas during these times. For discussions and controversies on migrations of people versus diffusion of ideas during the Late Woodland, see Bragdon 1996; Chilton, in press; Grumet 1990; Fiedel 1991; Funk 1997; Lavin 1995; Snow 1995; and Starna and Funk 1994.

27. McManamon and Bradley 1985:98.

28. The domestication of the dog (*Canis familiaris*) has attracted a great deal of archaeological interest (Kerber 1997; Morey and Wiant 1992; and Schwartz 1997). The native dogs in the United States are currently considered to be descended from an Asian wolf (Kerber 1997:82).

29. Cantwell and Wall, n.d.

30. R. P. Bolton 1909 and Finch 1909. The article was written for the *New York Herald,* according to a manuscript on file at the National Museum of the American Indian, CRC Archives, OC 20 #11.

31. The reports of these other dog burials are sketchy, but these were clearly burials and not simply animals that had been discarded along with other refuse. We do not know the ages or the sexes of the dogs, nor do we know how they met their deaths. Additional dog burials were found at Ward's Point (Skinner 1909), at the Throgs Neck and Clasons Point sites (Skinner 1919), at Bowmans Brook (Skinner 1909), in Pelham Bay Park and Van Cortlandt Park (R. P. Bolton 1934; Kaeser 1970), at Century Golf Club in the Bronx (M. R. Harrington 1909), and at Ferris Point and Schurz (Lopez and Wisniewski 1958). The last two burials were reported to have been in human graves. There is only one clear report of a dog sacrifice, and that is from the College Point site in Queens, where a decapitated and de-tailed dog was found in a burial pit accompanied by a decapitated fisher (Lopez and Wisniewski 1958; see their article for additional listings of dog burials).

32. R. P. Bolton 1924:42. Although in other parts of the Northeast, especially among Iroquoian peoples, dogs were part of ritual meals and ceremonies, early colonial accounts suggest that when dogs were eaten in the coastal area it was usually in times of famine, when there was nothing else to eat (Butler and Hadlock 1949; Kerber 1997).

33. Cantwell 1980. There is some disagreement on the

importance of dogs in hunting in this part of the country (Butler and Hadlock 1949; Kerber 1997).

34. Tantaquidgeon 1942:36. In other cases when the child died, there might be a "release ceremony," in which the child's family would tie a string of wampum about the guardian dog's neck, thereby releasing the animal from its responsibilities.

35. Dean 1978:3. See also Weslager 1973:87.

36. See Lopez and Wisniewski 1958 for reports of other such burials.

37. Dean 1984:62; Butler and Hadlock 1949:26. Speck (1937) discusses twentieth-century Delaware and other Algonquian peoples' concept of the Milky Way as the "Spirit or Ghost Path." The role of dog as psychopomp may date back to the Middle Woodland (Anderson 1971).

38. The first quotation is from Henry Wadsworth Longfellow, as cited in Butzer 1990:369, and the second is from Francis Parkman, Jr., as cited in Nash 1982:99. The artifacts recovered give few clues as to the nature of the economy. A few stone hoes have been found, although it is unclear whether they are Late Woodland or Contact tools. In the Northeast, shell hoes and digging sticks were used in historic times, and these may not have been recognized archaeologically. Grinding stones have been found, but these may have been used for grinding nuts or seeds. The concept of a necessary relationship between sedentism and agriculture has been under siege recently. A number of sedentary societies have a hunting, fishing, and gathering economy. See Fagan 2000; Wenke 1999; and Bragdon 1996. There is a large literature on the nature of sedentary life, the complexities of hunting-and-gathering societies, and the meanings of such often loosely defined terms as *village, central base camp,* and *settlement* (Fagan 2000; Flannery 1972; Luedtke 1988; Ceci 1990; and Wenke 1999).

39. Bendremer et al. 1991; Bendremer and Dewar 1994; Bendremer 1999; Cassedy and Webb 1999; Chilton 1999; Dimmick 1994; J. Hart 1999; Little and Schoeninger 1995; Demeritt 1991; McBride and Dewar 1987; and Heckenberger et al. 1992. The effects of a cooling period, the Little Ice Age (ca. A.D. 1450–1850), on local subsistence decisions are not known at this time (Nicholas 1988).

40. Ceci 1977.

41. For details on the dating of these sites and their multicomponent nature, see Ceci 1990. See also Bendremer and Dewar 1994 and Ceci 1989.

42. See Bragdon 1996 on the possible interconnections among trade, wampum, and maize and other social relations between coastal and interior peoples.

43. D. H. Thomas 1998:346–51.

44. See Pepper 1904 and Jacobson 1980 for accounts of these burials, Ceci 1990 for dating, and Bridges 1994 for skeletal analysis. These are the only known examples of violence in Late Woodland New York, and their significance is unknown.

45. Bridges 1994:15.

46. Bridges 1994:22. See her article for details of the analysis. See also Carlson et al. 1992; Little and Schoeninger 1995; and Bragdon 1996 for similar analyses in New England. Only three individuals plus the dog can be confidently dated to this critical Late Woodland period (Ceci 1990:6).

47. The men also showed signs of minor cases of porotic hyperostosis (Bridges 1994).

48. Cohen and Armelagos 1984; Carlson et al. 1992; and Buikstra and Milner 1991. Conversely, agriculture may be related to population growth (see, e.g., Wenke 1999).

49. McManamon and Bradley 1988 and McManamon et al. 1986. For a discussion of the complexities of sedentism, see Wenke 1999. Based on evidence from sites in other coastal areas, a great variety of wild plant foods may also have been part of the diet (Lightfoot et al. 1987; Bernstein 1990; Lavin 1988; McBride and Dewar 1987; McManamon et al. 1986; Mulholland 1988; and Little and Schoeninger 1995).

50. In discussing southern New England, Bragdon (1996:58) uses the concept of "conditional sedentism" developed by Frederick Dunford. This involves sedentary groupings, of various sizes, that are focused on estuarine adaptations. This appears to have been the case in New York. See also Bernstein 1999; Bendremer 1999; and Chilton 1999. For discussions of the economic security provided by coastal resources, see Heckenberger et al. 1992: 142–44. For eastern Long Island, Bernstein (1999) suggests that protected estuaries and harbors pro-

vided areas where nonfarming year-round communities may have lived.

51. Lavin 1988:113. In eastern North America, no agricultural group, no matter how intensively it relied on farming, ever entirely gave up wild plant and animal foods. See also Bernstein 1990, 1999; Bragdon 1996; Demeritt 1991; Dimmick 1994; Heckenberger et al. 1992; Little and Schoeninger 1995; and McBride and Dewar 1987.

52. On the environmental risks that agriculture poses, see Salwen 1975; Bendremer 1999; Demeritt 1991; Heckenberger et al. 1992; and Mulholland 1988. The major role of women in farming is not surprising, as traditionally they were associated with the collection and processing of wild plant foods. See Watson and Kennedy 1991 for the role of women in domesticating plant foods in the East.

53. N. White 1987:3, 5.

54. The archaeological record is too fragmentary to reconstruct the Late Woodland settlement system, but it likely included sites over a broad area in tidewater New York, possibly including some inland areas. Van Cortlandt Park and Throgs Neck may also have been substantial settlements (C. Smith 1950). Some sites appear to have been shellfishing stations that were temporarily occupied by a variety of groups, including Late Woodland peoples. These include the Dyckman Street (Skinner 1920) and Kaeser (Rothschild and Lavin 1977) sites, which may have been used by peoples living on the coast or by related inland peoples who came down to the shores to gather oysters, hard- and soft-shell clams, scallops, and crabs. At the Kaeser site, hide working appears to have been an important activity. There are a number of other small Late Woodland sites, such as Milo Rock in Pelham Bay Park and Wilkins and Grantville in Queens (C. Smith 1950; Lopez 1958). A Native American quartz quarry has recently been discovered in the Bronx, but its temporal affiliation is not known. In addition, there were probably fishing stations used during the large spring runs, fall nut-harvesting stations, winter deer-hunting camps, and the like.

55. Cronon 1983:12.

56. Calloway 1999:11. The phrase "crusader ideology" is from Jennings 1976:3. On immigrants' experiences

and the difficulties they had in interpreting Native American landscapes, see Kehoe 1992:569; Calloway 1997, 1999; and Cronon 1983. See Silverberg 1968 and Kennedy 1994 for ways this myth and its attendant politics affected interpretations of archaeological sites and the legitimacy of the Native American past.

57. Wroth 1970:137. For place names, see Grumet 1981:2. Europeans fished off the coasts of Maine and Newfoundland in increasing numbers throughout the sixteenth century. They were also contacting Indian tribes to the north and south of the Munsees. Although some of these Europeans may well have visited coastal New York, there are no unequivocal records of any such direct contacts after Verrazano until Henry Hudson's 1609 voyage (H. Kraft 1991).

Chapter 8: A Tumultuous Encounter

1. Anonymous, in J. F. Jameson 1909:293. See also Heckewelder 1841 for an extended Delaware version from the late eighteenth and early nineteenth centuries.

2. Dowd 1992:31. See Weslager 1972:492 for the Munsee calendar. In using the Munsee calendar, we are influenced by Snow 1994. See J. F. Jameson 1909 for Juet's account of Hudson's voyage.

3. See R. P. Bolton 1920; Goddard 1978; and Grumet 1981, 1995a. The identification of specific groups with specific locations is problematic. During this period, Indian peoples, having fluid concepts of property and borders, moved across the landscape. The Europeans had difficulty identifying and locating such flexible independent groups. The naming of these groups also presents some confusion (Goddard 1978). South of the Munsee speakers was a related group of Unami dialect speakers. Collectively these two groups later became known as Delaware or Lenape (see Goddard 1978 and Orr and Campagna 1991 for the subsequent formation of a corporate Munsee identity). To the north of the Munsees were the Mahicans, and the Iroquoian peoples were to the north and west (Trigger 1978). For primary sources and ethnohistorical accounts of the Munsees, see J. F. Jameson 1909; Van der Donck 1968; Danckaerts 1941; Gehring and Grumet

1987; Newcomb 1956; Goddard 1978; Ruttenber 1872; R. P. Bolton 1920, 1922, 1924, 1934; and Weslager 1972.

4. The first quotation is from the Rev. Michaelius, in J. F. Jameson 1909:126–27, the second from Van der Donck 1968:72–74. See Ronda 1984 and H. Kraft 1991 for discussions of the concept of wilden.

5. Heckewelder 1841, 1876. The quotation is from Weslager 1972:112.

6. For general discussions of Contact, see Delâge 1993; Trigger 1991; Grumet 1995a; Salisbury 1996; and Axtell 1985, 1989, 1992.

7. For Late Woodland material culture, see chapter 7; H. Kraft 1986; C. Smith 1950; and Snow 1980.

8. Skinner 1909, 1919. Trade goods have been found at Ryders Pond (Lopez and Wisniewski 1978a, 1978b) in Brooklyn; Old Place (Skinner 1909), Bowmans Brook (Skinner 1909, 1919), and Ward's Point in Staten Island (Jacobson 1980); the Inwood area in Manhattan (Skinner 1920); and Van Cortlandt Park (Skinner 1920), Clasons Point, and Throgs Neck (Skinner 1919) in the Bronx. These goods could have come either from the Dutch or from other groups, European or Indian, to the north. Surprisingly, no Munsee burials containing European trade goods have been found in the city, as has been the case in other parts of Lenapehoking and adjacent areas (Brenner 1988; H. Kraft 1978, 1986; Heye and Pepper 1915).

9. See Cronon 1983; Delâge 1993; and Trigger 1991.

10. Calloway 1997:198.

11. The title of this section, "The Nations Are Warring with Each Other" (*Keekhockewitschik Mamachtagewak*) is a quotation from Heckewelder 1876:440.

12. J. F. Jameson 1909: 230.

13. Trelease 1960 remains the best source on Kieft's War. See also O'Callaghan 1845 and J. F. Jameson 1909.

14. De Vries, in J. F. Jameson 1909:231. In colonial times, corn was sometimes referred to as Turkish wheat.

15. O'Callaghan 1845:265. On July 4, 1641, Kieft had offered ten fathoms of wampum for every Raritan head brought to him.

16. See Delâge 1993:331; Trigger 1991:1214; and Newcomb 1956:84 as well as Cave 1996; McBride 1994;

and R. B. Ferguson 1992. Munsee leaders traditionally were "simply the first-among equals . . . [and] lacked coercive prerogatives" (Goddard 1978:216). They served as mediators, ritual figures, and spokesmen. Military leadership was based on ability and not heredity. Many important decisions were made by consulting group members, including women. Initially, the Munsees may have found it difficult to unite to fight the larger and better-organized groups of Europeans, but by mid-century there seems to have been some "agglomeration of interacting local groups" (Goddard 1978; see also Grumet 1989c). By the final decades of the seventeenth century, some individuals representing these consolidated groups did emerge as political leaders.

17. De Vries in J. F. Jameson 1909:209. For the two fronts, see Salisbury 1996:413.

18. Cited in H. Kraft 1986:223.

19. J. F. Jameson 1909: 227–29.

20. O'Callaghan 1845:269. Van Tienhoven, whose Pearl Street property was excavated by archaeologists (see chapter 10), served as a scout for the Pavonia attack.

21. For Hutchinson's land acquisition, see R. P. Bolton 1920:32.

22. Van der Donck (1968:99) notes that it was unusual for the Indians to kill women and children. Hutchinson's daughter was in fact taken by the Munsees and lived with them until the peace treaty of 1645 ordered her return to the English. Both she and the Munsees met this condition reluctantly (Salisbury 1982; Shonnard and Spooner 1900). See R. P. Bolton 1920 for An hoock's role in land sales and variations of his name.

23. Cited in Trelease 1960:83.

24. "Recalling a Massacre" 1886:8. Although Skinner (1919:51) speculated that some of the burials at Throgs Neck might also be those of victims of Kieft's War, there is no evidence to substantiate that claim.

25. R. Bolton 1881:517.

26. Skinner 1919:116. See also R. P. Bolton 1920.

27. See Trelease 1960; H. Kraft 1986; and Danckaerts 1941 for the havoc that alcohol wreaked on the Native population. See Heckewelder 1876 for the Delaware version of the introduction of alcohol. For descriptions of artifacts, see Skinner 1919; Jacobson

1980; and Lopez and Wisniewski 1978a, 1978b. The small amount of European military hardware may reflect the Dutch ban on trading arms to the Munsees and their policy forbidding armed Indians in New Amsterdam after 1655. See Salwen 1989 on the difficulties of interpreting these large multicomponent sites. For Munsee settlements (some of which were fortified), see R. P. Bolton 1920. For weapons, see Skinner 1909 and Jacobson 1980.

28. Quoted in Skinner 1919:52; see also his discussion of Clasons Point as well as that of C. Smith (1950:169). There are reports of other sites, including wampum workshops, near Throgs Neck and Clasons Point (R. P. Bolton 1920, 1976). Five points made from recycled European metals were found at Ward's Point, as were a few gunflints, rum-bottle fragments, a coin, pipe fragments, and table-knife blades (Jacobson 1980:64). For brass points and other trade goods from Bloomfield and Old Place, see Skinner 1909:28.

29. Lopez and Wisniewski 1978a, 1978b; Strong 1977:168; and R. P. Bolton 1920:50, 1934:146. Iron points were also found at Ryders Pond and at Ward's Point.

30. For spiritual qualities of copper, see Hamell 1983, 1987, and the discussion of wampum later in this chapter. See Trigger 1991 and Bradley 1987 for discussions of the utilitarian versus the ideological importance of trade goods in Native economies. For recycling of kettles, see Bradley 1987 and Williams 1988.

31. Nassaney 1989.

32. Strong 1997:188; Grumet 1995b. For Massapequa linguistic affiliations, see Goddard 1978. The legend quoted here is taken from a communication written by Judge Samuel Jones to the New-York Historical Society and delivered by De Witt Clinton in 1811. It refers to a massacre that was presumed to have taken place in 1653 at Fort Massapeag (Solecki, n.d.:16–22).

33. Solecki 1985, n.d.

34. Le Jeune in Thwaites 1896–1901 VI:297–99.

35. Van der Donck 1968:113.

36. For a definitive discussion of wampum, see Williams and Flinn 1990.

37. The quotations are from Miller and Hamell 1986:

318. See also Hamell 1983, 1987; Bradley 1987; and Trigger 1991.

38. The literature on wampum is enormous. See bibliographies in Williams and Flinn 1990 and Ceci 1977, 1990. On significance of pre-Contact wampum, see Ceci 1977, 1989, and Salisbury 1982.

39. Weeden quoted in Williams and Flinn 1990:13.

40. Williams and Flinn 1990; Ceci 1977.

41. See Williams and Flinn 1990; Ceci 1977, 1990; and Salisbury 1982 for wampum in the colonies and Williams 1972; Bragdon 1996; and Chilton, in press, for the role that the developing wampum trade may have had in centralizing leadership and competition among various groups.

42. Southern New England and Long Island were the centers for the wampum industry. See various works by Ceci for the complexities of wampum and the notion she introduced of the triangular trade of which it was a part.

43. Ceci 1977; Skinner 1919; Smith 1950; Solecki, n.d. Solecki (pers. comm., 1999) argues that evidence for wampum making should include grit rubbing stones, whelk columellae, and fragments of the blue lips of quahogs, as well as both the anterior and posterior ends of the whelks and evidence of abrading or abrasion from the rubbing stones on the columellae. By his definition, with which we agree, many sites referred to in the literature as wampum producing do not meet the required criteria.

44. Solecki, n.d.:16–17, 22. Solecki mentions reports that there was another fort in the immediate area. The village site is multicomponent.

45. Solecki (n.d.:38) notes that because of impenetrable plant growth, only a small part of the interior was tested. McBride (1994) reports a similar lack of interior domestic debris at Fort Island on Block Island. See also Salwen and Mayer 1978 and Williams 1972. Van der Donck (1968:81) notes that forts frequently contained twenty or thirty houses. See Solecki 1994 for summaries of colonists' accounts of techniques used by Indians to build forts.

46. Solecki and Grumet 1994:18.

47. Most of the trade goods were from the Dutch trade (Solecki, n.d.). Although some of the Indian pottery, the Shantok ware, could have been made at any time starting at the end of the Late Woodland,

it is similar to pottery found at other Indian mid-century sites (Solecki and Williams 1998). The Indian pottery suggests contacts of some sort with other Indian groups in Connecticut, the Hudson and Delaware Valleys, and central and northern New Jersey (Solecki, n.d., and Solecki and Grumet 1994).

48. Burgraff 1938; Solecki and Williams 1998; Solecki 1994; Solecki, pers. comm., 1999.

49. Hicks 1896–1904(1):43–44. The treaty stated that the fort was to be built on the "north-side." Most people have assumed that this meant the north shore of Long Island, especially because there is a later reference to a proposed fort on the north shore in Oyster Bay to control English smuggling (Brodhead 1853–71 I:622). But this later reference to the Oyster Bay fort, made on May 13, 1656, as Solecki and Grumet (1994:204) note, emphasizes "the more defensive purposes of a fort ordered built to shelter local colonists" rather than a trading post. To add to the confusion, the modern town of Massapequa, on the south shore, was also known as Oyster Bay. See Solecki 1994, n.d., and Solecki and Grumet 1994. Other town records suggest that for a number of reasons, including the lack of available enslaved Africans to quarry and transport stone, lime, and other materials, the Oyster Bay fort had not been built by 1661. In 1675, when the English controlled the area, their governor wrote that he was having trouble finding people to build the Oyster Bay fort (Cox 1916–40 II:697–98). Although these references do not clarify the relationship of that fort to the one offered to Tackapausha, or the "north-side" reference, the proposed Oyster Bay and the Massapeagua forts appear to be very different. Massapeag was a wooden palisade with no stone or lime used in its construction; the trade goods found there are mid-century Dutch (Solecki and Grumet 1994:25), not English goods dating to the last quarter of the century. For these reasons, Solecki's conclusion that Massapeag may be a mid-century Indian-Dutch trading post, Indian wampum manufactory, and refuge, and not this long delayed Oyster Bay redoubt, seems reasonable. But whether the Massapeag earthworks are all that is left of that *particular* post that Stuyvesant promised to build for Tackapausha or of another undocumented one is unclear. Nor is it known whether it was built by Indians, Europeans, or Africans or by some combination of these groups.

50. Solecki and Grumet 1994:21.

51. See Strong 1997 and Trelease 1960 for Tackapausha's role in regional politics.

52. See McBride 1994 for Dutch-Indian trading strategies.

53. Initially, many Munsees favored red because it was a color with supernatural associations, but men, especially, soon abandoned it for more muted colors because, as one Dutch trader put it, "the Indians say that it hinders them in hunting, being visible too far off. They all call for black, the darker the color the better, but red and green they will not take" (De Rasieres, quoted in H. Kraft 1986:202).

54. R. P. Bolton 1920:75 and Newcomb 1956: 82–83. A bead maker could make only between thirty-two and forty-two beads a day. Yet in one instance in 1651, thirty-two fathoms of tribute were demanded, each fathom representing nearly three hundred of these beads and many days' labor (Ceci 1977:262–64; Solecki, n.d.:81–84; Williams and Flinn 1990: 21–27).

55. Bragdon 1996; Salisbury 1982; and Williams 1972.

56. Solecki, n.d.:13–14, 154.

57. See P. Thomas 1985:143–44 on this interdependency. For similar posts, see Salwen and Mayer 1978; Williams 1972; and McBride 1994.

58. Hicks 1896–1904 (1):43–44.

59. Axtell 1992:13.

60. Peña 1990 and Williams and Flinn 1990.

61. Grumet 1990:36.

62. Meltzer 1993:153; Dobyns 1983:11. The phrase "virgin soil," which Dobyns quotes, is taken from Crosby 1976. For the effects of disease on the peoples in the Northeast and failures of traditional healing practices, see Dobyns 1983; Jennings 1976; Snow 1992, 1994; Snow and Lamphear 1988; Spiess and Spiess 1987; Starna 1992; Grumet 1990; and H. Kraft 1986.

63. Van der Donck 1964:64; Denton [1670] 1902:45.

64. For difficulties in estimating population and mortality figures, see Snow 1980; Snow and Lamphear 1988; Dobyns 1983; Salwen 1975; Grumet 1989a;

and Goddard 1978. For social, fertility, and economic repercussions, see Cronon 1983; Snow 1994; and Starna 1992.

65. Jennings 1976:30.

66. This account was told to Heckewelder in the early nineteenth century (1876:75; see also 1841:74). See also Bierhorst 1995:85–86.

67. O'Callaghan and Fernow 1856–87 I:37–38; R. P. Bolton 1934:128, 1920, 1975. Weslager (1972:37) points out that the Indian concept of land "was subtly related to the basic Indian belief in hospitality whereby a stranger's physical needs were fully satisfied by his host." See also Cronon 1983:70; H. Kraft 1991; and P. Thomas 1985.

68. Heckewelder 1876:102.

69. Grumet 1989a:4. See Grumet 1989b, 1990, and R. P. Bolton 1920, 1975.

70. Quoted in Dowd 1992:43. In the years between 1680 and 1720, for example, the European population in the Middle Atlantic region jumped from 14,900 to more than 103,000 (Grumet 1989a, 1989b). There were also a number of fraudulent land deals, the most infamous of which is the Walking Purchase (Weslager 1972:173–95).

71. Grumet 1990:36.

72. Skinner 1919:113, 118, 123, 1909:29.

73. Skinner (1919:118) notes that pig bones were also found at the Pelham Knolls site in the Bronx and at the Bowmans Brook site in Staten Island.

74. Cronon 1983:14–15.

75. For a discussion of movements and migrations of Munsees to the Delaware Valley Minisink region, see Goddard 1978; Grumet 1991, 1995a; and H. Kraft 1986.

76. Grumet (1981:230, 1992) notes that the name *Manhattan* may be derived from the Delaware word *menatan*. Today most Delawaran peoples can be found in communities along the East Coast, in Ontario, Wisconsin, and Oklahoma. Over the years, other Indian groups from many parts of the Americas moved to New York City, including the Mohawks, who were involved in the high-steel construction industry. The 1990 census showed 27,531 Indians living in the city, constituting about 0.4 percent of the population (Grumet, in Jackson 1995:28). For the diaspora and modern communi-

ties, see Goddard 1978; Grumet 1986, 1989b, 1989c; Heckewelder 1876; H. Kraft 1986; Lenik 1989a; Oestreicher 1991; and Weslager 1972, 1978.

Chapter 9: The Arrival of the Global Economy

1. This discussion of Dutch mercantilism is adapted from Fayden [Janowitz] 1993.

2. The first non-Indian known to have stayed on Manhattan Island was Jan (or Juan) Rodriguez, described in contemporary accounts as a "mulatto" from San Domingo (in today's Dominican Republic). He had been dropped off by Mossel in 1613, presumably to make arrangements for future trade (S. Hart 1959). But before Mossel returned in the fall, Christiaensen had anchored in Lenapehoking, and Rodriguez signed on to work for him. The story of Orson and Valentine is recounted by Nicolaes van Wassenaer (in J. F. Jameson 1909:78, 81). Their names are derived from a French legend about twins who were abandoned in a forest; one (Orson) was raised by a bear, while the other was raised at court (Williamson 1959:3). We do not know if the Indian brothers were captives or if they undertook their travels voluntarily. The episode appears to have had an unhappy ending: van Wassenaer accuses Orson of having been responsible for the deaths of Christiaensen and many of his crew a few years later.

3. The first quotation is from the *Breeden Radiate*, a 1649 tract reputed to have been written by Cornelis Melyn, as quoted in Brodhead 1853–71:48. The second is from De Vries (in J. F. Jameson 1909:230–31).

4. Adapted from Rink 1986:41–44 and Huey 1991a:28–29.

5. Adapted from Solecki 1974.

6. See Williamson 1959. The wooden remains were brought to the Museum of the City of New York, where they remain today.

7. Adapted from Solecki 1974.

8. Bird and DeJong in Jackson 1995:111.

9. Rink 1986:27–28.

10. Heermans' relations with Stuyvesant were not always smooth; he was one of the signers of a 1649 protest complaining to the States-General about the

running of the colony, complaints that led to New Amsterdam's becoming a municipality in 1653. A watercolor of New Amsterdam attributed to him is in the Austrian National Library; fig. 2.2 is thought to be based on it. In 1659 Heermans was sent to Maryland to help settle a border dispute between that colony and the Dutch settlements along the Delaware. Shortly thereafter, he began a survey and map of the colonies of Maryland and Virginia. Lord Baltimore, the English proprietor of Maryland, rewarded him for this ambitious undertaking with the grant of a huge tract of land on Chesapeake Bay. There he built an estate, called Bohemia Manor, where he moved with his family in 1662. It was on this estate that the Labadists established their community (see chapter 3). The biographical information on Heermans is from Stokes 1915–28 II:266–67 and Grossman 1985.

11. Grossman 1985:chap. 10, p. 9; Innes 1902:53–54.

12. The first quotation is from Fernow 1976 VI:215, the second from Stokes 1915–28 I:176, and the third from City of New York 1917 II:18. Discussion adapted from Wall in Rothschild et al. 1987:121–23. In discussing the building just to the north of the tavern, we use the Dutch name of Stadt Huys when referring to it during the Dutch period of its history and the English name of State House when referring to it during the English period.

13. The tax records listed the property as a "lott" and not a "house" for that year; they did not mention that it had been destroyed in a fire.

14. Rothschild et al. 1987:130–66.

15. Adapted from Rockman [Wall] and Rothschild 1984:112–21.

16. This discussion of the pipe dump is based on Diane Dallal, in Grossman 1985:chap. 7, pp. 28–35.

17. Dallal discovered that there had been a warehouse on the property in the 1690s and that Obadiah Hunt kept his tavern next door. It is possible that either the merchant who owned the warehouse or the tavernkeeper had imported pipes in bulk primarily from the Tippets in Bristol and also from Worden in London. An association with a tavern is supported by some of the other artifacts that were found in the outbuilding: there were several drinking vessels, including a delft posset pot and a Ger-

man stoneware tankard. Interestingly, the stoneware tankard, like some of the pipes, was seriously flawed: its bottom had a crack that had formed during firing and which would have made the tankard useless for holding liquids (one can tell that the crack was there during firing because its sides are covered with the salt glaze that formed in the kiln; see Stehling in Grossman 1985:chap. 5, p. 23). Archaeologists found evidence of an early nineteenth-century paving made up of pipe fragments in the backyard of the Schermerhorn Row block in the South Street Seaport (Kardas and Larrabee 1991).

18. Based on Geismar 1983 and Dickinson 1991.

19. Based on appendix 2 in the report of the Assay excavations (Berger 1991).

20. The places of origin of the goods found on the grocer's floor and their locations on the floor are from Berger 1991.

21. Based on Berger 1991.

22. The technique Gilbert uses to match the clays is called Inductively Coupled Plasma Emission Spectroscopy. He chose this method because it is inexpensive, accurate, and can determine the quantities of a great variety of different elements that are naturally present in clays. Some of the elements—like aluminum, iron, calcium, and magnesium—are present in the clays in abundance, while others—like copper, cobalt, and strontium—are measurable only in parts per million. Samples of clays characterized by the amounts of thirty of their constituent elements can be sorted by computer to show which samples are chemically most alike and thus which might have come from the same place. Gilbert et al. 1993; Gilbert, pers. comm., 1999.

23. Gilbert et al. 1993; Gilbert, pers. comm., 1999; Fayden [Janowitz] 1993:309–12.

Chapter 10: Daily Life in New Amsterdam and Early New York

1. The data on the Dutch immigrants are from Rink 1986, while those on the population of New Amsterdam are from contemporary estimates; there was no formal census. The figures are from Rosenwaike 1972:2–3.

2. The quotation is from Jogues, in J.F. Jameson 1909: 259. See D. S. Cohen 1981; Rink 1986:155. The ranges for the figures on the enslaved Africans in the Dutch colony in 1664 are from Goodfriend 1975:137, 1992: 112; Kammen 1975:58; and Foote 1993:122; we have no reliable population estimates for the Native Americans. Foote (1993:122) lists the names of the enslaved Africans. The heavy dependence on enslaved labor was unusual for a northern American city, but the Dutch West India Company, the company that ran New Amsterdam, was deeply involved in the African slave trade, which may account (at least in part) for this phenomenon. In 1679 the English governor banned the enslavement of local Indians; the enslavement of members of other Indian groups continued until the 1740s (Davis, in Jackson 1995:1076).

3. Boorstin 1987:14.

4. As Goodfriend (1992:55–56, 135) points out, unlike the other English American colonies, New York City contained relatively few European indentured servants in the seventeenth or early eighteenth centuries, perhaps because of the institutionalization of enslavement there. The percentage is from Foote 1991:91. See D. Wall 2000 for discussions of the problems of seeing the African experience in these complex households in the archaeological record, and of slaveholding in the van Tienhoven and Kierstede families.

5. The information on van Tienhoven is from Stokes 1915–28 II:129, 266, 384–85; E. S. Fisher 1918:44–45; Innes 1902; J. F. Jameson 1909:340; and van der Zee and van der Zee 1978:276–79.

6. The data used for dating the privy are from Grossman 1985:chap. 10, pp. 6–8 and Stokes 1915–28 I:129.

7. Edward Bird was one of the many English pipe makers who settled in the Netherlands and married Dutch women after James I made it difficult for pipe makers to make a living in England. His pipes were very popular among both the European and Indian populations of New Netherland, and they were also found at Fort Massapeag (see chapter 8). Dallal (1995) discusses Bird and the emigration of the pipe makers from England to the Netherlands.

8. E. S. Fisher (1918) discusses the family of Lucas van Tienhoven. Janowitz (Fayden [Janowitz] 1993) describes and analyzes the ceramics in this feature; the dating information and the description of the other artifacts in this feature are from Grossman 1985.

9. The pipes are described by Dallal (in Grossman 1985).

10. The information on Kierstede is from Stokes 1915–28 II:263–64; that on Sara Roelofs is from van der Zee and van der Zee 1978:99; Totten 1925; and Randolph 1934. The description of the Kierstedes' relationship with the Indians is from Riker 1981–83:13 and Mrs. J. K. van Rensselaer 1898:22, 26.

11. Stokes 1915–28 I:227; Totten 1925:222–23. The Labadist community was located on land acquired from Augustine Heermans' estate, Bohemia Manor. Although Peter Bayard later left the Labadist sect, his and Blandina's son Samuel remained there (S. Van Rensselaer 1909:230–31; Totten 1925:222–23). We do not know for sure whether enslaved Africans were among those who lived in the Bayard house, but we do know that Blandina Bayard did own at least one slave; in 1693 she inherited "a negro boy, Hans," from her mother, Sara Roelofs. Roelofs' will is summarized in Pelletreau 1893–1913 I:225–26.

12. Dallal (1995:90) discusses Gerdes and Anna Maria Van de Heijden.

13. Samford (1996:104) and Russell (1997:75) discuss the discovery of ceramic gaming pieces at plantation slave quarters in the South and in Jamaica; see Huey (1991b; pers. comm., 1999) for the Albany Almshouse.

14. Diamond (in Grossman 1985) describes and dates the wineglass stem. To date, we have not been able to identify the names of the people living in this house around 1710.

15. Grossman 1985. Huey (1974) discusses reworked pipe stems.

16. Examples of studies of other colonies include Deagan 1974, 1983, and Reitz and Scarry 1985 for the Spanish in sixteenth-century Florida; Cumbaa 1975 for eighteenth-century Florida; H. Miller 1984 for the English in seventeenth-century Maryland; and Reitz and Honerkamp 1983 for the Georgia coastal plain.

17. Deetz 1977; Deagan 1983.

18. Although European men and Indian women had

sexual relations with each other (see, e.g., De Vries, in J. F. Jameson 1909:231), they did not tend to marry for reasons that are not completely clear. Rothschild (1995) compares Dutch marriage practices with those of the indigenous peoples of the Dutch colonies of New Netherland and Indonesia; Schrire and Merwick (1991) compare the attitudes of the Dutch toward the indigenous peoples of New Netherland and South Africa.

19. For New Amsterdam, see Fayden [Janowitz] 1993; Grossman 1985; Greenfield 1989; Janowitz 1993; Rothschild 1990a; and Rothschild et al. 1987. For Fort Orange, see Huey 1988, 1991a.

20. Huey 1985:73, 1991a:48–49. The quotation is from Huey 1991a:61.

21. Deetz 1977:50; Fayden [Janowitz] 1993:3.

22. Janowitz 1993; Fayden [Janowitz] 1993. The other archaeologists whose work Janowitz drew on include Huey (1988), Grossman (1985), and Rothschild (1990a), who, taken together, directed the excavations at all of the major sites that have been excavated in New Netherland.

23. We can see this avoidance of sheep expressed in the animal bones from the two seventeenth-century privies described above: the van Tienhoven and early Kierstede privies both included more cow and pig bones than sheep bones (Fayden [Janowitz] 1993).

24. Huey 1991a:58; Grossman 1985:chap. 10, p. 22. Janowitz (Fayden [Janowitz] 1993) notes the prevalence of the bones of deer and wild fowl and their luxury status in the Netherlands.

25. Janowitz 1993; Fayden [Janowitz] 1993; Rothschild 1990a:148.

26. Fayden [Janowitz] 1993:283–87; Van der Donck reports on the prevalence of "sapaen" in Native American homes in the seventeenth century, and the Swedish naturalist Peter Kalm reports that the Dutch were eating "sappan" in Albany in the middle of the eighteenth century (Fayden [Janowitz] 1993:285).

27. Fayden [Janowitz] 1993; Janowitz 1993.

28. Goodfriend (1992) discusses the nature of the Dutch community in early English New York.

29. Condon 1968:viiii.

30. Adapted from Kammen 1975.

31. See Kammen 1975:121–27 and Burrows and Wallace 1999:96–102.

32. The quotation is from Archdeacon 1976:113. Some historians have interpreted Leisler's motivations for his role in the rebellion as religious in origin (Leisler was an extremely orthodox Calvinist who was genuinely concerned about whether the fate of Protestants in England and the English colonies might be the same as that of the French Huguenots after the Revocation of the Edict of Nantes; see Voorhees 1994) as well as related to class and ethnicity. Bonomi (1971:75–81) discusses the legacy of the rebellion in New York's politics in the last decade of the seventeenth century and the first decade of the eighteenth.

33. Archdeacon 1976; Goodfriend 1992. For Goodfriend's conclusions, see particularly pp. 161–69 and 188–98.

34. Goodfriend 1992:213–16; Rothschild 1990a; Wilkenfeld 1976.

35. Goodfriend 1992:210; see also Burrows and Wallace 1999:89–90 and Kammen 1975:91, 94.

36. Janowitz (Fayden [Janowitz] 1993:351) discusses the possible triumph of English-style ceramics in the second quarter of the eighteenth century. The privy linked to the Huguenot family's tenure was excavated at the Stadt Huys Block; the ceramics from the feature are analyzed in Fayden [Janowitz] 1993. See chapter 11 of this book for an example of the expression of a resurgence of Dutch identity in the late eighteenth century.

37. Historians have identified two different sites where the Dutch West India Company's enslaved Africans lived: on the East River near today's 74th Street, as shown on the 1639 Manatus Map (this settlement, which is not substantiated in other records, may be apocryphal [Stokes 1915–28 II:207]), and a house on the west side of William Street between Broad and Nassau Streets, where the company housed its slaves from before 1643 until 1662 (Stokes 1915–28 II:297). The West India Company gave farmland between Lafayette, the Bowery, and Houston and 8th Streets to some of its slaves in the 1640s along with, first, their "half freedom" and, later on, their full freedom (Foote 1991:12–13, 1993:120–22). The experience of Africans in New York can add an ur-

ban dimension to the understanding of the African diaspora that is being gleaned from studies of plantations throughout the Americas and the Caribbean as well as in other parts of the world. Plans are currently under way for the excavation of the Dutch East India Company's slave quarters in Cape Town, South Africa (Gabeba Abrahams, pers. comm., 1999).

Chapter 11: Urban Space in the Colonial and Post-Revolutionary City

1. The concept of Manhattan growing uptown is from Lockwood, who entitled one of his books *Manhattan Moves Uptown* (1995); Blackmar (1979) described New York as a walking city. The quotation is from Haswell 1896:86.
2. Blackmar 1979, 1989.
3. Winters 1969:111.
4. D. Wall 1987, 1994; Rothschild 1990a.
5. Abbott (1974) discusses the neighborhoods of colonial New York.
6. This discussion is based on Rothschild 1990a. The statistics are from Wilkenfeld 1976, as cited in Rothschild 1990a:111.
7. Although Dutch policy required outward conformity to the Dutch Reformed Church, the practice of holding the services of other religions in private homes was usually tolerated. After the Portuguese conquest of New Holland in Brazil, a number of Jews arrived in New Amsterdam. Peter Stuyvesant, a strict Calvinist, wanted to banish them but was forbidden to do so by the Dutch West India Company, which reminded him that many of its stockholders were Jewish. Stuyvesant was also admonished by the company for his harsh policy toward Lutherans and Quakers (Rink 1986:228–37).
8. This discussion of ethnicity is based on Rothschild 1990a:83–85.
9. The ethnic transformations of Charles Bridges are recorded in Archdeacon 1976:38; Rothschild 1990a:87.
10. See chapter 3 in Rothschild 1990a for this discussion of ethnicity in the early city.
11. See chapter 4 in Rothschild 1990a for this discussion of wealth in the early city.
12. Rothschild 1990a:99. For this discussion of eth-

nicity in the city in 1789, see chapter 3 in Rothschild 1990a.
13. The African neighborhood centered on Fair, Beekman, Nassau, and Gold Streets; the Jewish neighborhood was located on Broad, Water, and Stone Streets.
14. A Lutheran church was located near the German enclave, on Rector Street near Broadway. Scots lived on Crown and Pearl Streets and, along with people of African descent, on Fair Street. Presbyterian churches were located on Little Queen Street near Broadway and at the intersection of Nassau and Beekman Streets (Rothschild 1990a:99–102).
15. See chapter 4 in Rothschild 1990a.
16. Rothschild 1990a:183.
17. Dallal and Reckner 1995. Dallal notes the curious fact that although the original members of the Holland Lodge (who were ethnically Dutch) split from the main lodge ostensibly so that they could keep their minutes in Dutch, and although they continued to protest for many years the decision on the part of the Grand Lodge that they had to keep minutes in both Dutch and English, in fact, "no evidence exists to indicate that minutes were *ever* kept in the 'low Dutch language'"—all their surviving records are in English (Dallal, pers. comm., 1999, citing Mark Parthemer, master of Holland Lodge, pers. comm., 1996).
18. This section on the Van Voorhis family is based on D. Wall 1994.
19. This discussion of the Robson family is based on D. Wall 1994.
20. This discussion is based on D. Wall 1994.
21. See D. Wall for the methods that were used in this study (1994:appendixes A, B, and C and chapters 2 and 3).
22. Hone, in Nevins 1927:202.

Chapter 12: Daily Life in the Nineteenth-Century City

1. The members of the Van Voorhis household in the 1790s are discussed in D. Wall 1994:85. The figures on enslaved Africans are from S. White 1991:5; slavery in New York is discussed at greater length in chapter 16 of this book.
2. The quotations are from the titles of Demos 1970

and Lasch 1977. The enslaved were emancipated in New York State in 1827.

3. For the methodology used, see appendixes A–D in D. Wall 1994. The following discussion on household composition is adapted from chapter 4 of D. Wall 1994.

4. The census records for this early period are very general and do not list the names of the individuals who lived in each household; they simply supply the numbers of people in different age and sex categories under the name of the household head. Therefore Wall had to make inferences to derive information about household composition: a decrease in the numbers of children in the households over time meant that the birth rate in these households was declining; the decline in the average number of men in the households over time meant a decline in the numbers of male employees or boarders who lived with their employers; and an increase in the numbers of women living in the households over time showed that there were more domestic servants at work in these homes than there had been in the past.

5. The discussion of the changing structure of meals is adapted from chapter 5 in D. Wall 1994.

6. Clark (1987:154–55) discusses the absence of dinner parties among the middle class. Modern sources on the structure and content of nineteenth-century meals include Belden 1983; Dickinson 1985; and R. J. Hooker 1981; contemporary sources include Beecher 1855; Leslie 1844; Carter 1796:129; Hall in Pope-Hennessey 1931:19, 65, 149; and works quoted in Sherrill 1971:74, 83–85.

7. Calvert Vaux, *Villas and Cottages* (1857:44; referred to in Clark 1987).

8. See Roth 1961 for the classical discussion of tea in the eighteenth century; Hall (in Pope-Hennessey 1931:63, 81) and Sherrill (1971:92) provide contemporary accounts of tea parties.

9. Bleecker 1799–1806; the entries referred to here include those for July 3, 14, and 16; August 9; and September 2 and 5 (all in 1800).

10. The households were located on the following archaeological sites: the Broad Financial Center site (Grossman 1985), the 7 Hanover Square site (Rothschild and Pickman 1990), the 175 Water Street site (Geismar 1983), the Sullivan Street site

(Salwen and Yamin 1990), the Telco Block site (Rockman [Wall] et al. 1983), and the Barclays Bank site (Berger 1987). This methodology is discussed in appendix E of D. Wall 1994. The discussion of the ceramics is adapted from chapter 6 in D. Wall 1994.

11. D. Wall 1994, 1999.

12. George Miller, a historical archaeologist, devised the method that Wall used to examine the relative cost of dishes (G. Miller 1991).

13. This irony was noted by Ortner (1984) for similar kinds of interpretations and by Ryan (1979) for the restructuring of the gender system in nineteenth-century America in particular.

14. Adapted from D. Wall 1999 and based on Gutman and Berlin 1987 and Wilentz 1984; the population figures are from Rosenwaike 1972:16, 42 and Stott 1990:72, respectively.

15. Rosenwaike 1972:42; Stott 1990:92; Stansell 1986; Wilentz 1984; Griggs 1996:9. The figures on domestic servants are from Stansell 1986:72.

16. The excavations at the Courthouse site were conducted under the direction of Leonard Bianchi and Edward Rutsch (of the archaeological consulting firm Historic Conservation and Interpretation); the artifacts were analyzed and the report on the excavations was written under the direction of Rebecca Yamin (of John Milner and Associates; Yamin 1997, 1998). The Five Points intersection was formed by Orange (now Baxter), Cross (now Park), and Anthony (now Worth) Streets. The only other extensive excavation at a tenement in New York to date was directed by Joel Grossman (1995) at a site on East 8th Street on the Lower East Side, in a neighborhood that was called Kleindeutschland in the nineteenth century.

17. Dickens 1957 [1842]:88–89.

18. Yamin and Milne 1994, adapted from Blackmar 1989:176.

19. Stott (1990) talks about the standard of living among the city's poor; Groneman Pernicone (1973) did the first study of the social history of the Sixth Ward, the political ward where the Five Points was located. See also Mayne (1993).

20. The quotation is from Yamin and Milne 1994, as revised by Yamin (pers. comm., 1999). One of the problems with using archaeological data to look at ways of life in tenements and other multiple-

occupancy buildings is that it is hard to ascribe particular artifacts to the members of particular groups. In studying tenements, the artifacts could have come from any of the households in the building, and they could have come from just one household or from many. In cases where tenement residents belonged to different ethnic or class groups (as is often the case), it may not be possible to ascribe the artifacts to the correct ethnic or class group. Although most tenants might be Irish, some might be German or Polish or Italian; although most might be working class and work as wage laborers, some might be bourgeois entrepreneurs like saloonkeepers or grocers who own their own businesses and real estate. In addition, although many people associated with a tenement might simply live in it, others might work there as well (such as grocers, saloonkeepers, tailors, or prostitutes). The artifacts found in a backyard feature might therefore reflect aspects of these economic activities as well as of domestic life. Archaeologists have to remember all these strictures when they are interpreting their finds (D. Wall 1999).

21. Adapted from Griggs 1999.

22. Griggs 1999:96–98; the quotation is from Griggs 1999:95.

23. This discussion of the brothel at the Courthouse site is adapted from Yamin 1998. In discussing the brothel here, we remember our own strictures about interpreting the archaeological evidence from multiple-occupancy housing: it is impossible to tell with certainty whether any particular artifact came from the brothel rather than from the homes of the families who also lived in the tenement. For our discussion, we have made the assumption that the artifacts from this feature that differed in some way from those found in other features at the Courthouse site came from the brothel.

24. Adapted from D. Wall 1998; based on Gilfoyle 1992; Hill 1993; Hobson 1987; Stansell 1986. Archaeological excavations directed by Donna Seifert uncovered deposits associated with a brothel run by a successful madam in Washington, D.C. (Seifert et al. 1998; Clines 1999).

25. This and the following paragraphs are based on Yamin 1998.

26. Thomas Crist is the physical anthropologist who analyzed the bones of the infants (1998). The study of prostitutes in mid-nineteenth-century New York City was conducted by Dr. William Sanger (the father of Margaret Sanger, the champion for women's reproductive rights) and cited in Yamin 1998. Although abortion was not technically legal in the mid-nineteenth century, it was commonly practiced and seldom prosecuted. Infanticide, then, as now, was considered to be murder. See Mohr 1978 for the classic study of abortion throughout American history.

27. Faunal analysts have noted that, on the whole, boneless cuts tend to be less expensive than in-bone ones. Because the Five Points was a poor neighborhood, this fact could be important in analyzing diet (Henn 1985).

28. Milne and Crabtree 1996; Yamin 1997.

29. Yamin 1997:52; De Voe (1969 [1862]:505 and passim) and Henn (1985:205) talk about the costs of different kinds of meat in nineteenth-century New York. Griggs describes the condiments from the cesspool; the quotation is from Griggs 1999:94. The bones found in a privy associated with an Irish-American grocer's family on Broome Street showed that pigs' feet continued to be a favorite with the next generation, at least in this case (Richard Clark, pers. comm., 1997).

30. Milne and Crabtree 1996:10–11.

31. Crabtree and Milne 1997:49.

Chapter 13: Building the City

1. After Blackmar 1989, who refers to this legend as the creation myth for the birth of the city's real estate market.

2. Brouwer 1980: 21. See Harris Sapan 1985 for a discussion of some of the charges of corruption that resulted from the setting of prices for the water lots that were granted to some of the city's most powerful merchants in the mid-eighteenth century.

3. Huey (1984:24) argues that although these slips began to typify the city's shoreline only after the English conquest of New Amsterdam, they may have been a cultural legacy of the Dutch.

4. Rothschild and Pickman 1990; Berger 1987.

5. The discussion of yellow fever is from Shyrock 1971; the quotation is from Bayley 1798:125.

6. Geismar 1987a, 1987b, 1987c.

7. Different kinds of plank bulkheads have been recorded at the Telco Block (Rockman [Wall] et al. 1983), Assay (Berger 1991), and 7 Hanover Square (Rothschild and Pickman 1990) sites. Cobb wharves have been discovered at the Telco Block site, the site at 175 Water Street (Geismar 1983), site 1 of the Washington Street Urban Renewal Area (Geismar 1987c), and the Assay site. The Crevecoeur quotation is from Still 1956:170.

8. In many ways the Assay project was a model of how not to run an archaeological excavation. Three sets of archaeologists worked at the Assay site: for the documentary phase and part of excavation planning, Joel Grossman, then of Greenhouse Consultants, was the principal investigator. When the project was about to move into the field, the Landmarks Preservation Commission asked that the principal investigator be changed, as Grossman was still in the process of analyzing another site (he had just finished excavations at the Broad Financial Center site, and his report had naturally not yet been completed). At that point, Greenhouse Consultants hired Roselle Henn and Diana Wall as co-principal investigators; they directed the project throughout the field phase. At the close of fieldwork, the developer, the Howard Ronson Organization, closed down the project and, for reasons apparently connected with cost, subsequently awarded the laboratory and analysis phases of the project to another archaeological firm, Louis Berger and Associates. An archaeological team from that firm, led by Charles LeeDecker and Terry Klein, analyzed the finds and wrote the final report of the excavations (Berger 1991). Needless to say, from an archaeological perspective, the project suffered from this lack of continuity through its different phases.

9. For a more extensive description of the Assay site wharves, see Berger 1991.

10. Geismar 1987c:chap. 5, p. 12 refers to the regulation requiring the use of block-and-bridge piers.

11. For example, in retrospect it is obvious that the portion of Cruger's wharf uncovered in 1969 at Old Slip (Huey 1984) and the wharf discovered lining Beekman Slip at the Telco Block (Rockman [Wall] et al. 1983) were both originally parts of block-and-bridge piers. Geismar also notes that the wharf recorded during monitoring at site 1 of the Washington Street Urban Renewal Area may well have been a block-and-bridge pier (Geismar 1987c).

12. Geismar 1983. This is the same site that Geismar used in her study of the trash content of landfill, discussed above. Howard Ronson was a developer who had to finance three of the large-scale excavations in lower Manhattan: the Broad Financial, Assay, and 175 Water Street sites.

13. See Brouwer 1980 and Henn, n.d., for a discussion of the ship in the basement.

14. Riess and Smith 1985.

15. Geismar 1983, 1987b; Geismar, pers. comm., 1999.

16. Greer (1984) describes the search for a home for the ship.

17. Rothschild and Pickman 1990; Pickman, pers. comm., 1999.

18. This discussion is adapted from Rothschild and Pickman 1990; similar deep walls were also found at the Barclays Bank site (Berger 1987), another late seventeenth-century landfill site located a block to the north of 7 Hanover Square.

19. In fact, the back wall of one of the buildings whose side walls were supported by pilings did rest on a spread-footer complex, which was located on the part of the block that had been filled earlier, before 1797.

20. Selwyn in Rothschild and Pickman 1990:app. C.

21. L. Ferguson 1992; D. Wall 2000.

22. The quotation is from L. Ferguson 1992:114; see Wall 2000 for more on the spoon from the Assay site.

23. See chapter 16 of this book and New York City Landmarks Preservation Commission 1993:39 for a discussion of the landfill at the African Burial Ground, and Pickman 1980 for a discussion of the landfill at the Aqueduct site.

Chapter 14: Building in the City

1. For gardens in seventeenth-century New Amsterdam, see Schaefer and Janowitz 1996.

2. Geismar (1989, 1993) reports that the night soil

from a nineteenth-century privy in Greenwich Village contained the egg casings from a human parasite, whipworm, as well as pollen and microscopic seeds that provided insights into the diets of the property's inhabitants.

3. Barrel features were found at the Stadt Huys Block (Rothschild et al. 1987) and the Broad Financial Center site (Grossman 1985). The latter include the Van Tienhoven and Kierstede barrel features whose contents we described in chapter 10. Because the properties where the barrels were found were the only ones that had been both the sites of homes in the mid-seventeenth century and relatively undisturbed by later construction, they were probably ubiquitous at domestic sites in New Amsterdam. The description of the barrel features is based on information describing the privy at the Stadt Huys Block (Boesch in Rothschild et al. 1987:112–14).

4. The dating information is from Grossman 1985: chap. 10, pp. 6–8.

5. Brick-lined pits were found at the Stadt Huys Block (Rothschild et al. 1987) and at the Broad Financial Center (Grossman 1985) sites; in chapter 10 we discussed the one found on the Kierstede lot.

6. These features have been found at many eighteenth- and early nineteenth-century landfill sites: at the Assay (Berger 1991), 175 Water Street (Geismar 1983), Telco Block (Rockman [Wall] et al. 1983), and Courthouse sites (Leonard Bianchi, pers. comm., 1991; Rebecca Yamin, pers. comm., 1997].

7. Geismar 1993.

8. Stone-lined privies have been excavated at the Stadt Huys Block (Rothschild et al. 1987), 7 Hanover Square (Rothschild and Pickman 1990), Telco Block (Rockman [Wall] et al. 1983), 175 Water Street (Geismar 1983), Barclays Bank (Berger 1987), Assay (Berger 1991), Courthouse (Rebecca Yamin, pers. comm., 1997), African Burial Ground (P. Perazio, pers. comm., 1991), Greenwich Mews (Geismar 1989), Sullivan Street (Salwen and Yamin 1990), and Twelfth Street (Nancy J. Brighton, pers. comm., 1991) sites in Manhattan, and the Weeksville (Roselle Henn, pers. comm., 1989), Bishop Mugavero Geriatric Center (Geismar 1992), and Atlantic Terminal Urban Renewal Area (Fitts and Yamin 1996) sites in Brooklyn.

9. Several privies straddling property lines were found at the Telco Block (Rockman [Wall] et al. 1983) and Barclays Bank (Berger 1987) sites.

10. The placement of privies near the rear property line was prescribed by law in the 1830s (Geismar 1993), but the practice had begun decades earlier.

11. N. White 1987:39–43. Burr's water company is alleged to have been a front; his goal in establishing it was to create a bank that could compete with the Bank of New York, which had been formed with the help of Alexander Hamilton, Burr's arch-enemy. Burr persuaded the state legislature to empower the Manhattan Company to conduct business as a bank at the time the company was created. Construction crews still find the Manhattan Company's wooden pipes while digging under the streets in the old part of Manhattan. Both the South Street Seaport Museum and the Museum of the City of New York have these pipes in their collections.

12. These features were found at both the late seventeenth-century landfill sites that have been excavated: 7 Hanover Square and Barclays Bank. The description of the features is adapted from Rothschild and Pickman 1990:234–35 and Berger 1987:chap. 6, p. 12.

13. Morin's interpretation is adapted from Berger 1987: chap. 6, p. 12; it should be noted that although Morin was not able to rule out the possibility that the features were for storing ice, subsequent data from other sites show that this function is unlikely. The quotation is from the *New York Gazette,* August 28, 1758, as given in Berger 1987:chap. 7, p. 30 (emphasis added). Archaeologists have also found wooden cisterns that were made out of barrels and sunk into the ground (see, e.g., Berger 1991). Like the wooden boxes, these barrels were encased in clay to ensure that they were watertight.

14. Archaeologists found a stone platform supporting a cistern at the Telco Block (Rockman [Wall] et al. 1983:122) and one made of stone and wood at the Stadt Huys Block (Rothschild et al. 1987: 109–10).

15. Archaeologists have found dry wells at the Telco Block (Rockman [Wall] et al. 1983), the Sullivan Street (Salwen and Yamin 1990), and the Merchant's House (D. Wall 1997) sites. They found

troughs connecting the dry wells to cisterns at the Telco Block site.

16. Burrows and Wallace 1999.

17. Rockman [Wall] et al. 1983. The figures for the cholera epidemics are from Markel in Jackson 1995: 219.

18. Spann (1981) discusses the public fanfare that greeted the arrival of the Croton water into the city; Philip Hone, a former mayor of New York, noted in his diary his hopes that the city's moral tone would be improved by the adoption of water as the city's drink (referred to in Spann 1981:117).

19. Howson 1987, 1994.

20. Spann 1981:120.

21. Howson 1987, 1994. Stansell (1986:50) describes the work of women and children in the city's tenements.

22. Michael Devonshire, historical architect with Jan Hird Pokorny, Architects and Planners, contacted Wall; they had both dug at the Stadt Huys Block a decade earlier.

23. Adapted from D. Wall 1993, 1997, and Pokorny 1993.

24. Disponzio, app. 2 in Pokorny 1993.

Chapter 15: Beyond the City's Edge

1. S. White 1991:16.

2. Early in the twentieth century, avocational archaeologists excavated at several colonial and nineteenth-century farmsteads, particularly in northern Manhattan and the southern Bronx. More recently, archaeologists have excavated at farms in Brooklyn, Queens, and the Bronx in preparation for modern construction work, which could destroy archaeological traces of the farmhouses' history. Farm sites excavated by early avocational archaeologists include the Dyckman, Nagel, Teunissen, Oblienis, Kiersen, and Kortwright farms in northern Manhattan (which were explored by William Calver and Reginald Bolton and the New-York Historical Society Field Exploration Society; see R. P. Bolton 1924) and the Walton-Stillwell farmhouse in Oude Dorp, Staten Island (excavated by Anderson and Sainz [1965]). Other farmhouse lots tested by modern professional archaeologists include: for Brooklyn, the Wyckoff House (by several different groups,

including Arthur Bankoff of Brooklyn College), the Christian Duryea House in New Lots (by Arthur Bankoff), and the Lott house in Flatlands (by Arthur Bankoff, Fred Winter, and Christopher Ricciardi; Ricciardi et al. 2000); for Queens, the Vander Ende Onderdonk House (by several different groups, including Rothschild [1978]), the Rufus King House (by several different groups, most extensively by Linda Stone [1998]), the Bowne House (by Queens College archaeologists, including Lynn Ceci [1985] and James Moore), and the Adriance Farmhouse at the Queens County Farm Museum (by several different groups, most extensively by Arnold Pickman and Eugene Boesch [Pickman and Boesch 1994; Pickman 1995]); for the Bronx, Van Cortlandt Mansion and Rose Hill Manor (discussed later in this chapter); for Staten Island, the Conference House and the Voorlezer House (both excavated by Sherene Baugher [Baugher and Baragli 1987; Baugher et al. 1985]). The reports on these excavations are on file with the New York City Landmarks Preservation Commission, the Department of Parks and Recreation, or the associations that run the historic houses.

3. Arthur Bankoff, pers. comm., 1995; Bankoff 1999.

4. Arnold Pickman, pers. comm., 1998.

5. Stone 1998. The King Manor Association runs this historic house-museum.

6. See Cantwell et al. 1983. The Greenwich Village Trust for Historic Preservation and the Sheridan Square Triangle Association alerted the archaeologists and sponsored the project. The trust provided both logistical and financial support, and Regina Kellerman, its executive director, conducted the historical research for the project.

7. The discussion of Fordham Manor and Rose Hill is adapted from Allan S. Gilbert, pers. comm., 1998, 1999; and Gilbert and Wines 1999, in press.

8. Gilbert and Wines 1999.

9. This discussion of the history of Van Cortlandt Mansion is based on Bankoff et al., in press; Loorya 1995; Ricciardi 1997; and Rothschild and Matthews, n.d.

10. Part of a Late Woodland settlement had been uncovered on the Van Cortlandt estate at the end of the nineteenth century (James 1896, 1897).

11. See Ricciardi 1997 for a discussion of the transformation of the topography of the estate with its conversion to public land.

12. The discussion of the ceramics from these features is based on Loorya 1995.

13. The Van Cortlandts had 64 plates (34 Canton, 8 willow, and 22 other) and 27 cups and saucers; the Robsons had 38 plates (8 Canton, 12 willow, and 18 other) and 53 cups and saucers. Data from Loorya 1995 and D. Wall 1994.

14. This discussion is adapted from Loorya 1995:15–20. Baugher and Venables (1987) have shown that as long as sites are located on waterways and social class and economic power are constants, site location does not seem to be a variable affecting access to consumer goods and consumer choices in rural areas.

15. This discussion is adapted from Winter 1981; the quotation is from Winter 1981:58.

16. McManus 1966:187. A project currently under way (directed by Cynthia Copeland, Nan Rothschild, and Diana Wall) focuses on Central Park's Seneca Village. Both historical research and remote-sensing studies have been done on the village, but there have yet to be excavations there.

17. Maynard in Jackson 1995:1251; Banks 1997.

18. Archaeologists Bert Salwen and Sarah Bridges did a study of the more than 2,500 ceramic sherds that the Hurley and Harley team collected (Salwen and Bridges 1974). Subsequently, Robert Schuyler organized a City College field school at Weeksville that was directed by his student, Roselle Henn. The students excavated two privies that had been abandoned and filled in around the beginning of the twentieth century, after the village had become an integrated working-class community (Henn 1985). Some of the artifacts from the City College excavation are on view at New York Unearthed, the archaeological museum at 17 State Street in New York.

19. Adapted from Askins 1988:64–70. Several of the descendants of the African Americans of Sandy Ground continue to live there today and have formed the Sandy Ground Historical Society.

20. Adapted from Askins 1985:211–12, 1988:91–110.

21. Schuyler 1977; adapted from Askins 1988.

22. After Askins 1985:215–16; the quotation is from Askins 1985:216.

23. Askins 1985:216.

24. Adapted from Askins 1985:214–17; the quotation is from Askins 1985:217.

25. Jackson (1985:25) makes the case for Brooklyn Heights as the world's first commuter suburb.

26. The projects in Greenwich Village are described in D. Wall 1991, 1994, 1999; Bodie 1992; Brighton, pers. comm.; Geismar 1989; and Salwen and Yamin 1990. Those in Brooklyn are described in Fitts and Yamin 1996; and Geismar 1990, 1992.

27. Burrows and Wallace 1999:234.

28. Ruins of defensive earthworks survive today in northern Central Park; see Hunter Research 1990. An outdoor exhibit showing part of a War of 1812 fortification (which was discovered by archaeologists) is on view on Ellis Island in New York Harbor. For the work of Calver and Bolton, see particularly Calver and Bolton 1950 and R. P. Bolton 1924. Although their excavation records are not up to modern standards, their collection, which is at both the New-York Historical Society and the Dyckman House, is invaluable.

29. This discussion of Fort Independence is adapted from Lopez 1978, 1983.

30. The archaeologists who worked on this project include Joel Grossman (1991), whose firm did the background study and field testing; Sherene Baugher (then of the Landmarks Preservation Commission), and Arthur Bankoff and Fred Winter, whose Brooklyn College field school performed the excavation; see Baugher et al. 1990 for the analysis of the excavation. See also Baugher and Lenik 1997. Linda Stone (1997) discovered a footing from the second Almshouse, built in 1796 and destroyed by fire in 1854, in City Hall Park during archaeological testing for another utility trench. In 1999 Petar Glumac led extensive excavations in City Hall Park as part of the park's renovation (Barry 1999); the results of this work are not yet available.

31. Baugher and Lenik 1997:18.

Chapter 16: "We Were Here"

1. This statistic is from Rosenwaike 1972:8.

2. For scholarly treatments of enslavement in the city, see, most recently, Foote 1991; S. White 1991; and Wilson 1994. Foote (1991:57, 73) has noted that between 1664 and 1737, the enslaved tended to work either as skilled artisans or in domestic service, while between 1737 and 1771, the labor needs of the city determined that most of the enslaved worked as unskilled labor. S. White (1991) discusses the high numbers of the enslaved who worked on farms.

3. Foote 1991:91; S. White 1991:9. It should be noted that the enslaved who were owned by the Dutch West India Company did live in separate quarters (Stokes 1915-28 II:207, 297). Although Foote (1991) emphasizes the isolation of the enslaved who lived in small numbers in European households, S. White (1991) emphasizes the fact that they could slip in and out of these homes unobserved and were thus able to build solidarity with their African neighbors.

4. They studied two sites for their report, only one of which, the "Broadway site," concerns us here; Ingle et al. 1990.

5. The property was first granted to Van Borsum for Roelofs by the Dutch during their brief takeover of New Amsterdam in 1673-74. When the grant was confirmed by the English in 1696 after Roelofs' death, the property was granted to Roelofs' son Lucas Kierstede and sons-in-law Johannes Kip and William Teller, who were all executors of her estate. Roelofs, however, had left her property in equal shares to all her eight surviving children. The other children disputed the claim by the executors that the property had been granted to them personally rather than as executors of the estate. The city itself took advantage of this controversy, contested the legality of the grant, and claimed that the property was still part of the Commons. For a fuller discussion, see New York City Landmarks Preservation Commission 1993:7.

6. Ingle et al. 1990:73; New York City Landmarks Preservation Commission 1993:20. Wilson (in Jackson 1995:9) discusses the fact that Trinity churchyard had been the burial ground for the city's paupers before the church was chartered.

7. Valentine, quoted in Ingle et al. 1990:76, and New York City Landmarks Preservation Commission 1993:19.

8. Ingle et al. 1990:77-78; see also Foote 1991 and Davis 1985.

9. It is thought that more than eleven thousand prisoners of war died in New York, but most had been imprisoned on ships and their bodies were simply thrown overboard or buried in mass graves nearby (Burrows and Wallace 1999:254). Some others were buried in the African Burial Ground (Stokes 1915-28 IV:394, cited in Ingle et al. 1990:79).

10. Ingle et al. 1990:70-71, 78-79, 84-88.

11. Ingle et al. 1990:99, 128-29.

12. Rutsch and Staff 1992:11-13; Cantwell (1994) describes MFAT's work with Pierre Toussaint. The MFAT team was headed by James Taylor of Lehman College and was made up of a number of scholars from the New York area.

13. Rutsch and Staff (1992:16) describe the discovery of the humic layer.

14. Dinkins and Diamond are both quoted in Dunlap 1991a.

15. Dunlap 1991b, 1991c.

16. Paterson is quoted in Dunlap 1991b and 1991c; see also "Paterson to Monitor Dig" 1991. We, the authors, as representatives of the Professional Archaeologists of New York City, were members of Paterson's Task Force.

17. Dunlap 1992.

18. The responsibilities of federal agencies in the historic preservation process are spelled out in U.S. Government et al. 1995.

19. Cantwell 1994.

20. La Roche and Blakey 1997:84; Francis is quoted in S. P. M. Harrington 1993:34.

21. For the W. Montague Cobb collection, see Masters 1992. The Blakey quotation is from Cook 1993:25. There were other serious disagreements as well; see Cook 1993:26-27 and La Roche and Blakey 1997:88-89.

22. The commission's chair, Laurie Beckelman, was quoted by S. P. M. Harrington (1993:34), who also discusses the switch to JMA.

23. The members of the community were not allowed

to hold rites on the site itself until the summer of 1992 (Jean Howson, pers. comm., 1999).

24. Barron 1992a, 1992b; Dinkins' quotation is from Seifman 1992.

25. Savage's quotation is from S. P. M. Harrington 1993:36; his remarks about Diamond are from Cottman 1992. It turned out that Savage had been alerted to the situation by Alton Maddox, a New York civil-rights lawyer and activist (Shipp 1992), and that members of the congressional Black Caucus had also been putting pressure on the GSA.

26. E. Brown 1994.

27. The African Burial Ground is the first instance in New York where anthropologists and a descendant community came into direct conflict over the disposition of human remains, and where anthropologists fought among themselves over who should study such remains. But that does not mean that there has been no precedent for such conflicts (see the Hone entry for December 10, 1839, in Nevins 1927, for different views of treating the remains of Lady Cornbury, the English governor's wife, which were exhumed during the demolition of the ruins of Trinity Church after the 1835 fire) or for the study of human remains by anthropologists (see Shapiro 1930 for a study of burials exhumed in the Nagel cemetery in northern Manhattan). See Cantwell 1994 for a discussion of the recent role of anthropologists in the transformation of the dead into symbols for the living in New York City. Beyond the local level, Fowler (1987) and Silberman (1990) discuss how some nation-states have used the past to legitimize their power and authority; see also Silverberg 1968 for a discussion of the use of the past in justifying the seizure of Indian lands in the United States in the nineteenth century, and Lowenthal 1985 and Gathercole and Lowenthal 1990 for more general discussions.

28. Perry 1997, 1998.

29. Handler 1994.

30. Blakey 1999:11. The DNA analysis was of mito-chondrial DNA, cytoplasmic DNA that is inherited only through the female line.

31. Blakey's role in the identification of the symbol is described in Coughlin 1996; the quotations are from Ofori-Ansa 1995.

32. Perry (1997:14) discusses multivalence in the material culture of the African Burial Ground.

33. Perry 1997, 1998.

34. La Roche 1994:14. R. P. Bolton (1924:204) reports that at the colonial Nagel family cemetery in northern Manhattan, a section reserved for the enslaved was discovered in 1904 near Tenth Avenue and 212th Street when workmen leveled the hill on which it stood. One of the burials uncovered was of a child who wore a little bead necklace.

35. La Roche 1994.

36. The quotation is from Blakey in Coughlin 1996:10

37. The figures here are from African Burial Ground Project 1998.

38. Blakey 1997.

39. Blakey 1997; Coughlin 1996:10.

40. Blakey 1997.

41. The information given here about Burial 101 and the quotation are from an interview with Blakey (Daly 1997).

42. Blakey 1997.

43. Blakey has discussed his responsibilities in D. H. Thomas 1998:547 and in an interview with Coughlin (1996:13); the quotation is from Blakey (in D. H. Thomas 1998:547). The figure of $5.2 million is from Coughlin 1996:8.

44. The quotations are from Boakyewa and Wright 1995.

45. Dinkins in 1994, quoted in La Roche and Blakey 1997:100.

Chapter 17: Common Ground

1. Basso 1996:32; Bellow 1970:190.

2. The quotation, made in a different context, is cited in Kennedy 1994:243.

References

Abbott, Carl. 1974. The Neighborhoods of New York, 1760–1775. *New York History* 55:35–54.

Adovasio, James, J. Donahue, and R. Stuckenrath. 1990. The Meadowcroft Rockshelter, 1973–1977: A Synopsis. *American Antiquity* 55:348–54.

African Burial Ground Project. 1998. New York African Burial Ground: Skeletal Biology Report, First Draft. Report prepared by Howard University for the United States General Services Administration, Northeast and Caribbean Region.

Anderson, Albert. 1967. Burial No. 9, Site 1, Tottenville, S. I. *Chesopiean* 5:138–43.

———. 1971. A Child and His Dog. *Chesopiean* 9:75–80.

Anderson, Albert J., and Donald R. Sainz. 1965. Excavations at Oude Dorp. *Staten Island Institute of Arts and Sciences, the New Bulletin* 14 (9):82–95.

Archdeacon, Thomas J. 1976. *New York City, 1664–1710: Conquest and Change*. Cornell University Press, Ithaca, N.Y.

Askins, William Victor. 1985. Material Culture and Expressions of Group Identity in Sandy Ground, New York. In *Urbanization and Social Change in Historical Archaeology,* ed. N. A. Rothschild, J. H. Geismar, and D. diZ. Wall. *American Archaeology* 5 (3):209–18.

———. 1988. Sandy Ground: Historical Archaeology of Class and Ethnicity in a Nineteenth-Century Community on Staten Island. Ph.D. dissertation, Department of Anthropology, City University of New York.

Axtell, James. 1985. *The Invasion Within: The Contest of Cultures in Colonial North America*. Oxford University Press, New York.

———. 1989. *After Columbus: Essays in the Ethnohistory of Colonial North America*. Oxford University Press, New York.

———. 1992. *Beyond 1492: Encounters in Colonial America*. Oxford University Press, New York.

Bakeless, J. 1950. *The Eyes of Discovery: The Pageant of North America as Seen by Early Explorers*. J. B. Lippincott, New York.

Bankoff, H. Arthur. 1999. H. Arthur Bankoff Responds. "New York's First Landmark" section, *Archaeology* 52(1):11–12.

Bankoff, H. Arthur, Frederick A. Winter, and Christopher Ricciardi. In press. Archaeological Excavations at Van Cortlandt Park, the Bronx, 1990–1992. In *The Buried Bronx,* ed. A. S. Gilbert. Bronx County Historical Society, Bronx, N.Y.

Banks, William H., Jr. 1997. Weeksville: Brooklyn's Hidden Treasure. *American Legacy* 3 (3):26–34.

Barlow, Elizabeth. 1971. *The Forests and Wetlands of New York City*. Little, Brown, Boston.

Barron, James. 1992a. Dinkins Seeks to Halt Excavation at Cemetery for Blacks. *New York Times,* July 21.

———. 1992b. U.S. Rejects Dinkins Plea for Old Burial Site. *New York Times,* July 24.

Barry, Dan. 1999. Preserving a Buried Legacy. *New York Times,* March 6.

Basso, Keith. 1996. *Wisdom Sits in Places*. University of New Mexico Press, Albuquerque.

Baugher, Sherene, and Judith Baragli. 1987. Archaeological Investigation of the Conference House Site, Staten Island, New York. Report on file with the New York City Landmarks Preservation Commission.

Baugher, Sherene, Judith Baragli, and Louise DeCesare. 1985. The Archaeological Investigation of the Voorlezer House Site, Staten Island, New York. Report on file with the Staten Island Historical Society.

Baugher, Sherene, and Edward J. Lenik. 1997. Anatomy of an Almshouse Complex. *Northeast Historical Archaeology* 26:1–22.

Baugher, Sherene, Edward J. Lenik, Thomas Amorosi, Diane Dallal, Judith Guston, Donald A. Plotts, and Robert Venables. 1990. An Archaeological Investigation of the City Hall Park Site, Manhattan. Report prepared by the New York City Landmarks Preservation Commission for the New York City Department of General Services.

Baugher, Sherene, and Robert W. Venables. 1987. Ceramics as Indicators of Status and Class in Eighteenth-Century New York. In *Consumer Choice in Historical Archaeology,* ed. Suzanne Spencer Wood. Plenum, New York.

Baugher, Sherene, and Diana diZerega Wall, 1996. Ancient and Modern United: Archaeological Exhibits in Urban Plazas. In *Presenting Archaeology to the Public,* ed. John H. Jameson, Jr. AltaMira, Walnut Creek, Calif.

Bayley, Richard. 1798. Appendix in An Inquiry into the Cause of the Prevalence of the Yellow Fever in New York. Letter. *Medical Repository* 1.

Beecher, Catharine. 1855. *A Treatise on Domestic Economy, for the Use of Young Ladies at Home and at School.* Harper and Brothers, New York.

Belden, Louise Conway. 1983. *The Festive Tradition: Table Decoration and Desserts in America, 1650–1900.* W. W. Norton, New York.

Belknap, D. F., and J. C. Kraft. 1977. Holocene Relative Sea-Level Changes and Coastal Stratigraphic Units on the Northwest Flank of the Baltimore Canyon Trough Geosyncline. *Journal of Sedimentary Petrology* 47: 610–29.

Bellow, Saul. 1970. *Mr. Sammler's Planet*. Viking, New York.

Bendremer, Jeffrey. 1999. Changing Strategies in the Pre- and Post-Contact Subsistence Systems of Southern New England: Archaeological and Ethnohistorical Evidence. In *Current Northeast Paleoethnobotany,* ed. J. Hart. New York State Museum, Albany.

Bendremer, J., and R. E. Dewar. 1994. The Advent of Prehistoric Maize in New England. In *Corn and Culture in the Prehistoric New World,* ed. S. Johanessen and C. Hastorf. Westview Press, Boulder.

Bendremer, Jeffrey, Elizabeth Kellogg, and Tonya Baroody Largy. 1991. A Grass-Lined Maize Storage Pit and Early Maize Horticulture in Central Connecticut. *North American Archaeologist* 12:325–49.

Berger, Louis, and Associates. 1987. Druggists, Craftsmen, and Merchants of Pearl and Water Streets, New York: The Barclays Bank Site. Report on file with the New York City Landmarks Preservation Commission.

——. 1991. Archaeological and Historical Investigations at the Assay Site, Block 35, New York, New York. Report on file with the New York City Landmarks Preservation Commission.

Bernstein, David J. 1990. Trends in Prehistoric Subsistence on the Southern New England Coast: The View from Narragansett Bay. *North American Archaeologist* 11:321–52.

——. 1999. Prehistoric Use of Plant Foods on Long Island and Block Island Sounds. In *Current Northeast Paleoethnobotany,* ed. J. Hart. New York State Museum, Albany.

Bernstein, David, Robert Cerrato, and Heather Wallace. 1994. Late Woodland Use of Coastal Resources at Mount Sinai Harbor, Long Island, New York. Paper presented at the Annual Meeting of the Society for American Archaeology, Anaheim.

Bettinger, Robert. 1987. Archaeological Approaches to Hunter-Gatherers. *Annual Review of Anthropology* 16:121–42.

Bierhorst, J. 1995. *Mythology of the Lenape*. University of Arizona Press, Tucson.

Blackmar, Elizabeth. 1979. Rewalking the "Walking City": Housing and Property Relations in New York City, 1780–1840. *Radical History Review* 21: 131–48.

——. 1989. *Manhattan for Rent, 1785–1850*. Cornell University Press, Ithaca.

Blakey, Michael L. 1997. The African Burial Ground: The Biology of Enslaved Africans in Colonial New York. Paper presented at the conference "Race and Ethnicity in American Material Life," October 3–4, Winterthur, Del.

———. 1999. Michael L. Blakey . . . Responds. "Tenuous Connection" section, *Archaeology* 52 (1):10–11.

Bleecker, Elizabeth. 1799–1806. Diary Kept in New York City. Rare Books and Manuscripts Division, New York Public Library.

Boakyewa, Ama Badu, and Deborah Wright. 1995. Fihankra Tour '95: Reuniting the Divided House. *Update: Newsletter of the African Burial Ground and Five Points Archaeological Projects* 1 (9):1, 18.

Bodie, Debra C. 1992. The Construction of Community in Nineteenth Century New York: A Case Study Based on the Archaeological Investigation of the 25 Barrow Street Site. Master's thesis, Department of Anthropology, New York University.

Bolton, Reginald P. 1909. The Indians of Washington Heights. In *The Indians of Greater New York and the Lower Hudson*. Anthropological Papers of the American Museum of Natural History 3:77–109. American Museum of Natural History, New York.

———. 1920. *New York City in Indian Possession*. Indian Notes and Monographs 2, no. 7. Museum of the American Indian, Heye Foundation, New York.

———. 1922. *Indian Paths of the Great Metropolis*. Indian Notes and Monographs, Miscellaneous Series 23. Museum of the American Indian, Heye Foundation, New York.

———. 1924. *Washington Heights, Manhattan, Its Eventful Past*. Dyckman Institute, New York.

———. 1934. *Indian Life of Long Ago in the City of New York*. Bolton Books, New York.

———. 1975. The Purchase of Manhattan. *Bulletin of the Archaeological Society of New Jersey* 32:30–32.

———. 1976. An Indian Settlement at Throg's Neck. *Indian Notes* 11:111–25.

Bolton, Robert. 1881. The History of the Several Towns, Manors, and Patents of the County of Westchester. Volume 1. Charles Roper, New York.

Bonomi, Patricia U. 1971. *A Factious People: Politics and Society in Colonial New York*. Columbia University Press, New York.

Boorstin, Daniel. 1987. *Hidden History*. Harper and Row, New York.

Booth, Nathaniel. 1982. The Archaeology of Long Island. In *The Second Coastal Archaeology Reader,* ed. J. Truex. Suffolk County Archaeological Society, Stony Brook, N.Y.

Boyd, Glenda F. 1962. The Transitional Phase on Long Island. *American Antiquity* 27:473–78.

Boyle, Robert H. 1979. *The Hudson River, a Natural and Unnatural History*. W. W. Norton, New York.

Bradley, James W. 1987. *Evolution of the Onandaga Iroquois: Accommodating Change, 1500–1655*. Syracuse University Press, Syracuse.

———. 1989. The Grove Field Ossuary, Bourne, Massachusetts (19-BN-612). *Bulletin of the Massachusetts Archaeological Society* 50 (1):19–34.

Bragdon, Kathleen. 1996. *Native Peoples of Southern New England, 1500–1650*. University of Oklahoma Press, Norman.

Braun, David. 1974. Explanatory Models for the Evolution of Coastal Adaptation in Prehistoric Eastern North America. *American Antiquity* 39:582–96.

———. 1987. Co-evolution of Sedentism, Pottery Technology, and Horticulture in the Central Midwest. In *Emergent Horticultural Economies of the Eastern Woodlands,* ed. W. F. Keegan. Southern Illinois University at Carbondale Center for Archaeological Investigations Occasional Paper No. 7. Carbondale, Ill.

Braun, Esther, and David P. Braun. 1994. *The First Peoples of the Northeast*. Lincoln Historical Society, Lincoln, Nebr.

Brennan, Louis A. 1974. The Lower Hudson: A Decade of Shell Middens. *Archaeology of Eastern North America* 2:81–93.

———. 1977. The Lower Hudson: The Archaic. In *Amerindians and Their Paleoenvironments in Northeastern North America,* ed. Walter S. Newman and Bert Salwen. Annals of the New York Academy of Sciences 288:411–30.

Brenner, Elise. 1988. Sociopolitical Implications of Mortuary Ritual Remains in 17th-Century Native Southern New England. In *The Recovery of Meaning: Historical Archaeology in the Eastern United States,* ed. M. L. Leone and P. Potter, Jr. Smithsonian Institution Press, Washington, D.C.

Bridenbaugh, Carl. 1968. *Cities in the Wilderness: The First Century of Urban Life in America, 1625–1742*. Alfred A. Knopf, New York.

Bridges, Patricia. 1994. Prehistoric Diet and Health in a Coastal New York Skeletal Sample. *Northeast Anthropology* 48:13–23.

Brodhead, John Romeyn. 1853–71. *History of the State of New York*. Harper and Bros., New York.

Brose, D., J. Brown, and D. Penney. 1985. *Ancient Art of the American Woodlands*. Harry N. Abrams, New York; Detroit Institute of Arts, Detroit.

Brose, D., and N. Greber, eds. 1979. *Hopewell Archaeology: The Chillicothe Conference*. Kent State University Press, Kent, Ohio.

Brouwer, Norman. 1980. The Ship in Our Cellar. *Seaport* 14 (3):20–23.

Brown, Emilyn. 1994. The Ties That Bind: A Political Celebration. *Update: Newsletter of the African Burial Ground and Five Points Archaeological Projects* 1 (3): 2–3.

Brown, James A. 1995. On Mortuary Analysis—with Special Reference to the Saxe-Binford Research Program. In *Regional Approaches to Mortuary Analysis,* ed. L. Beck. Plenum Press, New York.

———. 1997. The Archaeology of Ancient Religion in the Eastern Woodlands. *Annual Review of Anthropology* 16:465–85.

Browning, Kathryn. 1974. Indian Textiles as Reconstructed from the Impressions Left on Long Island. *Archaeology of Eastern North America* 22:94–98.

Browning-Hoffman, Kathryn. 1979. Can Incised Pottery Give Clues to Prehistoric Basketry? *The Bulletin and Journal of New York State Archaeological Association* 76:26–34.

Broyles, B. J. 1971. *Second Preliminary Report: The St. Albans Site: Kanawha County, West Virginia*. West Virginia Geologic and Economic Survey, Report of Investigations. Morgantown, W.Va.

Brumbach, Hetty Jo. 1986. Anadramous Fish and Fishing: A Synthesis of Data from the Hudson River Drainage. *Man in the Northeast* 32:35–66.

Buikstra, Jane E., Jill Bullington, Douglas K. Charles, Della C. Cook, Susan Frankenberg, Lyle Konigsberg, Joseph Lambert, and Liang Xue. 1987. Diet, Demography, and the Development of Horticulture. In *Emergent Horticultural Economies of the Eastern Woodlands,* ed. William F. Keegan. Southern Illinois University at Carbondale Center for Archaeological Investigations Occasional Paper No. 7. Carbondale, Ill.

Buikstra, Jane E., Lyle Konigsberg, and Jill Bullington. 1986. Fertility and the Development of Agriculture in the Prehistoric Midwest. *American Antiquity* 51:528–46.

Buikstra, Jane E., and George R. Milner. 1991. Isotopic and Archaeological Interpretations of Diet in the Central Mississippi Valley. *Journal of Archaeological Science* 18:319–29.

Burgraff, James D. 1938. Some Notes on the Manufacture of Wampum Prior to 1654. *American Antiquity* 4:3–58.

Burrows, Edwin G., and Mike Wallace. 1999. *Gotham: A History of New York to 1898*. Oxford University Press, New York.

Bushnell, David I., Jr. 1920. *Native Cemeteries and Forms of Burial East of the Mississippi*. Bureau of American Ethnology Bulletin 71, Smithsonian Institution, Washington, D.C.

Butler, E. M., and W. S. Hadlock. 1949. Dogs of the Northeastern Woodland Indians. *Bulletin of the Massachusetts Archaeological Society* 10:17–35.

Butzer, Karl. 1990. The Indian Legacy in the American Landscape. In *The Making of the American Landscape,* ed. M. Conzen. Unwin Hyman, Boston.

Callahan, E. 1979. The Basics of Biface Knapping in the Eastern Fluted Point Tradition. *Archaeology of Eastern North America* 7:1–180.

Calloway, Colin G. 1994. *The World Turned Upside Down: Indian Voices from North America*. Bedford Books, Boston.

———. 1997. *New Worlds for All: Indians, Europeans and the Remaking of Early America*. Johns Hopkins University Press, Baltimore.

———. 1999. *First Peoples: A Documentary Survey of American Indian History*. Bedford Books, Boston.

Calver, William L. 1948. Recollections of Northern Manhattan. *New-York Historical Society Quarterly* 32:20–31.

Calver, William L., and Reginald Pelham Bolton. 1950. *History Written with Pick and Shovel*. New-York Historical Society, New York.

Cantwell, Anne-Marie. 1980. Middle Woodland Dog Ceremonialism in Illinois. *Wisconsin Archeologist* 61:480–97.

———. 1990. The Choir Invisible: Reflections on the Living and the Dead. *Death Studies* 14:601–16.

———. 1994. "Something Rich and Strange": Reburial in New York City. In *From Prehistory to the Present:*

Studies in Northeastern Archaeology in Honor of Bert Salwen, ed. N. A. Rothschild and D. diZ. Wall. *Northeast Historical Archaeology* 21–22 (1992–93): 198–217.

Cantwell, Anne-Marie, Arnold Pickman, and Diana Rockman [Wall]. 1983. Archaeological Investigations at Sheridan Square: A Preliminary Report. Report on file with the New York City Landmarks Preservation Commission.

Cantwell, Anne-Marie, and Diana Wall. n.d. A History of New York City Archaeology. Manuscript.

Carlson, C., G. Armelagos, and A. Magennis. 1992. Impact of Disease in the Precontact and Early Historic Populations of New England and the Maritimes. In *Disease and Demography in the Americas,* ed. J. Verano and D. Ubelaker. Smithsonian Institution Press, Washington, D.C.

Carter, Susanna. 1802. *The Frugal Housewife.* Matthew Carey, Philadelphia.

Cassedy, Daniel, and Paul Webb. 1999. New Data on the Chronology of Maize Horticulture in Eastern New York and Southern New England. In *Current Northeast Paleoethnobotany,* ed. J. Hart. New York State Museum, Albany.

Cave, Alfred. 1996. *The Pequot War.* University of Massachusetts Press, Amherst.

Ceci, Lynn. 1977. The Effect of European Contact and Trade on the Settlement Pattern of Indians in Coastal New York, 1524–1665. Ph.D. dissertation, Department of Anthropology, City University of New York.

———. 1979. Maize Cultivation in Coastal New York: The Archaeological, Agronomical and Documentary Evidence. *North American Archaeologist* 1:45–74.

———. 1982. Method and Theory in Coastal New York Archaeology: Paradigms of Settlement Behavior. *North American Archaeologist* 3:5–36.

———. 1985. Historical Archaeology at the 1661 John Bowne House, Flushing, Queens. Report on file with the Bowne House Historical Society.

———. 1989. Tracing Wampum's Origins: Shell Bead Evidence from Archaeological Sites in Western and Coastal New York. In *Proceedings of the 1986 Shell Bead Conference: Selected Papers,* ed. C. Hayes III and L. Ceci. Research Records 20. Rochester Museum and Science Center, Rochester, N.Y.

———. 1990. Radiocarbon Dating "Village" Sites in Coastal New York: Settlement Pattern Change in the Middle to Late Woodland. *Man in the Northeast* 39:1–28.

Charles, Douglas. 1985. *Corporate Symbols: An Interpretive Prehistory of Indian Burial Mounds in Westcentral Illinois.* Ph.D. dissertation, Department of Anthropology, Northwestern University.

Charles, Douglas, and Jane Buikstra. 1983. Archaic Mortuary Sites in the Central Mississippi Drainage: Distribution, Structure, and Implications. In *Archaic Hunters and Gatherers in the Midwest,* ed. James Phillips and James Brown. Academic Press, New York.

Chilton, Elizabeth. 1999. Mobile Farmers of Pre-Contact Southern New England: The Archaeological and Ethnohistorical Evidence. In *Current Northeast Paleoethnobotany,* ed. J. Hart. New York State Museum, Albany.

———. In press. The Archaeology and Ethnohistory of the Contact Period in the Northeastern United States. *Review of Archaeology.*

City of New York. 1917. *Minutes of the Common Council,* ed. A. E. Peterson. City of New York, New York.

Claassen, Cheryl. 1991. Gender, Shellfishing, and the Shell Mound Archaic. In *Engendering Archaeology: Women and Prehistory,* ed. J. Gero and M. Conkey. Blackwell, Cambridge, Mass.

Claassen, Cheryl, ed. 1995. *Dogan Point: A Shell Matrix in the Lower Hudson Valley.* Occasional Publications in Northeastern Anthropology 14. Archaeological Services, Bethlehem, Conn.

Clark, Clifford Edward, Jr. 1987. *The American Family Home, 1800–1960.* University of North Carolina Press, Chapel Hill.

Clines, Francis X. 1999. Archaeology Find: Capital's Best Little Brothel. *New York Times,* April 18.

Coe, Joffrey. 1964. *The Formative Cultures of the Carolina Piedmont.* Transactions of the American Philosophical Society 54. Philadelphia.

Cohen, David Steven. 1981. How Dutch Were the Dutch of New Netherland? *New York History* 62 (January):43–60.

Cohen, N. M., and G. Armelagos. 1984. *Paleopathology at the Origins of Culture.* Academic Press, New York.

Cohn, Michael, and Robert Apuzzo. 1988. The Pugsley

Avenue Site. *Bulletin, Journal of the New York State Archaeological Association* 96:5–7.

Colden, Cadwallader A. 1825. *Memoir, at the Celebration of the Completion of the New York Canals*. New York.

Condon, Thomas J. 1968. *New York Beginnings: The Commercial Origins of New Netherland*. New York University Press, New York.

Cook, Karen. 1993. Bones of Contention. *Village Voice*, May 4.

Cotter, John L., Daniel G. Roberts, and Michael Parrington. 1992. *The Buried Past: The Archaeological History of Philadelphia*. University of Pennsylvania Press, Philadelphia.

Cottman, Michael H. 1992. Burial Site Bungled, Dinkins Tells Panel. *Newsday*, July 28.

Coughlin, Ellen. 1996. Sankofa: The African Burial Ground Project, a Dialogue Between Past and Present. *Howard Magazine* (Fall):8–15.

Cox, John, ed. 1916–40. *Oyster Bay Town Records*. Vol 2. Tobias Wright, New York.

Crabtree, Pam, and Claudia Milne. 1997. Monkey in the Privy! *Archaeology* (March–April):49.

Crist, Thomas A. J. 1998. Bioarchaeological Evidence of Infanticide and Abortion from an Antebellum Brothel Privy in New York City's Five Points District. Paper presented at the symposium "Sin City," organized by Donna Seifert, at the annual meeting of the Society for Historical Archaeology, Atlanta, Ga.

Cronon, William. 1983. *Changes in the Land: Indians, Colonists, and the Ecology of New England*. Hill and Wang, New York.

———. 1995. The Trouble with Wilderness. *New York Times Magazine*, August 12.

Crosby, Alfred W. 1976. Virgin Soil Epidemics as a Factor in the Aboriginal Depopulation in America. *William and Mary Quarterly* 33:289–99.

Cross, Dorothy. 1956. *Archaeology of New Jersey, Volume II: The Abbott Farm*. Archaeological Society of New Jersey and the New Jersey State Museum, Trenton.

Crumley, Carole. 1987. A Dialectical Critique of Hierarchy. In *Power Relations and State Formation*, ed. T. Patterson and C. Gailey. Sheffield Publishing, Salem.

Cumbaa, Steven. 1975. Patterns of Resource Use and Cross-Cultural Dietary Change in the Spanish Colonial Period. Ph.D. dissertation, Department of Anthropology, University of Florida.

Curran, M. L. 1996. Paleoindians in the Northeast: The Problem of Dating Fluted Point Sites. *Review of Archaeology* 17:2–11.

Curry, Dennis. 1999. *Aboriginal Ossuaries in Maryland*. Archeological Society of Maryland, Myersville; Maryland Historical Trust Press, Crownsville.

Custer, Jay. 1987. Problems and Prospects in Northeastern Prehistoric Ceramic Studies. *North American Archaeologist* 8:97–123.

———. 1988. Coastal Adaptations in the Middle Atlantic Region. *Archaeology of Eastern North America* 16:121–35.

Custer, J., K. Rosenberg, G. Mellin, and A. Washburn. 1990. A Re-Examination of the Island Field Site (7K-F-17), Kent County, Delaware. *Archaeology of Eastern North America* 18:145–212.

Dallal, Diane. 1995. "The People May Be Illiterate but They Are Not Blind": A Study of the Iconography of 17th Century Dutch Clay Tobacco Pipes Recovered from New York City's Archaeological Sites. Master's thesis, Department of Anthropology, New York University.

Dallal, Diane, and Paul Reckner. 1995. Masons, Motifs, and Meanings: Contextualizing Masonic Pipes. Paper presented at the Council for Northeast Historical Archaeology annual meetings, Louisbourg, Nova Scotia.

Daly, Michael. 1997. Some Brass Tacks of Slavery Revealed. *Daily News*, December 7.

Danckaerts, Jasper. 1941. *Journal of Jasper Danckaerts, 1679–1680*, ed. B. James and J. Jameson. Barnes and Noble, New York.

Davis, Thomas J. 1985. *A Rumor of Revolt: The "Great Negro Plot" in Colonial New York*. Free Press, New York.

Deagan, Kathleen. 1974. Sex, Status, and Role in the Mestizaje of Spanish Colonial Florida. Ph.D. dissertation, Department of Anthropology, University of Florida.

———. 1983. *Spanish St. Augustine: The Archaeology of a Colonial Creole Community*. Academic Press, New York.

Dean, Nora Thompson. 1978. Delaware Indian Reminiscences. *Bulletin of the Archaeological Society of New Jersey* 35:1–17.

——. 1984. Lenape Funeral Customs. In *The Lenape Indian: A Symposium,* ed. Herbert Kraft. Seton Hall Archaeological Research Center Publication No. 7, South Orange, N.J.

Deetz, James. 1977. *In Small Things Forgotten.* Anchor Books, New York.

Delage, Denys. 1993. *Bitter Feast: Amerindians and Europeans in Northeastern North America, 1600–64.* University of British Columbia Press, Vancouver.

Deloria, Vine, Jr. 1995. *Red Earth, White Lies: Native Americans and the Myth of Scientific Fact.* Scribner's, New York.

Demeritt, David. 1991. Agriculture, Climate, and Cultural Adaptations in the Prehistoric Northeast. *Archaeology of Eastern North America* 19:183–203.

Demos, John. 1970. *A Little Commonwealth: Family Life in Plymouth Colony.* Oxford University Press, New York.

Denevan, William. 1992. The Pristine Myth: The Landscape of the Americas in 1492. *Annals of the Association of American Geographers* 82:369–85.

Denton, Daniel. 1902. *A Brief History of New York Formerly Called New Netherlands.* Burrows Brothers, Cleveland.

De Voe, Thomas F. 1969 [1862]. *The Market Book.* Burt Franklin, New York.

Dickens, Charles. 1957 [1842]. American Notes. In *American Notes and Pictures from Italy.* Oxford University Press, London.

Dickinson, Nancy S. 1985. The Iconography of the Dinner Table: Upper and Middling Customs, 1760s to 1860s. Manuscript in the possession of the author.

——. 1991. Invoices, Correspondences, and Archaeology: Daily Life in Federal New York. Paper presented at the Winterthur Conference on Historical Archaeology and the Study of American Culture, Winterthur, Del.

Dimmick, Frederica. 1994. Creative Farmers of the Northeast: A New View of Indian Maize Horticulture. *North American Archaeologist* 15:235–52.

Dincauze, Dena. 1968. *Cremation Cemeteries in Eastern Massachusetts.* Papers of the Peabody Museum of Archaeology and Ethnology, Harvard University, 59 (1). Cambridge.

——. 1975. The Late Archaic Period in Southern New England. *Arctic Anthropology* 12:23–24.

——. 1976. *The Neville Site: 8,000 years at Smoskeag, Manchester, New Hampshire.* Peabody Museum Monographs, No. 4. Cambridge, Mass.

——. 1980. Research Priorities in Northeastern Prehistory. In *Proceedings of the Conference on Northeastern Archeology,* ed. J. A. Moore. Department of Anthropology Research Report 19. University of Massachusetts, Amherst.

——. 1981. The Meadowcroft Papers. *Quarterly Review of Archaeology* 2:3–4.

——. 1988. Tundra and Enlightenment: Landscapes for Northeastern Paleoindians. *Quarterly Review of Archaeology* 9:6–8.

——. 1989. Geoarchaeology in New England: An Early Holocene Heat Spell? *Quarterly Review of Archaeology* 10:1–4.

——. 1990. A Capsule Prehistory of Southern New England. In *The Pequots in Southern New England: The Fall and Rise of an American Indian Nation,* ed. L. Hauptman and J. Wherry. University of Oklahoma Press, Norman.

——. 1993a. Antecedents and Ancestors, at Last. *Quarterly Review of Archaeology* 14:12–22.

——. 1993b. Centering. *Northeast Anthropology* 46: 33–37.

Dincauze, D., and M. Mulholland. 1977. Early and Middle Archaic Site Distributions and Habitats in Southern New England. In *Amerinds and Their Paleoenvironments in Northeastern North America,* ed. W. Newman and B. Salwen. Annals of the New York Academy of Sciences 288.

Dobyns, Henry F. 1983. *Their Numbers Become Thinned.* University of Tennessee Press, Knoxville.

Dongoske, Kurt, Mark Aldenderfer, and Karen Doehmer, eds. 2000. *Working Together: Native Americans and Archaeologists.* Society for American Archaeology, Washington, D.C.

Dowd, Gregory. 1992. *The Indians of New Jersey.* New Jersey Historical Commission, Trenton.

Dunlap, David W. 1990. A Taste of the Past to Emend a Builder's Blunder. *New York Times,* May 6.

——. 1991a. Dig Unearths Early Black Burial Ground. *New York Times,* October 9.

——. 1991b. U.S. Asks Faster Excavation at Black Cemetery. *New York Times,* early edition, December 6.

——. 1991c. Excavation Stirs Debate on Cemetery. *New York Times,* final edition, December 6.

——. 1992. Mistake Disturbs Graves at Black Burial Ground: Despite Promises, Workers Unearth Bones. *New York Times,* February 21.

Edwards, R., and K. Emery. 1977. Man on the Continental Shelf. In *Amerinds and Their Paleoenvironments in Northeastern North America*, ed. W. Newman and B. Salwen. Annals of the New York Academy of Sciences 288.

Edwards, R., and A. Merrill. 1977. A Reconstruction of the Continental Shelf Areas of Eastern North America for the Times 9,500 B.P. and 12,500 B.P. *Archaeology of Eastern North America* 5:1–43.

Eisenberg, Leonard. 1978. Paleoindian Settlement Pattern in the Hudson and Delaware River Drainages. Occasional Publications in Northeastern Anthropology, No. 4. Franklin Pierce College, Rindge, N.H.

Eisenberg, Leslie. 1982. The Goodrich Site (Std 11-1). *Proceedings of the Staten Island Institute of Arts and Sciences* 31 (2, 3).

Emery, K., and R. Edwards. 1966. Archeological Potential of the Atlantic Continental Shelf. *American Antiquity* 31:733–37.

Erlandson, Jon. 1988. The Role of Shellfish in Prehistoric Economies: A Protein Perspective. *American Antiquity* 53:102–9.

Fagan, Brian. 1987. *The Great Journey*. Thames and Hudson, London.

——. 2000. *Ancient North America: The Archaeology of a Continent*. 3rd ed. Thames and Hudson, New York.

Fayden [Janowitz], Meta. 1993. Indian Corn and Dutch Pots: Seventeenth-Century Foodways in New Amsterdam/New York City. Ph.D. dissertation, Department of Anthropology, City University of New York.

Ferguson, Leland. 1992. *Uncommon Ground: Archaeology and Early African America, 1650–1800*. Smithsonian Institution Press, Washington, D.C.

Ferguson, R. Brian. 1994. Old-Fashioned Ethnic Cleansing. *New York Newsday,* April 29.

Fernow, Berthold. 1976. *Records of New Amsterdam and Court Minutes from 1653–1674*. Knickerbocker Press, New York.

Fiedel, Stuart. 1990. Middle Woodland Algonquian Expansion: A Refined Model. *North American Archaeologist* 11:209–30.

——. 1991. Correlating Archaeology and Linguistics: The Algonquian Case. *Man in the Northeast* 41:9–32.

——. 1999. Older Than We Thought: Implications of Corrected Dates for Paleoindians. *American Antiquity* 64: 95–115.

Finch, James. 1909. Aboriginal Remains on Manhattan Island. *Anthropological Papers of the American Museum of Natural History* 3:65–73.

Fisher, Emily Steelman. 1918. Luijkas van Thienhoven. *National Genealogical Society Quarterly* 7:44–45.

Fisher, Ian. 1994. The Compleat Urban Angler. *New York Times,* August 21.

Fitting, James. 1968. Economic Potential and the Postglacial Readaptation in Eastern North America. *American Antiquity* 33:441–45.

Fitts, Robert, and Rebecca Yamin. 1996. The Archaeology of Domesticity in Victorian Brooklyn: Exploratory Testing and Data Recovery at Block 2006 of the Atlantic Terminal Urban Renewal Area, Brooklyn, New York. Report on file with the New York City Landmarks Preservation Commission.

Flannery, Kent. 1972. The Origins of the Village as a Settlement Type in Mesoamerica and the Near East. In *Man, Settlement, and Urbanism*, ed. R. J. Ucko, R. Tringham, and G. Wembley. Duckworth, England.

Foote, Thelma Wills. 1991. Black Life in Colonial Manhattan, 1664–1786. Ph.D. dissertation, History of American Civilization, Harvard University.

——. 1993. Crossroads or Settlement? The Black Freedmen's Community in Historic Greenwich Village, 1644–1855. In *Greenwich Village: Culture and Counterculture,* ed. Rick Beard and Leslie Cohen Berlowitz. Museum of the City of New York and Rutgers University Press, New Brunswick.

Fowler, Don. 1987. Uses of the Past: Archaeology in the Service of the State. *American Antiquity* 52: 229–48.

Fritz, G. 1990. Multiple Pathways to Farming in Precontact Eastern North America. *Journal of World Prehistory* 4:387–435.

Funk, Robert E. 1976. *Recent Contributions to Hudson Valley Prehistory*. New York State Museum Memoir 22. Albany.

———. 1991. Late Pleistocene and Early Holocene Human Adaptations in the Lower Hudson. In *The Archaeology and Ethnohistory of the Lower Hudson Valley and Neighboring Regions: Essays in Honor of Louis A. Brennan,* ed. Herbert C. Kraft. Occasional Publications in Northeastern Anthropology 11. Bethlehem, Conn.

———. 1996. Holocene or Hollow Scene? The Search for the Earliest Archaic Cultures in New York State. *Review of Archaeology* 17:11–25.

———. 1997. An Introduction to the History of Prehistoric Archaeology in New York State. *Bulletin: Journal of the New York State Archaeological Association* 113:4–59.

Gathercole, Peter, and David Lowenthal. 1990. *The Politics of the Past.* Unwin Hyman, London.

Gehring, Charles T., and Robert S. Grumet. 1987. Observations of the Indians from Jasper Danckaerts's Journal, 1679–1680. *William and Mary Quarterly* 44:104–20.

Geismar, Joan H. 1983. The Archaeological Investigation of the 175 Water Street Block, New York City. Report on file with the New York City Landmarks Preservation Commission.

———. 1986. 17 State Street, An Archaeological Evaluation. Report on file with the New York City Landmarks Preservation Commission.

———. 1987a. Landfill and Health, a Municipal Concern, or, Telling It Like It Was. *Northeast Historical Archaeology* 16:49–57.

———. 1987b. Digging into a Seaport's Past. *Archaeology* 40 (1):30–35.

———. 1987c. Archaeological Investigation of Site 1 of the Washington Street Urban Renewal Area, New York City. Report on file with the New York City Landmarks Preservation Commission.

———. 1989. History and Archaeology of the Greenwich Mews Site, Greenwich Village, New York. Report on file with the New York City Landmarks Preservation Commission.

———. 1990. Archaeological Assessment of the Proposed Bishop Mugavero Geriatric Center Site, Block 189, Brooklyn. Report on file with the New York City Landmarks Preservation Commission.

———. 1992. Teacups and Opium: The Bishop Mugavero Geriatric Center Archaeological Field Report, Block 189, Brooklyn. Report on file with the New York City Landmarks Preservation Commission.

———. 1993. Where Is the Night Soil? Thoughts on an Urban Privy. In *Health, Sanitation, and Foodways in Historical Archaeology,* ed. Joan H. Geismar and Meta F. Janowitz. *Historical Archaeology* 27 (2): 57–70.

Gilbert, Allan S., Garman Harbottle, and Daniel DeNoyelles. 1993. A Ceramic Chemistry Archive for New Netherland/New York. *Historical Archaeology* 27 (3):17–56.

Gilbert, Allan S., and Roger Wines. 1998. From Earliest to Latest Fordham: Background History and Ongoing Archaeology. In *Fordham: The Early Years,* ed. Thomas C. Hennessey, S.J. Something More Publications, distributed by Fordham University Press, Bronx, N.Y.

———. In press. Twelve Years Excavating at Rose Hill Manor, Fordham University. In *The Buried Bronx: Recent Archaeology in the Boroughs,* ed. A. S. Gilbert. Bronx County Historical Society, Bronx, N.Y.

Gilfoyle, Timothy J. 1992. *City of Eros: New York City, Prostitution, and the Commercialization of Sex, 1790–1920.* W. W. Norton, New York.

Goad, Sharon. 1978. *Exchange Networks in the Prehistoric Southeastern United States.* Ph.D. dissertation, Department of Anthropology, University of Georgia.

Goddard, Ives. 1978. Delaware. In *Northeast,* ed. Bruce Trigger. Handbook of North American Indians, Vol. 15. Smithsonian Institution Press, Washington, D.C.

Goldstein, Lynne. 1989. The Ritual of Secondary Disposal of the Dead. Paper presented at the 1989 Theoretical Archaeology Group meetings, Newcastle upon Tyne, England.

Goldstone, Harmon H., and Martha Dalrymple. 1974. *History Preserved: A Guide to New York City Landmarks and Historic Districts.* Simon and Schuster, New York.

Goodfriend, Joyce D. 1975. "Too Great a Mixture of Nations": The Development of New York City Society in the Seventeenth Century. Ph.D. dissertation, Department of History, University of California, Los Angeles.

———. 1992. *Before the Melting Pot: Society and Culture in Colonial New York City, 1664–1730.* Princeton University Press, Princeton.

Goodyear, A., J. Foss, and G. Wagner. 1999. Evidence of Pre-Clovis in the Savannah River Basin, Allendale County, South Carolina. Paper delivered at the Annual Meeting of the Society for American Archaeology, Chicago.

Gramly, R. M., and R. E. Funk. 1990. What Is Known and Not Known about the Human Occupation of the Northeastern United States until 10,000 B.P. *Archaeology of Eastern North America* 18:5–31.

Grayson, D. 1991. Late Pleistocene Mammalian Extinctions in North America: Taxonomy, Chronology, and Explanations. *Journal of World Prehistory* 5: 193–231.

Greenfield, Haskell J. 1989. From Pork to Mutton: A Zooarchaeological Perspective on Colonial New Amsterdam and Early New York City. *Northeast Historical Archaeology* 18:85–110.

Greer, William H. 1984. City Seeks Help for a Homeless Ship. *New York Times,* December 23.

Griggs, Heather J. 1996. "By Virtue of Reason and Nature": Competition and Economic Strategy in the Needletrades in Mid-Nineteenth Century New York City. Paper presented at the annual meeting of the Council for Northeastern Historical Archaeology, Albany.

——. 1999. *Go gCuire Dia Rath Blath Ort* (God Grant That You Prosper and Flourish): Social and Economic Mobility among the Irish in 19th-Century New York. *Historical Archaeology* 33 (1):87–101.

Groneman Pernicone, Carol. 1973. The "Bloody Ould Sixth": A Social Analysis of a New York Working Class Community in the Mid-Nineteenth Century. Ph.D. dissertation, Department of History, University of Rochester.

Grossman, Joel W. 1985. The Excavation of Augustine Heerman's Warehouse and Associated 17th Century Dutch West India Company Deposits: The Broad Financial Center Mitigation Final Report. Report on file with the New York City Landmarks Preservation Commission.

——. 1991. The Buried History of City Hall Park: The Initial Archaeological Identification, Definition and Documentation of Well-Preserved 18th Century Deposits and the Possible Structural Remains of N.Y.C.'s First Almshouse. Report on file with the New York City Landmarks Preservation Commission.

——. 1995. The Archaeology of Civil War Era Water Control Systems on the Lower East Side of Manhattan, New York. Report on file with the New York City Landmarks Preservation Commission.

Grumet, Robert S. 1981. *Native American Place Names in New York City*. Museum of the City of New York, New York.

——. 1986. *New World Encounters: Jasper Danckaerts' View of Indian Life in 17th-Century Brooklyn*. Brooklyn Historical Society, Brooklyn.

——. 1989a. Strangely Decreast by the Hand of God: A Documentary Appearance-Disappearance Model for Munsee Demography, 1630–1801. *Journal of Middle Atlantic Archaeology* 5:129–45.

——. 1989b. The Selling of Lenapehoking. *Bulletin of the Archaeological Society of New Jersey* 44:1–5.

——. 1989c. *The Lenapes*. Chelsea House, New York.

——. 1990. A New Ethnohistorical Model for North American Indian Demography. *North American Archaeologist* 11:29–41.

——. 1991. The Minisink Settlements: Native American Identity and Society in the Munsee Heartland: 1650–1778. In *The People of Minisink*, ed. D. Orr and D. Campana. National Park Service, Mid-Atlantic Region, Philadelphia.

——. 1992. Magical Names. In *AMERICA Invention*, ed. L. Baumgarten. Solomon R. Guggenheim Museum, New York.

——. 1995a. *Historic Contact: Indian People and Colonists in Today's Northeastern United States in the Sixteenth Through Seventeenth Centuries*. University of Oklahoma Press, Norman.

——. 1995b. The Indians of Massapeag. *Long Island Historical Journal* 8:26–38.

Gutman, Herbert G., with Ira Berlin. 1987. Class Composition and the Development of the American Working Class, 1840–1890. In *Power and Culture: Essays on the American Working Class,* ed. Herbert G. Gutman. Pantheon, New York.

Hall, Robert. 1997. *An Archaeology of the Soul: Native American Indian Belief and Ritual*. University of Illinois Press, Urbana.

Hamell, George. 1983. Trading in Metaphors: The Magic of Beads, Another Perspective Upon Indian-European Contact in Northeastern North America. In *Proceedings of the 1982 Glass Trade Bead Conference,* ed. C. F. Hayes III. Research Records 16. Rochester Museum and Science Center, Rochester, N.Y.

———. 1987. Mythical Realities and European Contact in the Northeast During the Sixteenth and Seventeenth Centuries. *Man in the Northeast* 33:63–87.

Handler, Jerome S. 1994. Determining African Birth from Skeletal Remains: A Note on Tooth Mutilation. *Historical Archaeology* 28 (3):113–19.

Harrington, Mark R. 1909. Ancient Indian Shell Heaps Near New York City. *Anthropological Papers of the American Museum of Natural History* 3:169–82.

Harrington, Spencer P. M. 1993. Bones and Bureaucrats: New York's Great Cemetery Imbroglio. *Archaeology* 46 (2):28–37.

Harris Sapan, Wendy. 1985. Landfilling at the Telco Block. In *Urbanization and Social Change in Historical Archeology,* ed. Nan A. Rothschild, Joan H. Geismar, and Diana diZ. Wall. *American Archeology* 5 (3):170–74.

Hart, John. 1999. Dating Roundtop's Domesticates: Implications for Northeast Late Prehistory. In *Current Northeast Paleoethnobotany,* ed. J. Hart. New York State Museum, Albany.

Hart, Simon. 1959. *The Prehistory of the New Netherland Company.* City of Amsterdam Press, Amsterdam.

Harvey, David. 1985. *Consciousness and the Urban Experience: Studies in the History and Theory of Capitalist Urbanization.* Johns Hopkins University Press, Baltimore.

———. 1990. *The Condition of Postmodernity: An Inquiry into the Origins of Cultural Change.* Blackwell, Cambridge, Mass.

Haswell, Charles H. 1896. *Reminiscences of an Octogenarian of the City of New York.* Harper and Brothers, New York.

Haviland, William A., and Marjory Power. 1994. *The Original Vermonters: Native Inhabitants, Past and Present.* Second Edition. University Press of New England, Hanover, N.H.

Heckenberger, Michael J., James B. Petersen, Ellen R. Cowie, Arthur E. Spiess, Louise A. Basa, and Robert E. Stuckenrath. 1990. Early Woodland Period Mortuary Ceremonialism in the Far Northeast: A View from the Boucher Cemetery. *Archaeology of Eastern North America* 18:109–44.

Heckenberger, Michael J., James B. Petersen, and Nancy Asch Sidell. 1992. Early Evidence of Maize Agriculture in the Connecticut River Valley of Vermont. *Archaeology of Eastern North America* 20:125–49.

Heckewelder, John. 1841. Indian Tradition of the First Arrival of the Dutch at Manhattan Island. *Collections of the New-York Historical Society,* 2nd ser., 1:69–74.

———. 1876. *History, Manners, and Customs of the Indian Nations Who Once Inhabited Pennsylvania and the Neighboring States.* Historical Society of Pennsylvania, Philadelphia.

Henn, Roselle E. 1985. Reconstructing the Urban Food Chain: Advances and Problems in Interpreting Faunal Remains from Household Deposits. In *Urbanization and Social Change in Historical Archaeology,* ed. Nan A. Rothschild, Joan H. Geismar, and Diana diZ. Wall. *American Archaeology* 5 (3):202–8.

———. n.d. The Water Street Site: Final Report on 209 Water Street. Report on file with the South Street Seaport Museum.

Hertz, R. 1907. Contribution à une étude sur la représentation collective de la mort. *Année Sociologique* 10:48–137.

Heye, G., and G. Pepper. 1915. Exploration of a Munsee Cemetery Near Montague, New Jersey. Contributions from the Museum of the American Indian, Heye Foundation 2. New York.

Hicks, Benjamin, ed. 1896–1904. *Records of the Towns of North and South Hempstead, Long Island, New York.* Jamaica, N.Y.

Hill, Marilynn Wood. 1993. *Their Sisters' Keepers: Prostitution in New York City, 1830–1870.* University of California Press, Berkeley.

Hobson, Barbara Meil. 1987. *Uneasy Virtue: The Politics of Prostitution and the American Reform Tradition.* Basic Books, New York.

Hooker, Richard J. 1981. *Food and Drink in America: A History.* Bobbs-Merrill, Indianapolis.

Howson, Jean E. 1987. The Archaeology of Nineteenth-Century Health and Hygiene: A Case Study from Sullivan Street, Greenwich Village, New York City. Master's thesis, Department of Anthropology, New York University.

———. 1994. The Archaeology of 19th-Century Health and Hygiene at the Sullivan Street Site, New York

City. In *From Prehistory to the Present: Studies in Northeastern Archaeology in Honor of Bert Salwen,* ed. Nan A. Rothschild and Diana diZerega Wall. *Northeast Historical Archaeology* 21–22 (1992–93): 137–60.

Huey, Paul. 1974. Reworked Pipe Stems: A 17th Century Phenomenon from the Site of Fort Orange, Albany, New York. *Historical Archaeology* 8:105–11.

——. 1984. Old Slip and Cruger's Wharf at New York: An Archaeological Perspective of the Colonial Waterfront. *Historical Archaeology* 18 (1):15–37.

——. 1985. Archaeological Excavations in the Site of Fort Orange, a Dutch West India Company Trading Fort Built in 1624. New Netherland Studies. *Bulletin KNOB* 84 (2–3):68–79.

——. 1988. Aspects of Continuity and Change in Colonial Dutch Material Culture at Fort Orange. Ph.D. dissertation, Department of Anthropology, University of Pennsylvania.

——. 1991a. The Dutch at Fort Orange. In *Historical Archaeology in Global Perspective,* ed. Lisa Falk. Smithsonian Institution Press, Washington, D.C.

——. 1991b. The Almshouse in Dutch and English Colonial North America and Its Precedent in the Old World: Historical and Archaeological Evidence. Paper presented at the Society for Historical Archaeology annual meeting, Richmond, Va.

Hunter Research, Inc. 1990. Preliminary Historic and Archaeological Assessment of Central Park to the North of the 97th Street Transverse, Borough of Manhattan, New York. 2 vols. Report on file with the Central Park Conservancy.

Ingle, Marjorie, Jean Howson, and Edward S. Rutsch. 1990. A Stage 1A Cultural Resource Survey of the Proposed Foley Square Project in the Borough of Manhattan, New York, New York. Submitted as Appendix B of Draft Environmental Impact Statement, Foley Square Proposed Federal Courthouse and Federal/Municipal Office Building, New York City, New York. U.S. General Services Administration, Washington, D.C.

Innes, J.H. 1902. *New Amsterdam and Its People: Studies, Social and Topographical, of the Town Under Dutch and Early English Rule.* Charles Scribner's Sons, New York.

Jackson, Kenneth T. 1985. *Crabgrass Frontier: The Suburbanization of the United States.* Oxford University Press, New York.

Jackson, Kenneth T., ed. 1995. *The Encyclopedia of New York City.* Yale University Press, New Haven.

Jacobson, Jerome. 1980. *Burial Ridge: Archaeology of New York City's Largest Prehistoric Cemetery.* Staten Island Institute of Arts and Sciences, St. George, N.Y.

James, John Bradley. 1896. Ancient Mohican Interments. *Popular Science News* (August): 180–81.

——. 1897. An Ancient Mohican Village. *Popular Science News* (April): 83–84.

Jameson, F. 1984. Postmodernism or the Cultural Logic of Late Capitalism. *New Left Review* 146:179–86.

Jameson, J. Franklin, ed. 1909. *Narratives of New Netherland, 1609–1664.* Charles Scribner's Sons, New York.

Janowitz, Meta Fayden. 1993. Indian Corn and Dutch Pots: Seventeenth-Century Foodways in New Amsterdam/New York. In *Health, Sanitation, and Foodways in Historical Archaeology,* ed. Joan H. Geismar and Meta F. Janowitz. *Historical Archaeology* 27 (2):6–24.

Jefferson, Thomas. 1788. *Notes on the State of Virginia.* John Stockdale, London.

Jennings, Francis. 1976. *The Invasion of North America: Indians, Colonialism, and the Cant of Conquest.* W. W. Norton, New York.

Jirikowic, Christine. 1990. The Political Implications of a Cultural Practice: A New Perspective on Ossuary Burial in the Potomac Valley. *North American Archaeologist* 11:353–74.

Joyce, Arthur. 1988. Early/Middle Holocene Environments in the Middle Atlantic Region: A Revised Consideration. In *Holocene Human Ecology in Northeastern North America,* ed. G. Nicholas. Plenum Press, New York.

Kaeser, Edward. 1963. The Morris Estate Club Site. *New York State Archaeological Society Bulletin* 27:38–45.

——. 1968. The Middle Woodland Placement of Steubenville-Like Projectile Points in Coastal New York's Abbott Complex. *New York State Archaeological Society Bulletin* 44:8–26.

——. 1970. Archery Range Ossuary, Pelham Bay Park, Bronx County, New York. *Pennsylvania Archaeologist* 40:9–34.

———. 1972. Inference on the Northern Dispersal of CONY Projectile Points and Net-Impressed Pottery, Based on Data from Coastal New York. *New York State Archaeological Society Bulletin* 54:12–31.

———. 1974. The Oakland Lake Site (Har-13-4). *New York State Archaeological Bulletin* 60:1–27.

Kammen, Michael. 1975. *Colonial New York*. Oxford University Press, New York.

———. 1993. *Mystic Chords of Memory: The Transformation of Tradition in American Culture*. Vintage Books, New York.

Kardas, Susan, and Edward Larrabee. 1991. Summary Report of 1981–1983 Archaeological Excavation, the Schermerhorn Block. Report prepared for the Bureau of Historic Sites, New York State Office of Parks, Recreation, and Historic Preservation and the New York City Public Development Commission.

Kehoe, Alice B. 1992. *North American Indians: A Comprehensive Account*. Prentice Hall, Englewood Cliffs, N.J.

Kennedy, Roger. 1994. *Hidden Cities: The Discovery and Loss of North American Civilization*. Penguin, New York.

Kerber, J. 1997. Lambert Farm: Public Archaeology and Canine Burials along Narragansett Bay. Harcourt Brace, N.Y.

King, T., P. Hickman, and G. Berg. 1977. *Anthropology in Historic Preservation: Caring for Culture's Clutter*. Academic Press, New York.

Klein, Joel I. 1990. J. C. Harrington Medal in Historical Archaeology: Bert Salwen, 1990. *Historical Archaeology* 24 (2):4–8.

Kraft, Herbert. 1973. The Plenge Site: A Paleo-Indian Occupation Site in New Jersey. *Archaeology of Eastern North America* 1:56–117.

———. 1977. The Paleo-Indian Sites at Port Mobil, Staten Island. *New York State Archaeological Association, Researches and Transactions* 17:1–19.

———. 1978. *The Minisink Site: A Reevaluation of a Late Prehistoric and Early Historic Contact Site in Sussex County, New Jersey*. Archaeological Research Center, Seton Hall University, South Orange, N.J.

———. 1986. *The Lenape: Archaeology, History, and Ethnography*. New Jersey Historical Society, Newark, N.J.

———. 1991. European Contact and Trade in the Lower Hudson Valley and Coastal New York. In *The Archaeology and Ethnohistory of the Lower Hudson Valley and Neighboring Regions: Essays in Honor of Louis A. Brennan*, ed. Herbert C. Kraft. Occasional Publications in Northeastern Anthropology 11. Bethlehem, Conn.

Kraft, J. 1985. Marine Environments: Paleogeographic Reconstruction in the Littoral Region. In *Archaeological Sediments in Context*, ed. J. Stein and W. Farrand. Center for the Study of Early Man, Orono, Me.

La Roche, Cheryl J. 1994. Beads from the African Burial Ground, New York City: A Preliminary Assessment. *Beads: Journal of the Society of Bead Researchers* 6: 3–20.

La Roche, Cheryl J., and Michael L. Blakey. 1997. Seizing Intellectual Power: The Dialogue at the New York African Burial Ground. *Historical Archaeology* 31 (3):84–106.

Lasch, Christopher. 1977. *Haven in a Heartless World: The Family Besieged*. Basic Books, New York.

Latham, Roy. 1953. Notes on the Orient Focus of Eastern Long Island, New York. *Pennsylvania Archaeologist* 23:108–10.

———. 1978. More Notes on the Stone Utensils in the Orient Burials. In *The Coastal Archaeology Reader*, ed. G. Levine. Suffolk County Archaeological Association, Stony Brook, N.Y.

Lavin, Lucianne. 1980. Harik's Sandy Ground: A Report of the 1967 Salvage Excavations. *Bulletin and Journal of the Archaeology of New York State* 78:17–30.

———. 1986. Pottery Classification and Cultural Models in Southern New England Prehistory. *North American Archaeologist* 7:1–14.

———. 1987. The Windsor Ceramic Tradition in Southern New England. *North American Archaeologist* 8:23–40.

———. 1988. Coastal Adaptations in Southern New England and Southern New York. *Archaeology of Eastern North America* 16:101–20.

———. 1995. Pottery Production and Social Process along Long Island Sound. Paper presented at the Eastern States Archaeological Federation, Wilmington, Del.

Lavin, Lucianne, Fred Gudrian, and Laurie Miroff. 1994. Pottery Production and Cultural Process:

Prehistoric Ceramics from the Morgan Site. *Northeast Historical Archaeology* 21–22 (1992–93): 44–63.

Lavin, Lucianne, and Rene Kra. 1994. Prehistoric Pottery Assemblages from Southern Connecticut: A Fresh Look at Ceramic Classification in Southern New England. *Bulletin of the Archaeological Society of Connecticut* 57:35–52.

Lenik, Edward J. 1989a. New Evidence on the Contact Period in Northeastern New Jersey and Southeastern New York. *Journal of Middle Atlantic Archaeology* 5:103–20.

———. 1989b. Cultural Contact and Trade in Prehistoric Staten Island. *Proceedings, Staten Island Institute of Arts and Sciences* 38:25–32.

Leslie, Eliza. 1844. *The House Book, or, a Manual of Domestic Economy for Town and Country*. Carey and Hart, Philadelphia.

Lightfoot, Kent, Robert Kalin, and James Moore. 1987. *Prehistoric Hunter-Gatherers of Shelter Island, New York: An Archaeological Study of Mashomack Preserve*. Contributions of the University of California Archaeological Research Facility 46. Berkeley.

Lindestrom, Peter. 1925. *Geographia Americae with an Account of the Delaware Indians Based on Surveys and Notes Made in 1654–1656 [1691]*, ed. Amandus Johnson. Swedish Colonial Society, Philadelphia.

Little, E. 1987. Inland Waterways in the Northeast. *Midcontinental Journal of Archaeology* 12:55–76.

Little, E., and M. Schoeninger. 1995. The Late Woodland Diet on Nantucket Island and the Problem of Maize in Coastal New England. *American Antiquity* 60:351–68.

Lockwood, Charles. 1995 [1976]. *Manhattan Moves Uptown: An Illustrated History*. Barnes and Noble, New York.

Loorya, Alyssa. 1995. The Van Cortlandt Park Estate: Tea or Dinner? Manuscript in the possession of the author.

Lopez, Julius. 1955. Preliminary Report on the Schurz Site (Throgs Neck, Bronx County, New York). *Nassau Archaeological Society Bulletin* 1:6–16.

———. 1958. The Milo Rock Site, Pelham Bay Park, Bronx County, N.Y. *Pennsylvania Archaeologist* 28:127–42.

———. 1961. The Areal Distribution and Complexities of "Abbott" Ceramics. *Bulletin of the Archeological Society of New Jersey* 18–19:7–11.

———. 1978. The History and Archaeology of Fort Independence on Tetard's Hill, Bronx County, N.Y. *Bulletin, New York State Archaeological Association* 73 (July):1–28.

———. 1982a. Some Notes on Interior Cord-Marked Pottery from Coastal New York. In *The Second Coastal Archaeology Reader*, ed. J. Truex. Suffolk County Archaeological Society, Stony Brook, N.Y.

———. 1982b. Curvilinear Design Elements in the New York Coastal Area. In *The Second Coastal Archaeology Reader*, ed. J. Truex. Suffolk County Archaeological Society, Stony Brook, N.Y.

———. 1983. Fort Independence—Regimental Data. *Bulletin, New York State Archaeological Association* 87 (Summer):40–44.

Lopez, Julius, and Stanley Wisniewski. 1958. Discovery of a Possible Ceremonial Dog Burial in the City of Greater New York. *Bulletin of the Archaeological Society of Connecticut* 29:14–16.

———. 1978a. The Ryders Pond Site, Kings County, New York. In *Coastal Archaeology Reader*, ed. G. Stone. Suffolk County Archaeological Association, Stony Brook, N.Y.

———. 1978b. The Ryders Pond Site II. In *Coastal Archaeology Reader*, ed. G. Stone. Suffolk County Archaeological Association, Stony Brook, N.Y.

Lowenthal, David. 1985. *The Past Is a Foreign Country*. Cambridge University Press, Cambridge.

Luedtke, B. 1988. Where Are the Late Woodland Villages in Eastern Massachusetts? *Bulletin of the Massachusetts Archaeological Society* 49:58–65.

Lynott, Mark, and Alison Wylie, eds. 2000. *Ethics in American Archaeology*. Society for American Archaeology, Washington, D.C.

MacKenzie, Clyde. 1992. *The Fisheries of Raritan Bay*. Rutgers University Press, New Brunswick.

Masters, Brooke A. 1992. Howard U. Skeleton Collection Gets Grant. *Washington Post*, August 3.

Mayne, Alan. 1993. *The Imagined Slum, Newspaper Representation in Three Cities, 1870–1914*. Leicester University Press, Leicester, England.

McBride, Kevin A. 1994. The Source and Mother of the Fur Trade. In *Enduring Traditions: The Native Peoples of New England,* ed. Laurie Weinstein. Bergin and Garvey, Westport, Conn.

McBride, Kevin A., and Robert E. Dewar. 1987. Agriculture and Cultural Evolution: Causes and Effects in the Lower Connecticut River Valley. In *Emergent Horticultural Economies of the Eastern Woodlands,* ed. William F. Keegan. Southern Illinois University at Carbondale Center for Archaeological Investigations Occasional Paper No. 7. Carbondale, Ill.

McManamon, Francis P., and James W. Bradley. 1988. The Indian Neck Ossuary. *Scientific American* 258 (5):98–104.

McManamon, Francis P., James Bradley, and Ann Magennis. 1986. *The Indian Neck Ossuary, Chapters in the Archaeology of Cape Cod, V.* Cultural Resources Management Study No. 17. National Park Service, Boston.

McManus, Edgar J. 1966. *The History of Negro Slavery in New York.* Syracuse University Press, Syracuse, N.Y.

McNett, C. A., ed. 1985. *Shawnee Minisink.* Academic Press, New York.

Mead, J. I., and D. Meltzer, eds. 1985. *Environments and Extinctions: Man in Late Glacial North America.* Center for the Study of Early Man, Orono, Me.

Meltzer, David. 1988. Late Pleistocene Human Adaptations in Eastern North America. *Journal of World Prehistory* 2:1–52.

———. 1993. *Search for the First Americans.* St. Remy Press, Montreal.

Meltzer, David, and Tom Dillehay. 1999. The Search for the Earliest Americans. *Archaeology* 52:60–61.

Miller, Christopher, and George Hamell. 1986. A New Perspective on Indian-White Contact: Cultural Symbols and Colonial Trade. *Journal of American History* 73: 311–28.

Miller, George L. 1991. A Revised Set of CC Index Values for Classification and Economic Scaling of English Ceramics from 1787 to 1880. *Historical Archaeology* 25 (1):1–25.

Miller, Henry M. 1984. Colonization and Subsistence Change on the 17th Century Chesapeake Frontier. Ph.D. dissertation, Department of Anthropology, Michigan State University.

Milne, Claudia, and Pamela J. Crabtree. 1996. Revealing Meals—Dinner at the Five Points. Paper presented at the session "Tales of Five Points: Working Class Life in Nineteenth Century New York," at the annual meeting of the Society for Historical Archaeology, Cincinnati, Ohio.

Moeller, Roger W., ed. 1980. *6LF21: A Paleo-Indian Site in Western Connecticut.* Occasional Paper 2, American Indian Archaeological Institute. Washington, Conn.

———. 1990. *Experiments and Observations on the Terminal Archaic of the Middle Atlantic Region.* Archaeological Services, Bethlehem, Conn.

Mohr, James C. 1978. *Abortion in America: The Origins and Evolution of National Policy, 1800–1900.* Oxford University Press, New York.

Morey, D., and M. Wiant. 1992. Early Holocene Domestic Dog Burials from the North American Midwest. *Current Anthropology* 31:224–29.

Mulholland, Mitchell T. 1988. Territoriality and Horticulture: A Perspective for Prehistoric Southern New England. In *Holocene Human Ecology in Northeastern North America,* ed. G. P. Nicholas. Plenum, New York.

Nash, Roderick. 1982. *Wilderness and the American Mind.* Yale University Press, New Haven.

Nassaney, M. 1989. An Epistemological Enquiry into Some Archaeological and Historical Interpretations of 17th Century Native American–European Relations. In *Archaeological Approaches to Cultural Identity,* ed. S. Shennan. Unwin Hyman, London.

Nassaney, M., and K. Pyle. 1999. The Adoption of the Bow and Arrrow in Eastern North America: A View from Central Arkansas. *American Antiquity* 64: 243–62.

Nevins, Allan, ed. 1927. *The Diary of Philip Hone, 1828–1851.* Dodd, Mead, New York.

Newcomb, W. N., Jr. 1956. *The Culture and Acculturation of the Delaware Indians.* Anthropological Papers, Museum of Anthropology, University of Michigan, No. 10. Ann Arbor.

Newman, W. 1977. Late Quaternary Paleoenvironmental Reconstructions: Some Contradictions from Northwestern Long Island, New York. In *Amerinds and Their Paleoenvironments in Northeastern North America,* ed. W. Newman and B. Salwen. Annals of the New York Academy of Sciences 288.

Newman, W., and B. Salwen, eds. 1977. *Amerinds and*

Their Paleoenvironments in Northeastern North America. Annals of the New York Academy of Sciences 288.

New York City Landmarks Preservation Commission. 1966, 1980. 71 Pearl Street File, LP-0041.

——. 1993. African Burial Ground and the Commons Historic District Designation Report, by G. Harris, J. Howson, and B. Bradley. On file at the Landmarks Preservation Commission, New York.

Nicholas, George P. 1987. Rethinking the Early Archaic. *Archaeology of Eastern North America* 15:99–124.

Nicholas, George P., ed. 1988. *Holocene Human Ecology in Northeastern North America*. Plenum Press, New York.

O'Callaghan, E. B. 1845. *History of New Netherland*. Appleton, N.Y.

O'Callaghan, E., and B. Fernow, ed. 1856–87. *Documents Relating to the Colonial History of New York*. 15 vols. Albany, N.Y.

Oestreicher, David. 1991. The Munsee and Northern Unami Today. In *The Archaeology and Ethnohistory of the Lower Hudson Valley and Neighboring Regions: Essays in Honor of Louis A. Brennan*, ed. H. C. Kraft. Occasional Publications in Northeastern Anthropology. Bethlehem, Conn.

Ofori-Ansa, Kweku. 1995. Identification and Validation of the Sankofa Symbol. *Update: Newsletter of the African Burial Ground and Five Points Archaeological Projects* 1 (8):30.

Orr, David, and Douglas Campagna, eds. 1991. *The People of Minisink: Papers from the 1989 Delaware Water Gap Symposium*. Mid-Atlantic Region of the National Park Service, Philadelphia.

Ortner, Sherry B. 1984. Theory in Anthropology since the Sixties. *Comparative Studies in Society and History* 26:126–66.

Pagano, Daniel N. 1992. How It Happens. In *Archaeology in New York City*, ed. Anne-Marie Cantwell and Diana diZerega Wall. *Professional Archaeologists of New York City, Special Publication No. 1.*

Parris, David, and Lorraine Williams. 1986. Possible Sources of Mica from the Abbott Farm Site, Mercer County, New Jersey. *Bulletin of the Archaeological Society of New Jersey* 40:1–6.

Paterson to Monitor Dig at Burial Ground. 1991. *New York Times*. December 7.

Pearce, Roy Harvey. 1988. *Savagism and Civilization: A Study of the Indian in the American Mind*. University of California Press, Berkeley.

Pelletreau, W. S., ed. 1893–1913. Abstracts of Wills on File in the Surrogate's Office, City of New York. 17 vols. *Collections of the New-York Historical Society for the Years 1893–1909* 25–41.

Peña, Elizabeth. 1990. *Wampum Production in New Netherland and Colonial New York: The Historical and Archaeological Context*. Ph.D. dissertation, Department of Archaeology, Boston University.

Pepper, George. 1904. When Red Men Battled on Staten Island. *New York Herald* (Magazine Section), March 3.

Perry, Warren R. 1997. Analysis of the African Burial Ground Archaeological Materials. *Update: Newsletter of the African Burial Ground and Five Points Archaeological Projects* 2 (2):1, 3–5, 14.

——. 1998. Archaeological Update from the Foley Square Laboratory. *Update: Newsletter of the African Burial Ground and Five Points Archaeological Projects* 2 (6):3–5.

Petersen, James B., and David E. Putnam. 1992. Early Holocene Occupation in the Central Gulf of Maine Region. In *Early Holocene Occupation in Northern New England*, ed. B. Robinson, J. Petersen, and A. Robinson. Occasional Publications in Maine Archaeology No. 9. Maine Historic Preservation Commission, Haffenreffer Museum of Anthropology and Maine Archaeological Society, Augusta.

Pfeiffer, John. 1980. The Griffin Site: A Susquehanna Cremation Burial in Southern Connecticut. *Man in the Northeast* 19:129–33.

——. 1990. The Late and Terminal Archaic Periods of Connecticut Prehistory: A Model of Continuity. In *Experiments and Observations on the Terminal Archaic of the Middle Atlantic Region*, ed. R. Moeller. Archaeological Services, Bethlehem, Conn.

Pickman, Arnold. 1980. Nassau Expressway, Cross Bay Boulevard to Atlantic Beach Bridge, Technical Support Document, Archaeological Survey (Sections A, B, C, D and Aqueduct Site Assessment). Report submitted to the New York State Department of Transportation.

——. 1982a. Reconnaissance Level Cultural Resources Investigation, Jones Inlet—Freeport Channel,

Nassau County, New York City. Report submitted to the U.S. Army Corps of Engineers, New York District.

———. 1982b. Phase Ia Cultural Resources Survey, Bay Park/Cedar Creek Sludge Transmission Main Rehabilitation, Nassau County, New York. Report prepared for Consoer, Townsend and Associates.

———. 1984. Considerations in the Evaluation of Possible Submerged Prehistoric Site Locations. Paper presented at the PANYC Symposium on Environmental Reconstruction, Barnard College.

———. 1995. Archaeological Investigation and Construction Monitoring, Queens County Farm Museum, Installation of Utilities and Reconstruction of Roadways. Report on file with the Queens County Farm Museum.

Pickman, Arnold, and Eugene Boesch. 1994. State II, Archaeological Site Examination, Queens County Farm Museum, Barn Reconstruction Project. Report on file with the Queens County Farm Museum.

Pietak, Lynn. 1996. The Use of Shell Beads and Ornaments by 17th and 18th Century Delaware and Munsee Groups. Paper presented at the 61st Annual Meeting of the Society for American Archaeology, New Orleans.

Pokorny, Jan Hird. 1993. Old Merchant's House Historic Structure Report. Report prepared for the Old Merchant's House.

Pope-Hennessey, Una, ed. 1931. *The Aristocratic Journey, Being the Outspoken Letters of Mrs. Basil Hall, Written During a Fourteen Months' Sojourn in America, 1827–1828*. G. P. Putnam's Sons, New York.

Randolph, Howard S. F. 1934. The Kierstede Family. *The New York Genealogical and Biographical Society Record* 65 (3):224–30.

Recalling a Massacre of Indians. 1886. *New York Tribune*, April 23.

Reitz, Elizabeth, and Nicholas Honerkamp. 1983. British Colonial Subsistence Strategy on the Southeastern Coastal Plain. *Historical Archaeology* 17 (2):4–26.

Reitz, Elizabeth, and C. Margaret Scarry. 1985. *Reconstructing Historic Subsistence with an Example from Sixteenth-Century Spanish Florida*. Special Publication Series 3, Society for Historical Archaeology.

Renfrew, Colin, and Paul Bahn. 2000. *Archaeology:*

Theories, Methods, and Practice. 3rd. ed. Thames and Hudson, London.

Ricciardi, Christopher. 1997. From Private to Public: The Changing Landscape of Van Cortlandt Park, Bronx, New York, in the Nineteenth Century. Master's thesis, Department of Anthropology, Syracuse University.

Ricciardi, Christopher, Alyssa Loorya, and Maura Smale. 2000. Excavating Brooklyn, New York's Rural Past: The Hendrick I. Lott Farmstead Project. Paper presented at the Society for Historical Archaeology meeting, Quebec, Canada.

Riess, Warren, and Sheli O. Smith. 1985. The Ronson Ship Finds a Good Home. *Sea History* 37.

Riker, David M. 1981–83. Surgeon Hans Kierstede of New Amsterdam. *De Halve Maen* 57 (3):11–13, 24.

Rink, Oliver A. 1986. *Holland on the Hudson: An Economic and Social History of Dutch New York*. Cornell University Press, Ithaca; New York State Historical Society, Cooperstown.

Ritchie, William A. 1944. *The Pre-Iroquoian Occupations of New York State*. Rochester Museum of Arts and Sciences, Memoir No. 1, Rochester, N.Y.

———. 1959. The Stony Brook Site and Its Relation to Archaic and Transitional Cultures on Long Island. *New York State Museum and Science Service Bulletin* 367.

———. 1965. *The Archaeology of New York State*. Natural History Press, Garden City, N.Y.

———. 1969. *The Archaeology of Martha's Vineyard*. Natural History Press, Garden City, N.Y.

———. 1971. A Typology and Nomenclature for New York Projectile Points. *New York State Museum and Science Service Bulletin* 384.

———. 1980. *The Archaeology of New York State*. Rev. ed. Harbor Hill Books, Harrison, N.Y.

Ritchie, William A., and Robert E. Funk. 1971. Evidence for Early Archaic Occupations on Staten Island. *Pennsylvania Archaeologist* 41:45–59.

———. 1973. *Aboriginal Settlement Patterns in the Northeast*. New York State Museum and Science Service Memoir 20. New York State Museum, Albany.

Robinson, Brian S. 1996. Archaic Period Burial Patterning in Northeastern North America. *Review of Archaeology* 17:33–44.

Robinson, Brian S., James B. Petersen, and Ann K.

Robinson. 1992. *Early Holocene Occupation in Northern New England*. Occasional Publications in Maine Archaeology No. 9. Maine Historic Preservation Commission, Haffenreffer Museum of Anthropology and Maine Archaeological Society, Augusta.

Rockman [Wall], Diana, Wendy Harris, and Jed Levin. 1983. The Archaeological Investigation of the Telco Block, South Street Seaport Historic District, New York, New York. Report on file with the New York City Landmarks Preservation Commission and the National Register of Historic Places.

Rockman [Wall], Diana diZ., and Nan A. Rothschild. 1984. City Tavern, Country Tavern: An Analysis of Four Colonial Taverns. *Historical Archaeology* 18 (2):112–21.

Ronda, James. 1984. "Singing Birds," European Perceptions of the Delaware People. In *The Lenape Indian: A Symposium*, ed. H. Kraft. Seton Hall University Museum, South Orange, N.J.

Rosenwaike, Ira. 1972. *Population History of New York City*. Syracuse University Press, Syracuse, N.Y.

Roth, Rodris. 1961. Tea Drinking in 18th-Century America: Its Etiquette and Equipage. *U.S. National Museum Bulletin 225, Contributions from the Museum of History and Technology* 14:61–91.

Rothschild, Nan A. 1978. Report on Excavation at the Vander Ende-Onderdonk Site, Queens, N.Y. —Spring 1977. Report on file with the Greater Ridgewood Historical Society.

———. 1990a. *New York City Neighborhoods, the Eighteenth Century*. Academic Press, Orlando, Fla.

———. 1990b. Bert Salwen, 1920–1988. *Historical Archaeology* 24 (1):104–9.

———. 1995. Social Distance Between Dutch Settlers and Native Americans. In *One Man's Trash Is Another Man's Treasure*, ed. Alexandra van Dongen. Museum Boymans-van Beuningen, Rotterdam.

Rothschild, Nan, and Lucianne Lavin. 1977. The Kaeser Site: A Stratified Shell Midden in the Bronx, New York. *Bulletin and Journal of Archaeology for New York State* 70:1–27.

Rothschild, Nan A., and Christopher N. Matthews. n.d. Phase 1A-1B Archaeological Investigation of the Proposed Area for the Construction of Six Tennis Courts on the Parade Grounds of Van Cortlandt Park, the Bronx, New York. Report submitted to

the City of New York Department of Parks and Recreation.

Rothschild, Nan A., and Arnold Pickman. 1978. Cultural Resource Report Nassau Expressway Phase 1 Report. Vollmer Associates. Report submitted to the New York State Department of Transportation.

———. 1990. The Archaeological Excavations on the Seven Hanover Square Block. Report on file with the New York City Landmarks Preservation Commission.

Rothschild, Nan, and Diana diZ. Rockman [Wall]. 1982. Method in Urban Archaeology: The Stadt Huys Block. In *Archaeology in Urban America: The Search for Pattern and Process*, ed. Roy Dickens. Academic Press, New York.

Rothschild, Nan A., Diana diZ. Wall, and Eugene Boesch. 1987. The Archaeological Investigation of the Stadt Huys Block: A Final Report. Report on file with the New York City Landmarks Preservation Commission.

Rubertone, Patricia. 1974. Inventory and Assessment of Archaeological Potential of Distrigas Property, Rossville, Staten Island, New York: Final Report. Report submitted to the Cabot Corporation, Boston.

Russell, Aaron. 1997. Material Culture and African-American Spirituality at the Hermitage. *Historical Archaeology* 31 (2):63–80.

Rutsch, Edward S., and staff. 1992. A Research Design for the Broadway Block, Including an In-Progress Fieldwork Summary Report. Historic Conservation and Interpretation, Inc., Newton, N.J.

Ruttenber, E. M. 1971 [1872]. *History of the Indian Tribes of Hudson's River*. Kennikat Press, New York.

Ryan, Mary. 1979. The Power of Women's Networks: A Case Study of Female Moral Reform in Antebellum America. *Feminist Studies* 5:66–85.

Sainz, Donald. 1962. The Fluted Point People. *New Bulletin of the Staten Island Institute of Arts and Sciences* 12:2–5.

Salisbury, Neal. 1982. *Manitou and Providence: Indians, Europeans, and the Making of New England, 1500–1634*. Oxford University Press, New York.

———. 1996. Native People and European Settlers in Eastern North America, 1600–1783. In *Cambridge History of the Native Peoples of the Americas: North*

America, ed. B. Trigger and W. Washburn. Cambridge University Press, New York.

Salwen, Bert. 1962. Sea Levels and Archaeology in the Long Island Sound Area. *American Antiquity* 28: 46–55.

———. 1965. *Sea Levels and the Archaic Archaeology of the Northeast Coast of the United States.* Ph.D dissertation, Department of Anthropology, Columbia University.

———. 1968a. New York University Test Excavations at the Charleston Beach Site STD 21-3. Report on File with the Department of Anthropology, New York University.

———. 1968b. Muskeeta Cove 2, a Stratified Woodland Site on Long Island. *American Antiquity* 33:322–40.

———. 1975. Post-glacial Environments and Cultural Change in the Hudson River Basin. *Man in the Northeast* 10:43–70.

———. 1989. The Development of Contact Period Archaeology in Southern New England and Long Island: From "Gee Whiz!" to "So What?" *Northeast Historical Archaeology* 18:1–9.

Salwen, Bert, and Sarah Bridges. 1974. The Ceramics from the Weeksville Excavations, Brooklyn, New York. *Northeast Historical Archaeology* 3 (1):4–29.

Salwen, Bert, and Susan Mayer. 1978. Indian Archaeology in Rhode Island. *Archaeology* 31:57–58.

Salwen, Bert, and Rebecca Yamin. 1990. The Archaeology and History of Six Lots: Sullivan Street, Greenwich Village, New York City. Report on file with the New York City Landmarks Preservation Commission.

Samford, Patricia. 1996. The Archaeology of African-American Slavery and Material Culture. *William and Mary Quarterly,* 3rd series, 53 (1):87–114.

Schaefer, Richard, and Meta Janowitz. 1996. Horticulture in New Netherland. Paper presented at the Council for Northeast Historical Archaeology annual meeting, Albany.

Schaper, Hans F. 1993. Oysters and Settlement in the Lower Hudson Valley. *Bulletin, Journal of the New York State Archaeological Society* 106:24–36.

Schrire, Carmel, and Donna Merwick. 1991. Dutch-Indigenous Relations in New Netherland and the Cape in the Seventeenth Century. In *Historical Archaeology in Global Perspective,* ed. Lisa Falk.

Smithsonian Institution Press, Washington, D.C.

Schuyler, Robert. 1977. Archaeology of the New York Metropolis. *Bulletin of the New York State Archeological Association* 69:1–19.

Schwartz, Marion. 1997. *A History of Dogs in the Early Americas.* Yale University Press, New Haven.

Sedgwick, Catharine Maria. 1837. *Home.* James Munroe, Boston.

Seeman, M. F. 1979. *The Hopewell Interaction Sphere: The Evidence for Interregional Trade and Structural Complexity.* Indiana Historical Society, Indianapolis.

Seifert, Donna J., Joseph Balicki, Elizabeth Barthold O'Brien, Dana B. Heck, Gary McGowan, and Aaron Smith. 1998. Archaeological Data Recovery, Smithsonian Institution, National Museum of the American Indian, Mall Museum Site. Report prepared by John Milner Associates, Inc., for the Smithsonian Institution, Office of Physical Plant, and Venturi, Scott Brown, and Associates.

Seifman, David. 1992. Dave to Feds: Halt Work at 1700s Black Burial Ground. *New York Post,* July 21.

Shapiro, H. L. 1930. Old New Yorkers: A Series of Crania from the Nagel Burying Ground, New York City. *American Journal of Physical Anthropology* 14 (3):379–404.

Sherrill, Charles. 1971. *French Memories of Eighteenth-Century America.* Books for Libraries Press, Freeport, N.Y.

Shipp, E. R. 1992. Unlikely Hero for Cemetery. *New York Times,* August 9.

Shonnard, F., and W. Spooner. 1900. *History of Westchester County, New York, from Its Earliest Settlement to the Year 1900.* New York History Company, N.Y.

Shyrock, Richard H. 1971. The Yellow Fever Epidemics. In *America in Crisis,* ed. Daniel Aron. Archon Books, Hamden, Conn.

Silberman, Neil Asher. 1990. *Between Past and Present: Politics, Ideology, and Nationalism in the Modern Middle East.* Anchor, New York.

Silver, Annette. 1980. Comment on Maize Cultivation in Coastal New York. *North American Archaeologist* 2:117–30.

———. 1984. The Smoking Point Site (Std 14-3), Staten Island, New York. *Proceedings, Staten Island Institute of Arts and Sciences* 33:1–46.

———. 1991. *The Abbott Interaction Sphere: A Consideration of the Middle Woodland Period in Coastal New York and a Proposal for a Middle Woodland Exchange System*. Ph.D. dissertation, Department of Anthropology, New York University.

Silverberg, Robert. 1968. *Mound Builders of Ancient America*. New York Graphic Society, Greenwich, Conn.

Sirkin, L. 1986. Pleistocene Stratigraphy of Long Island, New York. In *The Wisconsinan Stage of the First Geological District, Eastern North America*, ed. D. H. Cadwell. *New York State Museum Bulletin* 455.

Skinner, Alanson. 1909. The Lenape Indians of Staten Island. *Anthropological Papers of the American Museum of Natural History* 3:3–62.

———. 1915. *The Indians of Manhattan Island and Vicinity.* American Museum of Natural History Guide Leaflet 41.

———. 1919. *Explorations of Aboriginal Sites at Throgs Neck and Clasons Point, New York City*. Contribution from the Museum of the American Indian, Heye Foundation, V(4).

———. 1920. *Archaeological Investigations on Manhattan Island, New York City*. Indian Notes and Monographs 2. Museum of the American Indian, Heye Foundation.

———. 1925. A Staten Island Petroglyph. *Indian Notes* 10:313–15.

Smith, Bruce D. 1986. The Archaeology of the Southeastern United States: From Dalton to deSoto, 10,500 to 500 B.P. *Advances in World Archaeology* 5:1–92.

———. 1992. Prehistoric Plant Husbandry in Eastern North America. In *The Origins of Agriculture: An International Perspective,* ed. C. W. Cowan and P. J. Watson. Smithsonian Institution Press, Washington, D.C.

Smith, Carlyle S. 1950. The Archaeology of Coastal New York. *American Museum of Natural History, Anthropological Papers* 43 (2).

———. 1987. The Archaeology of Coastal New York in Retrospect. *Bulletin of the Archaeological Association of New Jersey* 42:44–46.

Snow, Dean. 1980. *The Archaeology of New England*. Academic Press, New York.

———. 1992. Disease and Population Decline in the Northeast. In *Disease and Demography in the Americas,* ed. J. W. Verano and D. H. Ubelaner. Smithsonian Institution Press, Washington, D.C.

———. 1994. *The Iroquois*. Blackwell, Oxford.

———. 1995. Migration in Prehistory: The Northern Iroquoian Case. *American Antiquity* 60:59–79.

Snow, Dean, and Kim M. Lanphear. 1988. European Contact and Indian Depopulation in the Northeast: The Timing of the First Epidemics. *Ethnohistory* 35:15–33.

Solecki, Ralph. 1947. An Indian Burial at Aqueduct, Long Island. *Bulletin of the Archeological Society of Connecticut* 21:44–49.

———. 1950. The Archeological Position of Fort Corchaug, L.I. and Its Relations to Contemporary Forts. *Bulletin of the Archaeological Society of Connecticut* 24:3–40.

———. 1974. The "Tiger," an Early Dutch 17th Century Ship, and an Abortive Salvage Attempt. *Journal of Field Archaeology* 1:110–16.

———. 1985. A Contemporary View of Some Archaeological Sites in New York City. *Professional Archaeologists of New York City Newsletter* 26:8–14.

———. 1986. New York City Archaeology and the Works of Robert Moses. *Professional Archaeologists of New York City Newsletter* 29:15–16.

———. 1994. Indian Forts of the Mid-17th Century in the Southern New England–New York Coastal Area. *Northeast Historical Archaeology* 21–22 (1992–93): 64–78.

———. n.d. The Archaeology of Fort Neck, Massapequa, Long Island, New York and Vicinity. Manuscript in possession of the author.

Solecki, Ralph, and Robert Grumet. 1994. The Fort Massapeag Archaeological Site National Landmark. *The Bulletin, Journal of the New York Archaeological Association* 108:18–28.

Solecki, Ralph, and Lorraine Williams. 1998. Fort Corchaug Archaeological Site National Historic Landmark. *The Bulletin, Journal of the New York Archaeological Association* 114:2–11.

Spann, Edward K. 1981. *The New Metropolis: New York City, 1840–1857*. Columbia University Press, New York.

Speck, Frank G. 1937. Oklahoma Delaware Ceremonies, Feasts, and Dances. Memoirs of the American Philosophical Society 7. Philadelphia.

Spiess, A. E., and B. D. Spiess. 1987. New England Pandemic of 1616–1622: Cause and Archaeological Implication. *Man in the Northeast* 34:71–83.

Stansell, Christine. 1986. *City of Women: Sex and Class in New York, 1789–1860*. Knopf, New York.

Starna, William. 1992. The Biological Encounter: Disease and the Ideological Domain. *American Indian Quarterly* 26:511–19.

Starna, William, and Robert Funk. 1994. The Place of the In-Situ Theory in American Archaeology. *Northeast Anthropology* 47:45–54.

Steinberg, Jacques. 1994. Anglers Ignore Hudson Warning. *New York Times*, September 3.

Stewart, R. Michael. 1989. Trade and Exchange in Middle Atlantic Region Prehistory. *Archaeology of Eastern North America* 17:47–78.

———. 1998. Ceramics and Delaware Valley Prehistory: Insights from the Abbott Farm. Trenton Complex Archaeology 14. The Cultural Resource Group, Louis Berger and Sons Inc., East Orange. Report prepared for the Federal Highway Administration and the New Jersey Department of Transportation, Trenton.

Still, Bayrd. 1956. *Mirror for Gotham: New York as Seen by Contemporaries*. New York University Press, New York.

Stokes, I. N. Phelps. 1915–28. *The Iconography of Manhattan Island*. 6 vols. Robert H. Dodd, New York.

Stone, Linda. 1997. Monitoring, Testing, and Mitigation of Impacts to Archaeological Resources Within the 31–52 Chambers Street Utility Trench Project, Manhattan, New York, DGS Job # PW-77102F. Report on file with the New York City Landmarks Preservation Commission.

———. 1998. Report on Archaeological Testing in Advance of Improvements Associated with the Drainage and Termite Project at Rufus King Park, Jamaica Avenue at 150–153 Streets, Jamaica, Queens: Contract # Q023–195 and CNYG 497. Report on file with the New York City Landmarks Preservation Commission and the King Manor Museum.

Stott, Richard B. 1990. *Workers in the Metropolis: Class,* *Ethnicity, and Youth in Antebellum New York*. Cornell University Press, Ithaca.

Strong, John A. 1997. *The Algonquian Peoples of Long Island from Earliest Times to 1700*. Heart of the Lakes Publishing, Interlaken, N.Y.

Tankersley, Kenneth. 1998. Variation in the Early Paleoindian Economies of Eastern North America. *American Antiquity* 63:7–20.

Tantaquidgeon, Gladys. 1942. *Folk Medicine of the Delaware and Related Algonkian Indians*. The Pennsylvania Historical and Museum Commission Anthropological Series 3. Harrisburg, Pa.

Thomas, David Hurst. 1998. *Archaeology*. Holt, Rinehart and Winston, New York.

———. 2000. *Skull Wars: Kennewick Man, Archaeology, and the Battle for Native American Identity*. Basic Books, New York.

Thomas, Gabriel. 1912. An Historical and Geographical Account of Pennsylvania and of West New Jersey. In *Narratives of Early Pennsylvania*, ed. A. Meyers. Scribner's, New York.

Thomas, Peter. 1985. Cultural Change on the Southern New England Frontier, 1630–1665. In *Cultures in Contact: The European Impact on Native Cultural Institutions in Eastern North America, A.D. 1000–1800*, ed. William W. Fitzhugh. Smithsonian Institution Press, Washington, D.C.

Thorbahn, Peter F. 1988. Where Are the Late Woodland Villages in Southern New England? *Bulletin of the Massachusetts Archaeological Society* 49: 46–57.

Thwaites, Reuben Gold, ed. 1896–1901. *The Jesuit Relations and Allied Documents*. 76 vols. Burrows Brothers, Cleveland.

Totten, John Reynolds. 1925. Anneke Jans (1607–8?–1663) and Her Two Husbands. *New York Genealogical and Biographical Society Record* 56 (3).

Trelease, Allen W. 1960. *Indian Affairs in Colonial New York: The Seventeenth Century*. Cornell University Press, Ithaca.

Trigger, Bruce. 1991. Early Native North American Responses to European Contact: Romantic Versus Rationalistic Interpretations. *Journal of American History* 78:1195–1215.

Trigger, Bruce, ed. 1978. *Handbook of North American*

Indians 15: *Northeast.* Smithsonian Institution Press, Washington, D.C.

Truex, James, ed. 1982. The Second Coastal Archaeology Reader: 1900 to the Present. In *Readings in Long Island Archaeology and Ethnohistory.* Suffolk County Archaeological Association, Stony Brook, N.Y.

Tuck, James. 1975. Archaic Burial Ceremonialism in the "Far Northeast." In *Essays in Honor of Marian E. White,* ed. W. Engelbrecht and D. Grayson. Occasional Publications in Northeastern Anthropology 5. Franklin Pierce College, Rindge, N.H.

United Nations. 1991. *World Urbanization Prospects 1990.* Department of International Economic and Social Affairs, United Nations.

United States Government, the Advisory Council on Historic Preservation, and the GSA Interagency Training Center. 1995. *Participants Desk Reference: Legislation, Regulations, Guidelines, and Related Information about Historic Preservation Policies and Requirements under the National Historic Preservation Act of 1966.* U.S. Government Printing Office, Washington, D.C.

Van der Donck, Adriaen. 1968. *A Description of the New Netherlands,* ed. T. F. O'Donnell. Syracuse University Press, Syracuse, N.Y.

Van der Zee, Henri, and Barbara van der Zee. 1978. *A Sweet and Alien Land: The Story of Dutch New York.* Viking Press, New York.

Van Rensselaer, (Mrs.) John King. 1898. *The Goede Vrouw of Mana-ha-ta at Home and in Society, 1609–1760.* Charles Scribner's Sons, New York.

Van Rensselaer, Schuyler. 1909. *History of New York in the 17th Century.* Macmillan, New York.

Voorhees, David. 1994. The "Fervent Zeale" of Jacob Leisler. *William and Mary Quarterly* 51:447–72.

Wall, Diana di Zerega. 1987. At Home in New York: The Redefinition of Gender among the Middle Class and Elite, 1783–1840. Ph.D. dissertation, Department of Anthropology, New York University.

——. 1991. Sacred Dinners and Secular Teas: Constructing Domesticity in Mid-19th-Century New York. In *Gender in Historical Archaeology. Society for Historical Archaeology Special Publication* 9, ed. Donna Seifert.

——. 1993. Archaeological Report. In Old Merchant's

House Historic Structure Report. Report prepared for the Old Merchant's House by Jan Hird Pokorny.

——. 1994. *The Archaeology of Gender: Separating the Spheres in Urban America.* Plenum, New York.

——. 1997. The Archaeological Excavations at the Old Merchant's House, 29 East 4th Street, New York, New York: Second Interim Report, on the 1993 and 1995 Seasons. Report on file with the Merchant's House Museum.

——. 1998. Comments on the Papers in the Sin City Symposium. Presented at the symposium "Sin City," organized by Donna Seifert, annual meeting of the Society for Historical Archaeology, Atlanta, Ga.

——. 1999. Examining Gender, Class, and Ethnicity in 19th-Century New York City. *Historical Archaeology* 33 (1):102–17.

——. 2000. Twenty Years After: Re-Examining Archaeological Collections for Evidence of New York City's Colonial African Past. *African American Archaeology* 28:1–6.

Wall, R., R. Stewart, J. Cavallo, D. McLearen, R. Foss, P. Perazio, and J. Dumont. 1996. *Prehistoric Archaeological Synthesis.* Trenton Complex Archaeology: Report 15. Cultural Resource Group, Louis Berger and Associates, Inc. Report prepared for the Federal Highway Administration and the New Jersey Department of Transportation, Bureau of Environmental Analysis, Trenton.

Watson, Patty Jo. 1988. Prehistoric Gardening and Agriculture in the Midwest and Midsouth. In *Interpretations of Culture Change in Eastern Woodlands During the Late Woodland Period,* ed. R. Yerkes. Department of Anthropology, Ohio State University, Columbus.

Watson, Patty Jo, and Mary Kennedy. 1991. The Development of Horticulture in the Eastern Woodlands of North America. In *Engendering Archaeology: Women and Prehistory,* ed. J. Gero and M. Conkey. Basil Blackwell, Oxford.

Weil, Jim. 1971. Excavations at Wort's Farm in 1971. *Proceedings of the Staten Island Institute of Arts and Sciences* 28:3–17.

Wenke, Robert J. 1999. *Patterns in Prehistory.* Oxford University Press, New York.

Weslager, C. A. 1942. Ossuaries of the Delmarva Peninsula and Exotic Influences in the Coastal Aspect of the Woodland Pattern. *American Antiquity* 8:142–51.

———. 1972. *The Delaware Indians*. Rutgers University Press, New Brunswick, N.J.

———. 1973. *Magic Medicines of the Indians*. Middle Atlantic Press, Somerset.

———. 1983. *The Nanticoke Indians—Past and Present*. University of Delaware Press, Newark.

White, Norval. 1987. *New York: A Physical History*. Atheneum, New York.

White, Shane. 1991. *Somewhat More Independent*. University of Georgia Press, Athens.

Wilentz, Sean. 1984. *Chants Democratic: New York City and the Rise of the American Working Class*. Oxford University Press, New York.

Wilkenfeld, Bruce M. 1976. New York City Neighborhoods, 1730. *New York History* 3:165–82.

Williams, Lorraine. 1968. The Wort Farm: A Report on the 1963/1964 Excavations. *Proceedings of the Staten Island Institute of Arts and Sciences* 22:39–46.

———. 1972. Fort Shantok and Fort Corchaug: A Comparative Study of the Seventeenth Century Culture Contact in the Long Island Sound Area. Ph.D. dissertation, New York University.

———. 1988. *The New Sweden Colony*. New Jersey State Museum, Trenton.

Williams, Lorraine, and Karen Flinn. 1990. *Trade Wampum, New Jersey to the Plains*. New Jersey State Museum, Trenton.

Williams, Lorraine, David Parris, and Shirley Albright. 1982. Interdisciplinary Approaches to WPA Archaeological Collections in the Northeast. In *The Research Potential of Anthropological Museum Collections,* ed. Anne-Marie Cantwell, James Griffin, and Nan Rothschild. Annals of the New York Academy of Sciences 375.

Williamson, W. M. 1959. *Adriaen Block: Navigator, Fur Trader, Explorer, New York's First Shipbuilder, 1611–1614*. Marine Museum of the City of New York, Museum of the City of New York, New York.

Wilson, Sherrill D. 1994. *New York City's African Slaveowners: A Social and Material Culture History*. Garland, New York.

Winter, Frederick A. 1981. Excavating New York. *Archaeology* 34 (1):56–58.

Winters, Howard D. 1969. *The Riverton Culture: A Second Millennium Occupation in the Central Wabash Valley*. Illinois State Museum, Reports of Investigations, No. 13, and Illinois Archaeological Survey, Monograph 1, Springfield, Ill.

Wisniewski, Stanley H. 1986. The Bay Terrace Creek Site. *Bulletin and Journal of the New York State Archaeological Association* 93:1–26.

Wroth, Lawrence. 1970. *The Voyages of Giovanni da Verrazzano, 1520–1528*. Yale University Press, New Haven.

Yamin, Rebecca. 1997. New York's Mythic Slum: Digging Lower Manhattan's Infamous Five Points. *Archaeology* (March–April):45–53.

———. 1998. "Wealthy, Free, and Female": Prostitution in Nineteenth-Century New York. Paper presented at the symposium "Sin City," organized by Donna Seifert, at the annual meeting of the Society for Historical Archaeology, Atlanta, Ga.

Yamin, Rebecca, and Claudia Milne. 1994. Defining New York City's Five Points: Boundaries and Biases. Paper presented at the annual meeting of the Council for Northeast Historical Archaeology, Williamsburg, Va.

Zeisberger, David. 1910. History of the North American Indians. Ohio Archaeological and Historical Society Publications 19.

Index

Page numbers in italics refer to illustrations.

Abbott Farm, 79; pottery, 79, *79*, 80, *80*

abortion, 222, 324*n*26

Adegbolola, Alegba Egunfemi, *286*

Adkins site (Maine), *45*

Adriance Farmhouse, 259–60

Africa, 168, 240, 277, 289–94; cultural traits, 289–90, *290*, 292

African Americans, 10, 12, 176, 193, 194, 195, 196, 277–94; discrimination against, 269, 279, 283; nineteenth-century, 199, 204, 208, 218; ritual life of, 240–41, 279, 289–92; Sandy Ground, 268, 269–72, *270–71*; enslaved, 154, 155, 168, 170, 174, 186, 189, 192, 194, 207, 234, 240–41, 259, 277–94, 299, 320*nn*2, 4, 11, 321*n*37, 329*nn*2, 3; towns, 268–72, *270–71*

African Burial Ground, 241, 278–94, *280–92*, 329*n*9, 330*nn*27, 34; research and excavation, 278–82, *282*, 283–89, *289*, 290–92, *292*, 293–94

agriculture, 87, 155, 234, 311*n*5; colonial, 146, 176, 180, 259, 267; farms, estates, and plantations, 259–67, *260–65*; labor, 113–14, 180, 259, 277; Late Woodland, 94–95, 97, 103, 109–14, 311*n*6, 313*n*38, 314*nn*51, 52; maize, 109–14, 180, 311*n*6; Middle Woodland, 76, 87; Munsee, 125, 126, 144, 145; nineteenth-century, 267, 269; slash-and-burn, 94, 103; trade, 155, 158; transportation, 267, 269

Albany, 119, 142, 149, 151, 153, 173, 177

Algonquians, 133, 135, 313*n*37. *See also specific groups*

almshouses, 279; kitchen, 275–76, *276*

American Indian Ritual Object Repatriation Foundation, 96

American Museum of Natural History, 15, 82, 110

Amity Street, 251–52

Amsterdam, 35, 179

Anabaptists, 267

Anderson, Albert, 40–42, 43, 48, 51, 82, 305*n*11

Anderson, Robert, 40–42, 48, 51

anemia, 84, 112

Anglican Church, 193

Anglo-Dutch Wars, 169, 181–82

An hoock, 123, 127, 128, *128*, 129, 145

animals, 275; ancient, 38, 42, 43, 44, 46–47, 57; Contact period, 119, 122, 125, 132, 133, 145–46; European domesticated, 145–46, 179, 299, 321*n*23; Late Woodland, 94, 99, 101, 104, *104*, 105–9, 111, 112, 114; Middle Woodland, 87–88, *89*, 90; nineteenth-century, 222–23, 230. *See also* hunting; *specific animals*

apprentices, 207, 208, 229

Aqueduct site, 97–98, 102, 114, 135, 241, 311*n*11

archaeology, 3–14, 15–16, 299–301, 303*n*1; African Burial Ground project, 278–94, *280–92*, 329*n*9, 330*nn*27, 34; contract, 12–13, 16; coroner's method of excavation, 283; costs, 16, 19, 23, 28, 30, 235, 293; digging in New York, 15–32, *19–31*; equipment, 23–24; ethical issues, 96, *96*, 97, 282–88; excavation procedures, 24–29, *25–26*, 110; historic preservation movement, 10–12, 13, 17, 104–5, 284; of landfill, 227–39, *228–39*; modern, 9–13. *See also specific sites and archaeologists*

Archaic period, 12, 46–49, *50*, 51–61, *58–61*, 64, 71, 306*nn*12, 17, 307*nn*19, 21, 22, 25, 27; Early, 46–54, 82;

Archaic period (continued)
    Late, 46, 57–61, *58–61*, 81, 87, 307*nn*22, 27; Middle,
        46, 47, 54–57, 307*n*21
Archdeacon, Thomas, 183
Archer, John, 261
Archery Range, *5*, 100–102, 104, 109, 114; artifacts, 101,
    101, 102
architecture: Dutch-style, 169, 177, *182–83*, 184, *185*, 198,
    237, *237*, 262, 270; Federal, *199*; Georgian, 263, 264,
    265, 270; I-house, 270, *270*, 271; nineteenth-century
    brownstone, 253–54, *254*, 255; Sandy Ground, 270–71,
    270–71
argillite points, reddish-purple, 78, 79, *79*, 80, 81, 309*n*12
arrows and arrowheads, 49, 94, 228; Late Woodland,
    94, 108; Munsee, 129, 130, *130*, 136, 145
Arthur Kill, 42, 51, 82
artisans and craftsmen, 194, 197, 202, 206, 219, 252, 277
Askins, William, 270, 271
Assay site, *6*, 162, *190*, 229–33, *230–32*, 238–39, *238–39*, 240,
    245, 325*n*8
Astor, John Jacob, 196
Atlantic Ocean, 37, 38, 42, 149, 154
atlatl weight, *59*, 307*n*25
axes, stone, 58, *58*
Axtell, James, 142

backyards, urban, 242–56, *243–55;* cisterns and dry wells,
    246–47, *246–47*, 248–49, *249*, 250–52; colonial, 242,
    243–44, *244*, 245, *245*, 247, 248, 249, *249*; health
    issues, 249–52; nineteenth-century, 243, *243*, 245–47,
    246–47, 248–56, *254–55;* privies, 243–47, *243–47*,
    248–52
bags, 89, 90
Bakongo, 240–41
Bankoff, Arthur, 259, 263, 267, 328*n*30
bannerstones, 58–59, *59*, 66
Barclays Bank site, *6*, 196, 198, 249
barrel-lined privy, 244, *244*
barrier-lagoon systems, 305*n*12
basements, 22–23, 247
baskets, 89, 90
Battery Park City, 226
Baugher, Sherene, 275, 328*n*30
Bayard, Peter and Blandina, 173, 320*n*11
Bayard privy, 173–74, *173*
Bayley, Richard, 228

beads: African, 290–91, *292;* shell, 131, 132, *132*, 133–34,
    134, 135–39, *139*, 140–42, 315*n*15, 316*nn*27, 28, 41,
    43, 47, 317*n*54; Woodland, 84. *See also* wampum
    trade
beans, 94, 110, 113, 180
beaver, 132–34
Bedford-Stuyvesant, 268
Beecher, Catharine, *Domestic Receipt-Book,* 213
Belgium, 167
Bergen-op-Zoom, 165
Bering Strait, 38
bifurcates, 48, *50*, 51, 52
Bird, Edward, pipes by, 164, 172, 174, 320*n*7
birds, 179, 221; Woodland, 88, *89*, 114
Blackwell's Island, 275
Blakey, Michael, 285, 287, 288, *288*, 289–93
Bleecker, Elizabeth, 212–13
Block, Adrian, 150–52
block-and-bridge wharf, 232–33, *233*, 325*n*25
Block Island, 136, 150
Bloomfield, 129
Board of Standards and Appeals, 31
Bodnar, Joseph, 42, 48
Boesch, Eugene, 259
Bolton, Reginald P., 94, 104–6, 108, 274
bone(s), 44, 275; awls, 76; chemical analysis of, 111–13;
    comb, 175, *175;* needles, 76; Woodland, 83–85, 99
Boorstin, Daniel, 169
Booth, Nathaniel, 64
Boston, 155, 181, 182
Bowmans Brook, 100, 102, 110, 114
box privies, 245–46
brass trade goods, 130, *130*, 131, 136, *139*
breweries, 218
Brewster, Joseph, 252–54
brick, 13, 25, 165; cisterns, *246*, 249, 250; colonial, 165,
    171, 198; privies, 243, 245, *245*, 246, *246*, 326*n*5
Bridges, Charles, 193
Bridges, Patricia, 84, 111–12
Broad Financial Center, *6*, 170, 176, *245*
Broad Street, 17, 20, *21*, 24, *185*, 212, 225; #85 Broad
    Street, 29, *29*
Broadway, 4, 193, 194, 195, 202; African Burial Ground
    excavation, 278–82, 287
Bronx, 4, *5*, 36, 60, 77, 127, 135, 145, 257, 314*n*54; Archery
    Range, *5*, 100–101, *101*, 102, 104, 109, 114; Clasons

Point, 60, 114, 129, 145; Morris-Schurz, *5*, 78–79, *79*, 81, *81;* Rose Hill Manor, 261–62, *262,* 263; rural land, 257, 261–67, *262–65,* 267; Throgs Neck, *5*, 60, 63, 78, 100, 129, 131, 136, 145; Van Cortlandt mansion, 263–65, *265,* 266–67

Brooklyn, 4, *5*, 54, 64, 134, 135, 203, 225, 246, 257; rural land, 257, *258*, 259, 267, 268, 272–73; Ryders Pond, *5*, 129–30, 131, 136; Wyckoff House, 259–60, *260*

Brooklyn Bridge, 268

Brooklyn College, 263, 266, 267, 328*n*30

Brooklyn Heights, 250, 272

Buckmaster, Edward, 156

bundle burials, 99–104

Burgis View of New York, *182–83*

Burgraff, James, 137–38

burials. *See* dog burials; funerary rites; human burials

Burr, Aaron, 247, 326*n*11

Bushwick, 267

buttons, 25, 274, 275, 276, *276*

Calloway, Colin, 115, 123

Calver, William L., 94, 104–5, *105,* 106, 108, 274

Canada, 134

Canarsees, 120, 129–30

candleholder and candlesnuffer, metal, 173, *173*

canoes, 77, 89, 119, 139, *168*

Cantwell, Anne-Marie, 261

Cape Cod, 102, 103, 151, 157

carbon isotope values, 111–12

Carter, Susannah, *The Frugal Housewife, 212*

Castello Plan, *21*

Catholicism, 168, 181–82, 200, 262, 263

cattle, 125, 145, 146, 179, 223, 228

Ceci, Lynn, 110–11

celts, 52, 306*n*11

census records, 202, 209, 210, 211, 215, 323*n*4

Centre Street, 278

ceramics, 13, 25, 73–75; chamber pots, 220, 243, *243;* chemical analysis of, 166, 319*n*22; Chinese porcelain, 161, 164, 172, *172*, 214, 218, 221, 266, 275; clay tobacco pipe, 155, 157, 158, *158*, 159–60, 164, 319*n*17; colonial, 157, 158, *158*, 159–61, 165, 169, 171–75, *171–75*, 179, 180, 185, 186, 196–97, 275, 319*nn*17, 22, 321*n*36; colono-ware, 240–41; costs of, 214–15, *216;* creamware, 214, *215*, 275; decorative motifs, 171, *171*, 213–15, *215*, 221,

266; delft, 171, *171*, 172, *172*, 174, *175*, 177, 198; development of, 73–75; Early Woodland, 73–75, *75*, 309*n*5; earthenware, *31*, 161, 165, *172*, 174, *174*, *175*, 186, 196–97, 214, 240, *243*, 266; European, 136, *139*, 161, 162, 165, 171–75, *171–75*, 186; global market for, 161–66; Gothic, 272, 273; Italianate, 272, 273, *273;* Late Woodland, 94, *94*, 98, *101*, *105*, 109, 114, 316–17*n*47; Middle Woodland, 63, 78, 79, *79*, 80, *80*, 81, *81;* Munsee, 136, *139;* nineteenth-century, 161–63, 198, 200, 209, *209*, 211–15, *212–16*, 218, 256, 263, *264*, 265–67, 271–73; Orient, 308*n*5, 309*n*3; pearlware, 196, 214, *215;* "royal," 214, *215;* sherds, 75–76, *139*, 154, 161–62, 165, 171, *171*, 172, *172*, 196, 200, 209, 213, 256, 275, 308*n*15, 328*n*18; teawares, 212–15, *216*, 218, 219, *220*, 221, 267, 273, *273*, 275; tiles, 165, 171, *171*, 198; tin-glazed, 171, 180, 185; Wedgwood, 162; working-class, 218, 219–20, *220*, 221

ceremonial life. *See* ritual life

chamber pots, 220, 243, *243*

Charles, The (ship), 35

Charles II, King of England, 181

cheese, 178, 179

chickens, 179

childbirth, 114, 198, 289, 290

children, 8, 299; colonial, 186, 198; enslaved African American, 277, 289, *289*, 290–92; infanticide, 222, 324*n*26; Late Woodland, 98–99, 101, 107–8, 111; middle-class, 207, *208*, 209–10, *210*, 211–15; Munsee, 126–27, 143; nineteenth-century, 196, 204, 206–15, 219, 252, 272, 323*n*4, 324*n*26; Paleoindian, 44, 45; Ward's Point burial, 82–86; Woodland, 73, 74, 82–86; working-class, 219, 220, 222

Chinatown, 217

Chinese porcelain, 161, 164, 172, *172*, 214, 218, 221, 266, 275

cholera, 250

Christiaensen, Hendrick, 150, 151

churches, 193–94, 279, 286, 322*nn*7, 14

cisterns, 27, 242, 246, *246*, *247*, 248–49, *249*, 250–52, 326*nn*13, 14

City College of New York, 253, 270

City Environmental Quality Review (CEQR), 30–32

City Hall, 188, 204, 226, 275

City Hall Park, 188, *189*, 217, 248, 275, 278, 328*n*30

Clasons Point, 60, 114, 129, 145

clay. *See* ceramics

Clinton, DeWitt, 196, 316*n*32

clothing, 44; Archaic, 60; colonial, 175; European, 132, 140; Late Woodland, 114; Munsee, 139–40; nineteenth-century, 213, 218; Paleoindian, 44, 45; trade, 158

Clovis, 38–39, 40, 304*n*4, 305*n*10; point, 40, *41*, 305*n*10

clubs, war, 125, *125*

coastal environment. *See* waterfront

coffee, 163, 221

Cohn, Michael, 268, 274

coins, 29, *155*, 274

colanders, 172, *172*, 180, 185

Colden, Cadwallader, 9

collective guardianship of land, 72, 188, 298, 318*n*67

Collect Pond, 54, 203, 217–18, 247, 270, *280*

College Point, *104*

colonial period. *See* Dutch settlement; English colonial New York; New Amsterdam

colonoware bowls, 240–41

Columbia University, 17, 18

combs, 175, 222; bone, 29; ivory, 175, *175*

commerce, 21–22; English colonial New York, 155–58, *158*, 159–60; New Amsterdam, *20*, 154–55, *155*; nineteenth-century, 161–64, 200–206, 214–15. *See also* economy; industrialization; trade

Commons, 275, 279, 280, *280*

commuters, nineteenth-century, 199–205, 211, 267, 272

Condon, Thomas, 181

Connecticut, 63, 153, 267

Contact period, 12, 13, 120–48, *121–47*, 314*n*3, 315*nn*16, 18, 316*nn*27, 28, 41, 43, 47, 317*nn*49, 53, 318*n*76

contract archaeology, 12–13, 16

cooking: Archaic, 51–52; colonial, 169, 174, 180, 185–86, 260–61; nineteenth-century, 211, 248, 272; stone pots, 63, *63*, 64, *66*, 67, *67*, 68, 69; Transitional, 63–68; Woodland, 73, 78, 79, *79*, 94. *See also* food(s); hearths; *specific vessels and utensils*

copper, 84–85, 130, 133, *240*, 310*n*23; trade goods, 130–31

Corlear's Hook, 126, 127

Corsa, Benjamin, 261

cosmetics, 69, 140

Courthouse site, 217–23, 306*n*16, 323*n*16, 324*n*23; artifacts, 219–23, *220–21*

covered-table plan, 211, *212*

Crabtree, Pamela, 222

cremation, 64, 67; Transitional funerary pyres, 64–72, *63–72*, 308*n*12

Cronon, William, 53, 115, 147

Croton Aqueduct, 248, 250–51, 327*n*18

crucibles, 197, *197*

cultural resource management, 10–12

currency, 29, *155*; wampum as, 132–42

Cutchogue, 66, 308*n*5

dairy products, 178, 179, 259

Dallal, Diane, 159–60

Danckaerts, Jasper, 35–36, 97, 134, 173; Labadist General View by, *22*

Dauphin, La (ship), 115

Davids, Joseph, 156

Davis, William, 156

Dean, Nora Thompson, 108, *109*

deer, 88, *89*, 91, 94, 146, 179

Delaware, 35, 93, 100, 107–9, *109*, *133*, 300; ancestral blessing ceremony, *300*; Contact period, 119–48, *121–47*, 314*n*3, 318*n*76; diaspora, 123, 147, *147*, 148, 318*n*76; Late Woodland, 93–116, *94–115*, 119, *300*, 313*n*37

Delaware River Valley, 39, 60, 79, 80, 102, 148, 153

Denton, Daniel, 143

Department of Buildings, 22

Department of City Planning, 31

De Vries, David Pietersz, 124–28; illustration by, *89*

Diamond, William, 282, 283, 286, 287

dice, lead, 274

Dickens, Charles, 218

diet. *See* food(s)

Dincauze, Dena, 77, 92

Dinkins, David, 282, *283*, 286, 287, 294

dinner, nineteenth-century role of, 211–15, *212–16*

disease, 7, 84, 96, 108, 198, 289, 298; of African American enslaved, 291–92; cholera, 250; European, 123, 141, 142–43; Late Woodland, 97, 111–13; nineteenth-century, 198, 201, 220, 222, 228–29, 250, 272; smallpox, 142–43; venereal, 220, 222; yellow fever, 201, 228–29, 232

dishes. *See* ceramics; tablewares, nineteenth-century

doctors, 198–99

Dogan Point, 55

dog burials, 97, 299; Late Woodland, 97, 101, 104, *104*,

105–9, III, II4, 312nn28, 30, 31, 32, 313nn34, 37;
   spiritual role of, 107–9
Dollar Savings Bank, 17, 23, 28
dolls, 207, *208*
domestic servants, 201, 204, 207, 209, 210, 212, 217, 277,
   323n4
Dongan, Thomas, 156
Dongan Charter, 225
Dowd, Gregory, II9
"downtown," nineteenth-century development of,
   202–3
drills, 134–35; stone, 134–35, *139*
Druding, Henry, 153
drugs, 164
dry wells, 242, 246, *246, 247,* 249
Duane Street, 278, 279, 281
Dutch East India Company, 149
Dutch genre paintings, seventeenth-century, 178, *178*
Dutch Reformed Church, 193
Dutch settlement, 7–12, 16–30, 73, 88, 95, 102, 109,
   II5–16, II9, 217, 224, 225, 319nn10, 12, 320n2, 321n18;
   adaptations, 176–80, 194–96; commercial life, 153–55;
   Contact period, 120–48, *121–47;* daily life, 167–68,
   168, 169–81, *171–78;* ethnic identity, 170–87, 194–96;
   global economy, 149–66; Kieft's War, 124–28, 130,
   138, 151, 167; Stadt Huys Block, 16–30, *19–29,* 156, 176,
   200, *244;* trade with Indians, II9, 122–25, 130–42,
   146, 150, 315nn8, 15, 316nn27, 28, 41, 43, 47; waterfront development, 224–27. *See also* New Amsterdam; *specific sites*
Dutch West India Company, 20, II9, 133–34, 153, 154,
   167, 170, 172, 173, 177, 186, 263, 264, 320n2, 321n37,
   322n7, 329n3
Dyckman Farm, 274

Early Archaic period, 46–54, 82
Early Woodland period, 73–75, *75,* 76, 309n5
earthenware, *31,* 161, 165, *172,* 174, *174, 175,* 186, 196–97,
   214, 240, *243,* 266
East Broadway, 198, 199, 202
East River, *20, 21,* 24, 78, 81, 154, 156, 163, 169, 173,
   182–83, 194, 195, 197, 201, 202, 248; landfill, 224–41,
   228–40
economy, 3, 87, 224; Archaic, 56, 57, 59; colonial, 153–60,
   183, 201; Contact era, 120, 123–25, 131–42, *143,* 146;

Early and Middle Woodland, 73–74, 76–77, 87, 88,
   91, 298, 310n40; global, 124, 125, 131, 140, 149–66,
   227, 298, 299; Late Woodland, 95, 97, 109–14, 298,
   313n38; market, 206, 298; modern, 17; money,
   133–35; nineteenth-century, 195, 200–201, 206–7,
   209, 217, 221, 257, 271, 272; Paleoindian, 44–45,
   305n7; real estate, 223, 224–25; tavern, 155–58, *158.*
   See also commerce; labor; trade
ecosystems, 297; Contact era, 123, 146–47; Woodland,
   86–92
eggs, 178
eighteenth century, 21, 53, 155, 159, 186; Burgis View
   of New York, *182–83;* neighborhoods, 192–97; urban
   space, 188–89, *189,* 190, *190,* 191–202; waterfront
   development, *189–90,* 226–41, *228–40. See also* English
   colonial New York
Elk Street, 278, 281
Ellis Island, *300*
Emigrant Savings Bank, 219
England, 35, 155, 159–61, 162, 166, 172, 181–82, 193, 264,
   273–75; Anglo-Dutch Wars, 169, 181–82; conquest of
   New Amsterdam, 16, 20, 35, 138, 140, 142, 154, 169,
   181–83, 192, 193, 225, 324n3; Glorious Revolution,
   181–82; occupation of New York during Revolution,
   273–74, 281
English colonial New York, 16, 20, 35, 128, 140, 142,
   154, 167, 169–70, 181–87, *182–85,* 207, 217, 225, 257,
   273, 298–99, 324n3; African Americans in, 277–94,
   280–92; backyards, 242–45, *245, 247;* commercial
   life, 155–58, *158,* 159–60; daily life, 169–70, 182–87,
   182–85; Dutch ethnicity, 181–87, *182–85,* 194–96;
   Dutch transition to, 176–87; neighborhoods and
   ethnic identities, 192–96; rural land, *258,* 259–60, *260,*
   261–65; taverns, 20–21, *21,* 28–30, 155–58, *158;* urban
   space, 188–89, *189,* 190–94; waterfront development,
   189–90, 224–41, *228–40*
enslaved, 8, 168, 201, 207, 277; African American,
   154, 155, 168, 170, 174, 186, 189, 192, 194, 207, 234,
   240–41, 259, 277–94, 299, 320nn2, 4, II, 321n27,
   329n2, 3; emancipation, 201, 277; labor, 259, 277–94,
   320n2, 329n2; Native American, 168–69, 170, 277,
   320n2; physical hardship of, 291–93; revolts, 280;
   trade, 154, 155, 168, 240, 259, 279, 291, 320n2
environmental movement, 9, 10, 32
Erie Canal, 161, 163, 196

estates, farms, and plantations, 259–67, *260–65,* 327*nn*2, 10

ethnicity, 7–8, 168–69; colonial, 176–87, 192–96; Dutch, 170–87, 194–96; nineteenth-century, 200–201, 217–20, 270–72. *See also* immigrants; *specific groups*

European settlement. *See* Dutch settlement; English colonial New York; New Amsterdam

Fagan, Brian, 39

family life, 299; colonial, 169, 170, 185–86, 196–98, 207, 226, 261, 323*n*4; Early and Middle Woodland, 73–75, 80, 91; of enslaved African Americans, 277–78; Late Woodland, 94–95, 97, 98–104, 114–15; lineage, 71–72; meals and tablewares, 211–15, *212–16;* middle-class, 206–15, *210–16,* 266; Munsee, 125, 126–27, 133, 143, 146; nineteenth-century, 197–205, 206–23, 265–67, 272, 323*n*4; working-class, 217–20. *See also* children; men; women

farming. *See* agriculture

farms, estates, and plantations, 259–67, *260–65,* 327*nn*2, 10

Ferguson, Leland, 240–41

fertility, 73; Woodland, 73–74

fire, 73, 250; funerary, 64–72, *63–67;* Great Fire of *1835,* 162, 163; making, 69; Telco Block, 250; Woodland, 73

fish and fishing, 19, 40, 45, 228, 297; Archaic, 54–59; colonial, 178, 179–80; eighteenth-century, 180; Late Woodland, 95, 111–12, 114, 314*nn*54, 57; Middle Woodland, 77, 80, 87–88, *88,* 89, 90, 91; nineteenth-century, 223; plummets, *88. See also* shellfish

fishtail points, Orient, 63, *63,* 64, 69

Five Points, *204,* 206, 208, 217–23, 323*nn*16, 19; Courthouse site, 217–23, *220–21*

Flatbush, 267

Flatlands, 267

Florida, 176

fluted points, 40, *41,* 43, 305*nn*8, 13

food(s), 29; Archaic, 51–56, 58, 59, 307*nn*19, 22; colonial, 157, 169, 177–80, 185–86, 321*nn*23, 24, 26; Dutch foodways, 177–80, 186; Early Woodland, 73, 74; of the enslaved, 291; Late Woodland, 94, 95, 97, 106, 109–14; middle-class meals and tableware, 211–15, *212–16,* 223, 272–73, *273;* Middle Woodland, 87, 88, 91; Munsee, 146, 151; nineteenth-century, 163, 211–15,

212–16, 218, 221, 222–23, 263, 265–67, 272, 324*nn*27, 29; Paleoindian, 40, 43–45. *See also specific foods*

Fordham Manor, 261

Fordham University, 165, 261, 262–63, 264

forests: Archaic, 47, 53, 54, 57; Paleoindian, 38, 42; Woodland, 88–89, *89,* 90

forts and encampments, 273–75. *See also specific forts*

Fortuyn (ship), 150, 151

Fourth Street, 251, 252

Fox Creek spear points, 49, 78–79, *79*

France, 164, 170, 192

Franklin, Benjamin, 10

Fraunces, Samuel, 196

Fraunces Tavern, 196, 236

Freemasons, 195–96, 322*n*17

French Americans, 192, 193, 194

Fresh Water Pond, 54

Front Street, 162, 163, 226, 229–30, *230,* 234

Fulton Street, 250

funerary rites, 71–72; Middle Woodland, 81–86; Transitional, 64–72, *63–67. See also* dog burials; human burials

Funk, Robert, 48, 51

fur trade, 119, 133, 134–35, 149–50, 153–55, 158, 167, 169, 174, 298

Gabry (Peter) & Sons, 154

gambling, 174, 260–61, 263, 274

Geismar, Joan, 161, 228, 233

gender roles: Dutch-Indian, 320–21*n*18; nineteenth-century middle-class, 206–10, *210,* 211–15. *See also* men; women

General Services Administration (GSA), 278, 281–88, 293

George II, King of England, 274–75

Gerdes, Hendrik, pipes by, 174

German Americans, 192, 195, 196, 216–17, 222–23

Germany, 165, 172, 182

Gilbert, Allan, 165, 261–63

Gilfoyle, Timothy, 220

glass, 13, 25, 28, 129, 130, *139,* 157; colonial, 171, 174, 180; eighteenth-century, 174, *175;* nineteenth-century, 163, *163,* 164, 200, 218, 219, 220, 221, *221,* 263, 265–66, 271–72; prunts, 171, 180; urinals, 220, *221,* 222; wine bottles, *163,* 164, *175,* 221, 263 global economy, 124, 125, 131, 140, 149–66, 227, 298, 299

Goddard, Charles, 64

gold, 197

Goldman Sachs, 22, 29

Goodfriend, Joyce, 184

gorgets, stone, *61*

Gothic style, 272, 273

Governors Island, 153, 225

Gracht, 225

grains, 94, 109–14, 180, 259, 265

grapen, 174, *174*, 180, 185

grapes, 89, 163, 164

grave markers, African American, *282*

Gravesend, 267–68

Great Dock, *182–83*, 225

Great Fire of *1835*, 162, 163

Greenwich, 203, 204, 253, 266

Greenwich Street, 226

Greenwich Village, 30, 198–99, 203, 208, 246, 250, 261, 272, 273; Merchant's House, 252–55, *255*, 256

Griggs, Heather, 219, 223

Grossman, Joel, 154, 159, 170, 174, 325*n*8, 328*n*30

Grumet, Robert, 145

Hackensack, 120

hair, 175, 222

Halve Maen (ship), 119, 149

Hamell, George, 130, 133

Hamilton, Alexander, 326*n*11

Hanover Square, 197, 198; #7 Hanover Square, *5, 182–83, 228, 236–37, 237, 239, 249*

Hans, 134

Harbor Green, 135

Harlem, 267, 273

Harlem River, 44, 59, 106, 274

Harrington, M. R., 54, 82

health, 228–29, 271; regulations, 228–29; privies, cisterns, and, 249–52. *See also* disease; medicine

hearths, 53, 68; Archaic, 51–52; colonial, 177; Orient funerary pyres, 64–72, *63–67*

Heckewelder, John, 102, 143–45

Heermans, Augustine, 20, 154–55, 318–19*n*10; warehouse, *20*, 154–55, *155*, 159

hemp, 89, *90*

Henn, Roselle, 162, 229–30

Herbert, Bert, 196

hereditary rights, 71–72

Hesselius, Gustavus, 133

hide preparation, 52

hilltop cemeteries, Orient, 64–72, *63–67*, 102–3, 308*n*18

historic preservation movement, 9, 10–12, 13, 17, 104–5, 284

Hoboken, 272

Holland, Joseph, watercolor by, *185*

Holland Lodge, 195–96, 198, 322*n*17

Hollowell, Donald, 48, 51

Hollowell, H. F., 48

home and workplace, nineteenth-century separation of, 198–205, 210

home life. *See* children; cooking; family life; food(s)

Hone, Philip, 203

Hopewell, 76–77, 81, 85, 92, 310*n*18; pipes, 85

Howard University, 285, 287, 288, 293

Howe, General William, 264, 273

Howson, Jean, 251–52

Hudson, Henry, 119, 149–50

Hudson River, 37, 42, 46, 51, 55, 57, 87, 119, *137*, 149, 150, 151, 153, 177, 226; block-and-bridge wharf, *233*

Hudson River Valley, 39

Huey, Paul, 177

Huguenots, 186, 192, 193, 194, 321*nn*32, 36

human burials, 8, 297, 299; African Burial Ground, 241, 278–94, *280–92*, 329*n*9, 330*nn*27, 34; Archaic, 64; bundle, 99–104; ethical issues in excavation of, 96–97, 282–88; Late Woodland, 96–104, 108, 114, 312*nn*13, 15; Middle Woodland, 81–86, 310*nn*18, 20; Munsee, 128–29; nineteenth-century, 220; Orient, 61, 62–72, *63–67*, 102–3, 308*nn*10, 12, 14, 51, 17–21; primary, 99, 102, 108; secondary, 99–104, 108, 114, 300; segregation, 279; status markers, 86

Hunter College, 18

hunter-gatherers, 44, 69, 94, 112, 297–98

hunting, 40; Archaic, 48, *49–50*, 52, 56, 58–59, *59*, 60; Munsee, 125, 130–31, 144, 145, 146; Paleoindian, 40–45; Transitional, 62–63, 69; Woodland, 76, 77, 80, 83, 91, 108, 114

Hurley, James, 268

Hutchinson, Anne, 127, 315*n*22

Ice Ages, 4, 36, 37–39, 46, 47, 115, 304*n*2

immigrants, 7, 142, 168, 300; eighteenth-century, 192–96, 200; nineteenth-century, 200–201, 206, 208, 216–23, 272, 324*n*20. *See also specific nationalities*

Independence, Fort, 274–75

Indians. *See* Native Americans

indoor plumbing, 243, 248, 251–52

industrialization, 161, 217–18, 272, 281

insects, 47

intertidal zone, 237

Inwood, *5*, 57, 58, *60*, 104, *107*, 114, *122*

Irish Americans, 200, 204, 208, 216–23

Iroquois, 132, 133, 134, 138, 312*n*32, 314*n*3

Italianate style, 272, *273*

Jamesport, 63, 64, 66–68, 308*n*5; excavations, *63*, 66–68, *66–67*

James II, King of England, 181

Jamestown Tavern (Virginia), 157, *158*

Janowitz, Meta, 177–80, 186

Jefferson, Thomas, 101

Jennings, Francis, 143

Jersey City, 272

jewelry, 69; African, 290–91. *See also* beads; ornaments

Jewish Americans, 192, 193, 194, 195

Jim Crow laws, 269, 270

Jogues, Father Isaac, 168

John Earthy's Tavern (Maine), 157, *158*

journeymen, 207, 208

Kaeser, Edward, 77–78, 81, 101–2

Kammen, Michael, 9

Kaufman, Melvyn, 32

Kaufman (William) Organization, 31

Kelly, James, 151–53

kettles, brass trade, 130, *130*, 131

Kettletas, Garret and William, 161–62

Kidd, Captain William, 237

Kieft, Willem, 124–28, 173

Kieft's War, 124–28, 130, 138, 151, 167

Kierstede, Blandina, 173, 185

Kierstede, Hans, 20, 22, 172–73, 278

Kierstede house and artifacts, *20*, *22*, 172–75, *173–75*, 177, 180, 185

King, John, 261

King, Rufus, 260–61

King (Rufus) House, 260–61

King's House Tavern, 20–21, *22*, 28–30, 156–57, *158*, 165; artifacts, 30, *31*, 156–57

Klein, Terry, 196

knappers, 43

knives: Archaic, *50*, 51, 58, 60, 307*n*27; colonial, *172*; European, 130, *172*; Munsee, 137; Paleoindian, *41*; Transitional, 62; Woodland, 78, 79, 108

Koch, Edward, 27, 235

Kraft, Herbert, 42, 43

Labadie, Jean de, 36

Labadists, 22, 35–36, 173, 319*n*10

labor, 8, 45; agricultural, 113–14, 180, 259, 277; colonial, 179, 180, 207, 259, 277–78; division of, 44–45, 74, 113, 207, 306*n*10; enslaved, 259, 277–94, 320*n*2, 329*n*2; nineteenth-century, 203–4, 207–10, 216–23; Paleoindian, 44–45; Woodland, 74, 91, 113–14; working-class, 203–4, 208, 216–23

landfill, 182, 188, *189–90*, 223, 224–41, *228–40*, 245, 282, 297, 325*nn*8, 11, 12, 18, 19, 326*nn*6, 12; archaeology of, 227–39, *228–39*; buried ground surfaces, 238–39, *239*, *240*. *See also specific sites*

Landmarks Preservation Commission, 10, 16, 17, 18, 23, 27, 28, 30, 31, 231, 285, 287

land ownership, 8, 72, 101, 188, 224; collective guardianship concept, 72, 188, 298, 318*n*67; colonial, 188, 279; Contact, 123; European concept of, 72, 143–45, 188, 298; Manhattan sold to the Dutch, 143–45, 224; Native American dispossession, 123, 143–45, 224; nineteenth-century, 250, 257–76; real estate economy, 224–25; rural, 257–76

Lappawainsoe, *133*

La Roche, Cheryl, 285

Late Archaic period, 46, 57–61, *58–61*, 81, 87, 307*nn*22, 27

Late Woodland period, 93–116, *94–115*, 122, *122–23*, 241, 263, 311*nn*1, 4, 312*nn*13, 26, 313*n*38, 314*n*54

Latham, Roy, 64, 66, 67

Lavin, Lucianne, 87

Law of Stratigraphic Association, 24

Lehman Brothers, 17

Leisler, Jacob, 182–84, 321*n*32

Leisler's Rebellion, 182–84

Le Jeune, Father Paul, 132

Lenape, 35–36, 93, 100, 102, 107–9, *109*, 119, 144, 314*n*3

Lenapehoking, 35, 119, 120, *121*, 122, 128, 129, 142, 148, 149, 150, 151, 300, 315*n*8; colonial adaptations to, 176–80

Lincoln, Abraham, 300

Livingston, Robert, 237

Livingston house, *182–83*, 237, *237*, 238

London, 160

Long Island, 37, 120, 136, 151, 267; Fort Massapeag, 131–32, 135–36, *136*, 137–38, *138*, 139, *139*, 140–42; Gravesend, 267–68; Orient funerary pyres, 64–72, *63–67*; Sebonac, 110–11

Long Island Sound, 78

Loorya, Alyssa, 266

Lopez, Julius, 130, 274–75

Lovelace, Francis, 20, 28, 156

Lower East Side, 208

Lynch, Timothy, 219

Lyne, James, "A Plan of the City of New York from an Actual Survey," *189*

Maerschalck's "A Plan of the City of New York from an Actual Survey," *280*

Mahicans, 126, 314*n*3

Maine, 157

maize, 94, 109–14, 180, 311*n*6

malnutrition, 112, 291

Manhattan, 4, *5*, *6*, 104, 134, 150–54, 257; African Burial Ground, 241, 278–94, *280–92*; Assay site, *6*, 162, *190*, 229–33, *230–32*, 238–39, *238–39*, 240, 245, 325*n*8; backyards, 242–56, *243–55*; Barclays Bank, *6*, 196, 198, 249; Broad Financial Center, *6*, 170, *176*, *245*; colonial, 181–85, *185*, 186, 188–89, *189*, 190, *190*, 191–94, 224–41, *228–40*, 278–94; Contact period, 120–48, 314*n*3; Courthouse, 217–23, *220–21*; daily life in nineteenth-century, 206–23, *208–21*; Hanover Square (#7), *5*, *182–83*, 228, 236–37, *237*, 239, *249*; landfill, 224–41, *228–40*; lower, archaeological sites in, *6*; Munsee sale of, to the Dutch, 143–45, 224; nineteenth-century, 188, 189, *191*, *199*, 202–4, *204*, 205, 206–23, *208–21*, 243–56, *246–47*; post-revolutionary, 188, 194–206; rural land, 257, *258*, 261, 267, 268, 272; separation of home and workplace, 198–205; seventeenth-century daily life, 167–68, *168*, 169–75, *171–75*; Stadt Huys Block, 16–30, *19–29*, 156, 176, 200,

244; Sullivan Street, *5*, 198–99, *246*, 251, 252; Telco Block, *247*, 250; Washington Heights–Inwood sites, 104, 105, *105*, *106*, 114, *122*; Water Street (#175), 228, 233–35, *235*, 236. *See also* English colonial New York; New Amsterdam; *specific sites, streets, and neighborhoods*

Manhattan Company, 247–48, 326*n*11

marbles, *31*

Maritime Museum, Newport News, Va., 235–36

marshlands, 87–88, 90, 97

Maryland, 102, 173, 319*n*10

Massachusetts Bay Colony, 127

Massapeag, Fort, 131–36, *136*, 137–38, *138*, 139–42, 316*n*32, 317*n*49; artifacts, 136, *139*

Massapequas, 120, 131–42

mastodon, 38, 42, 43, 44, 46

Mathew, Father Theobold, 219, *220*

Maurice of Orange, Prince, coin issued by, 155, *155*

Maynard, Joan, 269

McKinney-Steward, Susan Smith, 268

McLoughlin, Michael, 219

meat, 45, 52, 114, 178, 179, 212, 222–23, 324*nn*27, 29

Medford, Edna, 288

medicine, 218, 241; nineteenth-century, 218, 222; plants, 88

men: Archaic, 58; colonial, 184; enslaved African American, 277, 292; Late Woodland, 111–12, 114; middle-class, 206–10, *210*, 211, 215; Munsee, 140; nineteenth-century, 201, 202, 206–15, 217, 272; Paleoindian, 44; working-class, 217, 219

Menominee, 60

Merchant's Exchange, 156

Merchant's House project, 252–55, *255*, 256

Mesozoic period, 79

mestizo culture, 176

metal, 197; colonial period, 173, *173*, 174, 240, *240*, 241, 274; trade, 130, *130*, 131, 136, *139*, 316*n*28. *See also specific metals and objects*

Metropolitan Forensic Anthropology Team (MFAT), 281–72, 285

mica, 78, 79, 80–81, 85, 309*nn*10, 12

Michielsen, Reyer, 261

Middle Archaic period, 46, 47, 54–57, 307*n*21

middle class, 31, 194, 195, 257; nineteenth-century, 200–205, 206–15, 217–20, 221, 223, 251, 253, 266–67;

middle class (continued)
  tablewares and meals, 211–15, *212–16*, 223, 266, 272–73, *273*
Middle Woodland period, 76–92, *79–90*, 113, 309*nn*12, 17, 310*nn*40, 41, 311*n*1
Milborne, Jacob, 183
Miller, Christopher, 133
Milne, Claudia, 222
Milner (John) and Associates, 286
Minuit, Peter, 224
Mohawks, 126, 318*n*76
Montgomerie Charter, 225
Moody, Lady Deborah, 267
Morin, Ed, 248
Morris-Schurz, *5*, 78–79, *79*, 81, *81*, 309*n*9
Moses, Robert, 98
Mossel, Thijs, 150
mound building, 76, 81–82
Mount Washington Collegiate Institute, *199*
mouth harp, brass, 136, *139*
mugs, ceramic, *209*
multiculturalism, 9
Munsees, 35–36, 93–96, 98, 101, 119–48, 149, 150–51, 170, 298, 311*n*1, 314*nn*3, 57; colonial period, 168, 170–71, 173, 176–80, 184, 186, 192, 193; Contact period, 119–48, *121–47*, 314*n*3, 315*nn*16, 18, 316*nn*27, 28, 41, 43, 47, 317*nn*49, 53, 318*n*76; dialect, 119, 120; diaspora, 123, 147, *147*, 148; enslaved, 169, 170, 277, 320*n*2; Kieft's War, 124–28, 130, 138, 151, 167; land dispossession, 123, 143–45, 224; smallpox epidemic, 142–43
Museum of the American Indian, New York, 15, 60, 63
musical instruments, 58, 136, *139*
mutton, 222–23
mutual determination, 54

Nachtegael (ship), 150
nails, 136
Nanticoke, 102
Nassau Street, 21
National Historic Preservation Act (*1966*), 11, 16, 17, 30, 303*n*9, 304*n*7
National Museum of the American Indian, Smithsonian Institution, 60
National Park Service, 300

National Westminster Bank, 233
Native Americans, 4, 7–13, 19, 35–36, 167, *168*, 217, 227, 264, 297, 298, *300*, 304*nn*2, 3, 4, 15, 318*n*2; ancestral blessing ceremony, *300*; Archaic, 46–49, *50*, 51–61, *58–61*, 64, 71, 306*nn*12, 17, 307*nn*19, 21, 22, 25, 27; colonial period, 168, 170–71, 173, 176–80, 184, 186, 192, 193, 321*nn*18, 26; concept of land, 72, 188, 298, 318*n*67; Contact period, 120–48, *121–47*, 314*n*3, 315*nn*16, 18, 316*nn*27, 28, 41, 43, 47, 317*nn*49, 53, 318*n*76; Early and Middle Woodland, 73–75, *75*, 76–92, *79–90*, 309*n*5; enslaved, 168–69, 170, 277, 320*n*2; and European trade, 119, 122–24, 130–42, 146, 150, 315*nn*8, 15, 316*nn*27, 28, 41, 43, 47; Kieft's War, 124–28, 130, 138, 151, 167; land dispossession, 123, 143–45, 224; languages, 119, 120; Late Woodland, 93–116, *94–115*, 119, 122, *122–23*, 241, 263, 311*n*1, 4, 312*nn*13, 26, 313*n*18, 314*n*54; life disrupted by Europeans, 102, 109, 110, 115–16, 120–48; myths about, 93–94, 109, 115, 311*n*2; Paleoindians, 35–41, *41*, 42–45, *45*, 46, 304*nn*2, 3, 305*nn*7, 10, 11, 12, 14; Transitional, 61, 62–72, *63–67*, 307*n*1. *See also specific tribes and periods*
Nechtanc, 126, 127
Neck, Fort, 140, *141*
neighborhoods, 192–200; eighteenth-century, 192–97; nineteenth-century, 197–204, *204*, 205, 206; working-class, 203–4, *204*, 206, 208, 216–23. *See also specific sites and streets*
Netherlands, 149, 151, 164, 165, 166, 167, 168, 177, 178, 179, 181; Anglo-Dutch Wars, 169, 181–82
nets, 89, 90
New Amsterdam, 16, 20–22, 35, 95, *137*, 165, 167–80, 192, 217, 263–64, 277, 298, 319*n*10, 320*n*2, 321*n*18, 329*n*5; backyards, 242–44, *244*, 245, *245*, 247; commercial life, 153–55; Contact period, 120–48, *121–47*, 316*n*27; daily life, 167–68, *168*, 169–81, *171–78*; Dutch adaptations to, 176–80; English conquest of, 16, 20, 35, 128, 140, 142, 154, 169, 181–83, 192, 193, 225, 324*n*3; establishment of, 119, 131, 153; flora and fauna, *89*; foodways, 177–80; global economy, 149–66; Hartgers View, *168*; Kieft's War, 124–28, 130, 138, 151, 167; neighborhoods, 192–93; Stadt Huys Block, 16–30, *19–29*, 156, 176, 200, *294*; transition to New York, 181–87; urban space, 188, 192–93; waterfront development, 179–80, 224–27

New England, *137*, 176, 182, 267. *See also specific states*

New Jersey, 42, 51, 120, 134, 142, 148, 153, 165, 269, 272; Abbott Farm, 79, 80, *80*

New Netherland. *See* New Amsterdam

New York Bay, 119, 149

New York Botanical Garden, petroglyph in, *36*

New York City, 3–32; Archaic period, 46–49, *50*, 51–61, *58–61*, 64, 71, 306*nn*12, 17, 307*nn*19, 21, 22, 25, 27; as archaeological site, 4, *5–6*, 7–14, 15–32, *19–31*, 299; backyards, 242–56, *243–55*; boundaries, 257, *258*; colonial (*see* English colonial New York); common ground, 297–301; Contact period, 120–48, *121–47*, 314*n*3, 315*nn*16, 18, 316*nn*27, 28, 41, 43, 47, 317*nn*49, 53; daily life in nineteenth century, 206–23, *208–21*; digging in, 15–32, *19–31*; Dutch-to-English transition, 181–85, *185*, 186–87; Early and Middle Woodland, 73–75, *75*, 76–92, *79–90*, 309*n*5; global economy, 149–66; landfill, 224–41, *228–40*; Late Woodland, 93–116, *94–115*, 119, 122, *122–23*, 241, 263, 311*nn*1, 4, 312*nn*13, 26, 313*n*38, 314*n*54; modern, 4, *5*, 30–32, 188, 189, 257; Munsee sale of, to the Dutch, 143–45, 224; as New Amsterdam (*see* New Amsterdam); nineteenth-century, 188, 189, *191*, 192, *199*, 202–4, *204*, 205, 206–23, *208–21*, 243–56, *246–47*, 257–76, *258–76*; Paleoindian period, 35–41, *41*, 42–45, 46, 304*nn*2, 3, 305*nn*7, 10, 11, 12, 14; post-revolutionary, 188, 194–206; rural history, 257–76, *258–76*; Transitional period, 61, 62–72, *63–67*, 307*n*1; urban space in colonial and post-revolutionary New York, 188–205, *189–204*. *See also specific boroughs, peoples, sites, and streets*

New York City Archaeological Group, 274

New York Harbor, 4, 31, 37, 46, 51, 61, 82, 87, 119, 153, 181

New York Herald, 82

New York State Maritime Museum, 23

New York State Museum and Science Service Bureau, 48, 65

New York Times, 219, 283

New York Unearthed: City Archaeology (exhibition), 32

New York University, 18, 198, 251

Nicolls, Captain Matthias, 156

night soil, 243–45

nineteenth century, 21, 115, 150, 299, 323*n*4, 324*nn*20, 23, 26, 29; daily life, 206–23, *208–21*; rural land, 257–76, *262–76*; separation of home and workplace, 198–205, 210; urban space, 188, 189, *191*, 192, 196, *199*, 202–4, *204*, 205; waterfront development, 226, 228, 230, 233, *233*

nitrogen isotope values, 112

North Beach, *5*, 76

Nutten Island, 153

Ohio Hopewell, 76–77, 81

Old Dorp, 267

Old English table plan, 211, *212*

Old Place, 48, 129

Olfersz, Jacob, 124

omnibuses, 199, 272

Oneroad, Amos, 58, *60*, 307*n*23

Onrust (ship), 150, 151, 153

Orange, Fort, 119, 134, 153, 165, 173, 176–77, 179

Orient fishtails, 626–63, *63*, 64, 69, 307*n*2

Orient I, 64, 308*nn*5, 10

Orient peoples, 62–72, 99, 102, 307*nn*1, 2, 308*nn*3, 5, 9, 10, 14, 18, 19; ritual life, 62–72, *63–67*, 102–3, 308*nn*17–19

Orient II, 64, 308*nn*5, 9, 14, 19

ornaments, 60; African, 290–91, *292*; Archaic, 60, *61*; Contact, *122*; copper, 85; Late Woodland, *122*; nineteenth-century, 222; Orient, 69; Woodland, 76, 83, 84–85

Orson, 151, 318*n*2

ossuaries, Late Woodland, 99–104

outhouses, 27, 243, 247, 253

overkill theory, 305*n*14

ox-head motif, 171, *171*

Oyster Bay, 317*n*49

oysters, 54–56, 58, 87, 106, 179, 222, 269–70

Pagremanski, Hedi, 304*n*9

paint stones, 69, 76

Paleoindian period, 12, 35–41, *41*, 42–45, *45*, 46, 304*nn*2, 3, 305*nn*7, 10, 11, 12, 14

Parrington, Michael, 282

Pavonia, 126–27, 128

Pearl Street, 17, 154, 170–73, 186, 196, 197, 225, 236, 237; Courthouse site, 217–23, *220–21*

Pelham Bay Park, *5*, 100, 127, 128, 145

Pell, Thomas, 101

pendant, stone (Late Woodland or Contact), *122*

Penhawitz, 123, 124–27, 131, 145

Pennsylvania, 44, 63, 79, 102, 120, 143

pepper, 163

Pepper, George, 82–86, 111, 288

Perry, Warren, 288, 290

petroglyphs, 36, *36*

pewter, colonial, 173, 174, 240, 274

Philadelphia, 10, 16, 155, 282; African American burial grounds, 285, 286

Pickman, Arnold, 198, 236, 259, 261, 305*n*12, 311*n*11

pigs, 125, 126, 145, 146, 179, 223, 318*n*73, 324*n*29

pipes, 29, *31;* European, 130, 136, *139,* 157–60, 172–75, 184; Late Woodland, 114, *115;* Tippet, 159–60; tobacco, 155, 157, 158, *158,* 159–60, 164, 171–75, *175,* 227, 256, 290, 319*n*17, 320*n*7; trade, 157–60; Woodland stone, 81, 85, *85*

"Plan of the City of New York," *190*

plantations, farms, and estates, 259–67, *260–65,* 327*nn*2, 10

plants: Archaic, 47, 53–57; Contact period, 146; medicinal, 88; Native American uses, 88–90, *90;* nineteenth-century gardens, 253–55, *255,* 256; Paleoindian, 38, 42; textiles made from, 89, *90;* Woodland, 88–89, *89, 90, 90,* 109–14, 310*n*35

Pleistocene, 38

plummets, stone, *88*

points. *See* spear points

politics, 184, 226; identity, 9

Pollard, Calvin, architectural drawing by, *254*

pollution, 86, 217–18, 248, 250–51, 270, 297

poor, 10, 194, 195, 275; almshouse kitchen, 275–76, *276;* nineteenth-century, 201, 203, 204, 216–23, 251, 271, 272, 275, 324*nn*20, 23

population, 7–8; African American, 277–94; ancient, 47, 54, 56, 57, 59, 70; Dutch New Amsterdam, 167–68, 177, 181–84; English colonial, 181–87, 192, 318*n*70; immigrant, 216–17; Munsee, 128, 143, 147–48; nineteenth-century, 198–205, 216–17, 250, 257; Woodland, 73, 95–96, 104, 113

porridge, 178, 180

Port Mobil, 32, 40–41, *41,* 42–45, 48, 305*nn*10, 11

ports, 82, 154, 161, 200, 201, 225; East River landfill, 224–41. *See also* waterfront

post-glacial environments, 46–48, 53, 305*n*14, 306*n*1

postholes, Late Woodland, 98–99, 101

post-Revolutionary city, 194–206

pots, stone, 63, *63,* 64, *66,* 67, *67,* 68, 69, 74

pottery. *See* ceramics

privatization of the home, 198–205, 210

privies, 4, 24, 26, 27, 161, 242–47, *243–47,* 265, 326*nn*2, 3, 5, 8, 9, 10, 328*n*18; colonial, 170–75, *171–75,* 243–44, *244,* 245, *245;* health issues, 249–52; nineteenth-century, 198, 209, 213, 218, 220, 221–23, 243, 245–47, *246–47,* 248, 249–52; shafts, 243–47, *244–45,* 251

prostitution, 220–23, 324*nn*23, 26

Protestantism, 167, 168, 182, 198, 200, 321*n*32

Pueblo Indians, 9

pumpkins, 180

quahogs, 132, 133, 137, 316*n*43

quartz, 85, 137, 290, 314*n*54; Orient fishtails, 63, *63,* 64

Queens, 4, *5,* 18, 64, 77, 135, 257; Adriance Farmhouse, 259–60; Aqueduct site, 97–98, 102, 114, 135, 241, 311*n*11; College Point, *104;* North Beach, 76; Rufus King House, 260–61; rural land, 257, 259–61, 267

Queens College, 110

racism, 269–70, 279

radiocarbon dating, 15, 38–39, 43, 48, 110, 111, 152, 303*n*10, 304*n*4

railroads, 267, 269

Raritan, 126

Raritan River, 82

Ratzer's "Plan of New York," *258*

Reade Street, 281

real estate economy, 223, 224–25

Rechqua Akie, 124, 131

red ocher, 64, 68, 69–70, 308*n*17

religion, 8, 60, 193–94, 322*n*7, 14; Glorious Revolution, 181–82. *See also* Catholicism; churches; Protestantism; ritual life

Republican Alley, 281

Rescarrick, George, 156

Revolutionary War, 15, 150, 160–61, 169, 194, 195, 197, 206, 216, 257, 261, 264, 273–74, 280–81, 298

Rhode Island, 63, 127

Richmond Hill, 48

rickets, 292

Riess, Warren, 234

Ritchie, William A., 48, 51, 65–71; Jamesport excavation, 66–68, *66–67*

Ritchie-Fitting hypothesis, 306*n4*

ritual life, 60, 61, 299; African American, 240–41, 279, 289–92; Late Woodland, 96–109, 114–15, *115, 122–23, 300*; Middle Woodland, 76–92, *79–90*; Munsee, 130–31, 133, 144–45; Orient, 62–72, *63–67*, 102–3, 308*nn17–19*; social teas and family dinners, 211–15, 266–67, 272–73

Robertson, Archibald, watercolor by, *262*

Robson, Benjamin, 196, 198–200, 207, 251–52

Robson, Eliza, 196, 198, 207, 251–52

Robson home, 198–200, 202, 207, 210, 211, 223, 251–52, 261, 266–67, 272; tableware, 214, *215, 273*

Rodriguez, Jan, 318*n2*

Roelofs, Sara, 173, 239, 278, 279, 281, 320*n11*, 329*n5*

Ronson excavation, 234–36, *235–36*

Ronson (Howard) Organization, 231, 233, 234, 325*nn8, 12*

Roosevelt Street, 202

"Roots phenomenon," 303*n5*

ropes, 89, 90

Rose Hill Manor, 261–62, *262*, 263

Rothschild, Nan, 17–19, *19*, 22–23, 27, 28, 157, 191–95, 201, 202, 236

rum bottles, 129, 130

rural land, 257–76, *258–76*; colonial, *258*, 259–60, *260*, 261–65, 267–68; farms, estates, and plantations, 259–67, *260–65*, 327*nn2, 10*; forts and encampments, 273–75; nineteenth-century, 257–76, *262–76*; suburbs, 272–73; villages and towns, 267–72, *270–71*. *See also specific sites*

Rutsch, Edward, 278, 281, 285, 286

Ryders Pond, *5*, 129–30, 131, 136

Sage, Francis, 199, 203, 207, 210

Sage, Mary, 199, 207, 210

St. John de Crevecoeur, Hector, 229

St. John's College, 262–63; dishes, 263, *264*

Sainz, Donald, 48, 305*n11*

Salwen, Bert, 17, 18, 28, 153, 198, *198*, 304*n7*, 306*n17*, 328*n18*

sandstone fragment (Late Woodland or Contact), *123*

Sandy Ground, 268, 269–72, *270–71*

sanitation, 112, 228–29, 249–52

Sankofa symbol, 290, *290*, 292, 293

Savage, Gus, 287

Schermerhorn family, 226

Schuyler, Robert, 234, 270, 328*n18*

Scottish Americans, 192, 195

scrapers: Archaic, *50*, 51, 52; Transitional, 63, *63*

Sebonac, 110–11

secondary burials, 99–104, 108, 114, 300

sedentary lifestyle, development of, 73–75, 97, 103, 109–14, 313*nn38, 50*

Sedgwick, Catherine, 211

segregation, 203–4, 251–52, 272–73, 279

Seneca Village, 268

Seton Hall University, 42

settlement studies, 190–92

seventeenth century, 13, 16, 18, *20–22*, 73, 92, 119; Contact period, 120–48, *121–47*, 314*n3*, 315*nn16*, 18, 316*nn27, 28, 41, 43, 47*, 317*nn49, 53*, 318*n76*; Dutch-to-English transition, 180–84; Dutch settlement, 16–30, 167–68, *168*, 169–81, *171–78*, 224–27, 236–37, 244–45, *244–45*, 247, 259, 263–64, 267–68, 277, 298, 319*nn10, 12*, 320*n2*, 321*n18*; waterfront development, 224–27, 236–37. *See also* English colonial New York; New Amsterdam

Seven Years' War, 148

sewage system, 250–52

sewant. See wampum trade

sewing, 222

shamans, 69–70, 71, 81, 133

sheep, 179, 222, 321*n22*

shell(s), 106, 290; ancient heaps, 54–56; Archaic, 54–59, 306*nn15, 16*; ceramic motif, 214, *215*; Late Woodlands, 106, *107*; wampum, 131, 132, *132*, 133–34, *134*, 135–39, *139*, 140–42, 146, 315*n15*, 316*nn27, 28, 41, 43, 47*

shellfish, 54–56, 58, 59, 87, 95, 112, 114, 179–80, 221, 222, 269–70, 307*n19*, 314*n54*; for wampum, 132–33, 140

shelters, Native American, 44, 45, *45*, 57, 58

Sheppard, John, 156

Sheridan Square, 261

ships and shipbuilding, 70, 233; colonial, 150–53, 154, 233–35; *Ronson* excavation, 234–36, *235–36* shoes, 29, 44, 227, *228,* 240, *240,* 274

shoreline. *See* waterfront

shrouds and shroud pins, 288–89, *289*

sickle-cell disease, 291

Silver, Annette, 79

Siwanoy, 129

Skinner, Alanson, 58, *60,* 63–64, 70, 82, 100, 123, 129, 145, 288, 307*n*23

slash-and-burn agriculture, 94, 103

slaughterhouses, 217

slavery. *See* enslaved

slums, nineteenth-century, 217–23

Sluyter, Peter, 35, 134, 173

smallpox, 142–43

Smillie, James, engraving by, *199*

Smith, Carlyle Shreeve, 74–75

Smith, Sheli, 234

smoking, 81, 114, *115. See also* pipes

Snakapins, 129

social classes, 8, 194; nineteenth-century, 189, 200–205, 206–23, 251–52, 266–67, 270–73; segregation, 203–4, 251–52, 272–73, 279; separation of home and work-place, 198–205; tablewares and, 211–15, *215–16,* 223, 272–73, *273;* wealth and, 192–96, 200–205; working-class, 203–4, *204,* 206, 208, 216–23. *See also specific classes*

social history, 9, 10, 12

Society for the Diffusion of Useful Knowledge, map of New York, *191*

Solecki, Ralph, 17–18, 97–99, 135–36, *136,* 138–40, 153

soup, 212

South America, 38, 223, 304*n*3

South Street, 229

South Street Seaport, 250

South Street Seaport Museum, 32, 153, 234, 236

Spain, 149, 167, 176

spear points, 4, 48, 94, 228, 306*n*6; Archaic, 48, 49, *50,* 51, 52, 56, 58–59, *59,* 60, 307*nn*21, 27; chronological sequence of styles, 48, *49;* Fox Creek, 49, 78–79, *79;* Transitional, 62–63, *63,* 64, 66, *66,* 67, *67,* 69, 307*n*2; Woodland, 78, 83, 108

spoons, 130, 173, 240, *240*

spread-footers, 238, *238,* 239, 325*n*19

Spring Street, 246

Spuyten Duyvil, 263

squash, 76, 94, 110, 113, 180

Stadt Herbergh, 20, *20*

Stadt Huys Block, 16–30, 98, 156, 176, 200, 225, *244,* 319*n*2; excavations, 16–30, *19–29,* 156, 304*n*9

Staten Island, 4, *5,* 37, 39, 40, 48, 56, 63, 100, 115, 126, 129, 145, 257, 306*n*12; Bloomfield, 129; Bowman's Brook, 100, 102, 110, 114; Old Place, 48, 129; Port Mobil, 32, 40–41, *41,* 42–45, 48, 305*nn*10, 11; rural land, 257, 267, 268–72, *270–71,* 273; Sandy Ground, 268, 269–72, *270–71;* Ward's Point, 48, 51–54, 82–86, 112, 114, 131

State Street, 31, 32

steatite pots, 63, *63,* 64, *66,* 67, *67,* 68, 69, 74, 308*n*3

Steen, Jan, *Merry Family,* 178, *178*

Stewart, Michael, 80

stone, 13; boiling, 52; pendant (Late Woodland or Contact), *122;* privies, 243, 246, *246,* 249, 250, 326*n*8. *See also* stone tools

Stone, Linda, 260–61

stone tools, 53, 136, 305*n*13, 306*n*11; Archaic, 48, 49, *50,* 51, 52, 58, *58,* 59, *59,* 60; Late Woodland, 98, 114; Paleoindian, 39, 40, 41, *41,* 42–45; Transitional, 62–63, *63,* 64, 66, *66,* 67, *67,* 69

Stony Brook, 66, 308*n*9

storage pits, Late Woodland, 106, 109, 114

stores and shopkeepers, 8, 21, 162, 195, 197–98; nineteenth-century, 162–63, *163,* 164, 196–205, 217, 219, 222; separation from home, 199–205

striped bass, 87, 180

sturgeon, 87

Stuyvesant, Anna, 173

Stuyvesant, Peter, 128, 138, 141, 154, 173, 193, 318*n*10, 322*n*7

suburbs, 7, 258; nineteenth-century, 203, 204, 214, 250, 258, 271–73

subway, 105, 151, 152

Sugar Loaf Hill, 64, *65,* 66, 308*n*5

Sullivan Street site, *5,* 198–99, *246,* 251, 252

Surinam, 181

Susquehannocks, 125

syphilis, 222, 291

tablewares, nineteenth-century, 266; middle-class, 211–15, *212–16,* 266, 272–73; working-class, 218, 219, *220*

Tackapausha, 123, 131, 138–41, 145, 317*n*49

Tantaque, 35–36

taverns, colonial, 20–21, *21*, 28–30, 155–58, *158*, 196, 319*n*17

taxes, 126, 202; sewer, 251

Taylor-Roberts Plan, *230*

teas, social, 212–15, 266–67

teawares, 212–15, *216*, 218, 219, *220*, 221, 267, 273, *273*, 275

technology. *See* ceramics; tools; weapons; *specific periods*

teeth, 29, 112; of enslaved Africans, 289, 291, 292

Telco Block, *247*, 250

tenement life, nineteenth-century, 218–23, 247, 250–52, 324*nn*20, 24

textiles, plants used for, 89, *90*

Thomas, Gabriel, 100

Throgs Neck, *5*, 60, 63, 78, 100, 129, 131, 136, 145

Thunderbird, *123*

tidewater trade and ritual, Middle Woodland, 77–82, *79–81*

Tijger (ship), 150–52, *152*, 153

tiles, 165, 177; delft, 171, *171*, 174, 177, 198

Timucua Indians, 176

Tippet, Robert, pipes by, 159–60

tobacco, 76, 81, 134, 154, 155, 309*n*17; pipes, 155, 157, 158, *158*, 159–60, 164, 171–75, *175*, 227, 256, 290, 319*n*17, 320*n*7

tools: Archaic, *50*, 51, 52, 56, 58, *58*, 59, *59*, 60, 61; bone, 76; hide-working, 76; Late Woodland, 98, 108, 114; Middle Woodland, 76, 78, 85; Munsee, 122, 136; Paleoindian, 39, 40, 41, *41*, 42–45; Transitional, 62–63, *63*, 64, 66, *66*, 67, *67*, 69, 70; woodworking, 69, 70, 76

toothbrushes, 29

tortoise petroglyph, 36, *36*

Toussaint, Pierre, 282

toys, 207, *208*, 219

trade, 7, 149–66, 298; Contact period, 119, 122–25, 130, 131–42, 146, 50, 315*nn*8, 15; English colonial New York, 155–58, *158*, 159–60; fur, 119, 133, 134–35, 149–50, 153, 154, 155, 158, 167, 169, 174, 298; global economy, 124, 125, 131, 140, 149–66, 227, 298, 299; Indian-European, 119, 122–25, 130–42, 146, 150, 315*nn*8, 15, 316*nn*27, 28, 41, 43, 47; Late Woodland, 110–11, 114; Middle Woodland, 76–92; modern, 161;

networks, 164–66; New Amsterdam, 153–55, 167; nineteenth-century, 161–64, 200–201, 206, 220–21; slave, 154, 155, 168, 240, 259, 279, 291, 320*n*2; triangular, 135, 155, 234; wampum, 125, 132, *132*, 133–34, *134*, 135–39, *139*, 140–42, 146, 315*n*15, 316*nn*27, 28, 41, 43, 47

trade kettles, metal, 130, *130*, 131

Transitional period, 12, 61, 62–72, *63–67*, 307*n*1

transportation, nineteenth-century, 199, 203–4, 211, 267, 269, 272

trash pits, 4, 63, 242, 270; colonial, 170–75, *171–75*; Late Woodland, 98, 100–102, 106, 109, 114

Tredwell, Daniel, 54

Tredwell, Gertrude, 253

Tredwell, Seabury, 253, 254

Trenton, 79, 80

triangular trade, 135, 155, 234

Trinity Church, 193–94, 198, 279, 286, 329*n*6, 330*n*27

Trowbridge, Harry, 274

Tubby Hook, *5*, 57, 85, *60*

tundra, 37, 38, 47

turkeys, 88, *89*

Tweed Courthouse, 275

Underhill, Captain John, 131

upstreaming, 75

urban space, 7, 16, 19, 57; colonial period, 188–89, *189*, 190–94; post-Revolutionary, 194–206

urinals, glass, 220, *221*, 222

Utrecht, 155

Valentine, 151, 318*n*2

Valentine's Manual, 190, 204, 233

Van Cortlandt, Augustus, 264, 266

Van Cortlandt, Augustus White, 266

Van Cortlandt, Jacobus, 264

Van Cortlandt family, 226, 263–67

Van Cortlandt Mansion, 261, 263–65, *265*, 266–67, 327*n*10, 328*n*13

Van Cortlandt Park, 264

Van der Donck, Adrian, 143, 263–64

van Tienhoven, Cornelis, 20, 22, 125, 170–72

van Tienhoven, Lucas, 171, 172, 184

van Tienhoven house and artifacts, *20, 22*, 170–72, *171–72*, 174, 177, 180, 184, 185

Van Voorhis, Catherine, 196, 197, 206

Van Voorhis, Daniel, 196, 197–98, 200, 202, 206–7

Van Voorhis homes, silvershop, and artifacts, 196–97, *197*, 198, 206–7, 211, 214, *215*

veal, 221

venereal diseases, 220, 222

Vermeer, Jan, 178

Verrazano, Giovanni da, 4, 61, 115, 119

village life, Native American: Late Woodland, 94–95, 99–116, 311*n*6; Munsee, 125, 135–37, *137*, 138–43, 145–46

villages and towns, 267–72, *270–71*; colonial, 267–68; nineteenth-century, 268–72, *270–71*

Virginia, *137*, 157, 235, 236, 240, 241, 319*n*10

Visscher map, *137*

Wall, Diana, 17–19, *19*, 22–23, 27, 28, 157, 162, 191–92, 200–202, 208–10, 229–30, 236, 252–54, 261

Walloons, 167, *168*, 177, 186

Wall Street, 4, 21, *21*, 159, 169, 196, 198, 225, *230*, 244; nineteenth-century development of commercial district, 200–206; Stadt Huys Block project, 16–30, *19–29*, 156, 176, 200

Wampage, 123, 127, 128, *128*, 129, 145

wampum trade, 125, 132, *132*, 133–34, *134*, 135–39, *139*, 140–42, 146, 315*n*15, 316*nn*27, 28, 41, 43, 47

war clubs, 125, *125*

Ward's Point, 48, 51–54, 82–86, 100, 112, 114, 129, 131; Archaic, 51–54; artifacts, 50, *51*, 83–85, *85*, 123; child at, 82–86; Contact, *123*, 131; Woodland, 82–86, *123*

warehouses, 163, 239, 281; New Amsterdam, *20*, 154–55, *155*

War of *1812*, 161, 274, 328*n*28

Washington, Fort, 274

Washington, George, 196, 264, 273

Washington Heights, 57, 104, 105, *105*, 106, *107*, 114

Washington Square, 198–99, *199*, 203, 207, 209, 223, 251, 252, 261, 266, 272

Washington Street, 226

waterfront, 224–41, 324*n*2, 3; ancient, 37, *37*, 38–42, 54–58, 61, 239–40, 297–98; colonial, 179–80, *189–90*, 224–41, *228–40*; Contact period, 129; landfill, 182, 188, *189–90*, 223, 224–41, *229–40*, 325*nn*8, 11, 12, 19; Late Woodland, 94, 95, 114; Middle Woodland, 76, 82, 86–92; slips, 226

water lots, 225–26, 229, 234, *235*, 324*n*2

Water Street, 161, 196, 226; #175 Water Street, 228, 233–35, *235*, 236

water supply, 247–52, 326*n*11

Watts family, 261–63

wealth, 192, 198, 257; nineteenth-century, 192, 200–205, 206, 217, 251–52, 266–67, 272–73; urban space and, 192–94

weapons, 48, *49–50*; Archaic, 48, 49, *50*, 51, 52, 58, *58*, 59, *59*, 60; European metal, 129–30, *130*, 136, 145, 274; Late Woodland, 94, 108; Middle Woodland, 78, 83, 85; Munsee, 122, 125, *125*, 129, 130, *130*, 136, 145; Paleoindian, 40, 41, *41*, 42–45; Transitional, 62–63, *63*, 64, 66, *66*, 67, *67*, 69

Weeks, James, 268

Weeksville, 268–69

Wellfleet Tavern (Cape Cod), 157, *158*

wells, 26; dry, 242, 246, *246*, *247*, 249

West Africa, 168, 240, 289, 290, 291, 292

West Central Africa, 168, 289, 292

Westchester, 126, 250, 263, 267, 273

West Indies, 155, 174, 234, 259, 264

West Street, 226

whale oil, 155

wharves, *182–83*, 229–33, *230–32*, 240, 245, 325*n*11

whelk, 132, 133, *137*, 316*n*43

William and Mary, 182

willow pattern, 214, *215*, 266

Wilson, Sherrill, 288, 293

Winans, Anthony, 163–64; store of, 163, *163*, 164

wine, 154; bottles, 163, 164, *175*, 221, 263

Wines, Roger, 261

Winter, Frederick, 263, 267

Wisconsin, 36, 37

Wisniewski, Stanley, *104*, 130, 274

women, 8, 10; African American slaves, 277, 289, *289*, 290–93; Archaic, 52, 58; colonial, 142, 175, 184–85; cult of domesticity, 207–15, 272; Dutch, 184–85; English, 184–85; Late Woodland, 98–99, 113–14, 314*n*52; middle-class, 206–10, *210*, 211–15, 221, 272–73; Munsee, 126–27, 139–40; nineteenth-century, 204, 206–15, 217, 252, 271–72, 324*n*26; Paleoindian, 44, 45; prostitutes, 220–23, 324*nn*23, 26; Woodland, 73; working-class, 217, 220–23

wooden-box cistern, 248, *249*

Woodland period, 12, 13, 63, 73–116, 298, 309*nn*1, 5, 12,

17; Early, 73–75, *75,* 76, 309*n*5; Late, 93–116, *94–115,*
119, 122, *122–23,* 241, 263, 311*nn*1, 4, 312*nn*13, 26,
313*n*18, 314*n*54; Middle, 76–92, *79–90,* 113, 309*nn*12,
17, 310*nn*40, 41, 311*n*1

wood-lined privies, 244, *244,* 245–46, 248

Worden, Thomas, 160

working class, nineteenth-century, 203–4, *204,* 206, 208,
216–23

workplace and home, nineteenth-century separation of,
198–205, 210

World Trade center, 44, 151, 153, 226

World War II, 62, 75

Wyckoff House, 259–60, *260*

Yamin, Rebecca, 218–22

yellow fever, 201, 228–29, 232

zoned pottery, Abbott Farm, 79, *79,* 80, *80*

zoning regulations, 30–32

Illustration Credits

Courtesy African Burial Ground and U.S. General Services Administration: figs. 16.2, 16.3, 16.4, 16.5, 16.6, 16.7, 16.8, 16.9

Courtesy the Library, American Museum of Natural History: fig. 6.5 (negative no. 32163) and fig. 8.9 (transparency no. K18490)

Courtesy Department of Library Services, American Museum of Natural History (photo by W. L. Calver): fig. 7.5 (negative no. 24449)

Courtesy Department of Library Services, American Museum of Natural History (copied by J. Beckett): fig. 7.6 (negative no. 338948) and fig. 8.13 (negative no. 338949)

Adapted from Edwards and Emery 1977 with permission of the Annals of the New York Academy of Sciences: fig. 3.2

AP/Wide World Photos: fig. 17.1

Askins 1985: figs. 15.6 and 15.7

From Robert Bolton, Jr., *A History of the County of Westchester from Its First Settlement to the Present Time* (New York: Alexander and Gould, 1848): fig. 8.5

Adapted from R. P. Bolton 1934: fig. 4.4 (detail)

Courtesy Brooklyn College Archaeological Research Center: fig. 15.5

Courtesy of The Brooklyn Historical Society: fig. 2.4

Adapted from Kathryn Browning, *Indian Textiles as Reconstructed from the Impressions Left on Long Island* (1974): fig. 6.8

Photo courtesy Anne-Marie Cantwell: fig. 7.2

Etnofrasfiska Museet (photo courtesy the New Jersey State Museum): fig. 8.4

Collection of Stuart P. Feld, New York: fig. 15.3

Fordham Archaeological Project: fig. 15.4

Courtesy Joan H. Geismar: fig. 13.6

Courtesy Edith Gonzalez de Scollard: fig. 15.2

Courtesy Dr. R. M. Gramly; artist William Parsons: fig. 3.4

Adapted from Haviland and Power 1994: fig. 4.4 (spear thrower)

Photo courtesy Herbert C. Kraft: fig. 3.3

Reproduced or adapted, by permission of the author, from Herbert C. Kraft, *The Lenape-Delaware Indian Heritage: 10,000 B.C. to A.D. 2000* (Elizabeth, N.J.: Lenape Books, 2000): figs. 4.1, 8.1, and 8.15

Reproduced from a lithograph, in the collection of Herbert C. Kraft, from the series Thomas L. McKenney and James Hall, *The Indian Tribes of North America* (Philadelphia: E. C. Biddle, 1857): fig. 8.8

Drawings by William Fowler for the *Bulletin of the Massachusetts Archaeological Society,* reproduced with permission: fig. 6.1

Photo courtesy Kervin Maule: fig. 6.2

Courtesy the Milwaukee Public Museum (negative 106990): fig. 4.5

Museum of the City of New York, Gift of the Department of Parks, 43.165B: fig. 9.1

Museum of the City of New York, the J. Clarence Davies Collection, 34.100.29: fig. 2.2

Courtesy, National Museum of the American Indian, Smithsonian Institution: fig. 4.3 (N5548), fig. 4.6 (N5564), fig. 6.6 (N5554), fig. 7.1 (N5551), fig. 7.8 (N5567), fig. 8.2, and fig. 8.3

Netherlands Maritime Museum, Amsterdam: fig. 6.7

Photos courtesy the New Jersey State Museum: figs. 6.3, 8.4, 8.6, and 8.7

New York Botanical Gardens, Bronx, N.Y.: fig. 3.1

New York Public Library: figs. 8.11, 10.9, 11.2, 11.3, 12.4, 12.5, and 13.2

Courtesy New York State Museum, reprinted or adapted from Ritchie 1959: figs. 5.1, 5.2, 5.3, 5.4, 5.5

NYC Landmarks Preservation Commission, photo Carl Forster: fig. 15.9

Courtesy Arnold Pickman: figs. 9.3, 12.3, and 12.7

Photo courtesy James Rementer: fig. 7.7

Rijksmuseum, Amsterdam (slide courtesy AKG London, oil on canvas, 111 × 141 cm): fig. 10.7

Rockman (Wall) et al. 1983: fig. 14.5

Photo courtesy Ralph Solecki, from Truex 1982: fig. 7.4

Reproduced by permission of Ralph Solecki: fig. 8.10

Adapted from Ralph Solecki in Gaynell Stone, ed., *The Native Forts of the Long Island Sound Area* (Stony Brook, N.Y.: Suffolk County Archaeological Association, 2000): fig. 8.12

From the collections of the South Street Seaport Museum: figs. 9.2, 9.4, 10.2, 11.4, 13.3, 13.4, 13.7, 13.9, 13.10, 14.3, and 14.4

From the collections of the South Street Seaport Museum; photo Diana Wall: figs. 10.3, 10.4, 10.6, 12.2, 12.6, and 15.8

From the collections of the South Street Seaport Museum; photo Kervin Maule: figs. 13.11 and 14.1

Courtesy of Society for Pennsylvania Archaeology, *Pennsylvania Archeologist* 40 (11-2): fig. 7.3

Courtesy of Society for Pennsylvania Archaeology, *Pennsylvania Archeologist* 41 (3): fig. 4.2

The State Museum of Pennsylvania, Pennsylvania Historical and Museum Commission (photo courtesy the New Jersey State Museum): fig. 8.6

William Duncan Strong Museum, Columbia University, New York: figs. 2.1, 2.5, 2.6, 2.9, 10.5, 11.5, 13.1, 13.8, 14.2, and 14.6

U.S. General Services Administration: figs. 12.8 and 12.9

Courtesy Diana Wall: figs. 2.7, 2.8, 12.1, 14.8, and 14.9